ARNOLD WEINSTEIN is the Edna and Richard Salomon Distinguished Professor of Comparative Literature at Brown University and the author of *Vision and Response in Modern Fiction; Fictions of the Self: 1550–1800; The Fiction of Relationship;* and *Nobody's Home: Speech, Self, and Place in American Fiction from Hawthorne to DeLillo.* He also gives a series of audio and video lectures on world literature for The Teaching Company. He spends his time at Brown University, Block Island, Stockholm, and Brittany.

A SCREAM GOES THROUGH THE HOUSE

A SCREAM GOES THROUGH THE HOUSE

What Literature Teaches Us About Life

ARNOLD WEINSTEIN

RANDOM HOUSE TRADE PAPERBACKS

NEW YORK

2004 Random House Trade Paperback Edition

This work was originally published in hardcover by Random House, an imprint of
The Random House Publishing Group, a division of Random House, Inc., in 2003.

Owing to limitations of space, acknowledgments of permission
to quote from previously published material can be found on page 421.

Library of Congress Cataloging-in-Publication Data

Weinstein, Arnold.
A scream goes through the house: what literature teaches us about life/
Arnold Weinstein.—1st ed.
p. cm.
ISBN 0-8129-7243-0
1. Literature and society.   2. Literature—Philosophy.   3. Literature, Modern—
History and criticism.   I. Title.
PN47 .W45 2003
801'.3—dc21   2002031719

Printed in the United States of America

Random House website address: www.randomhouse.com

2 4 6 8 9 7 5 3 1

Book design by Casey Hampton

To Ann, as always

PREFACE

The heart of this book about life, literature, and art is precisely the human heart: the pump that keeps our body alive and the *feelings* that course through us and link us to others. Literature and art live in these two ways, as a bloodstream that connects us to the world, as a mirror for our emotions; and as a magic script that allows us both to sound our own depths and also to enter the echoing storehouse of feeling that goes by the name of Sophocles, Shakespeare, Dickens, Munch, Proust, and all the great writers and artists whose work exists to nourish us. I see the great books as a feast for the heart.

For too long we have been encouraged to see culture as an affair of intellect, and reading as a solitary exercise. But the truth is different: literature and art are pathways of feeling, and our encounter with them is social, inscribing us in a larger community, a community composed of buried selves and loved ones, as well as the fellowship of writers over time. Literature and art provide intercourse of a unique sort. Through art we discover that we are not alone. These discoveries can be as revelatory as those dreams in which the world turns fluid, so that the living and the dead, the far and the near, come together in a dance that recasts our life. That picture of connectedness, of a universe that is umbilical and strange—a picture that no camera can take—takes the measure of our true lives.

And so this book is framed by two dreams. The first one, prophetic, occurred in October 1960 when I was a student in France, and its annunciatory fable of a monster on the loose—representing our somatic fate—will be dealt with in Chapter Two, "Living in the Body." The second dream, about the reach of feeling, about the bloodstream of feeling that carries us into others and others into us, took place in the summer of 2001, also in France, when I was putting the final touches on this book. More than any daytime argument I might marshal, it captures, with frightening purity—frightening to *me*—the meaning and purpose of this study, and I therefore offer it as a prefatory note, first as the dream itself unfurled, and then as I unpack and understand it.

July 25, 2001. Brittany, France. My wife and I have been here a week. My daughter, her husband, and their two children—seven-year-old Anna and two-year-old Gustav—arrived today. We allow Anna a special treat: to sleep in the trundle bed in our bedroom. All are asleep and I dream. I am in Memphis, where I grew up, and my mother and father are speaking, in low but urgent tones, in the bedroom next to me. Their voices grow louder, more insistent, moving from what seems a lament to what I can only call a wail. My father, who is depressed and dying, expresses his misery over and over to my mother, but she too utters her pain and anguish. In waves, in a singsong, systolic and diastolic, like a dirge, these sounds of my parents' hurt traverse the wall and invade our room. And, sure enough, Anna, now awake, says to me, "They're making noise." "Yes," I reply. "Yes."

I awake. All is quiet. Anna sleeps in her trundle bed, and my wife sleeps next to me. A minute later, I hear, from the third bedroom, Gustav wake up and cry, and I hear my daughter go into his room to comfort him. He goes back to sleep. But I am awed by the cogency and reach of this dream. My father has been dead for twenty years, and my mother now lies, stroke-ridden, in a nursing home in Memphis. Yet, time avails not, and their plaint enters me, through this dream, with sweet and brutal force. A scream goes through the house, one person's pain becomes another's, across time and space; there are no borders separating us. Life is a shadow play, and we are mummers all, visited and doubled by the ghosts of the past, invested with their pain, living a continuous drama that does not know closure. Brittany is Memphis, my children and grandchildren are my parents, the dead still live, the voices are not stilled.

And I think: this is my book. Above all, this is my life. This dream expresses to perfection the true coordinates of my life, coordinates not to be found on any calendar or gravestone, coordinates that disappear in the harsh light of day, when, like most of us, I cease to be haunted. Yet dreams are evanescent, while art endures; the novel, the poem, the painting, even the film, are splendidly material, accommodating us whenever we visit, casting forth their net—and indeed their network— each time we experience them. They are a force field of coursing energy, containing the still living pulse of both the artist and his or her time, made accessible by the simple miracle of reading. The encounter with literature adds to who we are. And I realize this is why I have spent my life teaching literature and art—because they are reflecting pools, soliciting our entry and immersion so as to gift us with a new sense of self, a new awareness of our actual dimensions.

Henry James used the expression *figure in the carpet* to signal the secret pattern that unifies works of art. But the figure in the carpet that most matters to each of us is that of our *life,* the yearned-for picture that would render our true arrangements in time and space, in body and mind, in heart and soul. For surely the surface story of our quotidian lives—the story we find in a newspaper or a résumé, the story an outsider could tell—misses utterly these rich and secret extensions: our past, our loves and losses, fears and dreams. A new geography, indeed a new cosmography would be needed to represent our actual plenitude and reach. It is that new cosmography that I mean to chart in this book.

While dreams provide this magic map, so, too, does art—literature, painting, film. Art reveals and expresses our real but hidden story: that which lies under the surface, in the realm of feeling, unavailable to the naked eye; that which still resonates, though long past, through memories or fantasies or the thoughts that course through our minds. The literature discussed in this book quite simply reconceives our place in the world, and thereby redraws our own contours, showing us to be porous and connected. Literature and art move us into our fuller selves. The mirror they proffer enables more than seeing; it makes it possible for us to understand, even to hear our feelings. The scream that goes through the house is the heartbeat that makes audible, at last, who we are, how resonant we are, how connected we are. The subtitle of this book is "What Literature Teaches Us About Life." The word to remember is *Life:* mine, as the dream in Brittany suggests, yours too, as you enter the looking glass that art provides, and so come into and repossess your estate.

Contents

LIST OF ILLUSTRATIONS

WHAT THE HEART IS

That I may learn in my own life . . . what the heart is and what it feels.
—JAMES JOYCE, *Portrait of the Artist as a Young Man*

"How many of you are hurting now?" I once asked my students at the beginning of a literature course I was teaching. There was nervous silence, then a few students tentatively raised their hands. But gradually more and more of these young people acknowledged that they were in some kind of pain, whether physical or emotional. They seemed puzzled that I should be asking. What did their feelings have to do with literature? Was this merely personal solicitude on my part? For they thought there could scarcely be any connection between the books we were to read together and the pain they were dealing with. As for me, I sensed that I had stumbled on to something I had been moving toward for a long time, something large and important about the connection between art and life. The book you have in your hands grew out of that discovery.

My students were displaying a deep-seated, widely assumed conviction that pain is private and that literature can do little to assuage it. It's assumed we are isolated in our experience of pain, not because of decorum, but because we think it is locked inside of us, that it exists as a kind of bedrock personal reality that no one else can really know or feel or share. Literature, on the other hand, is assumed to be an affair of large themes and universal truths, of thoughtful utterances and fine words, with little direct connection to our private feelings or sensations or pain. But the truth is, I believe, that art and literature provide us with a reservoir of shareable human feelings and experiences, a storehouse of emotions and insights about body and mind, a storehouse we can visit and take from via the elemental magic of reading, of encountering works of art.

Here, then, are my twin beliefs: *feeling is the basic but invisible fact of life; feeling is the basic but unacknowledged fact of literature and art.* Literature—and painting and music and sculpture and film—offers us access to, and a way to share in, the entire range of human feeling over the ages. This is a gift like no other.

From Sophocles' ancient fable of Oedipus and his double transgressions of incest and parricide to Kathryn Harrison's contemporary novel of child abuse and breakdown, *Exposure,* literature explodes with news about the world of feeling. We move throughout history from Sophocles to Harrison, passing through such exemplary figures as Hamlet, the prophetically dysfunctional prince, or depictions of death and dying in the poetry of Walt Whitman and Emily Dickinson and in the prose of Tolstoy, Proust, and Joyce; from the renditions of trauma and injury in Kafka to full-scale accounts of warfare and abuse in Pat Barker and Toni Morrison, from the evocation of disease as both private secret and urban disaster in Defoe and Dickens to recent work such as Tony Kushner's play about AIDS, *Angels in America.* Not all is cosmic and extreme; art also conveys the mystery and pathos of the mundane and the quotidian: puberty and old age, desire and anxiety, marriage and divorce, love and loss. This is our world, seen through lenses not our own, reconfigured and constituted at different moments of history, yet always telling us about human feeling, about what is deepest and most enduring in our lives. Such is the public—and I would say, private, individual—role of art. In the story "Sonny's Blues," James Baldwin's character Creole sums up what I mean:

> Creole began to tell us what the blues were all about. They were not about anything very new. He and his boys up there were keeping it new, at the risk of ruin, destruction, madness and death, in order to find new ways to make us listen. For while the tale of how we suffer,

and how we are delighted, and how we may triumph is never new, it always must be heard. There isn't any other tale to tell, it's the only light we've got in all this darkness. (31)

"*The only light we've got in all this darkness,*" Baldwin says. The darkness he means goes beyond the miseries that life could mete out to you; it signifies the universal opaqueness in which we live: the opaqueness of others to us, of our own bodies and minds, the fuzziness of our real lives (despite the brave clarity of résumés, blueprints, and statistics). Art is light. This dazzling light illuminates us, enlarges our field of operation, enables us to have a bigger, richer, nobler take on things—things such as self and reality.

But my argument is not only that literature and art provide more light. Art also gives us access to more wisdom, more harnessing of our resources, a deeper grasp of how extensive those resources are, how much more dimensional our lives are or could be. I am focusing here on feeling, pain, and illness as ways to get at life. The biologists tell us that pain is nature's way of signaling trouble; I suggest that art reconceives this signal system by making feeling and pain *vehicular* as well as communicative, furnishing us entry into dramas, perspectives, and existences not our own. Such a journey is educative, in the etymological sense of the word: leading us out.

The education in question here is not about facts and data; art's purposes have little to do with information. No, the voyage is visceral and experiential, it entails vicarious immersion in others' lives, endowing us with new eyes and ears, perhaps changing our hearts. Such transactions are, of course, exciting, but their true rationale has a more ethical and existential cast to it: to bring us closer to the world's heartbeat, to bring to—and into—us something of the world's great theater, even to function like a lightning rod, so that the great energies and forces that have coursed through history might, via art, strike us, jolt us with their vibrancy and intensity.

Feeling moves, and feeling moves us. *A scream goes through the house,* and by this I mean that human feeling travels the world, passes from person to person, and especially stamps our connection to art. The books we read and the paintings we see are vital energy sources, rippling through us, however staid or contained we or they may appear. Art galvanizes. By this I do not mean a Gothic scenario of horror or hauntings. Nor does this scream that goes through the house have much to do with the dread facts of war and violence that crowd our newspapers and TV screens, reminding us over and over of old, sometimes ancient feuds and blood conflicts that pit one group against another in never-ending cycles of hate. Art honors what is best in feeling: pith and keenness of sensation, radiance of thought, enchantment of the heart. Art restores us to full circulation.

"How many of you are hurting?" I asked my students. I could have asked, "How many of you are delighted?" and they would have been equally surprised. Feeling—personal pain and personal pleasure—may well be the central currency of our lives, but we do not expect to find such items in a college curriculum. The curriculum, the materials of an education: theirs, mine, yours. Why is feeling absent from the list? My answer is: knowledge, as it is packaged in universities, as it seems packaged in books, is thought to be an affair of reason, consisting of concepts to be mastered and facts to be learned. From kindergarten to university, there seems to be a disconnect between education and the whole person—body, mind, feeling.

Yet, we are somatic creatures, living in bodies, having emotions, bathed by sensations, at times bubbling and simmering, at times dawdling and eddying, hot and cold, nervous and calm, fearful and yearning, hungry and satiated. We are pulsions. Life is feeling. Our lives are affective from the get-go: from infancy to death, from getting out of bed in the morning to getting back in it at night (not to mention the time spent in it, in between). We all know this, yet the knowledge we acquire in school, and are taught is in books, seems not to take into account these home truths.

Sometimes I think that the brave picture we have of humans as rational beings is utterly misleading, a kind of photograph of our surface composure, and thus unreflective of—and unattuned to—the seismic emotional and psychic reality underneath, *our true reality,* one of nerves and visceral traffic that is hard to measure. Art reflects this realm; art takes this measure. Novels and poems and plays are not just "stories." They are, to borrow Dostoevsky's title, *notes from underground,* or, to put it another way, *reports from the front:* our underground, our front. Literature illuminates who "we" are: the repertory of selves we harbor within, the countless feelings we experience but never express or perhaps even acknowledge, the innumerable other lives we could but do not live, all those "inside" lives that are not on show, not included in our résumés. The arts put onto the page or the stage or the canvas or the screen a special portraiture that does justice to our depths.

Without literature, we would be bereft and impoverished creatures, denizens of a flat and dimensionless world, a world with no more depth than a photograph, that has no more scope than a résumé or a medical report. Art and literature go *in.* Ask yourself: who could write your biography? The external data are available—birth, schooling, marriage, work—but what exact relation does this fact sheet have to your life? How much does it tell? We do not know the inner lives of others. And all too often we scant our own interior world. How strange it is, in a culture defined by information technology and globalization, that we are so often locked out of ourselves. We have electronic access to the globe, we can go on the most exotic trips, yet we are often exiled to our own surface. The encounter with art offers, then, a rare form of self-encounter; it enables a voyage into our own depths.

In his effort to make Gertrude see the true nature of her soul, Hamlet casts his words as "a glass / Where you may see the inmost part of you" (III.iv.18–19). In marshaling together works of art and literature that illuminate our heart of darkness—yes, I believe we are often in the dark when it comes to our hearts—I hope this book will do the work of

Hamlet's glass: enable us to see within, to reach the inmost part of being human, as expressed by great writers, painters, and filmmakers over time.

Because the special mirror that civilization has devised for this labor is art. Over the centuries writers and artists have at once mined their own personal experiences and also been weather vanes to their historical moments, so that the work they have left us is astonishingly resonant and murmurous, speaking in tongues both private and public, mapping out realms that we can not only visit, but make our own. Moreover, art does not know death, even though artists die, whereas each of us, even the most long-lived, is allotted, like actors strutting and fretting their hour upon the stage, precious little time and space. This, too, is why art matters: created and compiled over the ages, as much doubtless through suffering as through joy, art is a form of personal inheritance, waiting for our encounter and our use, a legacy for which no deaths are required.

This book is meant to help you access that legacy, to bring you more fully into the storehouse of human experience and possibility that artists have bequeathed to us. Such a trip is easier than you might expect, for a number of reasons. First of all, you may be more ready now than you were when you first read some of the works of literature I write about. Many of us initially encountered great works of art and literature at the wrong time and under the wrong circumstances: when we were altogether too young, too inexperienced, too distracted, too inundated, and we were perhaps badly taught, to boot. It's not surprising that many thoughtful people still feel either locked out of the classics, or that those much touted works have an exaggerated prestige. Having taught these books to students and laypeople for three decades now, I can say, with some assurance, that you can make your way into these writers and artists—that these writers and artists will make their way into you—for this simple reason: *art connects.*

The cardinal belief of this book, undergirding a view of both life and art that is umbilical to the core, is that the experience of art yields a view of human reality as something networked, crisscrossed with ties and bonds, quite at odds with the individuated world we take to be real: our private body and mind as the fixed enclosure where we think we live as individuals. My view of art is quite at odds also with the electronic network that stamps our age, because the Internet culture, however capacious it may be, is also largely soulless and solipsistic—informational rather than experiential—when contrasted with our engagement with art. Through literature, other lives enter our own as richly and mysteriously as air enters our lungs. Through art we access realms of experience that are life-enhancing, sometimes life altering. This encounter is properly Odyssean, because the journeys at hand lead us back to our own Ithaca. We are at once altered and homeward bound, where we are better able (like Odysseus himself) to meet life's challenges, richer for the trip.

Ralph Waldo Emerson coined the term "Oversoul" in order to reconceive the individual's connection to nature and to others: Oversoul as a kind of current in which we are all bathed, a spiritual medium that nourishes and links creatures with the creation. Not surprisingly, his view of literature and art follows the same model, and it also stamps the thinking of this book: great artists unfold a vision and map a territory that is as much ours as theirs, that we make our own by dint of discovering and experiencing it. It would be closer to Emerson's logic to say that the artist explores *our* space, making us heir to what he has charted. Whereas the conventional view is that the artist expresses his or her private landscape, Emerson turns this notion upside down, claiming that the great vistas in art—those of Homer, Shakespeare, and, I would add, those who come after Emerson, such as Munch, Proust, Faulkner, Morrison—make beautiful sense to us because they are "happening" inside us. How else could we understand them? Soul, on this account, is everywhere, albeit shrouded in darkness for many of us, and the mission of the artist is no less than to illuminate it, make it more available. We all know that material goods are unevenly distributed on this earth of ours, but in some quite wonderful sense, *spiritual* goods, the gift of art and literature, are a profoundly democratic resource, not only accessible to each of us, but actually residing within each of us.

One of Emerson's central motifs is that of a *waterway,* a kind of flow which we navigate in our engagement with art, and at times this image is richly corporeal, becoming no less than a *bloodstream.* In this vision, the capacious world of art can be seen as a living organism, so that the act of reading or seeing a painting or play or film can be understood as an arterial event, a cardiac proposition, while remaining a nurturance that is as much spiritual as it is material. To see art in these terms is to get clear of several clichés that might clutter our minds. First, the arts are not esoteric or frills, not at a remove from reality, but quite the opposite: they are immediate, experiential, and life-expanding. Secondly, this view envisions art as not a private affair, supposedly cued to the artist's personal world or even confined to your own personal sphere, but rather as an opening out, bidding to transport you (time-bound, land-locked you) to new times, new places, and ultimately new selves.

I come now to the rationale for my focus on feeling, pain, and illness. Precisely because art is visceral and experiential, precisely because it alters our vision and expands our stock, it can be a resource of inestimable value to those who hurt. Once again I go back to my students, who had not suspected that literature might speak to their individual condition, might reshape their ideas about pain, about disease, about doctors, about death and dying. On the contrary, the testimony of the arts teaches us things about living in a body, about the nature of feeling, about our condition as imaginative, somatic creatures, that we can find nowhere else.

I imagine that in most homes there are two shelves: one, the medicine shelf (in a room close to where you sleep, a room where you cleanse yourself and minister to your body), and the other, the bookshelf. On the medicine shelf you put those pills that you need to ingest when you're in trouble, when you feel emotional, mental, or physical pain, or all three. Many of us have recourse to this shelf several times a day, even when "well," because it contains the ingredients necessary for us to stay functional.

On a different shelf, the bookshelf (in a different room, a place where you usually go fully dressed), you seek out, when time permits or when you cannot sleep, materials for edification or relaxation. Some people, including those in my profession, may go to the bookshelf as often as they go to the medicine shelf, but most people don't. One of the purposes of this book is to show that the bookshelf is as basic a resource for body and mind, especially the body and the mind in pain, as the medicine shelf.

By this I do not mean that books will distract you, and of course I do not mean that books will reduce your fever or regulate your blood pressure or cholesterol. But I am saying that books—the so-called great books as well as contemporary fiction, and indeed all the arts: painting, film, music, and so on—have more to say to you about your mind and body, well or ill, than you will ever find if you look strictly in the sciences, in medicine, or in the pills on the medicine shelf.

The institution of modern medicine, derived from an ever-growing understanding of disease, approaches disorders of body and mind as biological or physiological events. Western organ-based medicine constitutes a sort of zoned map, and your particular ailment must be aligned within this cartography. Put most reductively, we take our parts to specialists. The sights of medicine are focused on your somatic makeup, not on your hurt. Whether it is your yearly checkup or a life-threatening event in the hospital, at issue is invariably your *disease* (the bio-science problem you present), not your *illness* (the existential dilemma you experience). This helps us to understand the glaring paradox of modern Western medical culture: never has there been such a sophisticated scientific grasp of disease, and never has the individual patient, the person who hurts, felt more out of the loop. And that is not all: not only is the individual *story* elided here, but so too are the larger social and ethical dimensions of illness beyond the scrutiny of science proper.

Might there be another story to tell here, a varied and capacious story that both honors the private sphere of individual feeling and also reflects on the larger ramifications of the body's experience and medicine's aims? And might this fuller story do justice to the reach and primacy of feeling, enabling us to see that the great issues of pain—sickness, fear, death—are also the great issues of life? The dread hallmark of illness is the reduction and diminishment that it brings to our lives, the apprenticeship with pain and worry that close in on us, make us closed to others, and to ourselves. However, could we not see it the other way: illness as threshold, pain as opening, feeling as conduit to something larger, not smaller, something that draws us out of ourselves into a deeper relationship with others, art, and life.

I call this book *A Scream Goes Through the House* to signal the staggering *reach* of feeling and pain, to denote its role as pathway and journey. Art writes large and luminous the penitential experience of illness, and in so doing, it opens the prison. The great wealth of artistic testimony about emotion and disease, about breakdown, about doctors and death, translates directly into *our wealth,* and such riches are all the more precious given the impoverishment of body and mind that illness (and even aging) can bring on. When our own straits seem to have narrowed and we feel bereft, the glimpse of new territories (for thinking, feeling, and living) in literature can be priceless. But make no mistake about it, these discoveries are no less valuable even when we are well, inasmuch as such exposure to humanity jars and stirs us, makes us readier to reach out. Ultimately, the scream that goes through the house communalizes us, puts us in touch with the sentience of others, quickens (through its tidings) our own sense of life and possibility. There is a startling economy at work here, a two-way street, inasmuch as the books we read flow inward into us, add to our stock, enrich our perceptions, stir our inmost feelings; yet art and literature also, quite wonderfully, draw us out, hook us up (imaginatively, emotionally, neurally) into other circuits, other lives, other times.

In gathering together art's testimony about bodies, feelings, pain, and life, I have wanted to cast my net wide, to show just how far-reaching and eye-opening these vistas are. After all, even if pain itself can be dreadfully numbing, the story of somatic life is astonishingly broad and various, and I choose to be adventurous and exploratory, to move inward into the psychic and experiential landscapes that scientific notation ignores, but also to move outward into the social and even ideological issues that are woven into the story of pain and illness. Each of my chapters is meant to generate new horizons, to move you from the agreed-on notions we all share to the more surprising and challenging depictions art provides. My ultimate aim is enrichment rather than provocation as such, but some of the artistic performances on show here may disturb. It is my hope that, by book's end, your ideas about bodies, illness, art, and life will not be quite the same as they were.

Chapter One spells out the central truth that informs my vision: a scream goes through the house. The house is your own body when animated by feeling or racked by pain. We enter life screaming, and I contend that our entire journey through life is parsed by (unheard, unsounded) screams. The house is the larger world of living beings to whom feeling relates us. Finally, the house betokens the very institutions of literature and art, those capacious structures and dwellings we enter when we read a book or gaze at a painting, and there, too—there especially—we encounter the ongoing, unfurling scream, the music of human sentience that is life's blood and art's blood. The ramifications of this view are key: pain courses outward, into the world, into art (rather than remaining imprisoned in us, as is generally assumed); art constitutes an imaginative and affective bridge that allows us to exit our cramped quarters and enter the flow, to accede to other worlds and other times, always following the royal road of feeling as our means of entry and understanding. At its most transcendent, art simply remakes the world, reshuffles that tired deck, stuns us with a larger apprehension of human affairs *and our place within them,* for we see how tentacular and linked the world really is, how arterial art's pathways truly are.

To make good on these claims, I focus on single exemplary works of art in each genre (poetry, fiction, theater, painting, and film) that explore with immense power the vision of feeling-as-connective-tissue I have articulated. Each of these artists—William Blake, James Baldwin, Eugene

O'Neill, Edvard Munch, and Ingmar Bergman—makes us see and hear the scream that goes through the house, by presenting a world that is linked and meshed, a world in which pain and feeling bind us rather than divide us, an ecosystem that flaunts the primacy of emotion itself as human bridge. Such art makes at last visible nothing less than a new map for displaying our true arrangements. But the complacent cover of conventional wisdom and everyday logic—received ideas about boundaries that are supposed to separate me from you, now from then, here from there—is blown sky-high in these bold, revelatory works.

Chapter Two is about living in a body. We customarily define where we live in geographical terms: New York or Paris, New England or the West Coast, perhaps Europe or the Far East. We might even be metaphorical: "I am living in the dark . . . in misery . . . in pain." Prior to these spatial or figurative arrangements, however, is the stark fact that we are, first and foremost, from birth to death, inhabitants of bodies. Bodies that we did not choose, bodies with a will of their own. Here is a lifelong form of bondage and housing that we incessantly negotiate, as witnessed by the extraordinary body culture of contemporary life, as witnessed also (and more profoundly) by crucial somatic events that structure every existence: puberty, desire, anxiety, and, of course, illness and death. Less visible, perhaps, is the sheer alterity and authority of the body we live in, a creature with its own laws, language, and agenda. Literature and art can be especially provocative here, inasmuch as they are capable of radically *defamiliarizing* our givens, casting off our blinders, and thus illuminating the peculiar yet generic tug-of-war between I and It (identity and body) that no one escapes.

As far back as Oedipus' solution to the Riddle of the Sphinx— "Man," Oedipus replied, in answer to the question, What is on four legs in the morning, two legs at midday, and three legs in the evening?—writers and thinkers have pondered the transition from animal to human. Literary testimony—from Shakespeare's *Othello* to Charlotte Brontë's *Jane Eyre*, and into the twentieth century with Kafka's beetle-protagonist in "The Metamorphosis" and William Burroughs's bestiary in *Naked Lunch*—reminds us that the "animal" is with us forever, that the project of becoming exclusively mental or spiritual beings—free of flesh—is a fantasy. And perhaps a harmful fantasy, inasmuch as basic drives such as desire, appetite, even emotion, have an inescapable somatic dimension, so that any fuller view of our condition must come to terms with the animal.

But the animal-body is no less the site of our richest human experiences—tenderness, pleasure, passion—and this chapter closes with Toni Morrison's masterpiece, *Beloved.* Here we actually see what a "writing of flesh" might look like, and how the story of slavery—the very system whereby your body is owned by another—might be translated into a somatic language of great beauty as well as horror.

Chapter Three makes its way more directly into the medical arena by focusing on the central issue of *diagnosis.* As a layperson I know relatively little about the incredibly complex systems that make my body the living thing it is. Doctors are trained precisely in this area. My peculiar knowledge and expertise are on the other side of the equation: the lifelong experience of being in the dark, of guessing about (worrying about) what is actually going on inside. Laypeople consult doctors because they—the physicians with their education, trained eyes, and assortment of imaging and scanning devices, blood tests, and the like—can *read the body.*

Here would be the great promise of science, and here is one of the skills at once clinical and personal that we tend to prize, in school, at work, and in life: the diagnostic gaze performing its semiotic labor by translating symptom into disease, random detail into cogent pattern. Analytic prowess is the hallmark of the good doctor.

Might it be more than that? Are there issues of power, too, even exploitation, that accompany, willy-nilly, the diagnostic act? To be sure, we value the power of the doctor when it comes to reading our symptoms right. But how do we feel about people who can "see through" us, who are preternaturally keen in figuring out the motivation, even the secrets of others? The testimony of art and literature is sharp, sometimes ferocious, in this area—as if artists sensed that diagnosis and scrutiny can all too easily turn invasive, can violate both the seer and the seen. In writers as distinct as Choderlos de Laclos, the author of *Les Liaisons Dangereuses,* or the Americans Nathaniel Hawthorne and Henry James, or the German playwright Georg Büchner or the supreme analyst in fiction, Marcel Proust, we discover how voracious and manic the diagnostic impulse can be, and also how victimizing, even lethal, its operation can be, in that most central arena of both life and art: human relations.

Chapter Four, "Plague and Human Connection," puts onto the world stage all the issues dealt with—the primacy of feeling, the authority of bodies, the hazards of diagnosis. A scream goes through the house: private illness makes its fateful itinerary to collective disaster and plague, writing large the mystery of human connection/infection and the crucial social mechanisms enlisted to save the community. Once again, Sophocles' *Oedipus* (among other works) comes to the fore, this time as the master plot for how a community copes with catastrophe. The apparent backdrop of the Greek play, plague—people dying like flies in Thebes, the Oracle's tracing of the scourge to a concealed murder—provokes a central question that recurs throughout history: who is responsible for this epidemic? The great Sophoclean theme of illicit connection, at once political and sexual—a man kills his father the king, sleeps with his mother the queen—is also to be understood bacterially. Of course, Sophocles was no epidemiologist, but his account of mass deaths intrigues us because it turns on the key issue of secrets, both erotic and communal, and thus tells us (in the way literature tells us things) that the story of plague is a shockingly broad, social story, a revelatory story that thrusts the culture's connections, both licit and illicit, into full view.

The Sophoclean story of a city or culture threatened with plague—with apocalypse—is replayed throughout history. In narratives by Daniel Defoe and Charles Dickens we see London under siege, and these stories echo strangely still today, evoking for us what it might well have looked like, had we been citizens of Thebes, of Sodom or Gomorrah, of Dresden or Hiroshima or Grozny, or what it could look like in the wake of bioterrorism, with its threats of anthrax and smallpox and other toxins.

The very word "plague" has—or used to have—a yesteryear ring to it, an archaic condition located either in the past or in underdeveloped societies where medicine has not made the advances we take for granted in the West. But we are increasingly aware that mass disease and lethal infection cannot be ruled out of modern life. For just this reason my chapter closes with several stunning works of the twentieth century: Albert Camus's allegorical novel, *The Plague;* Ingmar Bergman's groundbreaking film of 1956, *The Seventh Seal;* and Tony Kushner's epochal play about AIDS, *Angels in America.* All these works face up to apocalypse, but they use the specter of mass death to posit *human connection*—the mysterious bonds of love—as civilization's most precious legacy.

"Saying Death" is the title of Chapter Five, and it should be recognized for the impossible proposition that it is. Bergman may well outfit Death with black cape and clown face, but for most of us this most generic of all outcomes has no profile and no voice. Death is silent, but literature is constantly drawn to the finale that gives point and shape to so much of our performance. Death punctuates life. All our notions of growth, development, and maturation are hardwired with death's certainty. Life and love are precious because death is real. Still: how to say it?

One death all of us can say is the death of others. I investigate the testimony of literature on the subject of mourning, because mourning constitutes the great paradox of our life: our encounter with finality, the disappearance of those we love, the impossible absence of those who were ever present in our lives. I say "paradox" because the dead do *not* disappear: we see them in photographs and letters; we hear and speak to them in our minds and dreams; we incorporate them in our behavior and genetic makeup. No writer can rival Marcel Proust on this topic, and it will be seen that his extreme focus on the processes of loss and survival is both Herculean and Promethean, gifting us with something as precious as fire: a fresh grasp of our own most intimate doings.

If the deaths of others are survivable and sayable, our own, strictly speaking, is not. But we can spend years worrying about its schedule, and we can sometimes chart its approach, not unlike an air-traffic control tower that tracks incoming planes. Tolstoy's famous novella about dying, *The Death of Ivan Ilych,* is among our premier literary accounts of how botched and dreadful these matters are likely to be. Poets and dramatists have also sought to say death, and this chapter will close with a look at the remarkable nineteenth-century American duo of Walt Whitman and Emily Dickinson—one titanic, the other sibylline—as well as discussing the only effort I know to actually stage dying: Ionesco's tragicomic *Exit the King.* Contrary to all expectations, these meditations on death are not in the least morbid: instead, they possess a mix of pluck, humor, and radiance that exemplify the gift of art, enabling us to take a readier and richer stance when it comes to final things.

Finally, in the concluding chapter, death-in-life is my target: I am thinking of *depression* as a form of dying that can set in tragically early, well before our bodies give out, causing a wreckage that may be worse than death, producing that "mass of men who lead lives of quiet desperation," as Thoreau memorably put it. I consider depression to be arguably the greatest scourge now facing modern Western society, a form of plague without lesions or other telltale signs, a plague no amount of safe sex can protect you from.

Hence, I close with a brief discussion of *Hamlet* as Shakespeare's brilliant mapping of a new species, a species increasingly with us today. *Hamlet* is the ever-fascinating study of a life crisis, of a discovery that one's mission is impossible, and—much worse, much more prophetic— that one's self is unownable. Shakespeare has given us a portrait of dysfunctionality, and this melancholy prince casts a long shadow over the centuries to come. In Hamlet's predicament we will recognize each of the problems and crises illuminated in my book: the mutinous body that takes over (this is what Hamlet cannot forgive his mother), the merry-go-round self that defies diagnosis (this is the riddle that Hamlet presents to his peers), the plaguelike sickness that rots in the state of Denmark (this is Hamlet's discovery), the sovereign undoing of meaning and purpose that is death's awful legacy to the living (this is the secret of the grave diggers). Little surprise that this young man suffers from what the Elizabethans would have called *melancholy*.

This legacy of the afflicted prince carries through the centuries, and I close my conclusion with a glance at one of his most fascinating literary descendants, William Faulkner's Quentin Compson (from *The Sound and the Fury*) as my version of what Hamlet might look like in the twentieth century, speaking American prose. We close with two young men, one a Renaissance prince, the other sent by his family to Harvard, each fatally incapacitated, each encountering the randomness of self and the musical chairs of life, each head and heart rendered indelibly by the institution of writing, writing that goes so deeply into the maelstrom to deliver its tumult, its sound and fury, that our picture of mind and consciousness is irrevocably altered. Literature discovers for us who we are.

Depression, yes. Depressing, no. The sheer genius of these two portrayals is life-affirming, awakening. The boldness of vision, the pith of language, the keenness of feeling, and the beauty of art *lift* us rather than lower us, cut through our frozen sea (as Kafka put it), and restore to us a sense of life's actual plenitude, of our own echoing reaches. Hamlet claimed that "readiness is all," and I want, many centuries later, to claim that art makes us readier, provides rehearsals (workouts, if you will), expands the scene, enables us to envision, to see, to experience *vicariously* the range of human feelings and fates recorded over time. I mean this book to be something of a guided tour for that special voyage, a way into feeling via art, a way of reading literature as emotional highway, a way of attending to the scream that goes through the house.

My chapters chart the itinerary of that scream. Bodies are its privileged site, and we are stunned by literature's representation of bodies as the strange place where we live. Diagnosis seeks to see, hear, and map this unfurling scream, and literature spells out how much mystery and violence accompany all attempts to go *inside* the mind or body. Infection and plague denote the social and even political reaches of illness, but only in literature and art do we glimpse the larger riddle at hand: the riddle of human connection. Death would seem to close the trajectory, to constitute the scream's final phase, its end stop, but here too we are surprised, for literature refuses to abide by such closure or silence, but instead opens up the territory, shows us how resonant and sinuous dying is, how much illumination death itself yields. We close with depression because it—even more than chronic pain which can be its fellow traveler—may be thought of as a halfway house where the scream goes on forever, a scream now seen as inseparable from consciousness itself, as if the bloodstream that irrigates body and mind became audible at last, bringing our entire psychic system to cacophonous voice and impending collapse.

Yes, Hamlet enables us to eavesdrop on our own most intimate and profound doings, and thus he stands for all the mediating figures who appear in this parade: for Oedipus, Ivan Ilych, Gregor Samsa, Proust's Marcel, and so many more. They are all guides of a sort, assisting us in our move toward self-exploration; they help us to a keener sense of our own inner landscapes. Art equips. I'll feel my book is a success if you come away from it with a sense that art constitutes a personal as well as a cultural gift that is far more practical, useful, than had been suspected. Rousseau once described reading as a way of "peopling his solitude." In addition to the familiar resources on which we depend—health, love, money, intelligence, character, family, friends—I believe it is essential for us to see art as instrumental to life, as a resource we can use.

These works of art and literature make up that "other" world I have mentioned, that house traversed by a scream of human feeling, that capacious and fascinating mirror in which you see yourself and others anew, trying out some of the roles and vicarious lives that art makes available to us. Just as Alice went into the looking glass, you must take the plunge. These novels and poems constitute a huge resource that is one of the fundamental gifts of culture. When we consider how narrow our individual straits seem in many times of life, including in times of sickness and pain, when we seek help for our ills, when we think about how much we pay—in lost time as well as money, in lost life—for relief, then the wares discussed in this book must indeed be one of civilization's great and unacknowledged bargains.

I have tried to write this book in the language of everyday speaking. I have avoided scholarly footnotes or excursions into high theory. My topic may seem heavy and large, but I want my book to be vibrant and fun, the way I find literature and art to be. The greatest pleasure of my career in teaching is something that miraculously occurs over and over: the sheer excitement I see generated in students by the encounter with art. I think of this excitement as a kind of creatural nourishment, on the order of a transcendent meal, even of a blood transfusion, so that reading literature and looking at painting become a life-giving exercise. One thing is sure: I find and make my own voice through attending the voices of writers I love, just as I discover and fashion my ideas through visits to this same quarry. Art is sustenance. Art is transformation. Such transactions are properly *inspiriting,* not unlike the project of the cannibals of old: to ingest the body of warriors they revered was to take into themselves the spirit of those warriors. I don't think this is a bad way to characterize the nurturance that great literature and art make available to us. It brings us back to bodies; it brings us back to those two shelves, one with books and one with pills, each destined to enter and alter us. May these books do as much for you.

A Scream Goes Through the House

CHAPTER ONE

A Scream Goes Through the House

In every cry of every Man,
In every Infant's cry of fear,
In every voice, in every ban,
The mind-forged manacles I hear.
—WILLIAM BLAKE, "London"

I was walking along a road with two friends—the sun was going down—
I felt something like a breath of melancholy. The sky was suddenly blood-
red—I stopped, and leant against the fence, dead tired—I saw the
flaming clouds like blood and a sword—the bluish-black fjord and
town—My friends walked on—I stood there, trembling with anxiety—
and I felt as though Nature were convulsed by a great unending scream.
—EDVARD MUNCH

ARE WE ALONE?

This book is about the urgency, centrality, and reach of human feeling. I regard feeling as the driving force of our individual lives, and I see it as the very stuff of which art is made. These are radical beliefs, inasmuch as we are taught to think of ourselves as predominantly creatures of reason, as opposed to feeling. And we are also taught to think of art—literature, painting, film—as a largely intellectual enterprise. My argument goes entirely the other way.

Art is our supreme record of human feeling over the ages, and it enables us, quite wonderfully, to access our own emotional depths. These convictions may seem radical, because they challenge many prevalent views about both self and art. Let us examine some of these assumptions, in order to clarify what my book attacks.

Let us begin with the notion of *individuation,* of a person's being confined to the body and mind he or she is born with. This is one of our most common assumptions. When we are in pain, we feel we are alone. Of course, social interaction—family, work, friendship, community, love—can militate against this self-absorbed view of life, but in moments of great pain, whether physical or emotional, our islanded state can seem ever more true. We tend to close in, rather than open out, when there is pain, hurt. Yes, there are people who attend the scream and hurt of others. And we are, each of us, equipped with empathy and sympathy. But goodwill and compassion are only what they are, and they are rarely enough to cross the existential and creatural divide that separates me from you. We feel alone in our pain. We alone know our pain.

This book takes the premise that the opposite is true: human feeling connects us. Works of literature and art can be the bridge. A scream goes through the house. Pain, hurt, feeling, can be shared.

We all know what a scream is: the primordial human expression of feeling, usually the feeling of pain or anguish. Screams constitute the most primitive form of language, utterance at a level common to all living creatures, language that is unamenable to grammar, syntax, or control. Infants scream, children scream. Adults, we know, scream rather less, because they have learned to convert such raw sentience into distancing language, but it does not seem far-fetched to say that adults may be screaming *inwardly* a great deal, even though we do not hear them.

We can hurt from fear as well as from lesions, and such hurt can range from garden-variety stress to massive, incapacitating anxiety about our work, our relationships, and our engagement with the deaths that must come: those of loved ones and our own. Some may find my description of normal, everyday life exaggerated and melodramatic. You look outside and you do not see shrieking citizens. You meet people and you smile. Pleasure is not unreal. But hurt is more real than we often acknowledge; it has a frequency that no one has ever measured but that every sentient being knows.

This book recognizes the existential dilemma of aloneness and incommunicable pain, but then goes on to show that literature and art constitute a precious human resource for just this reason: they offer us a stunning map of human feeling, a map that displays a world of linkage and connection, in which solitude is overcome, and pain finds utterance.

Illness is one of the quintessential human experiences of such matters, illness understood, at least initially, as the body in pain. Put this way, illness and pain appear as the fate of flesh, the inevitable itinerary of life-in-bodies, beginning with the crying of the newborn, continuing with all the bouts of sickness that punctuate life (even the healthiest life), and extending to the final chapter of death and dying. Illness is also the mind in pain, and this distress seems, if anything, even more locked up within us, more incommunicable, more at odds with the data recorded on our résumés, more unrevealed and unshared and unshareable than physical hurt is. These seem to be stubborn facts of life, with us from cradle to grave.

I have written this book to challenge those facts of life.

THROUGH THE HOUSE: ART AS COMMUNITY

The belief at the heart of this book is that art—literature, painting, and film, as argued, but surely music and other forms of aesthetic experience as well—offers us a shocking new picture of human arrangements, a picture that is insistently collective, relational, and extended. In art we can find and tap into a reservoir of feeling, and this encounter not only breaks open our solitude but also makes audible and visible to us the emotional lines of force that bathe individual life, separate us, yet connect us to one another. Art and literature are the ears we do not have, to hear the sounds of sentience, the emotions of others, and even our own;

they are the eyes we do not always have, that can look beneath the surface to see revealed the currents of feeling that lie beneath our words, our actions, and our separate states, and also to delineate the larger community in which emotions inscribe us.

That is why I have called this book *A Scream Goes Through the House.* The scream originates inside as a sign of pain, but it does not stay inside, stop there: it moves out of us, *it goes through the house.* Our scream, our seemingly private, seemingly incommunicable expression of anguish or pain has a trajectory, even a career, out in the world and over time, and its "journey" constitutes a story, a capacious human narrative that has largely gone unseen and unheard. That story creates an inhabitable universe, a *world* of feeling, a world whose citizens we all are, when we hurt, yet it is also a world we can explore, when we hurt. It is my claim that human pain, human feeling more generally, is a pathway; it remakes reality, redraws the boundaries, reconceives the self: where self starts and stops. Unlike the Internet with its informational highway, I have in mind an altogether different network, a kind of emotional highway, a place we can visit via imagination, so that all our assumptions about self-enclosure and incommunicable feeling are utterly exploded: feeling is an umbilical cord that links us to others, is ultimately a mode of travel and transformation.

Where, you may well ask, is this other world I am describing? The answer, of course, is art. Art not only gifts us a picture of this broader sentient universe, a universe that extends across the usually accepted boundaries of time and space, but it offers us a ticket to travel there as well; art and literature enable us to see ourselves anew, to discern our own fit within these larger realms. The experience of art bestows on us something akin to new citizenship papers. Seen collectively, literature and art, including the works discussed in the pages of this book, constitute no less than a mirror and echo chamber, a universe in which our personal stories might be seen and aligned with or against those others on show. Art transports us, we know that; it ushers us into a larger relational scheme largely because *feeling* is a prime motor in the artistic energy system, a driving force with directionality, scope, and coherence.

Feeling makes art; art makes feeling. These matters are deeply personal, because the feelings in question are not only the artist's, but also the reader's, the spectator's, yours. This reciprocal "making" of art and experience through feeling is, in its own right, territorializing, geographical, constitutive of an actual space for living—with others, through others, as others—well beyond the cramped quarters we have thought to be "self" and "home." It may sound metaphoric, but the encounter with art is a colonizing experience. We explore the imaginative and emotional terrain of the work, and the work stamps us with its depiction of human life and feeling—and so it makes sense to view this form of mind travel as genuine outreach, a true extension of self. I state this despite the more common view that art is not only subjective but a doubly private matter, an affair of "appreciation" that mainly goes nowhere but "in."

It is worth pondering these matters, however, because art offers us a prodigious resource here—here in the realm of feeling, whether it be pain or pleasure—and it is a resource utterly unimagined and untapped by the scientific paradigm that governs Western thinking along these lines. Art that matters is rarely sermonizing or didactic (it does not tell us "what to do"), but the project of this book is to show that it is deeply instructive nonetheless, gifting us with tools of immeasurable value and vistas of what it means to be human. I am arguing the utility of art, not in the sense that a visit to the museum or library could be invigorating or could replace a visit to the doctor, but in the broader and more jarring sense that art rewrites our location on the map, reconceives what we take to be our actual contours, where you or I begin and end.

In making visible the revolutionary potency and range of feeling— feeling as collective rather than self-contained—art makes available to us a new model of affective pathways, a new understanding of "connective tissue." My viewpoint has nothing to do with some mushy sense of mutual "caring" or "concern" for others; on the contrary, I am claiming that art overwhelms us with its news of feelings and relationships, that it brothers and sisters us, binds us in some almost visceral way beyond our choosing. The mere encounter with an image, the absorption of a story, are events grafted onto your flesh, entered into your body and blood and heart as well as your brain.

The territory the artist colonizes, the vineyard he toils in, is you. It is precisely inside of us that art releases its meaning and its riches. Emerson calls the poet *representative* in this sense: he "apprises us not of his wealth, but of the commonwealth" (448), inasmuch as the poetic vision we apprehend becomes *ours,* perhaps always was ours, needed only the poet to complete the transaction, the gift.

In saying that art enters our bloodstream—not like an infection, but like a transfusion—I again have Emerson in mind, especially his view of the Oversoul which he defines utterly along cardiac lines: "And this, because the heart in thee is the heart of all; not a valve, not a wall, not an intersection is there anywhere in nature, but one blood rolls uninterruptedly an endless circulation through all men, as the water of the globe is all one sea, and, truly seen, its tide is one" (399). In echoing John Donne's famous line, "no man is an island," Emerson radically challenges our intuitive and empirical conviction of being contained within individual borders, bound within our skin, creatures who can be opened up only at great risk.

To see the human circulatory system as a version of the water of the globe is to posit flow and connectedness as the central facts of life. Self and other, self and world, partake of each other. Is it possible that the life-giving blood that animates us only seems to be housed in our organism? Might it also come from afar, just as the air we breathe does, just as the words we read and the sights we see do?

Not only is art our commonwealth, the larger estate that is ours, but *in* art we sometimes discover this same shocking sense of a world that is entirely networked, tentacular, linked: a waterway and bloodstream that all creatures share, are nourished by. *A scream goes through the house:* the utterance of human feeling floods out into the world through literature and art. But it is no less true the other way around: the voices of the world enter into us, move from house to occupant, from wind to word.

The *house* through which the scream goes is to be understood as the terrains of both time and space. Space signifies the larger stage—family, society, universe—on which we are located. Time would be the two-way flow from past to present and back. Time brings Sophocles and Shakespeare to us, and us to them. This flow conveys the still living power of the dead, the heritage of feeling that enters you via their texts, the living emotive current that constitutes the bloodline, the central traffic of all art.

Time would also be the historical flow of your own life, a flow that art is equipped to register, but which normal perception cannot. Just as dreams bring your entire life into composite form, so too does art yield something precious, on the order of a four-dimensional portrait, rendering the shape of your life in a way that neither the eye nor casual thinking can perceive.

At the end of Proust's very long novel, the narrator, now an old man, hears the tinkling of a bell that reminds him of the same portentous sounds of long ago when the neighbor Swann used to close his evening visits (portentous because now he would have Maman all to himself), and he then wonders, with terror, if this is not the same bell indeed, if the ringing has ever stopped, if somewhere deep within us some things go on forever. Is it possible that key moments in our lives—moments of pleasure or pain, moments that mark us—echo and resonate endlessly, ordinarily just below the threshold of consciousness, but suddenly perceivable in times of heightened experience? Do we ever stop screaming?

We all know the cliché of wearing one's heart on one's sleeve, and we think it a cliché because our emotional life is thought to be invisible. But what if it were not? What if literature and art were a new code that expressed the hidden story of feeling that truly tells who we are, who we have been? What if others could perceive this? When Sophocles' Jocasta finally sees, with inescapable certainty, that Oedipus is her son as well as her husband, she emits a scream: "Aieeeeee— / man of agony— / that is the only name I have for you, / that, no other—ever, ever, ever!" (223). Given that the entire play is devoted to the riddle of Oedipus' identity, the many different and transgressive roles he has played, Jocasta confers on this man perhaps his truest name: "Aieeeeee— / man of agony." Her scream also illuminates the horror of *her* life—whose fatal pattern is only now visible—constituting a tragic existence every bit as awful as Oedipus'.

Art helps us to see and to hear the "Aieeeeee" that may punctuate our lives, to feel the truth that the past—especially its injuries or transgressions—is rarely past. For many these may not be welcome tidings. After all, one wants to believe that the past is past, that pain can be truly over, the wound can heal, the damage be transcended. And it is true that people get well, survive trauma, live in the present, and have a shot at a future. But it is also true that the past and its screams break through, are real, that a life-in-time amounts to a prodigious amount of processing older materials, and that few of us are "clear" of the earlier events that have marked us.

True, too, is the sheer scale of a life that recovers its dimensionality and sweep, and I have long felt that Sophocles wanted, in some strange fashion, to tell the story of a man who came slowly into possession of his life and who had the courage to chart his real narrative line, even to the tune of embracing the horrors (of parricide and incest) that were his; and that Sophocles then presented this *recuperation* of a life as at once something noble and also the secret medicine for a dying community: Oedipus' life story becomes therapy for Thebes.

Our lives are so filled with days and years, with details and routines, that few of us possess that magic thread, that figure in the carpet, which would give a distilled picture of who we really are, of what our life really means. Art does just this. However you turn it, art challenges the thin, "over with" testimony of daily experience. Art is true to the stubborn, enduring, shaping power of feeling, the longitudinal reach of feelings. In the realm of feelings we cannot easily close up shop or leave it in the office; we bring it home with us, we relive it, we work through it, and it works through us. Art is echoing, committed to depths, hence shows the surface to be a shimmering thing that speaks in many tongues; literature is invested in orchestrating all the critical data of a life—and even of a culture—into a picture of depth, relationships across time, connections across space.

Art has common cause with dreams, those nightly experiences of the reaches and odd patterns of our lives, those episodes where longitude and latitude come together so that the people of the past and the present do their dance of musical chairs, displaying for us a tapestry of our doings (and failures to do) that bears little resemblance to our résumés and chitchat. Such vistas enlarge us even as they intimate that almost all human business is unfinished business. The familiar myths that we can "compartmentalize" and find "closure" may have some narrow authority, but art tends to take down, to deconstruct, these fences, to breach the dikes as dreams do, and to let the flow in. The resultant flux flows across boundaries and can take many forms: it can create a new amalgam of personal past and present; it can be a shocking conflation of people and things you'd thought separate, now seen as glued together, and glued to you.

What is wrecked in these configurations of art and dream is our conventional sense of self, our habitual view of personal contours and identity. In its stead, we perceive something wondrous and strange, not totally unlike those odd moments when we see ourselves in a three-way mirror, or worse still, in a fun-house mirror, and yet sense that this is also us, the side of us we ordinarily omit, the fuller shape we customarily miss. But the ultimate significance of the shock of recognition that art provides has to do with the now visible lineaments of feeling, the now visible emotional ties that have shaped us, that still shape us, even though no photograph can render them. *Epiphany* is one term that has been invoked to convey this moment of perceptual truth, when our "true form" is grasped. "Four-dimensional portraiture" is another way of characterizing the plenitude of self that art makes available.

All of these concepts are a way of attending to the scream that goes through the house, a way of seeing our lives as they truly are: crisscrossed with ties, bound to others, and as shot through with feelings as are those ultraviolet photos that reveal the presence of rays we normally cannot see.

JANE EYRE

Consider as an example of fourth-dimensional portraiture, of how the fully sentient self could be depicted, a seemingly realist novel such as Charlotte Brontë's *Jane Eyre*. The book starts, logically enough, with Jane's unhappy childhood as poor relation and orphan in the Reed family. This stint with misery is epitomized in the episode of the "red room," where Jane is locked up as punishment for resisting the Reeds' emotional, even physical abuse. Terrified of ghosts (she is in the dead uncle's room), Jane sees her own reflection in the mirror ("visionary hollow" is Brontë's term) and fails initially to recognize herself; she sees only "glittering eyes of fear," and thinks of phantoms, fairies, and imps. Shortly thereafter, Jane is certain a ghost is coming, sees a light moving, and then she experiences an extraordinary moment of visitation, of panic and capsizing: "My heart beat thick, my head grew hot; a sound filled my ears, which I deemed the rushing of wings; something seemed near me; I was oppressed, suffocated; endurance broke down"; a moment later, the servants unlock the door and rush into the room, claiming to have heard a scream, something prodigious: " 'What a dreadful noise! It went quite through me!' exclaimed Abbot" (49).

We, however, have read nothing of the sort: the text says nothing about Jane screaming. The servants leave, Jane is again locked up, and this time she falls unconscious: "a species of fit." Everything in this sequence broadcasts the imperiousness of feeling, feeling so strong that it makes you unrecognizable, travels as a ghost, is characterized by beating heart and hot head, bypasses consciousness altogether, snuffs out Jane's lights, has the run of the house.

In the next chapter Jane recounts awakening to the face of a kindly man standing over her, asking, " 'Well, who am I?' " Not a bad question for this book, it will turn out. Brontë is redrawing the map of the self, by attending to the scream that traverses it, the emotional injuries of which it is made. The novel then seems to go on its merry linear path, narrating Jane's subsequent adventures at Lowood School, then at Edward Rochester's Thornfield, then at Marsh End, and finally back to Rochester at book's close. But the only way to really understand *Jane Eyre* is to realize that the episode in the red room—a visit from phantoms and fairies and imps, sound in the ears, rushing of wings, eventuating into a scream that comes from her without her knowing it, but then goes "quite through" all those around her—sets the stage for the entire novel, gets replayed throughout Jane's life, is ultimately the scream that goes through the house. For Jane is presented already in childhood as split, fissured, porous, entered by spirits, a shrieker of screams.

How would you truly show the enduring effects of emotional injury, the actual reality of trauma? I'd want to say that the penetrating scream in the red room is a signal of Jane's own continual emotional turmoil *that will not be silenced or stay put,* a kind of libidinal flow that courses through the house and the story. In this regard, Brontë is stunningly Freudian (even though she antedates him by over half a century), in that the red room episode is given to us as a textbook illustration of the mechanics of child abuse, of a wound that stays open, so that the language of phantoms and shrieks becomes eloquent as an index of damage that leads to potent feelings and to alteration of self. Brontë has wanted to tell the story of an injured child, and it is no accident that the motif of abandoned or unsavable children runs in filigree throughout the novel, appearing in Bessie's songs and in Jane's own fitful dreams. After all, what does emotional abuse of a child truly look like? At the surface, with a camera or notebook, you could describe it in terms of *something happening,* a physical or sexual injury; but how would you graph what is happening *under* the surface, what continues to smolder throughout one's life?

Brontë's invasion of the spirits in the episode in the red room does exactly that, shows us a little girl in the process of becoming a haunted house. Yet her scream not only escaped, but it seems ultimately to script the key events of the novel. For Brontë writes her narrative in such a way that the surface realism—from episode A to episode B and so forth—is disrupted, imploded by the libidinal virulence generated in the red room. This virulence is so great that it becomes the novel's reality principle by *twinning* its characters. Hence, Charlotte Brontë has taken the fissured, spirit-ridden Jane, and has systematically *doubled* her in this novel by her raging, carnal, libidinally charged counterpart self: Bertha Mason Rochester, the madwoman in the attic.

To see that proper, diminutive, wrenlike Jane and libidinal, corpulent, murderous Bertha might be the *same person* is to break all the rules of both realist fiction and common sense, but the poetic logic here is irresistible. Punish a young girl enough—and this book loads on the punishment—and she'll either die or explode. To see Bertha's violence as Jane's revenge is to see how the scream that goes through the house sovereignly reshapes reality, gives it a devastating emotional cogency.

Brontë would hardly have understood the word *uncanny* in the way Freud did—as an intuition that the place we enter for the first time is oddly familiar, that we've been there before—yet her novel beautifully depicts just such a world. It is a deceptive physical world, deceptive because it is drenched in spirit and emotion, ordered by libido rather than Newtonian logic, a space that is entirely scripted by our past history. Is this not what it means when the scream inside goes through us, then through the house? It spills out, shapes what we see, governs and becomes our reality.

Freud invokes the uncanny because he knows that we *create* the world (rather than merely taking it in), and we do so by projecting onto its physical surface our own emotional and libidinal needs and circumstances. Art, on this heading, is the supreme subjective record of life, the personal vision of things that might be at complete odds with the objective picture. Proust once claimed that film was an inferior art form for just this reason: it was shackled to the existing physical world of appearances and could not represent our inner picture of life. Through art, however, all of us have access to these interior universes. And these inner realms brought to expression in art can reveal what actually matters in our lives, what our deep story is, what our personal take on (and from) life is. (If these notions seem exaggerated, just ask yourself what *meaning* or *aura* the objects that surround you might have for a camera or distant observer, objects such as the photographs on your desk, the old toys you've not quite discarded, the jewelry or clothing you've inherited, indeed the very faces that surround you, including the one that looks at you in the mirror.)

In serving both the dictates of realism (agreed-on public reality) and the inner vision, Brontë remains a shrewd writer, giving us large chunks of objective data, but nonetheless governing her story, at key moments, according to the laws of feeling, the power of injury and emotion. At its most extreme, however, when the private view is not even checked by objective conditions, such art can become outright visionary. The agreed-on physical world that our retinas take in is then quite simply metamorphosed, reshaped by the emotional and libidinal currents of the seer. I use that word *seer* advisedly: the visionary prophet and the ordinary human subject who sees—might they not be one and the same? Might it not be that all of us carry within us a pulsating world of emotions and experiences that is overflowing all the time, spilling into and onto the scene we inhabit, ultimately and deviously composing the scene we inhabit, transposing the people we see into figures from our inner worlds?

We all are familiar with the old chestnut that ten people sitting around a table repeating from one to the next the same story will alter it to the tune of being unrecognizable: version ten will have no relation to version one. Why is this so? It will not do to chalk this up to sloppiness or inattentiveness; closer to the mark would be an acknowledgment that listening—like seeing, like all thinking—is an aggressively shaping activity, a complex process of inserting what we hear into the ongoing story we are always thinking (if not telling). We are all lifelong artists, shaping (secreting) our hidden, inner story from birth to death.

This example may be banal, but in the hands of a great artist, the docile, contoured world we take for granted is liberated from its material envelope, transformed into vistas of startling traffic, yielding new amalgams, leading to a rich but staggeringly unified picture of both self and world. All this differs entirely from the humdrum, daily experience of life in the office or at home, life filled with objects that are there, but hardly "cohere" or express any sort of deep truth about who we are, and how we have lived. Those deep truths are on the inside, often resistant even to ourselves, which is why many of us go through life feeling that our true coordinates, our genuine melody, our actual meaning, remain hidden and unknown.

The work of art shocks us with its cogency, its way of ordering things so that the truer pattern of life—the unstilled longings of Proust's narrator, the actual shape of Oedipus' existence, the emotional wounds of Jane Eyre—comes to the fore. You may think that such "unity" is merely the private, obsessive vision of the artist, illuminating a hermetic inner world, and thus has no wider relevance for us, the readers or spectators. But at its best, the visionary model—the personal vision that does justice to feeling as the secret law of life, the form-giver of life—can be fiercely social, can be luminous in its reshaping of *our* world. Art that hallows feeling, art that heeds the scream that goes through the house, is ultimately public in nature, illuminating our own private arrangements within the larger family or culture in unforgettable ways. Yes, we are enriched, enlarged, and in some wonderful but awful sense, *implicated*— advised of our fit (our responsibilities) in arrangements we had not foreseen, in families and communities we had thought to be distant, unrelated, nothing to us. Art that is suffused by human feeling upends our complacent sense of individual sovereignty, our lazy certainty that we are freestanding and self-sufficient. "Nothing to us" may be our trusty safe-conduct pass through life, but art challenges such immunity.

Let us move now to the real evidence, by looking carefully at selected artistic visions, drawn from poetry, narrative, theater, painting, and film, each illustrating the reach and shaping power of feeling. The scream that punctuates individual life does not stop there, but goes out into the world, is shown to be the governing principle of reality; it recasts discrete phenomena into a new mesh, providing a startling discovery of linkage and connection, forcing us to reconsider what a family is, what a society is. Each of these works hallows the authority of feeling, seeks to show how feeling is the primary pulsion and cohesion of life, with enormous moral and political consequences. Ultimately, we discover, as we experience these works of art, that feeling is not only pulsion, but actually *propulsion,* propelling *us* into larger realms, larger selves. I begin with William Blake's canonical poem of 1794, "London," to show how one prodigious poem reconfigures the position of the human subject (and the human reader) in the bustling life of the metropolis.

IT ALL FLOWS TOGETHER: WILLIAM BLAKE'S "LONDON"

Blake's "London," a sixteen-line poem, has probably received as much critical scrutiny as any text in English literature. This piece is, I think, particularly beloved among teachers because it seems to speak even to the most unschooled readers, seems to resonate and to cohere in ways that every reader senses, even if obscurely. It goes like this:

> *I wander through each chartered street,*
> *Near where the chartered Thames does flow,*
> *And mark in every face I meet*
> *Marks of weakness, marks of woe.*
>
> *In every cry of every Man,*
> *In every Infant's cry of fear,*
> *In every voice, in every ban,*
> *The mind-forged manacles I hear.*

How the Chimney-sweeper's cry
Every blackening Church appalls;
And the hapless Soldier's sigh
Runs in blood down Palace walls.

But most through midnight streets I hear
How the youthful Harlot's curse
Blasts the new born Infant's tear,
And blights with plagues the Marriage hearse. (144)

This is an explosive poem, or rather a series of explosions happening stanza by stanza, sometimes line by line, or even image by image. If you negotiate it evenly and coolly right to the end, how do you maintain composure when hit by the apocalyptic last line? Much of the poem's power comes from the awesome view of human society as one of flux and inescapable linkage among disparate individuals; the view that it enunciates is awesome because it unseats, unhinges our notions of self and stasis.

"Self" and "stasis" are the best words I can muster for the fundamental notions of fixity that regulate and undergird ordinary perception and thinking. We take ourselves to be finite, bounded creatures, each of us an "I" who goes through life under those arrangements: that is *self*. And each thing we see or conceive is (and remains) that thing we see and conceive; our world behaves, stays inside its definitional skin, doesn't pirouette or go on outings: that is *stasis*. Blake's poem, even though it sits nicely in its sixteen lines, wrecks all this, and tells us—a bit the way a merry-go-round tells us—about collapsing boundaries and swirling pathways, about how other people inescapably collide into us, about new communities into which we find ourselves thrust as card-carrying members of humanity with heavy obligations for one another, like it or not. Put more simply, the poem makes us see and hear—what an astonishing verb *make* is here, as if poetry could be coercive and engendering, could actually force a change in our registers—the feelings of others, shatters us with its scream that goes through the house: we are interconnected, inevitably and across boundaries of all kinds.

The poem's first stanza rips apart the notion of "chartered," precisely by contrasting the man-made (government-ordained) order of city streets against the fluid, uncontrollable river whose course may be traced but whose power cannot be regulated. More than two centuries after the writing of this poem, at a time when we are numbed by the ecological disasters that seem almost routinely to lay waste to our orderly landscapes—floods, earthquakes, hurricanes (along with the famine, disease, and social catastrophes they leave in their wake)—we rediscover something of the inherent unruliness in Blake's ironic lines, an unruliness that points up the arrogance of complacent urban and political design. But that first stanza also broadcasts the quintessential breakthrough of the poem: the poet reads individual pain as a collective grammar ("marks of weakness, marks of woe"), sees every London face as luminous and legible, like a billboard announcing its message. Something insistently diagnostic, downright medical, is happening here: the translation of human countenance into affective and ideological symptom.

For this doctor-poet the city dwellers are indeed ill. It comes through the ears as well as the eyes. "Cry" is twice stated, to tell us that acculturated adults are hardly different from newborn babes in their expression of life's hurt. But the poet's aural apprehension reaches a new plateau altogether when he assesses London noise as "mind-forged manacles." Is there any formulation in English that quite rivals these terms for saying ideological repression? With remarkable economy and pith, these words denote culture itself as imprisonment, as internalized ("self-willed" in some horrible, almost artisanal sense) incarceration, a building project (it would seem) of lifelong duration whose (mad? tragic? evil?) purpose is penal. But perhaps the most striking feature of Blake's notation is this: this act of penitential submission and deformation, this systematic undoing of agency, far from being silently at work in the dark (as one would expect) is *heard*. The poet hears the manacles—

I think of Jacob Marley clanking up those stairs on his way to Ebenezer Scrooge—and we must wonder: just how metaphoric is this? Just as every urban face is an open book, so is every London sound rendered as the clink of chains and prison. One might cavil that such perception is reductive (after all, London is a big and various place), but it is also grand in its incessant translation of *inner life*—pain, misery, powerlessness—into *public notation,* indeed into spectacle, uncannily seen and heard. And this is the poem's central strategic gambit: to transform locked-in, hidden, personal hurt into explosive, luminous public script.

The force of such a move is felt only if we contrast it with what we know of common experience. The initial premise I began with, notably that we are alone in our misery, can be complemented by premise number two: we are likewise in the dark when it comes to the misery of others. But in this poem private misery crosses a representational threshold, becomes a common language. One might counter that only the visionary poet is privy to this public broadcast, but the very act of reading the poem forces us to realize that the institution of poetry is a public broadcast, bringing every reader into Blake's field of vision.

Reading is the visionary experience of civilized life. Reading Blake's "London" zones you into frequencies you've never heard, assaults you with images of the living city as carnivorous and corrupt as Moloch devouring its citizens. (Fritz Lang's great film of the 1920s, *Metropolis,* with its man-eating machines and herdlike workers, is not a bad analogue for Blake's vision of systemic exploitation.) On this head, art itself gets reconceived, moved from the esoteric margins as high-culture frill all the way to the center, now seen as nuts-and-bolts public utility, as basic as electricity, light, gas, and water, a means of articulating and disseminating news of the common weal, a barometric project that is always measuring and announcing the culture's weather. In today's electronic era of instantaneous and encyclopedic information gathering, we find nothing remotely comparable to the collective utterance brought about in this poem. The Internet can tally heads and bodies and data, but it does not have the "accessing reach" to tell us what is going on *inside*. Moreover, recent research has confirmed that traveling on the information highway is experienced by many as a lonely enterprise, reinforcing the anomie of modern life, contributing to a culture of data-drenched self-enclosure quite at odds with the empowerment rhetoric that heralds this new technology. Blake's poem moves toward solidarity.

I claimed that we think ourselves alone in our misery, and whereas this is true in general (even if banal), it is still truer, and less banal, when it comes down to those victimized and abused in society, those whose hurt is systemically caused and just as systemically ignored. In the second half of his poem, Blake gets down to business, spells out just whose pain and misery he has in mind.

He starts with the chimney sweepers, those very young children and orphans who often died in London's chimneys, sacrificial victims commemorated in some of his finest lyrics. Once again, the paradox leaps out at us: the cry of the small child is what we customarily fail to hear, and in this instance it is not fanciful to imagine this cry coming actually from the chimney-coffins themselves, transformed by Blake into an indictment *d'outre-tombe,* from beyond the grave. These voices, largely unhearable in reality, become terribly potent: they "appall" "every blackening Church."

Here, again, we encounter the potency, muscularity, and reach of art. The physical setting is transfigured: the cry of the child-victim alters the landscape, both frightens and makes pale the sooty church, makes graphically and obscenely visible the power relations (as Blake saw them) between religious institution and victims of society. The following lines extend this revolutionary logic, this weird boomerang that cries out for justice for the weak by showing exactly who is doing them in: the hapless soldier's sigh—a sigh that takes place far away from London, somewhere in the empire, a sigh that cannot possibly be noticed in any realist scheme—is not only *heard* (given Blake's sensibilities, we expect this much), but is stunningly *translated* into an elemental script: it

"Runs in blood down Palace walls." This line carries, for me, some of the terror associated with the Greek oracle: a voice becomes fate, a noise becomes destiny, an institution turns reality into language, and language into reality.

In recent years our TV screens seem to overflow with images of bodies buried under rubble or uncovered in mass graves, of silent, stony faces trekking out of war zones, and we, in our living rooms, take this in as the obscene underside of our history. As we have learned, it can sometimes even happen on home ground. But for the most part it comes to us, even on today's TV screens, as silent film, as distant as the newsreels of another era that were called *The March of Time.* Is it too much to say that our grasp of history itself—including its most unprocessible chapters such as the Holocaust or Hiroshima or even the twin towers at New York's World Trade Center—is finally a set of images depicting mute victims, or (worse still) pure rubble that guards its secret, that entombs its silent dead?

To sum up, have we not learned, over and over, that cries go unheard, that the powerless are indeed powerless? New York, in the wake of September 11, 2001, was dotted with posters of the missing, and *The New York Times,* for months afterward, published thumbnail sketches of the victims, to give at least some sense of the victims' humanity, their story. But this poem, in its own way, goes much further: each victim trumpets forth—not via scream but by a sigh—his fateful indictment, and the virulence of such utterance turns it into a liquid script, into the visible blood that runs down palace walls.

We all know that the institution of language is at a crucial remove from things themselves, that words are differential, part of an endless semiotic chain that signifies ever more words, never at one, as Kant said long ago, with the thing itself, *das Ding an sich.* And many have bemoaned the "prison house of language," not just theorists and scholars and revolutionaries, but all those who feel that words always come up short and are not commensurate with what one actually wants to utter.

For just these reasons, Blake's achievement matters. Blood running down palace walls has a clarity and immediacy that are shockingly eloquent. Here is a pre-dictionary language (no schooling required), a violent but cogent *text* of abuse-and-punishment, an unmistakable graphic display of power relations that says: palaces send soldiers to their deaths, and churches are complicit with the exploitation of the weak. Blake has remained true to his initial image of the flowing Thames that cannot, we now realize, be "chartered," that does indeed *flow,* flows into and becomes running blood. Blake presents "flow" as the motor principle of the world, a flux that links victim back to institution, that becomes a fluid script for how power actually works, that eternal spectacle of the strong hurting the weak now become an actual spectacle, a kind of urban sound and light show, *son et lumière,* in which our relations are at last on show.

To say that flow is the law of the world is to challenge all notions of fixity: here versus there, now versus then, even you versus me. Blake's poem overturns these binarisms and categories, and in this new dispensation the rulers and their victims are umbilically connected and exposed as such. Power is at last visible, yes, but so too is pain. We return to those "marks of weakness, marks of woe," and we see that it all began there, that pain and suffering are a language, are "marks" of a story that can be told. In "London," such "marks" seem demiurgic in their thrust, capable of reconfiguring the world, demanding to tell their story of hurt and abuse. The poem closes with Blake's darkest and most apocalyptic images, as we realize (with a jolt) that it is indeed midnight, and that London is as diseased venereally as it is morally and politically. The inclusion of the harlot not only echoes back to the biblical Babylon as den of iniquity, but caps the poet's series of exploited figures, thereby defining the modern city almost exclusively as a human market, a place for buying and selling humans themselves (chimney sweeper, soldier, prostitute), a serial parade of use and abuse. The young prostitutes participate in the life and logic of flow: they pass on their venereal disease to the husbands who give it to their wives who extend it to the babes, and a generation itself is now doomed.

The City's great needs—warmth, security, sex—are serviced by its victims, but their day comes, here, as we witness the great reflux, the insidious two-way traffic that is fatally egalitarian in its operation, exposing the trumps of privilege and power to be, ultimately, illusory. Finally, the last stanza keeps covenant with Blake's "liberation theology," his transmutation of hurt into indictment, of isolated victim into public revenge. Everything speaks. The harlot's curse has the clarity and virulence of ancient curses, those moments when language acts on the world: she helps tell the story of her city and her time, links her plaint with that of others, as the poet weaves her voice into the visionary tapestry at hand. A scream goes through the house, and we follow its ideological itinerary, as luminous and revelatory as a flare in the night. This connective vision annihilates privacy and protection, and it reveals a new creatural community linked by hurt and abuse. That revelation, every bit as articulated and interconnected as the "network" reality-picture that emerges from our computer screens, is the work of poetry.

The force of Blake's visionary poem is most fully felt if we contrast this pulsating portrait of a city—with its wounded and victimized up front, their pain and blood writ large, sprayed like graffiti onto the actual surface of the city, onto its proudest institutions—with any other depiction imaginable: your perception as tourist walking the London streets? your experience with a CD-ROM presentation of London? even, let's say, your effort to imagine (on your own, without Blake's aid) the extent of exploitation and abuse that were hardwired in early capitalist England? My view is that none of these renditions can possibly rival the surreal one provided in Blake's poem. Not only does he illuminate what is invisible to our customary sight, but I'd claim that he brings us into the picture, hurls us through Customs (both conceptual and immigration), makes us (by dint of merely reading his poem) fellow travelers, witnesses to the crime, called on to respond. We can hardly go back in time and rescue chimney sweeps. We cannot easily soften the lives of today's urban or industrial victims either. But we respond nonetheless, as Blake takes us into the looking glass, over the threshold, into the inte-

rior. And what we navigate is no less than the great river of pain that unifies the lives of all these casualties. Reading a poem like "London" is indeed a "trip" (as one says today), but a voyage of virtually cardiac
dimensions, entailing entry into the bloodstream and flux of a great metropolis, so as to feel—in that ever so dry economic term—*the cost of
living*.

JAMES BALDWIN'S "SONNY'S BLUES": SUFFERING, KINSHIP, AND ART

If Blake begins on a private visionary note, James Baldwin opens his
poignant short story "Sonny's Blues" with the public record: the narrator, Sonny's older brother, reads a newspaper account of Sonny being
busted for heroin use. Whereas the poem explodes with its strange testimony, the narrative works perspectivally, gradually bringing *us*—the
"straight" readers for whom the "straight" older brother is a perfect surrogate, a man who has escaped Harlem's blight by playing by the rules,
marrying, having a family, becoming a schoolteacher—into Sonny's tortured life. And, indeed, is this not how most of us know about Harlem,
about heroin, perhaps even about the blues: as dispassionate observers,
as newspaper readers, as straight folks going about our lives? Baldwin
knows what he is doing when he entrusts his story to the papers and the
straight man.

Soon enough, we realize that "Sonny's Blues" is about the casualties
produced by Harlem, about the possible escape routes and strategies
devised in order not to go under. Not London with its Church and
Palace, perhaps, but Harlem is no less an all-powerful toxic container of
human lives, a systematic foreclosure and contaminator of individual
human possibility. Race is, of course, the major key. Hence, when the
narrator, who is justifiably proud of his hard-won stability, ponders
what he owes his busted brother Sonny, he recalls a good bit of his own
early history, including a story he has heard only late in life, from his
mother the last time he saw her, when he was home from the army on

leave. The story was about his father, long dead now, who, as a young man, witnessed the obscene murder of *his* younger (music-playing) brother by a bunch of drunk white youths out on a joyride:

> They was all drunk, and when they seen your father's brother they let out a great whoop and holler and they aimed the car straight at him. They was having fun, they just wanted to scare him, the way they do sometimes, you know. But they was drunk. And I guess the boy, being drunk, too, and scared, kind of lost his head. By the time he jumped it was too late. Your father says he heard his brother scream when the car rolled over him, and he heard the wood of that guitar when it give, and he heard them strings go flying, and he heard them white men shouting, and the car kept on a-going and it ain't stopped till this day. (13)

This story conjures up a father unlike the one the narrator knew, a man who acted rough and strong but who carried inside him a wound and a fount of tears no one (except his wife) ever saw or suspected. Not only do we begin to measure the choral dimension of this story—a serial story of brotherly sacrifice and responsibility, passed on from father to son—but something else comes into view, something musical and expressive, something about the very sound of pain and death, registered in the noise of the crushed guitar and the noise of the broken strings, registered also in the sound of this silenced but still playing story, now assuming its melodic role in this family's life. And we learn that the narrator also has his own cross to bear: his daughter Grace has just died of polio, and this death too is rendered as an affair of sounds and screams:

> Isabel [the wife] was in the kitchen fixing lunch for the two boys when they'd come in from school, and she heard Grace fall down in the living room. When you have a lot of children you don't always start running when one of them falls, unless they start screaming or something. And, this time, Grace was quiet. Yet, Isabel says that

when she heard that *thump* and then that silence, something happened in her to make her afraid. And she ran to the living room and there was little Grace on the floor, all twisted up, and the reason she hadn't screamed was that she couldn't get her breath. And when she did scream, it was the worst sound, Isabel says, that she'd ever heard in all her life, and she still hears it sometimes in her dreams. Isabel will sometimes wake me up with a low, moaning, strangled sound and I have to be quick to awaken her and hold her to me and where Isabel is weeping against me seems a mortal wound. (21)

We are now in a position to see that this well-regulated life is punctuated by noises from the past: the father's brother's death and the busted guitar, along with the car that "kept on a-going and it ain't stopped till this day"; Grace's *thump* and ensuing scream, a scream that Isabel still hears, that the narrator also hears on the countless nights when the sleeping mother's "mortal wound" opens and speaks its tears.

We come gradually to understand that every Harlem life is *composed* in this fashion, possesses its pulsing undercurrent of suffering and tears. We see a revival meeting consisting of one brother and two sisters: "All they had were their voices and their Bibles and a tambourine" (22), but this very old, very simple music played to the crowd "seemed to soothe a poison out of them" (23). Sonny reflects on what goes into this music: " 'While I was downstairs before, on my way here, listening to that woman sing, it struck me all of a sudden how much suffering she must have had to go through—to sing like that. It's *repulsive* to think you have to suffer that much' " (25). Sonny wonders that Harlem hasn't actually exploded: " 'all that hatred and misery and love. It's a wonder it doesn't blow the avenue apart' " (28). To our question, "Where does pain go?" Baldwin suggests two distinct trajectories: either into song—into blues—or into raw violence.

With just a few deft touches, Baldwin conveys the echoing, collective dimensions of the personal story of Sonny, offering a picture of Harlem life (human life?) as incessant, throbbing pain. Not entirely unlike

Freud's view of homeostasis, whereby the human brain works constantly to ward off all stimuli, this depiction of urban life is a meditation on how one copes with stimuli, how anyone actually deals with suffering. Predictably enough, Sonny posits suffering as the origin of music, as the "etiology" of the blues; less predictably, I think, he implies that *all* life choices—becoming a musician, taking heroin, having a family life, being a teacher—are just so many strategies for containing hurt, staying alive: " 'No, there's no way not to suffer. But you try all kinds of ways to keep from drowning in it, to keep on top of it, and to make it seem—well, like *you*' " (25). Not only is every life a dance of or around pain, but it is also an act of domestication, of yoking suffering into personal style.

This brief, spare tale becomes outright majestic as it gathers together its threads and motifs in the final pages where, at long last, we encounter Sonny's blues. We realize—much the way Ken Burns's fine documentary on jazz has made us realize—that the blues are pain and suffering set to music, transformed into music. We are now approaching dead center as we witness the cathartic moment, the making of music:

> Then Creole stepped forward to remind them that what they were playing was the blues. He hit something in all of them, he hit something in me, myself, and the music tightened and deepened, apprehension began to beat the air. Creole began to tell us what the blues were all about. They were not about anything very new. He and his boys up there were keeping it new, at the risk of ruin, destruction, madness, and death, in order to find new ways to make us listen. For, while the tale of how we suffer, and how we are delighted, and how we may triumph is never new, it always must be heard. There isn't any other tale to tell, it's the only light we've got in all this darkness. (31)

Even though Baldwin is talking about the blues, it would be hard to find a richer and nobler definition of art itself. I think it crucial to measure how broad and capacious, how shockingly inclusive this concept of art is. All too often, one thinks of the tortured artist as giving expression to his or her private demons. It is fair to say that the narrator has had exactly this view of his brother Sonny. Such a view is facile in every sense: it construes the making of art as little more than opening up one's mouth and unloading; it is also facile in its move to "personalize" artistic expression as narrowly confessional. Baldwin blows this concept right out of the water. Making music is a cosmic event, on the order of a reverse hurricane where you tame nature's chaos. You don't just emote or emit; there is indeed an explosion, but you shape its very elements into song: "the man who creates the music is hearing something else, is dealing with the roar rising from the void and imposing order on it as it hits the air" (29).

Yes, it is personal, just as lion taming is personal, just as being Prospero and commanding the elements is personal; and all you have, to pull off this miracle of transmutation, is a modest piece of metal: "I had never before thought of how awful the relationship must be between the musician and his instrument. He has to fill it, this instrument, with the breath of life, his own" (30). Ralph Ellison described Louis Armstrong's quotidian miraculous achievement in similar fashion: "Louis bends that military instrument into a beam of lyrical sound." Making music is akin to Genesis, has parallels with God putting breath into Adam, returns us to the oldest Greek concepts of soul as inspiriting breath. Personal? Yes, in the sense that Prometheus' theft of fire from the gods was personal, but also altruistic, a gift for all of us, a gift that can claim the very life of the giver.

But the story's climax has even more grandeur than this. Listening to Sonny play the blues, the narrator realizes that not only Sonny's life is now filling the air, but that "that life contained so many others" (31). Listening to Sonny's blues is a very pure form of catharsis, in just the pharmaceutical and social senses that Aristotle meant when he used the term to describe the effect of tragedy: a purging of the soul, an opening of the closed self into something larger. And, so, the narrator takes the awesome measure of these blues, the generosity of art that tells our collective story, that brings at last out into language and life the buried history of our hurt:

> He had made it his: that long line of which we knew only Mama and Daddy. And he was giving it back, as everything must be given back, so that, passing through death, it can live forever. I saw my mother's face again, and felt, for the first time, how the stones of the road she had walked on must have bruised her feet. I saw the moonlit road where my father's brother died. And it brought something else back to me, and carried me past it. I saw my little girl again and felt Isabel's tears again, and I felt my own tears begin to rise. (32)

Now it all comes together. Sonny's blues resurrects the ghosts of the family's and community's past, but not in any spectral sense; on the contrary, one fuses with one's loved ones, feels their pain, feels the calvary some suffered (the stones of the road they walked on), recovers one's own walled-off, living dead (the father's brother, the dead Grace), repossesses the emotional plenitude of one's existence, extended long back into time and space, preceding even one's birth. The story began with a newspaper notation, and it closes with the music of the soul, a music that is built of, and out of, suffering. Sonny's blues are a scream that goes through the house, not strident but soulful, gathering together all the injuries time has wrought, weaving together the affective plaint of the entire family, forcing open the enclosures of silence and repression that have been constructed, turning it all into restorative art. Art positions us finally in that larger homeland of feeling, which constitutes the true parameters of any life, even though no geographer or biographer is likely to take its hidden measure.

Reading "Sonny's Blues" transforms you, for a moment, via the imagination, into a citizen of Harlem, just as Blake's "London" plunges you, momentarily, into the London of 1794. Art moves us into places we have never been. It can also bring back our dead haunts. In 1963 I was a student in Berlin, and I was standing only a few feet from John F.

Kennedy that spring when he spoke at the Free University. He also spoke at the Rathaus, and he uttered the famous words that call to mind the impact of Blake and Baldwin, words that still resonate: "*Ich bin ein Berliner*" ("I am a Berliner"). Kennedy was not a poet or novelist, but his magical phrase captured something of the solidarity and transcendence of art: a vision of the larger family, that larger commonwealth Emerson had in mind, in which the silhouette of the individual is merged into, fleshed out into something communal. The world heard Kennedy's words then—that is why he said them—and we are, of course, treated to them again and again on TV replays, in election years, or at moments of political nostalgia.

When I hear them, however, I feel a complex cluster of emotions: a never-to-be-repeated bond with a charismatic leader, and also a rumbling of time and space as 1963 Berlin—with its war-torn look, its still bombed-out buildings, its restless theaters and brilliant museums, its edginess as incendiary political fault line, its brand-new Wall dividing East and West, its interminable arctic winter, its setting for me in terms of my brand-new marriage, my brand-new pondering of Jewishness and Germanness, my brand-new immersion into German literature, my sense of adventure and endless open free years in front of me—reappears. All this comes back into my life, reminding me that I too, in a sense quite different from Kennedy, can say, "*ich bin ein Berliner*." That city of 1963 no longer exists: the dazzling new modern German capital now coming into existence as Europe's confident crown jewel has nothing in common with the grungy, anxious, fissured place where I then lived. Likewise, London today has little resemblance to the place of chimney sweeps, soldiers, and harlots memorialized by Blake in 1794. Not even Baldwin's Harlem of half a century ago has remained the same. And the "me" that heard Kennedy announce himself a Berliner in 1963 has also been dead for some time now, about as long as Kennedy has been dead. And yet, on some subliminal but vital level, the words of Blake and Baldwin and Kennedy *move* me, in every sense of the word, emotionally and geographically and temporally, into other realms and other selves.

EUGENE O'NEILL'S *LONG DAY'S JOURNEY INTO NIGHT:* FAMILY AS ECOSYSTEM

There is no more obvious check on individual authority, maneuvering room, and hegemony than *family*. Family medicine is a specialty that encourages doctors to consider their patients in an environmental perspective, attentive to the familial genetic factors that crisscross the entire unit, attentive also to the group attitudes, assumptions, and values that contextualize and confer a pattern on individual illness. But we hardly require doctors to tell us that our personal song and dance is inevitably part of a group show, so that our own performance must needs be shaped both by and for that intimate public we were thrust into, and lived with during the formative years of our lives: the family.

Yet, since bodies are bounded by individual skin and since consciousness is so easily taken as solo voice, there is little wonder that the echoing, choral dimension of life tends to be obscured, rarely given its measure (other than as a prison house one seeks to exit). And it is no secret that the ethos of modern American society is individualist to the core, with the family seen (at best) as a launchpad for the children we raise, or seen as relaxing (or infernal) hearth to which the fatigued breadwinners return at the end of the day.

It has been shown statistically how much erosion of family rituals has taken place in recent decades, much of it driven by the youth culture and the media, much of it also driven doubtless by the increased workload and professional tempo of adults themselves, especially at a time when both partners work. Family dinners are largely a thing of the past; even shared meals between spouses are rarer than they used to be. When I occasionally ask my students if they intend to return to the places where they grew up, where their families reside, I am usually met with blank incomprehension. Out of the nest and into the world; go where the jobs are; such thinking is legion, and it does not seem to put a great premium on family.

These are some of the reasons that Eugene O'Neill's play *Long Day's Journey into Night* may strike us initially as dated and sepia-tinted, as the torturous and perhaps melodramatic account of a family of yesteryear. We know that O'Neill wrote it as a reckoning of sorts, not in adversarial terms but as an act of forgiveness and reconciliation, as a statement about facing one's ghosts and demons. I think it deserves special mention in this book because I know of no other text that succeeds so brilliantly and tragically in bringing the familial mesh to life, in showing that the familial mesh *is* one's life. The theatrical medium, with its set of many characters outfitted with voice and feeling, affords O'Neill a capacious form for displaying the astonishingly interactive, virtually incestuous life that all of us lead. Theater, given its cast of characters, is the social art form par excellence, and it is egalitarian in a way that neither poetry nor fiction can be: it grants life to the whole consort, and asks us to see just how porous, how interdependent, how infected, our private "agenda" really is.

O'Neill's play is famously a study of *dependency,* seen overtly in Mary Tyrone's morphine habit, seen covertly in all the Tyrone men's incessant boozing, and seen perhaps most profoundly in the ecological view of life the play presents: each of us lives in others as well as in ourselves; each of us is what he or she is because of others; each word we utter and each feeling we express is irremediably social and collective, infected by others, infecting those same others. In this play that takes place in a summer house, a play that consists of incessant recriminations on the part of each tortured Tyrone against the others and against fate, we see indeed a scream that goes through the house. We see it because O'Neill has fashioned a language of extraordinary modulation and reach, in which the most common words are echoing and prismatic, announcing the continuing—palpable, unstoppable, usurping—life of other people and other times in the existence of the speaker.

The play opens innocuously with James and Mary Tyrone engaged in small talk, and it seems equally innocuous that they discuss their son

Edmund's summer cold. Who hasn't been here before? Soon enough, however, we begin to take the deeper measure and reach of this chitchat, and it seems hardly an exaggeration to say that part of O'Neill's power is in showing that family conversation is little less than a minefield, a terrain that is filled with explosives. James congratulates Mary for looking fat and happy, and we realize he does so *because* he fears she may be on the verge of returning to her drug habit, but of course he does not say so. We quickly sense that Edmund's cold is not a cold, but something more—the annunciatory symptoms of tuberculosis. The mesh this conversation is starts to take on resonance and pith, as we learn that these developments are themselves of long pedigree, inasmuch as Mary has been in asylums before to combat her addiction, inasmuch as Edmund's consumption repeats that of Mary's father, who died of it.

As we factor in these prior realities, we start to hear the special O'Neill music, a music that conveys how prodigiously freighted our tiniest utterances are, how stubbornly the dance of the past scripts our thoughts, our way of seeing the world, and therefore even our smallest moves and statements. And even this formulation is too lame to capture O'Neill's sinuousness, because it leaves out what he shows us of the massive program of defenses and denials that we set into action in order to ward off these tidings from the past; those tidings are brought to life in the present, leading to a spectacular kind of programmatic blindness on the one hand, and a maniacal surveillance system on the other. James Tyrone refuses to speak his fears of his wife's addiction, even as he monitors her every move.

But the play moves toward utterance. Consider this conversation between James Tyrone and his son Jamie:

TYRONE: Yes, this time you can see how strong and sure of herself she is. She's a different woman entirely from the other times. She has control of her nerves—or she had until Edmund got sick. I wish to God we could keep the truth from her, but we can't if he has to be sent to a sanatorium. What makes it worse is her father died of consumption. She worshiped him and she's never forgotten. Yes, it will be hard for her. But she can do it! She has the will power now! We must help her, Jamie, in every way we can!

JAMIE: *(Moved)* Of course, Papa. *(Hesitantly)* Outside of nerves, she seems perfectly all right this morning.

TYRONE: *(With hearty confidence now)* Never better. She's full of fun and mischief. *(Suddenly he frowns at Jamie suspiciously)* Why do you say, seems? Why shouldn't she be all right? What the hell do you mean?

JAMIE: Don't start jumping down my throat! God, Papa, this ought to be one thing we can talk over frankly without a battle.

TYRONE: I'm sorry, Jamie. *(Tensely)* But go on and tell me—

JAMIE: There's nothing to tell. I was all wrong. It's just that last night—Well, you know how it is, I can't forget the past. I can't help being suspicious. Any more than you can. *(Bitterly)* That's the hell of it. And it makes it hell for Mama! She watches us watching her—(37–38)

It is as if the so-called present tense were a mirage, because you are constantly on the lookout for the insidious signs of the past.

Later in this book, an entire chapter is devoted to the issue of *diagnosis,* but it is worth underscoring here just how central (and destabilizing) that drive is in O'Neill's play, yielding a kind of medical scrutiny of each other that is all the more unbearable because of the emotional ties between the watchers and the watched.

O'Neill indulges in stage directions which doubtless seem tiresome to today's readers, but they are the indispensable markers of precipitous change and alteration. We know that O'Neill experimented with some of the conventions of Greek tragedy in earlier plays such as *Mourning Becomes Electra,* and that an ambitious work such as *The Great God Brown* seeks to reinstate the convention of Greek masks as conveyors of senti-ment. *Long Day's Journey into Night* brilliantly reconceives the Greek masks, by offering us a human visage that is in almost constant meta-morphosis as it reflects its many moods, as it performs its dance in time. Sometimes it is all in the stage directions themselves: *"He gives her a kiss. Her face lights up with a charming, shy embarrassment. Suddenly and startlingly one sees in her face the girl she had once been, not a ghost of the past, but still a living part of her"* (28). At other times, we see it as a kind of verbal and facial ballet, the kind of thing only a great actress can pull off, as indeed Katharine Hepburn (who seems to have been born for this role) did in one filmed version of the play:

TYRONE: *(With dull anger)* I understand that I've been a God-damned fool to believe in you! *(He walks away from her to pour himself a big drink)*

MARY: *(Her face again in stubborn defiance.)* I don't know what you mean by "believing in me." All I've felt was distrust and spying and suspicion. *(Then accusingly)* Why are you having another drink? You never have more than one before lunch. *(Bitterly)* I know what to expect. You will be drunk tonight. Well, it won't be the first time, will it—or the thousandth? *(Again she bursts out pleadingly)* Oh, James, please! You don't understand! I'm so wor-ried about Edmund! I'm so afraid he—

TYRONE: I don't want to listen to your excuses, Mary.

MARY: *(Strickenly)* Excuses? You mean—? Oh, you can't believe that of me! You mustn't believe that, James! *(Then slipping away into her strange detachment—quite casually)* Shall we not go into lunch, dear? I don't want anything but I know you're hungry. *(He walks slowly to where she stands in the doorway. He walks like an old man. As he reaches her she bursts out piteously)* James! I tried so hard! I tried so hard! Please believe—!

TYRONE: *(Moved in spite of himself—helplessly)* I suppose you did, Mary. *(Then grief-strickenly)* For the love of God, why couldn't you have the strength to keep on?

MARY: *(Her face setting into that stubborn denial again)* I don't know what you're talking about. Have the strength to keep on what? (69-70)

There is a very dark moment in August Strindberg's hallucinatory late play, *The Ghost Sonata,* when the theory is put forth that language is always and ever a form of lying, with the corollary that people who know and live with one another turn ultimately silent, because they can no longer lie successfully, because each of them is so transparent to the other, by dint of time. O'Neill has taken this grim concept and released the poetry in it, by putting on stage a family that knows—of course they know! don't we always know the ugly truths of those we live with?—everything about one another, but keeps on talking nonetheless, keeps on with the endless performance of saving face, denying reality, turning on the other, emitting the poison, withdrawing, pulling back. The play codes this rhythmic dynamic as *fog* and *foghorn,* as the desire to withdraw into private fantasy and darkness, to a place where we can no longer be reached or hurt—and the morphine and the alcohol are our ticket to that place—counterpointed by the no less powerful opposing tug into reality, into recognition and light, out of the fog and into recognizing the horror of what life has done.

Pain and suffering are O'Neill's theme song, just as they are James Baldwin's, but it becomes stereophonic in *Long Day's Journey into Night,* an affective roller coaster through time and space, so that all the ghosts of the past make their presence known: Tyrone's impoverished childhood, his miserliness; Mary's memories of the convent, her desire to be a pianist or a nun; Jamie's expulsion from school, his descent into drink and whoring and boundless cynicism; Edmund's fragile health, his desperate adventures, his tumultuous self-exploration; and then the deforming accidents: Jamie's (intentional?) infecting of the infant brother Eugene with his measles, leading to the baby's death; Mary's unbearable pain in childbirth—giving birth to Edmund—leading to the quack doctor's morphine prescription, leading to her condition as a "dope fiend." All this, and much more, is flushed out in the open in this single day in a summer house, flushed out because it has been surreptitiously humming and buzzing there all along, moving ever more potently toward expression.

All of the Tyrones are scarred and formed by their pasts, and in the course of the play this occulted material moves from echo and refrain, a foghorn in the distance, to overt utterance, reaching its operatic crescendo in the final scene where each Tyrone confronts his or her ghosts and demons, and shares this confrontation with the others. James reveals to Edmund the act of complacency and cowardice that kept him a matinee idol rather than becoming the greatest Shakespearean actor of his day; Edmund articulates the epiphanic visions he has had during his seafaring days, confirms his identity as stammering poet; Jamie tells Edmund to beware, that he hates him as much as he loves him, that he has intentionally poisoned his values, that he wants his younger brother to fail (just as he has); and, grand finale, Mary, moving ever more fully into the morphine-fog, remembers the innocence of her convent days while she seeks for her lost soul. Each of these characters has needed considerable lubrication to arrive at these utterances, whether in the form of copious alcohol installments or repeated morphine doses. But their actions are cathartic, just as Sonny's blues are cathartic, inasmuch as the curtain at last lifts up fully on their damaged histories, illuminating the defining wounds that continue to bleed through their present-day speech, behavior, and interactions.

"Interactions" seems such a poor term to convey the sheer emotional *traffic* that O'Neill's play stages for us, as if the life of a family were exactly that: traffic, incessant circulation and interweaving, a quasi-molecular or -cellular picture of our place within the whole, but exposed and lit in such a way that we see the whirling molecules themselves, as visible and materially present as the fog itself. Such a scheme announces that the individual actor is always/already *permeated* with the life of the others, not merely their contemporary existence, but the whole dreadful sweep of their transactions over time. *Long Day's*

Journey into Night reveals the sticky glue that joins me to you, as if life in the family were a form of flypaper, a morass of sorts in which each figure is stuck, where your skin is attached to me, so that all the desired hegemony I claim for myself turns out to be a mirage.

That is what this family knows: Tyrone's childhood penury is *their* legacy; Mary's morphine habit is on *their* plate; Jamie's cynicism is *their* cross; Edmund's consumption writes large *their* history: past, present, and future. The notion that your life could have clean contours is as naïve as thinking you can track a *single thread* in the fabric you are wearing. We are made up of one another, despite appearances to the contrary. O'Neill shows this by sounding it. In doing so, he utterly cashiers the "realist" assumptions that many ascribe to him—after all, the dramaturgy itself does not seem revolutionary—by crafting a theatrical language to show how utterly saturated and infiltrated we are with one another. Living in a family reconceives the scream that goes through the house, refracts this plaint into a chorus of blood-related voices, each filled with the other, each extending back over time, each woven by O'Neill's genius into a dramatic tapestry that is unsurpassed in pathos and gathering power.

Let me close my discussion of O'Neill by again acknowledging the sepia, perhaps dated aura of the play. This story of two older adults and two grown-up children living and breaking bread together in the same house hardly seems a story for our time of vacated nests and hustling professionals. Likewise, it is a wonder that the text is not simply banned from the curriculum because of its humongous alcohol consumption, given today's culture of chemical dependency warnings (what would O'Neill have thought of this term?) and drinking disorders, given how acutely medicalized our vision of older social rituals has become. All this gave me considerable pause when I put this text in my university course on Literature and Medicine, but the result was not what I anticipated. My students had no trouble at all negotiating O'Neill's version of damaged families and problems of addiction. Moreover, several pointed out the (unaccented) gender dimensions of the play, especially concerning the bereftness of Mary—lonely figure without "home," without friends, without resources, obliged to beg the servant girl to keep her company as she waits for the fog to set in—as contrasted with the drinking and carousing male figures, bathed in a kind of camaraderie that O'Neill simply took for granted, able to go to bars or brothels or clubs, reassembled at play's end to share their grief and solace with one another as Mary departs from their midst.

Above all, these students were attuned to the familial melody that plays throughout the piece, the ways in which each person's pain was an integral part of another's life. It seems to me that that is perhaps O'Neill's ultimate gift: to make us actually hear the plaint of our loved ones, to make it real at last. At one juncture in the play, Mary (who has the most comprehensive, and therefore forgiving, view of anyone in the play) rehearses for Edmund the sad fact that his father had to go to work in a machine shop when he was only ten years old, at which Edmund grouses, "Oh, for Pete's sake, Mama, I've heard Papa tell that machine shop story ten thousand times." Mary's reply is undemonstrative but it cuts to the bone: "Yes, dear, you've had to listen, but I don't think you've ever tried to understand" (117).

This line—and this play—made me think back to my own family, especially to my dead father, about whom the equally clichéd story was that he had had to go to work at the age of six. Six. I too have heard this story ten thousand times, and, now, twenty years after his death, I could wish that my mother had told me what Mary told Edmund: you've had to listen, but have you ever understood? I don't think I ever did. I know I didn't. Other than in that halfway measure of all lazy conceptualizing, by which the key facts of our lives are there, all right, but there as dead letters, as inert data, never opened up as language of the heart, as indeed one of the keys to my father's life. *Long Day's Journey into Night* stirred me in just this way, caused me to grasp something of the deafness and thickness that wall us off from one another, a kind of perceptual and moral plaque that fills up our emotional arteries and veins, preventing the flow of blood and sympathy, occluding those passageways that could link us together. O'Neill has opened them up, so that the flow of sentience goes through them, and even though his play is a long, heavy, and ponderous read or evening in the theater, it is anything but morbid: it vitalizes us by making its people finally alive to one another. In this, art's work is done.

MAKING THE SCREAM VISIBLE: EDVARD MUNCH

Blake's "London" articulates urban and cultural disease in terms of victimization and "marking," and he succeeds in transforming private suffering into public and political indictment, so that it may at last become visible and legible. It is an affair of voice and metaphor. We call this piece "visionary," but have only the words encoded in a sixteen-line poem. But what would urban plague *look like*? Could the narrative of human feeling and illness actually be *shown*? The work of the Norwegian painter Edvard Munch is richly cued to the governing premises in this argument, because Munch's entire long career is devoted to finding a pictorial language for binding moments of intense emotion. Who else has titled his pictures *The Scream* or *Jealousy* or *Anxiety*?

We find in Munch's work an astonishing kind of creatural grammar, a syntax of sorts, that seems to say: our affective and experiential lives are punctuated by key episodes of explosive, unhinging feeling, episodes that attend the temporal trajectory of the body as it moves from birth to death, with all the varieties of sickness and mania and fear and desire in between. What seems to undergird this body of work is a conviction that our episodes of upheaval have a special graphic character and can be represented in painting, lithograph, and woodcut. Munch's fame, I would submit, hinges on these qualities, this fidelity to feeling that surfaces over and over in his work; it has earned him a reputation for precariousness, neurosis, melodrama, and even posturing, but it is time to reconceive these matters, and to appreciate his power as portrayer, not only of libido and affect, but of the social pathways such forces take, pathways of a new human geography.

Evening on the Karl Johan, Edvard Munch, 1892.

The irresistible segue from Blake and Baldwin to Munch passes through the painter's famous *Evening on the Karl Johan*, done in 1892 and fully illustrative of the mature Munch style. A century after Blake diagnoses his fellow Londoners, and well before Baldwin depicts Harlem suffering, Munch passes in review the citizens of Christiania (today's Oslo). He does not focus on the chimney sweeper or the soldier or the harlot or the teacher or the musician or the addict, to make his indictment; instead, he renders the parade of proud burghers themselves, making their ritual procession down the main thoroughfare, the Karl Johan, to see and to be seen, a consummate moment of social vindication, meant to shore up these citizens in their sense of gravity and purpose. Munch had dealt with crowd scenes earlier, in his realist portrayal of the *Military Parade on the Karl Johan*, and in a pointillist version as well.

But none of these earlier forays prepares us for the march of zombies that we encounter here. On the one hand, Munch's crowd is a new urban constellation, with a form and synergy that accompany the growth of city populations and that intrigue the nineteenth-century artist and writer: Poe's "Man of the Crowd" and Baudelaire's "Les Foules" ("Crowds") testify eloquently to the explosive albeit anonymous energies to be found here, the sort of thing already at hand in the mass uprisings of the French Revolution. But merely to mention this activist model of the crowd is to measure how radically different Munch's rendition is. These denizens of Christiania would appear to be ghouls, the walking dead, and if we seek parallels with literary figures, one might invoke Thoreau's contemptuous reference to "the mass of men who lead lives of quiet desperation," except that this mass is represented by Munch in surreal, ghastly form now.

Above all, Munch reveals here his soon-to-be trademark style of vacancy and blankness, of white, featureless, hollowed-out faces, spectral countenances with gaping, staring pinpoint eyes, frozen and hieratic in their ghostly parade. No rippling energy in sight here, not even any signs of the picturesque variety that engaged other writers and artists. Instead, Munch has, as it were, plunged into the interior, has laid waste to any psychologizing or affective signs, has produced a spectacle as eerie and depleted and ghostly as some of the arctic landscapes in Melville's sublime chapter in *Moby-Dick* on "The Whiteness of the Whale," where he too elects to go "in," to peel away all the colorful surface trappings that give point to our variegated phenomenal world, so as to settle into the Nothingness that is his real interest.

Munch is Melville's fellow traveler in this regard, and his spectral citizens seem risen from the dead, like some kind of Last Judgment where the dead resurface (resurface as surface), put on their frock coats and top hats and fine gowns, while remaining dazed mannequins, moving (being moved?) in mass formation, but will-less and soulless. We are tempted to fast-forward to the great Fascist crowds of the 1930s, but Munch's emphasis is on the spectral, insubstantial character of these denizens, already prefiguring T. S. Eliot's "hollow men." Their performance gives the lie to all notions of stability, solidity, and solidarity (virtues they seek to display), and the self-congratulatory belief system that finances such rituals and parades has been eaten away entirely, turned inside out.

Munch's breakthrough here is to have worked through negation and erasure, to have refrained from all surface notation, in such a way as to yield a result of shocking power and violence. *Evening on the Karl Johan* jolts us in his depiction of modern life, because it forgoes any minute particulars—grimace, pain, suffering, even delight—in order to land at rock bottom, to get to the horror that lies underneath. Munch's people have bottomed out, are shown to inhabit a sphere beyond emotion itself, a blankness that seems prior, a bedrock of Nothing that all our song and dance seeks to camouflage. Yet—and here is the miracle—this painting broadcasts the same "marks of weakness, marks of woe" that characterized Blake's Londoners and Baldwin's denizens of Harlem. This, too, is in some terrible sense, a community, even a family of sorts, a whole class of like-minded, like-appareled citizens, aware of the surface features that unite them, wholly unaware of the inner void that unites them. All of the vacancy, the sucked-out vacuum of these faces and lives, exerts an irresistible pull on the spectator, draws us in, makes us gauge the horrible theft (of feeling, or meaning, of reality) that has taken place here. Munch is cunning in his use of blankness and emptiness, as if he knew that the viewer not only would rush in to fill the gap, but would experience the affective black hole as the true horror of these lives, the final record of what life has done to them.

And that is what lays ultimate claim to our attention. Through Munch we see what is not otherwise visible: the sickness at the core of things. This mob-gestalt that seems to flow down the Karl Johan, less animated than even the windows of the buildings, is contaminated, sick unto death, as Kierkegaard might have said, a billboard for epidemic plague. Such a painting obliges us to ask if, indeed, the human soul might be representable, representable most horribly as absence, vacancy. These figures are demonstrably paying the price for the culture that has formed them: their hollowness seems to be a form of "scalp-

ing," a lifelong process of erosion that we now see in its graphic insolence. An entire material culture (of surface prosperity, of agendas and
plans, of "success" as something real) seems on the block here—seen,
drawn, painted, weighed, and found horribly wanting—as the artist
brings us into his field of vision. No plaint is heard, yet this piece seems
dirgelike all the same, an urban portrait of hell, not the fiery traditional
hell we usually imagine, but the icy hell of erasure and nullity. Could any
of us have seen this, had we been on the Karl Johan ourselves, even had
we been Edvard Munch, as depicted (very likely) in the isolated figure
who moves upstream, against the flow of the crowd?

The painting *Anxiety*, Munch's reworking of the same cast of characters, positioned this time on the bridge that is to reappear in some of
his most famous works, gives us a close-up into these vacuous faces, and
the backdrop of the swirling waters and sinuous orange-red sky announces even more clearly existential disaster at hand. No longer in
touch with the apparently solid pavement of the Karl Johan, these wan-
derers on a bridge are suspended over the void, heightening even further
their precarious ontological footing, hinting at the void within. Once
again we note the psychic cancellation, and their dazed pilgrimage, their
endless trek across a landscape of water and sky, makes them seem like
aliens from another world, trotted out in their bourgeois finery but with
no place to go. Again Munch's cunning art pays off: where, we ask, is the
anxiety itself, since these faces are so blank and inexpressive? But the
collective portrait of slipped gears, of hypnotic trance, looks like a ritual
mix of death-by-water and death-by-fire, as if the mouth of hell had
opened to expel this itinerant troupe, with lots more where they came
from, marching both from and to oblivion. Not only is purposiveness
cashiered, unthinkable, here, but we gather that this is what anxiety may
actually be: our structural exiled condition, our dance of sleepwalkers.
In painting after painting, Munch tells the story of the emperor's new
clothes, tells it by decking out his burghers in new clothes in order to
point up their absolute vapidness. Anxiety relates to our dawning awareness of fraud and deception, of the lie built into the system.

Anxiety (painting), Edvard Munch, 1894.

Yet, it seems to go still further than this: we sense here that anxiety—
a busy term, a notion of sound and fury turned inward, an aggressive notion, something implosive and energetic in its own way—is ultimately
not tumultuous at all, but is the core blankness that is all, and on this
reading anxiety is not so much a response to life as its ultimate precon-
dition, the originary, residual horror below the skin, simply *there*. This
view, while not very pretty, has at least the tonic virtue of restoring something of the priorities (priorities in literal sense: that which is prior) that
the sick and the hurting have always known, so that anxiety is the field
we reenter in moments of pain or capsizing, experienced now as an

Anxiety (lithograph),
Edvard Munch, 1896.

Anxiety (woodcut),
Edvard Munch, 1896.

awful homeland which convention and good luck and health have deceptively painted as accidental, occasional, and escapable. Munch knows it to be the place we live in. The "we" counts here, as strange counterforce to the solipsism usually identified with anxiety, as if Munch were intent on communalizing horror.

And he seems to revel in ways of saying and showing it. Consider the variations of this motif as they appear in lithograph and woodcut, yielding an ever-simpler and more drastic equation of exodus and fall. In the lithograph the swirling natural currents of sea and sky announce even more forcefully the theme of cosmic power and human incapacity, whereas the woodcut seems to go still further, to reveal the very scars and sores lodged in the soul, the scars and sores that are the soul. Anxiety as truth, not as response. Here is Munch's news: within us is the horror, just beneath our surface composure lies the sea of terror. Kafka once wrote that art is the ax that chops into our frozen sea; in Munch that sea is on show.

I realize that this account of both Munch and human feeling may appear impressionistic and sensational. But Munch's work announces a rival logic to that which regulates our daytime and scientific thinking (as well as the discourse of both the academy and the street). Blank though his pieces seem to be, they posit affect—not noisy affect, just horror—as the ground we live on (the vacuum under the ground we live on), and thereby give the lie to our brave postures of composure, control, and capability. Anyone who is sick or suffering, who has experienced anxiety, has bitten into Munch's sour apple, has sensed the frequent speciousness of civilized forms, ranging from the black suits of the bourgeoisie to more serious matters such as unified personality, meaning in life, and sanity itself.

If Munch is right in such depictions, how fraudulent are our customary forms and measures? Something tonic, perhaps even sustaining and inspiriting, may be brought about by such work, because it reconceives our libidinal bases, offers a kind of halfway house for all who know whereof he paints. I would argue that—contrary to popular belief—no one has ever been depressed by Munch, but that many have felt both gratitude and recognition at the tidings he brings. *Evening on the Karl Johan* and *Anxiety* do not quite say "Join the crowd," but they are strangely inviting nonetheless, implying that we, even at our lowest, especially at our lowest, have compatriots. The world, Munch seems to announce, only pretends to be bluff, healthy, and functional, but underneath it is all frozen sea. I hardly want to claim that such work makes anyone delirious with joy, but it is reassuring in its peculiar fashion, and it in fact reinstates something of that "solidarity" which seemed initially to be its great target.

Munch travels far down the road of psychic portraiture in his effort to redraw our map, to chart our actual emotional traffic and whereabouts. In many instances we end up with shimmering canvases that remain enigmatic, that seem to hint at a propriety and causality on the far side of our normal habits of reason. Among these *poetic* works I'd put *Red Virginia Creeper* close to the top of the list. Here we see the frontal suffering figure (based on Stanislaw Przybyszewski, who was a player in Munch's erotic entanglements, whose face Munch enlists over and over to depict misery) whose blank, hollow-eyed look defies us to make sense of things. And with good reason: all we can make out is a stately house covered with Virginia creeper (or "Red Vine" as the piece is also known), positioned in an exceptionally barren landscape, with truncated tree and prisonlike white fence. But the more you look at this piece, the curiouser it becomes, the more you start to negotiate the scream that is going through it, and thus you entertain the view that this haunted house that looks like it has skin cancer is somehow an expression of the sufferer's psychic condition. In this light, you can regard the path that seems to flow out of the house as a river of sorts, an imperious flow that then produces—lo and behold!—our hollow-eyed ghoul as its result, giving us the feeling that he is actually swept along by this current, that in about thirty seconds he will disappear from the canvas, carried off to wherever Munch's gallery of the damned ends up.

You'll note that I am treating this painting as if it were precisely a

Red Virginia Creeper, Edvard Munch, c. 1900.

kind of waterway, as if looking at it were an odd form of rafting, but the flux in question is sentience, not water. Reading the piece in this fashion entails parsing it, espying its odd emotive syntax, its riddling way of positioning us in the world, as if to say: the realist models you believe are harmless and nice enough in their way, but they are worthless when it comes to our actual arrangements, our actual proximities, distances, and relations. Here would be a form of portraiture that cashiers the Newtonian worldview by inventing its own psychic landscape—a landscape that is not fantastic at all, that consists of things we recognize, but now these things *speak* us—as a way of reconfiguring who we are. A house with red vines, a picket fence, a barren tree, and a man who looks like he has just come from a jaunt in hell: discrete items? or a fearful symphony? or a canny landscape that *says* this man's misery and lostness? or an infernal Halloween scene, replete with lit-up haunted house, that vomits out its diseased, crazed occupant? I am intentionally rhapsodic here, because I feel that our most intense emotional states *defy represen-tation*. Suppose you are feverish (with jealousy or fear or desire or just plain fever itself) and it all rages inside: how could someone depict this? Suppose you are chronically ill or severely depressed or just plain out of sorts: could this be shown? We need to see Munch's strange canvases along these lines, as the translation of a psychic state into a material language of form and color.

Munch's paintings imply that the true career of body and soul constitutes a social, spatiotemporal story that has never been told. Sickness and death are among the prime movers, but hardly the only ones. The discovery of *life* can be just as unhinging as that of death, as I will show in the following chapter when I discuss Munch's *Puberty*. Puberty, like sexual desire, can be experienced as something distinctly mutinous, as a revolt coming from quarters we (when prepubescent) have doubtless known but never paid attention to. All of a sudden, somatic alterations and "messages" such as tingling, yearning, even ecstatic capsizing, inform the occupant of the body of new and imperious tidings. Munch's work sensitizes us to our strange conditions as inhabitants of bodies, as subjects of a somatic order that follows its own rules, plays out its own logic, and leaves us with the challenge of domesticating and personalizing this generic activity.

Is this not also the chilling and inescapable message that illness brings home to us: that our bodies have a life of their own, a life we essentially follow rather than lead, despite the hubris of our conceptual habits? Fever makes joints that we never knew we had ache; makes walking and being upright as difficult and miraculous an event as the history of evolution tells us it is; pain skews our perceptions, addles our judgment, makes much of our well agenda meaningless (seen at last for its superficiality), while what really counts is: no more pain. Munch helps us understand the body's despotism. In pleasure and in pain, the body speaks and we—well, we listen. And must come to terms with the startling news that this speaking body is us. To be sure, many, many painters have done homage to the authority of the human body, but few have

The Family at the Road, Edvard Munch, 1903.

sought its peculiar grammar and syntax in the way Munch has; few have positioned it in our life trajectory—temporally and morally—quite the way he has. Looking at Munch's depiction of bodies in thralldom to the great forces welling up in and out of them helps us to citizenship rights in the somatic country we inhabit.

Battening on to crises and moments when the body speaks or alters, Munch turns out to be a wonderful painter of children, as if he knew that they were truly different, anthropologically different. The group por-

Self-Portrait: Between Clock and Bed, Edvard Munch, 1940.

traits of children that he did for many of his wealthy patrons are suffused with this awareness, and the dramatic contrast between ages is captured in works like *The Family at the Road* where clichés such as "generation gap" attain their full resonance, as we measure the vertiginous existential space that separates these four figures: doll, daughter, mother, and grandmother. And yet, here too, they are unforgettably framed as a unit, as a legend about the familial shape of passing time, the female contours of history.

Munch is arguably among our very greatest painters of old age, of aging itself as the fascinating and terrible cost of living. The ruthless self-portraits that Munch carried out in the last decades of his very long life, with special (often queasy, always scientific) emphasis on episodes of sickness and impending physical failure, reach their culmination in his *Self-Portrait: Between Clock and Bed,* done in 1940, a weird companion piece to *Puberty,* but now seen from the final phase of the trajectory, looking backward rather than forward. The frail, soon-to-die old man stands (barely stands) next to the two indicting fixtures that broadcast his insufficiency: the clock that serves as bell-toller, with or without hands, and the bed that awaits those who can no longer stay upright. Yet, as critics have recognized, this is a painting with great charm and wit. The bed cover is an explosion of saucy living color and vibrant pattern, seeming to speak a painterly language of gaiety that knows only life, not death. The old man stands in a doorway, and behind him we see not just a room but a world: a brilliant yellow wall filled with paintings, his paintings (his flesh and blood?) that cannot age or grow frail or die. And we espy still another door, this one darker, half open, leading to a shadowy corridor through which the painter will ultimately exit.

At farthest right we look at the painted human body that is the fundamental currency of Munch's art. This painting is, in its way, quite as philosophical as Picasso's *Les Demoiselles d'Avignon,* in that it proposes for our inspection a number of places, of sites, each asking us to gauge what lives and what dies. The fleshly tenement will fall, but the painted one will stand (however precariously) forever. One remembers, in looking at that vivid space behind the old man—lit by his work, yet containing dark passages—Montaigne's splendid phrase for the thinking subject's inner sanctum, *"l'arrière boutique"* (back room). Munch's *arrière boutique* is the world he has made, the material testimony of work and time: a room of one's own and a family of one's own. We would be hard put to name another painting that shows us more poignantly, more religiously, the fate of flesh and the triumph of art, with the additional, self-evident proviso that the painting itself, albeit done by a man approaching eighty, joins the fray, is forever on the side of the living.

I want to close my discussion of Munch by focusing on what is unquestionably his most notorious work, *The Scream,* a painting that stands in the minds of many as a watershed artwork, a prophetic gate-

The Scream, Edvard Munch, 1893.

way to all that is diseased and terrifying about modern life. Munch's figure on the bridge, shorn of all gender markings and psychological nicety, swaying frontally toward us with its terrible tidings, seeking feverishly to block its ears as its gaping mouth and ghoul-eyes fix upon us, personifies our most nightmarish notions of the modern era. That this piece has become a commercial, even "hip" icon today, seen in advertising and publicity, found on wrapping paper and greeting cards, appearing in graffiti on walls and under bridges, does not really diminish the virulence of the work. Munch has left us a record of this painting's genesis, how it began in a more meditative, melancholy symbolist form (with a gendered figure looking down into water), and how it sought to give visual form to an earlier memory Munch had had about a sky suddenly blood red, "flaming clouds like blood and a sword," "and I felt as though Nature were convulsed by a great unending scream" (quoted in Eggum, 81).

The congruence between Munch's words and the title of my book hardly needs pointing out, and this painting illustrates to perfection the range of our issues. "A scream goes through the house," and we now see that the "house" is no less than the cosmos itself, the sea and sky worked up to paroxysmal fury as the human creature . . . utters? . . . hears? the great shriek. Here we see, as never before, the power of human feeling, the awesome agency it has acquired. We cannot determine if the environment is shaken by the human's anguish, or if the human is shaken by the environment's fury, but what we can hardly miss is that these two seemingly disparate realms—environment and subject, outside and inside—are now fused, and with this fusion disappear all the protective barriers and boundaries that customarily (mercifully) mark off self from world.

Proust once described a dying character in terms of someone who suddenly felt the monstrous force of gravity itself pulling the body into the grave, and something similar is happening here: the fundamental contract that preserves human equilibrium—I am I, and the world is the world—has been scandalously breached. The world is hemorrhaging, the dike has collapsed, the flood rushes in. If the origin of such fury is external, it suggests a demonic world, yet also a world become familiar to us in its outbreaks of earthquake, hurricane, and the like; if the origin of such fury is internal, it suggests a tempest of a different sort, a psychic, affective storm that cannot be weathered, with analogues such as seizure, stroke, and infarction. The bridge that should offer safe passage is a tilted, elongated affair, a plane you could slide off into the maelstroms that surround it. Bad news is everywhere in this painting. But the most insidious reading is that outside and inside are in horrible collusion, and once we entertain this view, we understand it to be the greatest threat of all. Is that not the core incapacity on show here? Nothing can be kept "in" or "out." "Keeping" is a cultural myth, derived from fond notions of stability and control that make sense to those who are well.

Pain and sickness initiate us routinely into the maelstrom Munch has painted, even if we do not care to see our entry in such garish terms. In sickness, in old age, the body's circuits and channels play us false: obstructions can block pathways, fluids move where they shouldn't, the entire hydraulic, plumbing, and electrical arrangements go amok, the thermostat is off, the organs mutiny, viruses and bacteria invade, the immune system fails. This central drama of the human subject under siege, attacked from without and within, characterizes our somatic fate; it also has uncanny parallels with Munch's *Scream*. In studying Blake's poem "London," we saw that the "chartered Thames" is a lie, that the flow of elemental forces cannot be governed by law, political decree, or human will; we saw this most strikingly in the fateful return of the flow, in the form of blood that runs down palace walls. In *The Scream,* that blood is back. As the Ur-flow of human life, the corporeal Thames that each of us contains, the river that governs our life and death, it deserves place of pride in any depiction of actual somatic life.

Munch saw a bloodred sky, and we know from his correspondence that he agonized over this painting, agonized that he couldn't make a red that would make us feel indeed that we were looking at blood rather than paint. A work of art composed of real blood is hard to imagine, although doubtless some performance artists can manage it; but *The Scream* comes very close, I think, to realizing Munch's impossible desire, in that it is true to the law of flux, shows the human subject to be a sinuous flow of forces (energy, blood, paint, swirling lines) alike in nature to the force field that contains it. Everything is at the breaking point here: the subject vomits its anguish, the world convulses in a scream. Munch's painting is cardiac in the sense that it pulses over, washes away barriers and frames, inaugurates a regime of pure flux. As such, it reconfigures our place in the world, by erasing all customary contours: gender, nature/self, even painting/viewer. A new world is in sight.

One cannot imagine living very long in these precincts. Even Munch has his periods of calm and respite. Yet, the power of *The Scream* clearly derives from the shock of recognition experienced by every viewer: this is the bedrock truth of pain and despair; these are our most naked arrangements. Munch has challenged conventional notions about our real whereabouts: our lives in bodies, our lives with one another, our position on the planet. His paintings set forth a new geography, and yet this geography is also very old, in that it confirms what we actually sense when we are in pain or gripped by feeling. In the last analysis, Munch's paintings are territorial; they construct a terrible homeland, enabling us to encounter vistas such as we have never seen but have always known.

PATHWAYS OF FEELING:
BERGMAN'S *FANNY AND ALEXANDER*

Flux—a state where things ordinarily considered separate, such as past/present, here/there, you/me, merge into each other—has been posited as the rival logic at work in Blake's poem, Baldwin's prose, O'Neill's drama, and Munch's paintings, flux understood as the collapse of boundaries and the emergence of a meshed condition that wipes out individual self-sufficiency. Feeling is the motor force in all this, feeling now revealed as the supreme mover in human affairs. Yet even these art forms remain, in some ultimate sense, static; they are turned mobile only by the reader/spectator's active involvement. After all, the poem or the story or the play sits still on the page. But could there be a form of art that embodies movement and flux directly? Dance is obviously one answer. But film is another. The "moving pictures" offer a unique means of representing this fluid logic, and the final part of this chapter will be devoted to the work of Ingmar Bergman, who, in his great final opus, *Fanny and Alexander,* has fashioned a visual, "flowing" language of pain and feeling of remarkable intensity and splendor.

It is worth saying that all of Bergman's great films seek to chart the astonishing flow of feeling. *Wild Strawberries* (1957) is arguably Bergman's most lyrical and haunting evocation of a life from every angle—public record, memory, dream, hallucination—so as to illuminate the despotic affective material that has been repressed and demands to be acknowledged. Isak Borg, the doctor/protagonist of the film, has succeeded in a long professional medical career of great eminence, but the pot boils over nonetheless, and a kind of sentient lava fills the screen, in the guise of failed love, coldheartedness, fear of dying—as seen in the surrealist moments when the doctor encounters his own corpse in a coffin, when the doctor fails his medical exam, when the doctor watches his wife fornicating with a lover. Bergman constructs here, via the scenes of dream and hallucination, a gathering, withering indictment that Isak Borg's seemingly full life has been utterly hollow, not unlike the exposé that Munch performed on his preening burghers in *Evening on the Karl Johan.*

Persona (1965) finds still other ways to graph the libidinal currents that bind us in what we call pain or pleasure. In this dazzling, Picasso-like opus, Bergman jettisons realist storytelling entirely, obliging us to recognize that the fluid, incestuous, double portrait of two women merging with each other opens up new frontiers. Bergman's theme here is the cannibalizing of one person by another, the fusion of selves, and he wants these psychological notions to become startlingly visible. Film can do just that, can show one image consuming another, can fuse its figures together, can offer scenes where the spectator cannot determine if these events are happening or just fantasized.

In film after film, Bergman does homage to the seemingly unphotographable world of feeling. *Autumn Sonata* (1978) cargoes the full temporal span of a hurting family into its plot of (concert pianist) mother visiting (stayed at home) daughter, so much so that we may feel that the poor mother (played unforgettably by Ingrid Bergman in her sole Bergman role) is virtually smothered, buried alive in all this miasmic material, so many open sores that seem to live forever, invested with a quasi-radioactive virulence. Proust once said that time requires human bodies to write on, and I believe that Bergman's view is comparable, with a slight shift: feeling requires human bodies to write on, and

The vampirish embrace between Elisabet and Alma. *Persona* (1965).

it sovereignly does so over time, with the corollary that this system does not know "erasing." Bergman is notorious for the sheer length of some of his films—*Scenes from a Marriage* (1973) is about three hours in its short version, *Fanny and Alexander* (1983) is all of five hours in its original format—but this seems brief, given how much temporality is packed into these stories, stories that are epic as well as intimate.

Scenes from a Marriage is a longitudinal study of marriage and divorce covering the good years, the beginning, middle, and end of the split, and then the aftermath. And that is exactly why it hits the target: marriage and even divorce are longitudinal realities, and their measure cannot be taken in snapshots. They are longitudinal because they embody a scream that goes through the house, an affective current that cannot be turned off when divorce (or even death) comes. Divorce leaves emotional scars, the muck that refuses to go away even though both partners are now "free." With a little license I'd like to apply to divorce what they now say about jet lag: you will experience a full day of out-ofsyncness for each hour of time zone you have crossed; which means that those years of marriage (and all the affective materials of which they are made) will mathematically require their due, get their boomerang-like revenge at divorce, entailing an equal (if not longer) number of years to reestablish your equilibrium, to shut out and to still that noise going through the house.

We must turn to Bergman's great *summa* of 1983, *Fanny and Alexander,* for his most evolved account of the pathways of feeling, of a visual geography that would at last chart the forces that link humans together. In *Fanny and Alexander,* all the pieces fall into place: at stake is no less than the whereabouts of spirit, spirit now understood as a kind of power that many institutions may lay claim to, but whose workings film might depict. This film has a strangely Foucauldian dimension to it, as if the old filmmaker were out to reveal how power works in his culture, and thus wanted to stage a kind of discursive and institutional warfare.

In this final film, the Church, with its repressive order and tyrannical claims (issues Bergman, whose father was a minister, had altogether too much firsthand knowledge of) appears as the archenemy, an enemy that is incarnate in the form of the father. Edvard the bishop emerges as Bergman's death-dealing Lutheran father, indeed, a version of Swedish patriarchy itself. Against him are arrayed the counterforces that matter: imagination and fantasy, as located in the child Alexander, Bergman's portrait of the artist as young man; and then, the power of art forms themselves: masks, mummies, plays, stories.

Fanny and Alexander, while not preoccupied with illness or death as such, may still be the premier manifestation of this book's central thesis: art as rival to science, art as revelation of the way the universe actually works, art as graph of neural and emotional pathways (a higher EKG or EEG if you will, but in collective form), finally art as staggering human resource that helps us to a new picture of our situation. A mighty intensification is at hand, a gathering virulence, as Bergman opens wider and deeper his exploration of the manifold forces that bathe, inform, and co-

Alexander and his magic lantern.

erce human life. Hence we have the great battlefields of church, family and art, where the human players go through their moves, wrestle with their contingency, seek or suffer connection, with the result that the classical self, the individuated fortress that most of us take to be real, is going to be blown sky-high.

At first glance, *Fanny and Alexander* seems like a straightforward, realistic, slightly nostalgic evocation of life in small-town Sweden (Uppsala) at the turn of the twentieth century, a "user friendly" Bergman film markedly more accessible, say, than *Wild Strawberries* or *Persona*. Yet we see, soon enough, that Bergman's eternal conflict, his agon between life and art, logic and emotion, is still playing center stage. And the stage is indeed at the center, since Alexander's family, the Ekdals, are theater people, public servants, in some sense, whose mission it is to bring poetry, imagination, fantasy, and magic to the lives of the complacent Swedish burghers living in this town.

The film starts with the annual Christmas play, where we witness the sweetly innocuous rituals of art, enlisted to remind this stolid public of

Jesus' presence among them. This conventional performance is later followed by another installment of potent images, this time in the children's bedroom, as Alexander operates his magic lantern, casting upon the walls of the room the story of the pursued Arabella, playing out his favorite role as magician, wielder of power who offers thrills and chills to his young siblings and cousins. Again conventional, this scene is also personal (we know enough of the young Bergman's love affair with magic lanterns) and literary, evoking Proust's child-artist, Marcel, equally enthralled with the *"sorcellerie évocatoire"* ("evocative magic") of projecting images on a wall. One wants to add: the scene is also social, a little exercise in crowd control, a little incursion into the reality principles of what the film calls "the big world." In the long version of the film, this sequence closes with the father's (Oscar's) fulsome narrative of a magic chair, stressing still further the dual role of objects: inert and seemingly docile on the one hand, but secretly bristling as conduits of energy, passion, and history on the other.

This concern with the social and figurative reaches of art and narrative returns in a major key in the central episode of Oscar's death. Bergman needs this turn of events to launch his inquiry into patriarchy: Oscar the sweet man of theater (albeit not Alexander's blood father) versus Edvard, the repressive but passionate man of the cloth. Two fathers for Alexander: the fireworks that flow from this will carry the entire plot. But this oedipal story is brilliantly overdetermined by the stunning mediation of Shakespeare's *Hamlet.* Oscar suffers his (to be) fatal stroke on-stage during a rehearsal of *Hamlet* in which he plays the role of the ghost, the dead father. At his deathbed, Oscar tells Emilie that he will continue to be present, even in death, for her and her children. In short, he will become the ghost he played. And he does, making his entry (albeit visible only to Alexander and the spectators) into numerous scenes of familial morass: attending the wedding of Emilie and Edvard, visiting his mother to express his (justifiable) worries about the children, coming to Alexander in the attic after the bishop has cruelly whipped the boy for lying and defamation. The recurring presence of Oscar, Hamlet's ghost, onstage merely rachets up the ontological claims suggested by the magic lantern and the magic chair: the world moves in flow and flux; the apparently docile edges of things, people, and events—this is only a chair, that is an image, Oscar is dead—are only apparent, and at crucial moments things can alter, metamorphose, and disclose a new kind of traffic.

One reason that *Fanny and Alexander* is among Bergman's most lovable films is that the metaphysics of flow and flux is not presented as some form of occult theology or head game, but rather as the actual living pulse that moves our everyday world. It only *looks* still and docile. Bergman's camera gives us lingering close-ups of the masks, puppets, costumes, and other paraphernalia of Isak the Jew's lodgings—strategically counterpointed against the barrenness of the bishop's quarters—because these objects, these artifacts are the still living, soon to be activated, receptacles of spirit and power. And the human body ranks high among these energized things; it too is revered for its indwelling powers, expressed quite wonderfully in the scene where Carl (the failed Ekdal uncle), after ingesting the gargantuan Swedish *Julbord*, treats the children to some intestinal fireworks; the third of his ritual farts, religiously attended to by Alexander, match in hand, explodes the screen into darkness, and we are led to say that apocalypse comes in many guises, and a sufficient fart may be one of them (at least *in petto*).

Such carnal power is, of course, predominantly on show in erotic matters, and the now elderly Bergman treats fornication in this late film with a humor and warmth that are new and welcome, as seen in the bed that collapses under the strenuous activities of Gustav Adolf and Maj, or even in the sexual passion that brings Edvard and Emilie into their ill-fated union. Nowhere is Bergman's vision clearer than in the scene where Edvard sternly admonishes Alexander never to lie again, and then unctuously unites his new family in a moment of prayer; but when Edvard intones the pious words, Alexander hisses under his breath the obscene anthem of the body: "Piss-pot, fuck-pot, shit-pot, sick-pot, cock-pot, cunt-pot, arse-pot, fart-pot . . ." (94). It is a fine moment, because it stages the film's warfare—not body versus spirit, but body *as* spirit—with great pith. Edvard's major campaign against Alexander is cued to the dichotomy between truth and lie, since this is the demarcation that shores up his own worldview (and explains his suspicion of art and storytelling), but the film helps us to see that lies and fictions have an ontology of their own. Hence, when Alexander *lies* about Edvard's alleged murder of his first wife and children—the lie for which he is severely beaten—the entire film trumpets out the truth of the boy's fiction: Edvard is indeed, in front of our eyes, imprisoning his wife and children and is en route (at least emotionally) to murdering them; but their names are Emilie, Fanny, and Alexander.

In this light, the replay of *Hamlet*—with Alexander in the title role, Oscar as the ghost, Emilie as Gertrude, and Edvard as Claudius—is not predominantly a saga of revenge, but first and foremost an illustration of the film's weltanschauung or worldview: spirits live, move through the world, inhabit people and things, coerce lives. This is the truth of Bergman's film, and we see it manifested everywhere, in ghosts, mannequins, and bodies. And we hear it too, in a scream that goes through the house. That scream is worth attending to; it erupts at several critical moments in the film. One of them is when Isak the Jew goes to the bishop's quarters to retrieve the imprisoned children. This episode begins with a splendid shot of Isak serenely positioned in a horse-drawn carriage that is thundering toward us, as if to advertise the energy system that is about to go into action. Isak then waltzes through his consummately ingratiating performance with both Edvard and his sister, an exchange that is larded with Lutheran contempt, a dislike so powerful as to be visceral, as we soon enough note when Edvard later throttles Isak, accusing him of trying to steal his (!) children, the classic anti-Semitic indictment of all time. For our purposes, however, the episode's significance hinges on the magic act of rescuing the children. This is no simple matter. Isak has rushed upstairs while Edvard is counting the money (paid to him for a cupboard and a trunk), and he hurries the two children down, pops them into the trunk, just as Edvard returns to the room. The two chat amiably for a moment, then Edvard pounces on Isak, accuses him of stealing the children, and opens the trunk. And finds it empty.

Finds it empty. The bishop then rushes upstairs, to be certain the children are still there. At this point, something happens in the film that does not appear in the film script. Isak, brutalized and shaken by Edvard's assault of a moment earlier, stand up, gathers himself, looks up at the ceiling, and (with a transfigured face) emits a great scream. This image of human utterance so powerful that it overcomes the laws of reality is as emblematic for my book as Munch's signature painting, *The Scream,* is. That Bergman himself saw this scene as pivotal can be documented by a photo we have of the filmmaker instructing his actor, Erland Josephson, exactly how to deliver the fateful scream. One feels that Munch's own ghost is not far away, much less Shakespeare's or Hamlet's, because this scream through the house is Bergman's great leitmotiv for announcing the reign of spirits. And they (the spirits) do their job. Edvard opens the door and sees an eyeful (as do we): Fanny and Alexander are lying on the floor, still ("perhaps dead" says the film script), with the sweaty, bedraggled, pregnant Emilie standing guard over them, forbidding Edvard to touch them, threatening murder if he does. WHAT IS THIS? We "know" the children to be in the trunk, but Edvard has looked in it and found it empty; we now "see" the children in the bedroom, where they cannot logically be. Edvard returns downstairs as the workmen carry out the trunk, which the film script now calls "heavy." The children are indeed in it, and they escape to Isak's lodgings.

How to explain this matter of invisible children? facsimile children? There is no way to avoid Bergman's logic: Isak's scream, his spiritual intervention, reshapes the material world. As we might well say, "he spirits the children out of the house." We are very close here to the

ABOVE: Isak's scream. BELOW: Bergman instructing Erland Josephson (Isak) how to make the scream.

shape-shifting power embedded in Munch's *The Scream,* a representation of the cosmic reaches of sentience, now folded into a story about saving the children. But there is more to come.

One expects the children to be safely ensconced at Isak's quarters, so that the story can wind down. But Bergman has surprises for us. Alexander, unable to sleep and needing to pee, now makes his true inventory of the Jew's strange lodgings: a wild assortment of masks, puppets, dolls, and other mannequins, including the infamous mummy that still breathes even though it has been dead for more than four thousand years. In addition to these exotic and disturbing material objects, we get a closer look at the exotic and disturbing human objects too: Isak's nephew Aron, who enjoys terrifying Alexander by staging the entry of the great puppet God, and—most intriguing of all—the strange Ishmael (the other nephew), whom we initially only hear of. Ishmael is kept carefully locked up in the heart of the labyrinth, and we *know*—with that delicious and awful sureness of logic that all good narrative carries—that Alexander's destiny is to encounter this enigmatic figure. We are approaching dead center.

It is a strange encounter; it is a textbook example of what *encounter* actually means in the logic of this film. Ishmael, played by a very hermaphroditic-looking Stina Ekblad, announcing thereby already a major slippage of boundaries, asks Alexander to write his name; but when the boy dutifully writes "Alexander Ekdal," Ishmael shows him that it reads, instead, "Ishmael Retzinsky." I can become you. "Perhaps we have no limits; perhaps we flow into each other" (199), says Ishmael. The old Jew's philosophy, as cited by his nephew Aron, is indeed Bergman's core system of belief: "Uncle Isak says we are surrounded by realities, one outside the other. He says there are swarms of ghosts, spirits, phantoms, souls, poltergeists, demons, angels and devils" (194). But only now do we see this theory actualized in all its unsettling force. Ishmael fuses ever more intimately into Alexander, caresses the pubescent boy—what viewer is not jolted, at this sight, into an awareness that this is a coming-of-age story in the oldest, phys-

Ishmael holding Alexander.

iological sense?—caresses his flesh, and tries to ease his burden of hatred and rage.

Now the Hamlet project reaches its full pitch, as Ishmael taps into Alexander's fierce desire for revenge, and we begin to see that release is not only possible but inevitable. But whereas Shakespeare requires swords and cadavers, it all goes much faster in Bergman, as if revenge were part of the information highway, a click of the button away, and powerful feelings could achieve the immediacy and deadly accuracy of electronic currents. Ishmael midwifes Alexander's hatred, even as the boy resists and tries to keep it in, and the delivery is enunciated in terms that govern this book: "The doors are to be thrown open—a scream is to go through the house" (200).

What doors are these? Those of the bishop's quarters, to be sure, but also, one feels, those of the human subject who is now dropping his load, firing his shot, projecting his violence outward, like a guided missile, onto Edvard, who has received the fatal visit of his aunt in flames. But this fire is not to go out, and one even thinks of the footage we have seen of planes opening their bomb compartments, of rockets leaving their launchers. As we hear Ishmael's words, we also hear a scream. At first one thinks it to be that of the burning aunt. But, like the doors, it too is becoming symbolic, generic, echoing. We are entitled to think laterally here, to remember Munch's bloodred sky that is convulsed by an unending shriek, to recall Blake's soldier's muffled sigh that is also unending, that ultimately flows in blood down palace walls.

In fact we have heard this scream once before. Earlier. This is Emilie's voice, and the mind doubles back to an earlier crisis: Alexander, asleep, is awakened by muffled screams, wakes up Fanny, makes his way through the dark Ekdal house, opens door upon door, and comes to the final door, which opens only partway to frame the culminating vision of Oscar the father lying dead on the bed, center frame, and the keening, screaming figure of Emilie, who moves left to right, right to left across the scene, showing Alexander and us the awful mystery and mobility of death, its reality as hieratic spectacle and shrieking voice. All the screams now fuse together: the flaming aunt, the grieving Emilie, the shrieking Isak. That is the charged, resonant noise we hear as Ishmael lightens Alexander's load, liberates his hatred into winged instrument.

And it flies. With consummate craft, Bergman cuts back and forth, between Ishmael "delivering" Alexander, on the one hand, and its target, Edvard, fatally pursued by his sick, now burning, incandescent aunt, on the other. Film becomes magic here, illuminates the flux that is reality (because this systematic splicing is the very logic of Bergman's story), and writes large for us the shocking extension of human feeling. Alexander strikes Edvard as a rocket would, causing him to burn to death, and the filmic cutting initiates us into the spectacle of fateful linkage. This is Hamlet's revenge, but it is also a new human geography, in which the boundaries of self are erased, and the currents of feeling emerge in all their horrible force.

Alexander's murder of Edvard constitutes the purest example of the scream that goes through the house, the most perfect embodiment of the artist's rival universe that is now ordered entirely by the power of feeling. We may well decide that there is little to celebrate in this view of the reach of lethal emotions. We have long been taught that feeling is dangerous only privately, when inside: it gnaws within, eats us up, can cause dysfunction, cancer, or simple misery. But the unstated corollary has always been: feeling is invisible and inoperative in the public world, the phenomenal world. My pain may be the basic fact of my life, but it is doomed to be a fiction in yours. This book is written in full awareness that most of us subscribe to this view: that pain is considered ultimately incommunicable and unsharable. And because we believe that, our pain islands us, makes of our life a form of exile. All who have been in emotional pain, or very sick, or even a little sick, know this. The expressions to be seen on the faces of the suffering and the ill, whether in hospitals or in our memories, bear this out.

Here are exactly the reasons why I believe the views of feeling and pain put forth by art—and embodied in Blake, Baldwin, O'Neill, Munch, and Bergman—demand our attention. They help us to a radically different picture of our situation and our resources. Our bodies and our emotions neither begin nor end where we think they do. Our gut feeling that we are real, while others are ghosts—a gut feeling rarely acknowledged—may be egregiously wrong. Above all, our belief that our own hurt is private, fated to be our individual reality but no one else's, that conviction is challenged by art. Reality, art suggests, may actually be communal, networked. Blake's poem implies that the map of London is flawed, that the Thames (and, indeed, the City) cannot be chartered, that the victims of the ideological order—the poor, the exploited—are not only a community, but also the luminous and deafening agents of counterattack, trafficking in blood that runs down palace walls and apocalyptic revenge in the form of the "Marriage hearse."

Baldwin celebrates the immense and *homing* power of the blues, so that Sonny's dirge reverses the outcome of the Humpty-Dumpty story of human life (the center cannot hold, we fall apart, we are alienated from one another) by enabling the players actually to assemble the broken parts, to put it all back together again, via the power of feeling, as conveyed by the blues.

O'Neill records the symphony of the family as well as the cacophony of people living together over time, discovering ever more sharply and richly how intertwined they are, including their ghosts from past generations, how no single piece of any of them stands alone. His play stages our embeddedness in one another.

Munch actually illuminates the amazing reach and dimensionality of our feelings, our affective career—desire, anxiety, fear, sickness, dying—which is social and relational to the core. His paintings position us in shocking landscapes and postures, and his blank faces are almost unbearably eloquent about the pain and turmoil within.

These eruptive tidings are at once the flow that carries us, and the shapers of our life story. We waltz (or crawl) through our lives, keyed to a thin narrative of reason and surface truth—one person, one body— that is beggared and exploded by the testimony of art. Bergman exploits ever more brilliantly over his career the magic lantern that he loved as a child, so as to make visible to an audience the tentacular reach of feeling, to convey the depth, truth, and power of our experiential lives. Bergman closes my discussion of the scream that goes through the house, because in his work we finally see and hear that long trajectory that charts the length and breadth, the height and depth of feeling. The new dispensation brought into view by these works of art is utterly at odds with the post-Enlightenment worldview that informs modern life in the West, and many may find it fanciful, mad. But for those who are sick or in pain, those who know the law of sentience and the power of feeling, these tidings may be of value.

What value? you may ask. How can a body of film or paintings or literature alter what we know of our givens? especially our bodily givens? So much of the art under discussion here is about misery, suffering, human pain. Don't we have enough of that in the flesh, without signing on for more of it in art?

The greatest unhappiness that sickness produces is the *shrinkage* it occasions in our lives. We find ourselves confined to sickroom, to bed, to reduced function, to an intractable body that seems to have taken over. No work of art that I discuss can deny this state of affairs. The issue is: what can be done? And my answer is: literature and art *expand* our estate, enable us to move—conceptually, imaginatively, vicariously—out of the physical jail we (we the healthy, as well as we the sick) live in. This is not a cheat or an illusion. It is as real as the flesh that hurts, or even the death that is coming. The experience of art sets the brain and the heart going; it vitalizes and it quickens. I have argued, indeed, that it socializes and empowers, because it bids to redefine "home" for us: art from other lands and times comes into us and enriches our estate; we move outward, into new territories that become ours. By offering us its special mirror, by showing how resonant and capacious the human story can be, art restores feeling to its proper place in life.

CHAPTER TWO

LIVING IN THE BODY

As Gregor Samsa awoke one morning from uneasy dreams he found himself transformed in his bed into a gigantic insect.

—FRANZ KAFKA, "The Metamorphosis"

"Here," she said, "in this place, we flesh; flesh that weeps, laughs; flesh that dances on bare feet in the grass. Love it. Love it hard. Yonder they do not love your flesh. They despise it. They don't love your eyes; they'd just as soon pick 'em out. No more do they love the skin on your back. Yonder they flay it."

—TONI MORRISON, *Beloved*

SEEING THE BODY: THE VISION OF ART

In this book about human feelings, about art as a place where those feelings are illuminated and shared, I want nonetheless to say that the dominant fact of life that governs somatic creatures from birth to death is this: we are *embodied*.

Counterintuitive though it may seem, literature and the arts afford us a royal way into the body, and this is a trip worth making because the acquaintanceship in question is, of course, with ourselves.

You did not choose the body you were born in. You will spend your entire lifetime "following" (rather than leading) its dictates and nature. To be sure, contemporary society regards the body as ever more malleable to our aesthetic and personal wants, but you're still going to be stuck with (and stuck in) an apparatus that is, to say the least, strange: protuberances everywhere, holes in it, larded with organisms, animated by potent forces, changing over time. This creature who we are is, oddly enough, invisible to us most of the time, even though it is calling the shots and running the show; scientific description does not really convey it, and mirrors tend to keep its secret.

It is not easy to see our generic equipment for the strange apparatus it is. Eyes, ears, a nose and a mouth, a pair of arms and legs, hands with fingers and feet with toes: from infancy on, we regard these features and forms as natural, as inevitable. What might they look like to a Martian? Or to a bird or a dog? And that only covers the cover: what about the insides? Heart, lungs, liver, kidneys: surgeons may know what they look like, but most of us have long forgotten whatever images we may have seen in school science classes, and rarely stop to think that these entities live in us, and may indeed determine our fate.

When we are healthy, the body behaves. We do not need to command our organs to function: breathing and blood circulation miraculously just happen. And the commands that are necessary—the brain's relays and the operation of the nervous system—seem invisible, a gift of nature, bypassing our awareness, so that walking and talking, moving your body and using your head, seem natural, immediate, unlabored. Most of us live in a head-world, a world of ideas and images, often a realm of abstractions (such as money, success, happiness, failure, ambition, remorse, depression, etc.), where the corporeal, the somatic, play little if any role. You wake up in the morning, and although your first act may be to get out of bed, your thoughts are doubtless elsewhere: on breakfast, on today's agenda, on projects of all stripes. How often do you think about the wondrous set of cooperating bones, muscles, and brain commands that make it possible for your body to leave the bed in the first place?

Our schooling, our mental, verbal, and perceptual habits, everything conspires to make us think we are in the driver's seat. Our organic equipment is not all that different from the other equipment that we own and use. All of it—bodies, automobiles, computers, the whole list of "assets" that seem to be ours—is there to be harnessed, there to serve our purposes. In these last three sentences I have used the possessive pronoun *our* no less than five times, to signal a fundamental proprietary scheme that is so basic, so taken for granted that few of us ever think about it. So let me now ask: do we really own our bodies? Does anyone have a contract or a lease of this sort? Could our bodies be far more independent and autonomous than we realize? Aren't sickness and death shocking for just this reason: they remind us how illusory our ownership is.

In reflecting on the phenomenon of the death of the body, Faulkner's character Doctor Peabody, in *As I Lay Dying*, considers the nihilist view that death is the end, versus the fundamentalist view that death is the beginning, and decides that "in reality it is no more than a single tenant or family moving out of a tenement or a town" (29). That tenement is no docile habitation, but has its own laws and customs, and is strange to us in the way that other cultures are strange to anthropologists. To take the body for granted, to fail to *see* it, is to put on blinders or to *naturalize* a set of corporeal and visceral arrangements that is in fact most unruly. So unruly that I want to use the word *beast* to evoke that tenement of flesh and blood that we inhabit.

Art removes these blinders, puts the beast center stage. It shows us who we really are, as regards the body. *Beast* conveys something of the core alterity, independent volition, and occasional horror that characterize bodies. My other favorite term for this state of affairs is *monster*. Our bodies can be both monstrous and fantastic, and this unsettling view is to be found in the testimony of writers from antiquity to the present. Such writing is, you might say, "a return to basics," with the crucial corollary: these basics are a lot stranger than you may think.

FROM ANIMAL TO HUMAN: THE SOPHOCLEAN LEGACY

Let me start with the premier exemplar of Western humanism, Sophocles. In the *Oedipus* we find our most archetypal story about taking the measure of the human. This man, Oedipus, vibrant king of Thebes when the Sophoclean version opens, comes to learn that all of his assumptions about who he was and what he did are egregiously wrong: the violent altercation and murder at the crossroads was a parricide; the queen-wife he sleeps with is his mother. It might seem that the theme of animality is not foregrounded, but the body's scale and frailties loom larger than first appears. Medicine itself is a major topos in the play: the city of Thebes is dying of plague, and Oedipus is repeatedly imaged as the savior-physician, the man who possesses the skill to exorcise the miasma from the community, to cleanse it of pollution. The Greek audience is fully aware that Oedipus is the man who delivered the city from the prior curse of the Sphinx, and hence he is expected to save it again.

Now, Sophocles has not elected to treat the episode with the Sphinx, but its significance is central to the story. We know the riddle that Oedipus answered: what is the creature that is on four legs in the morning, two legs at midday, and three legs in the evening? The confident answer, "MAN,"—infancy, adulthood, old age—is commonly understood as the supreme shorthand expression of Greek humanism, and many scholars, such as Bernard Knox, point out that all of the pathos and ambiguity of the play hinges, in some sense, on whether "MAN" solves the riddle. Man, it will be further noted, is the only living creature that changes its locomotion over time, via crawling, then walking, then leaning.

Much is at stake with this question-and-answer at this moment in ancient history. What the French call the "human sciences" are burgeoning at the time of Periclean Athens: mathematics, architecture, sculpture, agriculture, navigation, medicine, philosophy, historiography, tragedy. The ensuing story of Oedipus' knowledge-cum-ignorance calls into question the very claims of humanism. And those issues are richly materialized in the encounter with the Sphinx: this monstrous creature of fable—body of a lion, head of a human, later feminized— seems to me to stand for an earlier culture of animal gods (consider Egyptian or Assyrian deities), for a world in which the so-called human scale, a scale tirelessly promoted by the Greeks, has little or no purchase.

It is worth recalling, at this juncture, the influential critique of the oedipal myth written by the anthropologist Claude Lévi-Strauss. He is drawn to the insistent pun entailed in Oedipus' name: "swollen-foot." Here is literally the telltale sign of Oedipus' origins, his stint as exposed infant, cast out and tied at the ankles (by his father, Laius, who had been told by the Oracle that he would be slain by his son). But Lévi-Strauss goes on to connect the name with that of both father and grandfather, Laius and Labdacos, meaning respectively "left-sided" and "lame" (traits further linked, in the ancient Greek mind, with abnormality in behavior, especially sexual behavior). Lévi-Strauss's interpretation of the myth (which interests him in all its variants, not merely the elements Sophocles marshaled together for his play) is complex and fascinating, cued to key issues of procreation, over- and underrating of blood relations, and, central for our purposes, the slaying of monsters. From an anthropological perspective, the myth is *thinking* about some crucial biological and cultural issues having to do with the origins, nature, and comportment of bodies. The most intriguing touch comes from the emphasis on walking-problems that is signaled by the male names, a set of problems that Lévi-Strauss finds (oddly) replicated in Pueblo myths concerning men born from the earth. With characteristic pithiness, the anthropologist sums up the problem as "difficulties to walk and to behave straight."

Is this not precisely the challenge posed by humanism: to replace a regime of monsters or animals, four-footed creatures, with a new concept and scale, man, the creature that may be four-footed at birth (on all fours) and three-footed in old age (on a staff or cane), but who is defiantly two-footed, erect and in fighting form, in his noontime. Oedipus' two disastrous actions in being an erect fighter—murdering his father and procreating with his mother—hardly constitute humanism's finest moment, and cast considerable doubt about man's successful passage from the animal to the human.

Let's now consider another Sophoclean play, the later and lesser known *Philoctetes*, which seems to continue the same meditation about man and beast. But the coloration of this play is much darker than *Oedipus*, as if the bright claims made for human knowledge and doing—after all, Oedipus does finally assume the burdens of his deeds, does achieve a stunning sort of self-possession—had been proven hollow. This story is set during the Trojan War, and its title character, Philoctetes, has been abandoned on a desert island, some ten years earlier, by the Greek cohort heading to Troy, abandoned because, when visiting the temple of the goddess Chryse, he was bitten in the foot by a venomous serpent, guardian of the shrine.

This wound turned out to be so noxious and unbearable, with its bleeding, its stench, and its unhealable nature, that the Greek warriors could not bear his presence among them, and ditched him on the island. But now, ten years later, the Oracle has explained to the Greeks that the Trojan War cannot be won without the participation of Philoctetes, because he is the possessor of a magic bow, given to him by Heracles, and this is what is needed for victory. To implement this policy, two Greeks are sent to the island to convince and retrieve Philoctetes and his bow: the wily Odysseus (whom Philoctetes hates with a passion only equaled by his hatred for Agamemnon and Menelaus, those leaders responsible for abandoning him) and the young Neoptolemus, son of the dead Achilles. Their job is to lie to the wounded man and trick him into coming back with them. The moral core of the play appears located in Neoptolemus' refusal to engage in such realpolitik, and we can hardly miss the paternal dimensions of this struggle: who will the young man without a father follow: the cunning Odysseus, or the suffering and bitter Philoctetes? What stuns us and stays with us in this play, however, is not the moral dilemma faced by the young man; it is the intensely, tragically physical depiction of Philoctetes and his fate.

If Lévi-Strauss focused our attention on the problems of walking and behaving straight in *Oedipus*, Edmund Wilson taught us to rethink *Philoctetes* in his memorable essay "The Wound and the Bow," in which he argues that the play is concerned with the role of the gifted in society, drawing the conclusion that the artist—be he ever so wounded or damaged or marginalized—nonetheless turns out to be indispensable for the society at large. The wound is inseparable from the bow; you can't win the war without reclaiming the sick Philoctetes. There is an appealing social dialectic at work here, a sort of ecosystem that jars traditional thinking by valorizing the sick and wounded.

More recently, the play has been examined as our premier depiction of what chronic pain is like: namely, it becomes a world you inhabit, from which no exit is conceivable. In this light, the very topography of the play is eloquent, for pain is an island; pain is exile. Sophocles is relentlessly social in his perspective, and this play shows us what kind of bitterness and misanthropy result from sickness and pain. Pain dehumanizes. Not just its sufferer, but all those around him as well. Sophocles dwells at great length on the desolation of Philoctetes' life, and in a number of brutal scenes we actually witness the outbreak of pain, the festering wound that opens up its mouth to issue its blood:

> PHILOCTETES (*collapsing to the ground*):
> I'm done for . . . no use trying to hide it.
> Oh! Oh! . . . it goes through me like a knife.
> I'm done for, boy . . . it's come for me now . . .
> (*racked with agony*) Pfff!
> Your sword, if you have it . . . For God's sake, boy.
> Cut off my foot! Off with it! Quick!
> O son, O son! O let me die.
> NEOPTOLEMUS: What is it? So suddenly coming upon
> you . . . These terrible cries . . .
> PHILOCTETES: You know!
> NEOPTOLEMUS: What is it?
> PHILOCTETES: You know . . .
> NEOPTOLEMUS: Tell me, what is it?

PHILOCTETES: You must . . . Ah!

NEOPTOLEMUS: It tortures you . . .

PHILOCTETES: Torture . . . I cannot tell you . . . O for pity!

NEOPTOLEMUS: What can I do?

PHILOCTETES: *(recovering a little):*

    Don't leave me now. There's nothing to fear.

    The demon comes from time to time

    After letting me alone for a little while.

(188–189)

Back and forth we see the collapse of speaking and knowing. We all know that language is better for some things than others, and that it is devilishly hard to find words to convey feelings and sensations. Pain ranks high here. And terrible pain, as in torture, quite simply cancels out language altogether, as Elaine Scarry has brilliantly argued in her book *The Body in Pain.* Sophocles is merciless in his emphasis on the human wreckage and havoc caused by pain, the revulsion and twistedness it brings and leaves; and readers quickly sense that there is no way this bitter, broken man is going to return willingly to Troy, once Neoptolemus has told him the dirty truth about their mission, no matter what the Oracle has said. Sophocles is obliged to bring the dead Heracles back on stage, a deus ex machina of the first order, if this mess is to be cleaned up and this man with his bow to be put back into circulation.

What does this fable tell us about bodies? Edmund Wilson properly focused on Philoctetes' magic bow as the integral counterpart to the stinking, unhealing wound, but I want to return our sights to this injury. Wounded by the serpent, guardian of the shrine, Philoctetes appears to have encountered the mark of the god. But what the play thrusts at us, through its unremitting depiction of pain, suffering, and despair, is the elemental truth that Philoctetes has encountered *the mark of the beast.* This festering wound, demon that comes "from time to time," that spreads its dark blood and poison and foulness and makes life unbearable for all parties, is unmistakably somatic, of the flesh. We see here the mark of the beast in both senses: the serpent beast that wounded Philoctetes, but also the marked human creature itself, carrying its wound as primary constituent of identity, as signature. Sophocles is exposing the scandal of flesh—not unlike what he did in *Antigone,* where so much hinges on getting dead flesh into the ground before it rots—and he makes us see that the body has a dreadful priority in human affairs.

Why not go further and say that the wound is originary with life—the somatic explosion or accident that is waiting to happen, the physiological liability that we are—and not some kind of occupational hazard that could occur if you trespass on the goddess's shrine. Customary medical logic views the body as whole and intact until the onset of disease or decay. Even as a layperson, I have some appreciation for what a miraculously complex and harmonious system the body is, how intricately ordered our biological and physiological arrangements are. Yet—and this may well be a sign of my aging—I have an ever-sharper sense of the body's mortality, its vulnerability to disease, its inevitable entropic journey toward death. If we can see the *Philoctetes* along these severe lines, as a play that offers a troubling and moving account of what it is like to live in a body, measuring the dehumanization that attends pain and injury, and presenting the body itself as essentially a locus of agony—pleasure is inconceivable in this scheme, real though it may be in our better days—then we may regard it as a dark sequel to the *Oedipus.* The first play hinges, as we saw, on the ability of humans to walk and behave straight. In factoring in the wound of Philoctetes, we may now conclude by saying that Sophocles tends to imagine humanism as the Walking Wounded, as a kind of defiant bid for agency in a somatic, animalistic scheme that will not have it.

To call Homo sapiens the Walking Wounded may seem like a bleak view of the classical legacy, but it has the tonic virtue of underscoring how astonishing the trajectory from animal to human actually is, how stubbornly real and authoritative the body is and remains, no matter how glittery our mental and moral achievements may be. And it helps us toward a more balanced view of the uneasy coexistence between soma and spirit that is with us from cradle to grave. That coexistence is, in itself, a fascinating story, filled with sound and fury, a story that seems to require the imagination and vision of the artist if we are to see its fullest dimensions. Art is there, in Kafka's words, to chop through our frozen sea, by which he meant, to pierce through the thickness of routine and habit, the dulled torpor of complacency. Kafka himself was thinking of spiritual vistas when he wrote those words, but I do not hesitate to apply his dictum to the affairs of the body, to its strange and unacknowledged rule over us. As we think through these matters via the testimony of writers and artists throughout history, we will encounter in many different guises the Sophoclean double legacy: the body as animal, the body as wound.

DOMESTICATING THE BODY: CAN IT BE DONE?

Of course this theory of the human as animal is not news to anyone. Writers have produced fables based on this motif ever since Aesop, and in seventeenth-century France La Fontaine produced some of the most sophisticated, elegant, satiric, and ironic fare of his day working in this vein. Need I even mention our Age of Disney with its immortal animal stars and *vedettes*? In fact, the cartoon culture for today's children in America—starring creatures such as Rugrats, SpongeBob, and the like—is such a fantasia of altered animal/human forms that one wonders if the next generation will have the same understanding of morphology as we do. But it is one thing to endow animals with human attributes, and quite another to peel away the human façade so as to expose the animal. As long as we stick to the metaphorical, there is no problem: sly as a fox, stubborn as a mule, strong as a horse, proud as a lion, evil as a snake; such epithets and similes have been around forever, and startle no one, even if we recognize the conventionality and overdetermined symbolism of such characterization. But what happens if we reverse direction, moving from the figurative to the literal, when the human body either acquires or exposes other, more disturbing features? Susan Sontag describes the age-old fears and prejudices related to disfiguring diseases, and she makes some crucial distinctions: "Not every kind of alteration to the face is perceived as repulsive or shaming. The most dreaded are those that seem like mutations into animality (the leper's 'lion face') or a kind of rot (as in syphilis). . . . What counts more than the amount of disfigurement is that it reflects underlying, ongoing changes, the dissolution of the person" (128–129).

People shy away from disfigurement for many reasons, including (I think) a primitive fear that it could be contagious. Whatever rationales are at work, there seems to be a rather narrow aesthetic range for the "normal," and works like *The Elephant Man* derive their pathos from the cruelty that results from such normative assumptions, a cruelty that denies the notion of "human" to those who do not fit within the frames. Throughout history, not only lepers, but hunchbacks, dwarves, people with clubfeet, and countless other "irregularities" have been subject to derision and contempt. But also to fascination, as the history of circuses suggests, with their stable of "misfits" such as giants, the fat woman, the man-woman, etc. In our time, critics like Leslie Fiedler have reflected on such matters (in his book *Freaks*), and photographers like Diane Arbus have exploited this mix of malaise and attraction in showing how much physical oddity there is even in everyday faces and bodies, once you look closely.

The flip side of these matters leads directly to a discussion of *beauty*. Beauty has a long history in the discourses of both philosophy and aesthetics, including a complex association with notions such as goodness and truth. Beauty is said to attract, just as ugliness repels, and we all know how much human excitement and misery have resulted from these beliefs. Needless to say, we live in a world where physical "beauty" can play a paramount role in all those arenas that count so much, especially for the young and fit: romance, friendship, happiness, professional success, self-esteem. Should any of us forget these facts of life, a casual glance at the blitz of images coming our way via advertising, TV, fashion, film, and mass culture in general will get the message across. All this has a great deal to do with bodies, especially with the postmodern view that our bodies are infinitely sculptable and alterable. Our moment is stamped by an unprecedented concern with dieting, exercising, muscle building, cosmetic surgery, and an ever-growing repertory of body-altering devices and aids. It is as if the old Pygmalion story were being played, but instead of transforming a sculpture into life, we seem to go at it from the other direction: to change our own bodies into sculpture.

It seems to me there is a considerable amount of hubris and over-reaching in our body-altering culture, inasmuch as the materials we are sculpting (the deck we were dealt) may have a will of their own. The desire to remake the body is essentially Faustian (in Goethe's play of two centuries ago, one of the Faust's first exploits in his quest for knowledge and power consists in acquiring a more youthful, more handsome body), and literature is drawn to the hubris involved here, the fantasy of significantly improving the physiological givens you were born with. One of the most fascinating early accounts of such overreaching is found in Hawthorne's well-known tale "The Birthmark," from the 1840s. Hawthorne's story fits in the "Frankenstein vein" of literature, in that it is a parable about the limits and limitations of science; but it engages us today also because of its glaring gender biases: the experimental scientist Aylmer is obsessed with removing from the otherwise perfect face of his wife, Georgiana, a tiny birthmark that mars (for him) her beauty—even though Hawthorne characterizes the tiny hand-shaped mark as the gift of "some fairy at her birth hour" (204).

Most unsettling of all is Georgiana's own growing self-hatred which results from her husband's critical mania, and she begs him to remove the birthmark, no matter how risky such a procedure might be: "Danger is nothing to me; for life, while this hateful mark makes me the object of your horror and disgust—life is a burden which I would fling down with joy. Either remove this dreadful hand or take my wretched life!" (207). Needless to say, Aylmer's experiment succeeds on both fronts: it removes the birthmark, and it takes her life. Hawthorne doubtless intended a kind of rebuke to scientific overreaching in this story, but he was prescient, indeed prophetic, in his awareness that male canons of beauty could lead women to despair and even to death. In the 1840s resculpting the body is portrayed, at least in literature, as a kind of black magic, and the cult of beauty turns out to be lethal.

Hawthorne's birthmark is shaped like a hand, and it seems to prefigure that omnipotent surgeon's hand that is called on, in today's culture, to rectify nature's mistakes. The well-known surgeon-writer Richard Selzer has given us, in "Imelda," a startlingly contemporary version of "The Birthmark," but more problematic and heartrending. Narrated in the first person by Selzer as a memory from his student days, the story is about a distinguished surgeon, Hugh Franciscus, who encounters during his yearly stint to Honduras the severely deformed Imelda, whose cleft lip and cleft palate—the child's shame and mark—are described with graphic detail. The surgeon confidently plans to remake the child's face (after mapping it out like an exercise in geometry), but things go amok, and the girl dies under the anesthesia before the surgery can be attempted.

Faust enters the picture here, as Franciscus elects to operate anyway, in the dead of night, with a candle to illuminate the scene, and thus the child placed in a coffin the next day has been surgically altered. So, too, is Franciscus, for whom this episode seems to have been a turning point, a sign that it is time to slow down, to stop. Much is packed into this brief tale: the arrogance of science but also its superhuman aspirations, leading doctor and patient, man and girl, into a professional ritual that is a double dance of death. Selzer's story is nonetheless a cautionary fable and acquires a special pathos by being refracted to us through the perspective of the medical student who is pondering its significance, looking for boundaries, trying to determine exactly what can be done to and with flesh.

If Imelda's wrecked face seems a viable candidate for surgical remaking, can one say as much for today's culture of wholesale "improvements"? In his provocative study *Illness and Culture in the Postmodern Age,* David Morris devotes an entire chapter to "Utopian Bodies" in which he discusses the "ethics and aesthetics of perfection"—so vividly on display in our bodybuilding mania as well as our media, with the corollary phenomena of anorexia and bulimia and other disorders—and he concludes with a moving plea that we make our peace with "imperfection" as our natural fate. He urges us to rethink our canons, to consider women who've had mastectomies and men who live with disabilities as candidates for a postmodern heroism.

Given the imperious role played by images in the media, and given the ongoing developments in genetic programming and reproductive technologies which seem to promise manufactured bodies to fit every specification, it is hardly surprising that the human body is thought by many today to be simply "material" that one alters at will. Hawthorne and Selzer relied on doctors for the bodywork they wanted to question, but the truly alluring question would be: could you go it alone? could this be a do-it-yourself job?

To shed still more light on the fantasies of body control and self-deification at play here, I turn now to an older text, Laclos's epistolary classic of the eighteenth century, *Les Liaisons Dangereuses.* Mme. de Merteuil, the astonishing female lead, is the grand predator of the novel, smarter by half than anyone in her entourage, shrewd about the role of vanity and desire in all human interactions, utterly cued to the signs of body language that advertise all erotic interest, and able to produce such physiological signs—blush, rapid pulse, trembling—whenever necessary. (Can you do this?) She and her (vastly inferior) male counterpart, Valmont, are embarked on an erotic search-and-destroy mission, entailing as many sexual conquests as possible, and their success depends in large measure on their readerly prowess: they decipher bodies. Merteuil is a Nietzschean figure of real proportions, and her soma comes across as a form of advanced weaponry, utterly under her control.

At the close of the novel, this unstoppable woman is stopped: she is

disfigured by smallpox. Critics have cried "foul," since such an authorial move reeks of poetic justice rather than real-life behavior, but I'd
argue it the other way: Laclos wants to show that we never own our bodies, docile though they may appear during our good days. There is a
Greek feeling to this ending, a recognition that the body obeys rules,
speaks a language, and performs acts beyond anything of our own devising. The moralists within the text delight at Merteuil's disfigurement:
her face, now hideous and monstrous, shows, according to them, the
last thing she'd ever choose to reveal: her soul.

BEASTIOGNOMY: OUR ETERNAL TUG-OF-WAR

Writers are drawn to the body's often frightening eloquence and authority, especially since it displays the untamable animal we also are. Shakespeare is everywhere alive to the traffic between man and beast, and one
could argue that *Othello* is entirely cued to this stark truth. The bedrock
for such a view is doubtless the bed itself, as Iago implies when he
screams up to Brabantio, Desdemona's father, that "Even now, now, very
now, an old black ram / Is tupping your white ewe" (I.i.89–90), to be followed in short order by the pithiest figure for copulation that I know of:
"your daughter and the Moor are now making the beast with two backs"
(I.i.116–118). The vexed transition from beast to human signaled by Lévi-
Strauss in the story of the Sphinx is not very esoteric at all, when we consider the basic drives of the body, especially the sex drive.

Iago's worldview is that we are, underneath our façade, entirely animal in nature, and his plot consists in making sure that Othello becomes
precisely that. At the play's exact center (III.iii) Iago feeds his poison of
sexual suspicion to Othello, and in the scope of this single scene we see
the noble Moor completely transmogrified. Worse is to come: driven to
madness by sexual jealousy, Othello moves ever further into the bestiary: raves of "Pish! Noses, ears, and lips" (IV.i.41–42), closes his greeting to the Venetian emissary Lodovico with "You are welcome, sir, to
Cyprus. Goats and monkeys!" (IV.i.265) and expresses his unbearable

sense of defilement thus: "But there where I have garnered up my heart, / Where either I must live, or bear no life, / The fountain from the which my current runs, / Or else dries up—to be discarded thence / Or keep it as a cistern for foul toads / To knot and gender it!" (IV.ii.56–61). We learn in these poignant lines how one's own inmost soul can be so tarnished through (imagined) sexual betrayal that the current runs dry and and becomes a locus of animal filth and fornication; here, too, is transformation, inasmuch as Iago's stock fable of black rams and white ewes becomes an act far more exquisitely vile and dirtying: spirit becomes hideously carnal, and *your* sexuality does that to *me*.

The nineteenth-century German playwright Georg Büchner, political agitator and lecturer in comparative anatomy (with special interests in neurology), offers an appropriately politicized and medicalized version of *Othello* in his amazing play *Woyzeck,* Europe's first proletarian drama. The play is larded with puns about "beastiognomy" and the like, and its central figure, Woyzeck, is certainly bestial, cannot refrain from pissing on the street, and will be driven mad in the course of the play, ultimately stabbing his woman dead. Büchner has prophetically included an inhuman doctor who uses Woyzeck as an ongoing lab experiment (replete with forced diet); in one of the most moving scenes, Woyzeck is insane with jealousy, speaking of being ice-cold while the earth is hellish hot, talking of driving a stake into the sky and hanging himself from it, and against this Shakespearean language the doctor emotes pure clinicalese: "Your pulse, Woyzeck, your pulse, short, hard, thumping, irregular," "Facial muscles rigid, taut, jerky at times, posture erect, rigid." This text stages, along with its show of medical torture, a kind of rhetorical warfare, lets the scientific and the visionary codes do battle with each other, asks us to judge which is most attuned to the passional experience of the human animal.

Other still more famous literary texts hinge on the eternal tug-of-war between the bestial and the human. Stevenson's tale of Dr. Jekyll and Mr. Hyde is doubtless our most celebrated depiction of this monstrous duality, and it is no accident that the entire fantasia is a medical one, that

Hyde is produced by ingesting potent chemicals. Stevenson, pre-Freudian that he was, was certainly pointing to the dark underside of the psyche, ruled out by Victorian properties, but we are entitled to think pharmacalogically as well, to foresee already what kind of R and D might be out there, needed to free up our animal spirits. Is it such a stretch to say that Stevenson's fable gestures—however unwittingly—toward our culture of Viagra and other sexual enhancements?

Other literary performances on this topic in the nineteenth century are less overt, but still more profound. I am again thinking of Charlotte Brontë's classic novel *Jane Eyre,* in which the gentle, diminutive Jane is doubled by the monstrous, intemperate, unchaste Bertha Mason Rochester, the "madwoman in the attic" whom we have learned to see as Jane's alter ego, thanks to the insights of modern feminist criticism. Much to ponder here: for more than a century, it never occurred, even to the boldest critics, that the "mad, bad and embruted" Bertha could be understood as Jane's "other." Certainly the advent of Freud matters here, in that his notion of repression signifies a kind of personal and cultural policing that we do to deny the animal side of things. And today anyone can see that the entire plot of Brontë's book depends on *locking up* the animal, a carceral project that fails, not only once (when Rochester leads the wedding party up to the infamous third floor of Thornfield where Bertha is kept caged) but over and over throughout the novel, as we hear the animal's infernal laugh, glimpse her bouts of violence, sense her roaming. The animal is nothing less than libido itself, i.e., the energy system that drives bodies, a view that Victorian thinking proscribes with all its might.

We will never know how much of all this Brontë intended—it is the first question my students ask when I suggest this libidinal interpretation of a book many of them have read in much more innocent fashion—and my only answer is: can we know what any author intends? what we ourselves intend? Novels are not subject to proof or disproof, like evidence in a courtroom, and we have everything to gain by taking liberties with Brontë, because the pieces of her story then fit together with an irresistible logic. *Jane Eyre* (the novel) is *thinking* about sexuality and animality, about the presumable transition from animals to humans, just as the *Oedipus* and the *Philoctetes* are. In Sophocles, incest, parricide, and misanthropy result, whereas the damage Brontë (unwittingly?) charts is of a different order. Bertha's potent mix of sexuality and rage gets quite a run: the animal tries to burn the bullying patriarch alive, ends up torching the castle and blinding/maiming him in the process. I'd say that some overdue nineteenth-century bills are being paid in this text. What other kind of map could possibly show us these things? I can think of few literary examples that display more perfectly why art matters, what it is good for, what it enables us to see and hear.

Jane Eyre speaks volumes about Victorian censorship, about the range of things between heaven and earth that its philosophy cannot comprehend, but that the artist intuits nonetheless. I say "volumes" are spoken, in that the "animalizing" of Bertha comes to us, more than 150 years later, as a double story of denial and liberation: the surface plot goes through its paces disciplining the unruly body, whereas the other plot offers a staggering critique of these moves, showing how ideologically resonant terms such as *mad, bad,* and *embruted* are, and how doomed the coercion scenario is.

In similar fashion, Büchner's *Woyzeck* tells us a great deal about a subject we encounter all too frequently today—the outbreak of domestic violence and murder; it is no accident that this play is based, at least in part, on three documented cases of men murdering their wives or mistresses in early-nineteenth-century Germany—and we are asked to ponder the connection between "beastiognomy" and social arrangements. Woyzeck, the lowest of the low, is systematically abused, and the author seems to be asking: how much does it take to push a man over the edge? The animals are everywhere: at the circus, on the street, in the beds. The critic Richard Schickel once suggested that a proper staging of the final scene in which Woyzeck is on trial for the murder of Marie should bring the animals back in, let them mosey into the courtroom and see what is being done to their kind. Büchner is very much the scientist and the political scientist in this play, seeking to gauge the nature and causes of violence, locating his answers both in the libidinal/neural equipment of the human species and in the economic order of the culture. We have not solved these questions. What causes domestic violence? why does someone walk into a subway car or a post office or a McDonald's and proceed to blow everyone away? One thing is certain: bodies, under sufficient pressure, explode. Literature helps us understand such eruptions as a social story.

KALEIDOSCOPIC BODY AND VISIONARY ART

I have said that our customary perception of the body cheats us by *naturalizing* what it sees. The entire project of visionary art and literature consists in *denaturalizing*, or, as William Blake famously put it in *The Marriage of Heaven and Hell*, restoring to us a true vision of things by dint of a perceptual cleansing: "If the doors of perception were cleansed everything would appear to man as it is, infinite./For man has closed himself up, till he sees all things thro' narrow chinks of his cavern" (73). Drawing doubtless on Plato's parable of the cave, according to which we see only shadows and reflections, Blake spells out one of the criteria of art: to open our doors of perception. Blake himself was a fierce social critic, looking at the power grid of late-eighteenth- and early-nineteenth-century England with the eyes of a visionary, and much of the destabilizing virulence we saw in Büchner and Brontë has a Blakean tinge to it. In particular, Blake celebrated what we today would call *libido*, but the word he used for it was *Energy*, which he saw as "the only life" and "from the body," which he also viewed as the source of "eternal delight."

But we can learn about the body's surprises and unruliness in other ways, too, from texts that have no cultural agenda whatsoever. I am thinking of Rilke's hallucinatory prose work, written during his youthful stint in Paris in the early years of the twentieth century, *The Notebooks of Malte Laurids Brigge*, in which the artist Malte seems almost cursed by having his perceptual doors cleansed. One of the motifs of the *Note-books* is the repeated refrain, "I am learning to see," "*Ich lerne sehen,*" and that is what art does: it teaches us to see. Not in the retinal sense of accurate information gathering, but in the inner, imaginative sense of grasping an emotional or psychological truth. Rilke's Malte is a man experiencing Parisian squalor, its carnival of down-and-out city dwellers who wear their misery on their faces, but he encounters them, as it were, without defenses, as an observer whose membranes are too thin, whose insides seem to be on the outside ("Electric trolley cars speed clattering through my room. Cars drive over me"). Not that Rilke has a program, wants you to improve urban conditions; rather, he shows how precarious and violent life is, how tumbling and dizzying it all is, how risky it is to *look*. To be sure, no reader would like to change places with him. Yet, we are enlarged by his explosive, jolting perceptions, helped toward a view of experience that is more generous, even if more turbulent and capsizing, than the firm scheme (our flesh included) we take to be stationary.

One of the text's most celebrated passages focuses on the body: not the body of a Parisian derelict, but Malte's own body. He is remembering an episode from childhood when he was coloring. At a certain point, the red crayon fell under the table, and the boy, numbed from the position he'd been in, went after it. Finding himself on a fur rug, no longer entirely clear what is his and what is the chair's, the child tries to accustom his eyes to this darkness and is obliged to rely on his sense of touch to find the missing crayon. Kneeling, propped up by one hand, the other combing the rug in search of the missing object, Malte is initially disoriented, but gradually his eyes adapt to the situation, and he sees the wall, the molding, and then something else:

> above all I recognized my own outspread hand moving down there
> all alone, like some strange crab, exploring the ground. I watched it,
> I remember, almost with curiosity; it seemed to know things I had

never taught it, as it groped down there so completely on its own, with movements I had never noticed in it before. I followed it as it crept forward; it interested me; I was ready for all kinds of adventures. But how could I have been prepared to see, all at once, out of the wall, another hand coming to meet it—a larger, extraordinarily thin hand, such as I had never seen before. It came groping in a similar fashion from the other side, and the two outspread hands blindly moved toward each other. My curiosity was not yet satisfied, but suddenly it was gone and there was only horror. I felt that one of the hands belonged to me and that it was about to enter into something it could never return from. With all the authority I had over it, I stopped it, held it flat, and slowly pulled it back to me, without taking my eyes off the other one, which kept on groping. I realized that it wouldn't stop, and I don't know how I got up again. (94)

What to make of this? The passage shrewdly prepares us for its discovery of one's own body as *other*: numbed body, darkened setting, groping hand. Anyone who has played the game of using fingers to cast animal shadows on a wall, anyone who has gazed a second too long at his or her hand or leg or other appendage, has sensed the estrangement in play here. An overlong look in the mirror will do the same job. In my view, the horror of the passage, the *other hand* that comes from nowhere and bids to usurp all (hand, child, world), is ultimately a repeat of what we see already in the first crablike hand making movements and knowing things it has never been "taught." Such writing brings home to us how *exotic* our bodies are, how crammed with pulsions and freewheeling our appendages are (again underscoring the mirage entailed in that pronoun "our," since these somatic performances don't seem to be carrying out "our" orders, but rather doing their own song and dance). How do we learn what may be at stake in such transactions, when the body flaunts its autonomy? Sickness—a limb or an organ threatens to quit, making you heinously aware of its power, of your dependency—is one kind of crash course. Literature can be another.

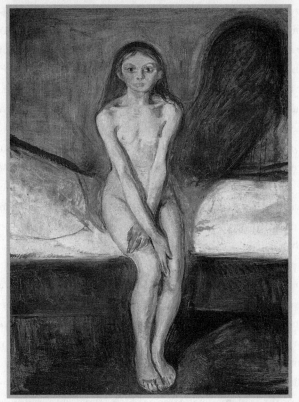

Puberty, Edvard Munch, 1894.

THE BODY'S CAREER OVER TIME: PUBERTY AND AGING

Rilke's depiction of the hand/crab is a lesson in metaphor. If we tried to visualize this as a real crab, it would be a grotesque joke. But the body's *otherness* can be captured visually, and to prove this, I want to invoke a familiar painting, Munch's *Puberty,* and to investigate what is so disturbing about it. Munch's sights are invariably focused on the career of the body, and although sickness and death are his favorite topics, he shows us here that the discovery of *life* is no less unhinging. This depiction of the naked, adolescent girl, vainly and fearfully trying to shield her burgeoning body from view, from *our* view, annihilates, for starters, any complacent notion that we might have of "spectating" as an innocent or neutral activity. Munch experiments frequently with frontal postures, but nothing quite matches the effect he achieves in *Puberty*. Merely to look at this painting is to do what this girl most fears: to ogle her body, invade her privacy. It is worth pondering the corrosive reach of these matters: how often do you factor yourself-as-viewer into the equation of art? You are a "player" in this piece, and the role you play is not nice. Looking—no less than the ontology of art, since it exists to be looked at—becomes tantamount to violation, and if you really think about viewing-as-voyeurism, you may find the next visit to the museum or the next browsing of an art book more uncomfortable and complicated than usual.

We pry when we look. And the girl knows it. The hands seek to hide the genitals but, as she seems to realize, the breasts are on view, and the expression on the face underscores the lopsidedness of the contest: naked bodies are vulnerable, cannot adequately shield themselves from harm or invading eyes. (How often do you have dreams or nightmares of being naked in public, unable to cover yourself, on show?) But we the spectators are only a part of this girl's problems. Her most unsettling discovery, the really traumatic one, is of her own body and its incredible trajectory-in-time, a trip she is just now understanding. There is a temporal treadmill on show here, an evolving curve of life that somatic creatures negotiate from birth to death, and the frightened eyes of this girl seem actually to see the woman she is starting to become, the child she is starting to leave. Puberty *itself* is no less drastic just because everyone goes through it, and in Munch's vision we recover something of its first-time shock value: the emergence of an entire physiological and sexual repertory, the actual machinery of a body that is now becoming adult-operational, shifting gears.

Some critics have suggested that the ominous black shadow that seems to grow out from the girl's genital area could signify menstruation or perhaps the dark and large space of female sexuality, but I'd want to look at it more broadly as a sign that a new regime is coming into being, a regime that houses "self" but has an "agenda" of its own. Somatic equipment that has been embryonically present since conception now starts to make itself seen and felt, inflecting personality in massive ways (ways camouflaged by our bland terms such as *growing up* or, indeed *puberty*). Young girls, now and since time immemorial, are acculturated to "know" that this chapter awaits them, but this painting, intended to restore the impact and turmoil of life's shaping events, illuminates the gulf between abstract information and visceral experience.

The body shifts gears in puberty. I think it shifts gears as long as we live, but aging gives this clanking operation an edge and insistence that are particularly hard to ignore. Everyday experience presents many of us with firsthand information of this sort, and it makes for tedious conversation. But in the hands of gifted writers, somatic entropy can be hilarious, and I want to cite Vernon here, a character from Don DeLillo's wicked novel *White Noise*, whose inventory of troubles is the perfect counterpoint to Munch's annunciatory painting:

> "Don't worry about me," he said. "The little limp means nothing. People my age limp. A limp is a natural thing at a certain age. Forget the cough. It's healthy to cough. You move the stuff around. The stuff can't harm you as long as it doesn't settle in one spot and stay there for years. So the cough's all right. So is the insomnia. The insomnia's all right. What do I gain by sleeping? You reach an age when every minute of sleep is one less minute to do useful things. To cough or limp. Never mind the women. The women are all right. We rent a cassette and have some sex. It pumps blood to the heart. Forget the cigarettes. I like to tell myself I'm getting away with something. Let the Mormons quit smoking. They'll die of something just as bad. The money's no problem. I'm all set incomewise. Zero pensions, zero savings, zero stocks and bonds. So you don't have to worry about that. That's all taken care of. Never mind the teeth. The teeth are all right. The looser they are, the more you can wobble

them with your tongue. It gives the tongue something to do. Don't worry about the shakes. Everybody gets the shakes now and then. It's only the left hand anyway. The way to enjoy the shakes is pretend it's somebody else's hand. Never mind the sudden and unexplained weight loss. There's no point eating what you can't see. Don't worry about the eyes. The eyes can't get any worse than they are now. Forget the mind completely. The mind goes before the body. That's the way it's supposed to be. So don't worry about the mind. The mind is all right. Worry about the car. The steering's all awry. The brakes were recalled three times. The hood shoots up on pothole terrain." (255–256)

While this tirade is not *King Lear,* DeLillo shares with Shakespeare a knowledge of bare, forked creatures, as well as a graveyard view of things that would not be out of place in *Hamlet.* Proust once wrote, in his rich and pathos-filled way, that bodies are the material of which time is made, and the well-known late scene, at the Guermantes reception, presents the spectacle of aging as a kind of masquerade in which people you used to know are now wearing white wigs, are now stooped and bent, obeying at last the tug of gravity that will carry them all the way into the earth.

All of us are positioned on this temporal treadmill, and it is fair to say that we are prone to be shocked by just these arrangements our whole life long: when we are stunned by the transformation of infants into "people," of our parents into old folks, of ourselves into our parents. The Sphinx knew what it was doing when it asked Oedipus what creature walks on four, then two, then three legs; borrowing Cecil B. De-Mille's famous words, I say it's the greatest show on earth. What is most endearing in DeLillo's paean to decay is its sheer pluck, its song and dance, its zest for turning nature's bad joke into a shtick of one's own. In our time- and gravity-defying culture of wellness, diets, workouts, and cosmetic enhancements, the gallows humor of this creatural countdown seems at once tonic and a reality check.

METAMORPHOSIS AND AGENCY:
THE MONSTER ON THE LOOSE

Rilke's Malte sees the strange other hand coming out of the wall and senses he is about to be taken over. Artist's neurosis or generic condition? How much control do we really have? One of the key terms enshrined in contemporary intellectual parlance is *agency*. There was a time when this word merely signified some bureaucratic office, but no longer, at least where I work. In today's academy it represents a cluster of crucial issues including authority, freedom, independence, and integrity. You will find it front and center in "emancipation" language of all stripes, and usually the forces preventing individual agency are cultural or ideological, having to do with patriarchy, late capitalism, sexism, and the like, frequently channeled through the media, but most often invisible to the naked eye, blithely *naturalized* as the "way things are."

A good bit of world literature, from all ages, is now assessed by critics along these lines, and the recurring plot that one encounters hinges on the struggle for agency. There can be stirring drama in this view, as well as a laudable focus on the workings of power within any culture. I have no quarrel with this, but am convinced that we are held in a somatic bondage that is distinctly prior to social arrangements. And I am not sure that any act of Congress or revolution is likely to alter this.

Art and literature, even film, open our eyes to this anarchic situation—this picture of enslavement that is fleshly rather than ideological—and I think that horror films derive much of their fascination from their attack on agency, an attack that is often located in the flesh. "Mutations into animality" was Susan Sontag's explanation of the widespread fear that attends disfigurement, and what better formula to describe the fascination enjoyed by the Dracula and Wolfman stories? All of us are familiar with those moments on-screen, usually in the reflection of the full moon, when the human face and body become animal, become covered with hair, acquire claws and fangs, exit from the human.

The more modern variants of this plot often have a sci-fi character.

The popular film *Men in Black* spoofs the serviceable convention that our planet is filled with aliens; in this case, we seem to have a cockroach fantasy at play, and the film is larded with roach innards and juices on the clothes and faces of the protagonists. Other films, like *The Matrix,* are more ambitious in their claim that the human-scale world we think we see is actually a vast illusion foisted on us by the beastlike machines that have taken over and reengineered our conceptual frames so as to naturalize the spectacle. And every so often we can count on a remake of *Invasion of the Body Snatchers,* since the topos of being taken over by the animals (or vegetables) is irresistible. It is worth asking what service these fables provide, since anything popular (that people are drawn to, want to see) is doing something for us, performing some sort of unstated cultural labor. My answer is that the successful outcome of such stories—the reestablishment of the human scale and human enterprise, the victory over the animals—is a story that ministers to our deepest fears and offers us a flattering fiction. In much the same way detective fiction closes with the arrest or death of the criminal, not merely as a way of restoring order itself, but as a shimmering proof that killers and monsters are caught, that it is "safe" out there once again.

I'd like to add one more story to this familiar genre. It concerns a dream I had more than forty years ago when I was a student; not only have I not forgotten it, but I suspect it underwrites a good bit of this book. In the dream I find myself amidst a nineteenth-century circus scene, a kind of *fête foraine* with hawkers and freaks (greatly resembling Fellini's *La Strada* or Bergman's *Sawdust and Tinsel,* which I had not yet seen), but all abustle with nervous energy, energy quickly approaching mass panic. The reason for this panic, one hears from countless figures scurrying about, seeking to escape, is that the Monster is loose, is headed our way, and there is a general, unstated certainty (the kind of certainty you have in dreams, the real kind) that he may be among us, but that we cannot recognize him.

Quickly the scene becomes paranoid and inquisitorial as we all scrutinize one another, trying to identify the Beast, and it gradually becomes clear that we have found him, a strange man, a "marked" man, marked only by our certainty that he is the scourge, the miasma. This man is then subjected to questioning and examination in which we apply every possible technique of analysis, at once legal and scientific, but he passes each test, documents repeatedly his innocence and his normality. We are still suspicious, but can prove nothing.

At this point, noise and hubbub enter the scene from the periphery, and voices start to scream that the Monster is sighted, is coming, is among us. In a rather fuzzy transition I then find myself in a small coach, trying to exit the circus, and I realize there is a second passenger as well: the "marked" man. Now the coach gathers speed, again the voices come, shrieking that the Monster is here, just outside the coach. Panic overtakes us all, and I desperately peer outside my window, glimpsing vaguely a figure being pounced on by the crowd, and I realize that this is It, that at last I will see the Beast. I then turn to my companion to share my news, and I see only his teeth as they approach my neck. I wake up, screaming and drenched in sweat, and the dream remains with me all my life.

For years I interpreted this dream as a parable about the failures of logic and security, about the limits of reason and analysis as guides to truth. In particular, once I became a professor, I saw the story as an allegory of the academy, with its carefully constructed postulates of truth testing and investigation, its aura of rationality. Of course, I was quite aware of the Gothic side of the story as well, the way it fit a Poe-like scenario, had a Jekyll-and-Hyde feeling to it, might even be a version of factual cases that were half mythic, such as the saga of Jack the Ripper or the Boston Strangler. In short, it proclaimed that a monster is loose in the community, and that none of our protective strategies or conventions—police, human reason, courage—will do us the least amount of good. Finally, the teeth at my throat smacked of Dracula, a particular kind of monster that battens on to human flesh and drinks our blood. In recent years, other aspects of the dream have taken on importance. Why the circus and carnival atmosphere? (Is this what lurks under the sober façade of professional activity: a roiling spectacle of tumbling forms? a no longer disguisable animality starting to break through the surface?) I now think that the most terrifying element of the dream is its mobility, its incessant slippage and shape-shifting, so that the world we think we know suddenly moves into action, sloughs off the perceptual skin we are used to, lurches into spasms, explodes into carnage.

It is no accident that J. K. Rowling reserves just such a Gothic moment to cap the terrors that make up Harry Potter's agenda in the first volume of her series, *Harry Potter and the Sorcerer's Stone;* Harry is in a tight place, trying to outsmart Quirrell (instead of Snape, whom he expected), and he hears the high, awful, unplaceable voice of Voldemort demanding a face-to-face. There is only the turbaned Quirrell in the room, but the boy, mesmerized, has a surprise coming:

> Petrified, he watched as Quirrell reached up and began to unwrap his turban. What was going on? The turban fell away. Quirrell's head looked strangely small without it. Then he turned slowly on the spot.
>
> Harry would have screamed but he couldn't make a sound. Where there should have been a back to Quirrell's head, there was a face, the most terrible face Harry had ever seen. It was chalk white with glaring red eyes and slits for nostrils, like a snake. (293)

Rowling seems to have conflated elements of the Medusa fable: the creature looks at you, but *it* (rather than you) turns into a snake. Yet, the real frisson at work here, in my view, comes from the shocking head-action itself, suggesting that the in-your-face violation of the human form is the most potent expression of evil imaginable.

Metamorphosis seems so sweet and innocuous when it comes to butterflies, but it spells catastrophe when we recognize it in the human sphere. Dreams work via metamorphosis, and this is one reason we experience such relief upon awakening: at last (at least) things are back in place. But are they ever? Bodies alter constantly, not only through aging, but through sickness and infirmity. Even garden-variety alterations, such as growing fingernails, toenails, hair, pimples, rashes, and countless other minor afflictions that flesh is heir to, should give us pause. (They do give us regular pause as we go about domesticating them with clippers, files, combs, brushes, powders, and ointments, but who construes such hassles as commerce with the beast?) Most unsettling, as we have noted, is when the body is no longer recognizable as "human."

Franz Kafka is a writer whose mind and work seem outright stamped by *metamorphosis*, and it is, of course, the title he gave to his most famous story. That story's opening lines are chilling: "As Gregor Samsa awoke one morning from uneasy dreams he found himself transformed in his bed into a gigantic insect" (1). The reference to bed and dreams has led many critics to psychoanalyze the story, but the full force of Kafka's genius is felt only if we grant him the literalness of that first sentence. Gregor *is* a bug (which is rather different from feeling *like* a bug). We also get to know what it might actually feel like, if you are a bug: how hard it is to get those "numerous little" legs off the bed, how to open a door when you have only a mouth but no hands, how garbage might gradually taste better than your favorite "earlier" dishes, how you might be more comfortable on the ceiling than on the floor, how strange liquids might issue from your body when your father makes craters in your flesh by hurling apples at it/you. In today's literary scene we are constantly asked to imagine the *other*—women, minorities, folks of a different race or ethnicity or sexual preference—but nothing quite matches the gauntlet Kafka throws down at us: to try out a new body, a horrendous insect body. If ever reading was an entry into something else, this is it.

Gregor's family debates endlessly over whether this can still be Gregor—my students invariably accuse the family of heartlessness, but put yourself in their place, I tell them, your son just acquired multiple legs and beetle paraphernalia—and much of the story centers around the question: what is a person? At what point does alteration alter you out of being human? (The deformed, the chronically ill, and the elderly know something about these matters.) We the readers grant Gregor human status largely because the story is written from his perspective, which is to say: this giant beetle has a consciousness that governs the story, and it is that consciousness we come to know. There is no one quite like Kafka in this department, inasmuch as every reader anticipates Gregor's voice to be one of horror and pathos—here, certainly, we expect a scream to go through the house—but finds, instead, the calmly (madly?) reasoning thoughts of a many-legged bug that still wants to go to work, still wants to play the role of loving son, still thinks he is human. Much of the power of stories such as that of the human beetle or the Elephant Man stems from our shocked awareness that this monstrous thing we see with our eyes is, yes, human.

In Kafka's most interesting work, human status is precisely what is being taken away. Not by any act of cruelty, but rather by a writerly imagination that sees the *human* as a category you could exit. The postmodern analysis of Kafka written by Deleuze and Guattari is provocative along just these lines: instead of "translating" these stories into allegory or psychology—according to which, Gregor might be the artist or Jesus or the schlemiel—they point out that Kafka's recurrent plot entails *becoming-animal.* We have Josephine the singing mouse, we have the ape who makes his "report to the academy," we have the astonishing narrator of "The Construction" (some kind of beast dug into the earth, insanely paranoid about attackers and threats, obliged to use its head as battering ram, offering up Kafka's grisly version of Homo sapiens). Literature performs its immemorial humanizing role in these fables by endowing these creatures with thought and speech, enabling (obliging) us to grant them human status. And that's fine. But they also strike terror in us by bracketing the human, by reminding us that the transition from animal to human—at issue since the encounter between Oedipus and the Sphinx—is a two-way street.

"I" VERSUS "IT": SELF VERSUS BODY

It does not take all that much for us to see the endless traffic on this two-way street. Disfigurement has been discussed already, but I'd argue that advanced senility, nervous tics, neurological dysfunction, the gestures of palsy or Parkinson's: these instances of motor impairment or spastic gesticulation signal the same kind of outbreak and alterity that was visible in the liberated hand that Malte was stunned by. Mutations into animality cause unease. One of Oliver Sacks's beguiling collection of stories, "clinical tales" he calls them, is entitled *The Man Who Mistook His Wife for His Hat,* and in these pieces the genial doctor shows us over and over how neurology itself is to be understood as the war between "I" and "It," between self and soma. Sacks has, I think, a rare gift for seeing what is human and precious in his patients, for illuminating how rich even the most impaired lives can be, and we can see his credo in the quotation from Ivy McKenzie that he offers as epigraph: "The physician is concerned [unlike the naturalist] . . . with a single organism, the human subject, striving to preserve its identity in adverse circumstances." In case after case—the amnesiac, the woman with proprioceptive dysfunction, those with phantom limbs, the aphasiac, the migraine visionary, the idiot savant, the autistic child—Sacks helps us to gauge the dance of our species, the tradeoffs and compensations and stunning adaptations we are capable of, in this struggle to maintain an "I." This dance is especially visible in figures like "Witty Ticcy Ray," who has Tourette's syndrome and manages a fragile truce between the mutinous high energy of his tics (which fuels his music, Ping-Pong, and repartee) and the constraining control of his drugs (making married life and work something manageable), leaving us with the conclusion that the "real" Ray is a composite of animal and medication.

Sacks claims that Ray's case is special because he must go to such lengths to control the animal, to yoke his rebellious system into at least partial submission; most of us, the neurologist implies, are blessed by our "normalcy" and do not require such ministrations. But is this true? In a culture that is increasingly aware of attention deficit disorder, dyslexia, anxiety disorders, and that much more familiar slew of somatic ailments such as high cholesterol, high blood pressure, and endless other little failings or deviations from the norm, do we know anyone who is not on medication of some sort, who doesn't require some adjusting? I have colleagues who say, only half in jest, that Prozac (or its successors) will soon be in the water supply, just as chlorine is. Witty Ticcy Ray breaks out in spectacular bouts of motor and verbal fireworks, and he receives medicine. The recent film *Shine* gave a heart-wrenching version of a similar conflict between physiological determinism and free will. I personally, who am not (yet) diagnosed as neurologically impaired, find increasingly that my whole life is a series of negotiations between "It" and "I"; I discover this in my sleeping patterns, the waxing and waning of appetites, my spells of temper, my dealings with colleagues and students, my bubbling fears, my unyielding features (physical as well as psychological). I doubtless owe large chunks of what is good as well as bad in my life to somatic givens of which I have no inkling. Hamlet signs a love letter to Ophelia: "Thine evermore, most dear lady, whilst this machine is to him, HAMLET" (II.ii.122–123). But there's the rub: these machines have a priority and agenda all their own, and we cannot answer for them, even though we are shackled to them.

Witty Ticcy Ray takes Haldol; I'll spare the reader a list of the substances I routinely ingest to remain me. Is this not a version of bodies eating bodies? American pills are so tiny and anodyne that they seem innocuous, but anyone who has filled a prescription in a French pharmacy knows how weighty and technicolor these matters can be: shiny colors, neon lights, glass vials, signs that this stuff means business.

In story after story, Oliver Sacks the doctor seduces us the readers by dint of his faith in the human person, his warm yet brilliant capacity to assist his impaired patients in their "I"/"It" conflict, their struggle to retain their form, their selves, despite the mutinies at hand. Some would have it that "being yourself" is a full-time job under any circumstances, with or without pills. Yet it seems to be the very basic drive of our lives, the supreme plot of a species that is born in a body but wants to maintain a self. Arguably, the most profound consequence of this philosophy, in my view, concerns medicine itself, by which I mean that the quintessential task of the physician is *maintenance of self* for his or her patients, entailing, especially in life-threatening situations where life-altering therapies may be on the docket, a complex understanding of the ill person's selfhood. The Hippocratic injunction, "at least do no harm," surely stems from a comparable belief in the integrity of the patient as that which antedates illness, and that which must not be compromised.

TAKEOVER

Dr. Sacks seeks to fashion some kind of harmonious existence for his impaired patients. He gives Witty Ticcy Ray Haldol in hopes that the pills can effect some kind of truce with Ray's skewed neurochemistry. At best, he reaches a compromise. Bodies have a will, sometimes an anarchic will of their own. The charade of civilization has it that we lead our bodies, but as we've seen, the truth may be the other way around. They are the controllers, the bullies. What if they could talk? Not just in ways we know about, via unbidden noises such as screams, laughs, hiccups, groans, belches, and farts, but really talk? I invoke here, for your delectation, one of the most dazzling passages in modern literature, William Burroughs's story of the man who taught his asshole to talk:

> "This ass talk had a kind of gut frequency. It hit you right down there like you gotta go. You know when the old colon gives you the elbow and it feels sorta cold inside, and you know all you have to do is turn loose? Well this talking hit you right down there, a bubbly, thick stagnant sound, a sound you could *smell*.
>
> "This man worked for a carnival you dig, and to start with it was like a novelty ventriloquist act. Really funny, too, at first. He had a number he called 'The Better "Ole" ' that was a scream, I tell you. I

forget most of it but it was clever. Like, 'Oh I say, are you still down there, old thing?'

" 'Nah! I had to go relieve myself.'

"After a while the ass started talking on its own. He would go in without anything prepared and his ass would ad-lib and toss the gags back at him every time.

"Then it developed sort of teeth-like little raspy in-curving hooks and started eating. He thought this was cute at first and built an act around it, but the asshole would eat its way through his pants and start talking on the street, shouting out it wanted equal rights. It would get drunk, too, and have crying jags nobody loved it and it wanted to be kissed same as any other mouth. Finally it talked all the time day and night, you could hear him for blocks screaming at it to shut up, and beating it with his fist, and sticking candles up it, but nothing did any good and the asshole said to him: 'It's you who will shut up in the end. Not me. Because we don't need you around here any more. I can talk and eat *and* shit.'

"After that he began waking up in the morning with a transparent jelly like a tadpole's tail all over his mouth. This jelly was what the scientists call un-D.T., Undifferentiated Tissue, which can grow into any kind of flesh on the human body. He would tear it off his mouth and the pieces would stick to his hands like burning gasoline jelly and grow there, grow anywhere on him a glob fell. So finally his mouth sealed over, and the whole head would have amputated spontaneous . . . except for the *eyes* you dig. That's one thing the asshole *couldn't* do was see. It needed the eyes. But nerve connections were blocked and infiltrated and atrophied so the brain couldn't give orders any more. It was trapped in the skull, sealed off. For a while you could see the silent, helpless suffering of the brain behind the eyes, then finally the brain must have died, because the eyes *went out,* and there was no more feeling in them than a crab's eye on the end of a stalk." (132–133)

Each time I read this passage aloud in a lecture hall (assigning and citing aloud Burroughs to Ivy League students furnishes a good argument for having—or abolishing—tenure), I encounter the same evolving response: giggles at first at the raunchiness of the topic, followed by full-throated laughter at the routines devised by both the asshole and the man in their joust, their fleshly pas de deux, and finally an increasing sense of unease that closes with utter silence. No one laughs at the end.

Burroughs has writ large for us a fable of somatic usurpation, in-flected initially with Rabelaisian humor but stamped finally by a tragic sense of human undoing. His story acknowledges the crucial coopera-tion between "I" and "It," man and animal, self and body, that charac-terizes our lifelong stint in flesh. And so long as this relationship is harmonious, we don't even know it exists, much less that we have grown accustomed to giving orders to the body every moment we live—I see myself typing these words on a page at this instant, see the docile fingers doing what the brain commands, and am grateful—even if we suspect that sickness and aging are likely to spoil this party whenever they crash the scene. Much of this tale's humor and malice derive from the crucial *education* it depicts: the man teaches his asshole how to talk. Speech, we know, is what distinguishes humans from animals, and one might argue that the asshole rises to the position of counterplayer via this transcen-dence of realms, almost as if this were a mythic fable, on the order of Prometheus stealing fire from the gods, but cast rather differently as an asshole with attitude and pretensions, an asshole that usurps human trumps, an asshole that declares war.

One thing is certain: the story has its place in the academy, not only because its salty language serves as an overdue reality check for the highfalutin professorial lingo of abstractions and fifty-dollar words we usually sling around, but because it is a parable about learning, about learning as power. It also graphs a kind of corrida in which the bull slays the matador. But this conflict doesn't have two actors, just one, yielding something on the order of a somatic civil war, a literally internecine struggle to the death. With a little exaggeration, I'd go on to say that a complete cultural belief system in socialization is going up in smoke.

After all, growing up consists in schooling the body, teaching it discipline, imposing decorous law on bladder and colon, repressing belches and farts, disapproving of nose-picking and scratching-where-it-itches, eating with utensils, hiding pain, postponing pleasure, not to mention learning to cultivate what is prized: physical beauty, good posture, our best features, perhaps voice, a winning smile, an entire host of mannerisms designed to please. *Il faut cultiver notre jardin,* Voltaire said, and the garden-body that is tended and pruned, clothed and perfumed, sent out into world as a chief engine in our schemes: all this is being cashiered in front of our eyes. Burroughs is announcing an end to the oldest tyranny of all: the self's control of the body. The former contracts are breached, the dike is broken, and we can see that the Terror is coming. Bye-bye, agency.

We know this liberated body all too well. The asshole that takes over the host is the dread cancer that is growing inside with a will of its own, undetectable until too late; the old diseases that have always cooked in our flesh and the newer ones that outsmart our medicines; the cellular and genetic regime that got there first, that constitutes the cards we have been dealt; the baffling mutinies that characterize immune disorders; today's inexplicable syndromes such as fibromyalgia and chronic fatigue, and the old explicable ones like pounding head, sore joints, and hurting back; the stubborn, low-profile, loyal, vulgar, quotidian aches and pains that punctuate our days and nights; the monster who will have his way.

THE BODY AS CULTURAL SCRIPT:
SOCIETY SPEAKS THROUGH THE FLESH

Up to now I have emphasized the unruliness of bodies and the shock value of art, so that we might recover a sense of the body's priority, its otherness. Now I'd like to shift my angle of vision and examine a rather different question: How does treatment of the body express our values? How does the body constitute a language? I do not mean "body language" as such—the corporeal semiotics (ranging from rash to erection, from MRI to body odor) decoded by physicians, radiologists, co-workers, and lovers that is central to both medical and psychological diagnosis, a huge issue that will be examined in the following chapter. Nor do I mean the body as inadmissible locus of animality or libido, such as we saw in Brontë and others. I want to examine the body as a kind of *cultural grammar.* This expression seems perhaps esoteric, but it may help us toward an understanding of the body as material graph, the index of civilization, and it follows that bodies serve as parchment, slate, clay, record, text, the place where culture's story is told.

One of Freud's earliest forays, "The Etiology of Hysteria," theorizes a view that we might term "the body as historical document." This (now infamous) essay posits the fundamental thesis that hysteria is the belated proof of earlier sexual abuse. Freud was later accused of "waffling" on this initial theory—which seemed to point to widespread abusive behavior, largely at the hands of fathers, sometimes nurses or governesses, in proper bourgeois families—when he subsequently devised the oedipal theory of desire to explain the family romance, now transforming the inappropriate sexual involvement between father and child from actual event (on dad's part) to projected fantasy (on child's part). Freud's actual views and motives have been hotly debated for decades, but my interest is in the trauma-model itself: certain kinds of damage are written on and into the body. There is something at once fierce and fine in this concept: nature, it would seem, keeps its books, and nothing can ultimately be concealed, so that injuries will eventually *show,* and the violence or abuse you have been subject to, far from disappearing or remaining just a dirty secret, comes out in the flesh.

This is not the place to dwell on the contentious issue of recovered memories—we now know that coaxing and invention play their role here, that memory is more a form of construction than some simple and reliable recall—but I am struck by the virtually Old Testament view of ills being visited upon the flesh, of history being written into the body, of flesh as ultimate terrain where one's story is to be seen and read. Trauma has long puzzled and engaged medical thinking, because the presence of undeniable injury where there is no physical lesion calls out for explanations that the bioscience model cannot easily provide.

In her book *Trauma and Recovery,* Judith Herman has powerfully argued that not only did Freud have it right the first time—yes, she says, plenty of real abuse in fin de siècle Vienna, no need to lay this on children's fantasies—but that we can see an entire serial history of collective abuse and body writing in the chain that links nineteenth-century hysteria to shell shock in World War I to contemporary phenomena such as the traumas experienced by battered or raped women as well as men suffering from combat trauma, especially that of the Vietnam War. Violence inscribes the bodies of those who experience it, leaving a legacy of disorder that requires decipherment. Whereas the traditional historian works in archives among faded written documents, whereas the archaeologist labors at restored sites of antiquity seeking material remnants of the past, we have something prodigiously different here: the human body as testimony.

The dysfunctional have a story to tell, and their dysfunction is its conclusion. We encounter here something well beyond the estrangement scenarios I have evoked in this chapter, something on the order of an ethical narrative we must learn to read. This challenge comes also as a language challenge, mandating that we translate the injuries we see back into the causes that produced them. I say *we* not to signal some kind of generosity or compassion we owe such victims, but to indicate that the narrative they embody may be rich (unbearably rich) in social significance. The French poet Mallarmé once defined the task of his art as "*rendre plus purs les mots de la tribu*" (make more pure the words of the tribe), and I'd like to suggest that the traumatized body can provide a somatic script of the tribe's experience.

In her superb novel *Regeneration* (the first of three volumes on World War I), the British novelist Pat Barker has sought to make good on exactly this challenge: making us see the horrible eloquence of the damaged body. The book is based largely on the true experiences of Dr. W.H.R. Rivers, an anthropologist/neurologist at Craiglockhart Hospital in 1917, at which time the poet/pacifist Siegfried Sassoon, along with other injured British officers, was treated for shell shock and trauma. Whereas Sophocles represented the wound of Philoctetes as the bite of the serpent guarding the shrine, Barker presents injury as the result of twentieth-century warfare. She offers us quite a panorama of the walking wounded: Anderson, the doctor/patient who can no longer bear the sight of blood; Willard, certain that his spinal cord is severed; Burns, virtually unhinged by his experience ("He'd been thrown into the air by the explosion of a shell and had landed, head-first, on a German corpse, whose gas-filled belly had ruptured on impact. Before Burns lost consciousness, he'd had time to realize that what filled his nose and mouth was decomposing human flesh" [19]); Prior, a major protagonist who (initially mute) has blocked his trauma and is hypnotized by Rivers back to the moment of horror when he is holding in his palm the eye of one of his exploded men; and Sassoon, prey to visions, eloquent, making his famous public declaration against the inhumanity and immorality of this war. Rivers, the gentle, wise, and caring doctor, fills the father role for these wounded men, and his job is to bring them sufficiently out of their traumas so that they can be sent back into the trenches.

But this may not be possible. Several times, Rivers wakes up feverish, sweating, with pains in his chest, and the reader understands that the doctor is "catching" the disorders of his patients: nightmares, hallucinations, the shakes. The novel's brilliance consists in showing that these symptoms of somatic distress and agony—all these hurting and dysfunctional bodies—constitute a new language that measures the actual reality of a key three-letter word: *war.* Barker makes these issues unforgettable by dint of her concern with actual speech: Rivers the psychotherapist bringing his tortured charges to some kind of verbal possession of their injuries, Rivers himself the son of a father who is both priest and speech therapist, Rivers himself possessed of a stammer that surfaces when he is distraught. The book obliges us to widen our sense of what language is: references are made to the "gift of tongues," a gift of Pentecost that "had made the Apostles *comprehensible* in all known languages" (153), and that is the goal here, to translate the war into an unbearably comprehensible physical code.

Hence, we are made to contrast the cheap, evasive slogans of war— "*Lost heavily in that last scrap*"—with the more painful, gathering, stammering report on human injury and sacrifice. The darkest episode occurs when Rivers's counterpart, Louis Yealland, appearing as the book's doctor from hell, tortures the traumatized and mute soldier Callan back into language by inserting electrodes in Callan's mouth and forcing him to speak the oppressor's code, shock jolt by shock jolt. It is a scene that might have been written by Michel Foucault, given its grue-some spectacle of subject formation (deformation) and disciplinary practice. Rivers has a nightmare about this scene, replete with deformed creatures who have horses' bits thrust into their mouths, reminding the doctor of the torture and punishment meted out to slaves in the Ameri-can antebellum South. Then the doctor has his horrible epiphany: he himself is performing this kind of oral rape, this form of social engineer-ing, on his own patients at Craiglockhart, in his efforts to send them back to France.

The body speaks. Barker's novel does not talk about war in the fa-miliar political and ideological terms we are accustomed to; instead, she writes this brutal chapter of English history in somatic terms. And she places at its center a doctor, a man who must gradually understand that the wounds he sees are luminous in their account of England itself: not only the violence and horror of combat across the Channel, but the blindness of a culture that lives by slogans and concepts, that blithely sends its young off to death while prattling about honor and glory. Rivers, stammering and riddled with personal pain, understands through his very patients the dreadful algebra at work here: war equals injured bodies, injured minds; war equals destruction of the human.

Guernica, Pablo Picasso, 1937.

The body speaks, and the artist listens, deciphers, and translates injury into the words of the tribe.

THE BODY: PIECED APART, PIECED TOGETHER

What Barker achieves in representing the trauma of the Great War is something we find in all real literature on war and violence, from Homer's *Iliad* to Grimmelshausen's depiction of the Thirty Years' War in *Simplicissimus* to Crane's *Red Badge of Courage* and Hemingway's vignettes of *In Our Time;* in each case the body renders testimony. And the body's testimony is most vivid, most unbearable when its very form is altered, remade.

Arguably the greatest work of modern art along these lines is Picasso's icon of war, *Guernica,* his painting done in remembrance of the Fascist bombing of a Basque village. The rending of human flesh and the destruction of home, family, man, child, and beast, all are immeasurably heightened by the Cubist and surreal elements in the painting. The shrieking creatures of flesh and legend have an unprecedented power because Picasso has wrecked the human form, has reconfigured face and body, annihilating older notions of integrity and propriety.

There is a convulsive explosion of energy in this piece, arguably as much demiurgic as it is destructive, for we cannot avoid the sense that the remaking of human and animal shapes reflects a monstrously potent can-do-ism on Picasso's part, a godlike reconfiguring of the world as we know and knew it. For me, this painting has always had the feeling of a nuclear explosion, inasmuch as I see here a frightening congruence between the violence of war and the violence of art, each understood as shape-shifting, as the unleashing of energies hitherto unknown. And yet, I tell myself, how better to honor this scene of human disaster?

War may seem an especially appropriate setting for a literature of the violated body, but it is by no means the only setting. No writer that I know helps us more in this regard than my favorite bad boy, William Burroughs, whose "talking asshole" we have already met. Burroughs's enduring legacy to American literature, *Naked Lunch,* remains absurdly underappreciated, and even when folks read it, they approach it as commentary on the Beat Generation. For my money, Burroughs qualifies as a genuine visionary whose worldview is radically body-centered. What would such a thing look like?

For starters, it is a universe of incessant *traffic.* The individual subject is immersed in a maelstrom of forces that he either craves or suffers: oxygen, food, drink, drugs, sex, electronic waves, print, ideas, politics, ideology. The Burroughs-human is an utterly porous body/mind, and is hence entered (read *violated, taken over*) both visibly and invisibly, all the time. Western metaphysics is so accustomed to granting privileges to actors and agents, so oversubscribed to the view that individuals initiate actions and that phenomena exist in discrete forms, that the Burroughs vision has been largely ignored. We assume that characters in both books and life *do* things, such as speaking, eating, loving, murdering, etc., but what about the ways they may be routinely penetrated and invaded: by air, by disease, by others' words, by images, by culture itself?

Naked Lunch seems like a surreal, hallucinatory carnival, a parade of scenes that we cannot easily label real or imaginary, but there is a grisly structure in all this turbulence: the opening of the body by a foreign object. This is Burroughs's only plot, because it is the only game in town. This is the *Urform* of reality, and we can see that it covers a lot of ground: eating, drinking, fornicating, infection, ingesting substances of any stripe (from aspirin to heroin), genetic engineering, and all of that crucial figurative stuff as well where we are entered: language, image, thoughts. Reading Burroughs, we understand that all bodies are porous, all bodies are the sites on which stuff (whether material or mental) goes in and out.

The novel goes on, in its shocking fashion, to chart the geometry and geography of such openings: the syringe penetrates the skin and the junk enters the bloodstream; the penis or its substitute enters the vagina or the rectum; the bacteria or the seed enters the body to grow; the scalpel or the rusty tin can cuts open the flesh; the genes are tampered with and "re-form"; the worm enters the egg; the pregnant woman carries the "little stranger"; the cells revolt through cancer and take over the body; the body's physiology is redesigned by doctors and scientists; the mind is altered by ideological and chemical programming. The actors may change, but the fable remains the same: the parasite enters the host to control it. No other writer has ever presented such a viral picture of the world.

This view of reality as body traffic cashiers a number of hallowed concepts: willpower, ethics, propriety (in every sense), integrity, agency. The picture it offers of the human subject is that of an organism held hostage to need, prey to invasion, meshed with others, from the moment of first breathing air to the moment of death. Burroughs picks up one of the oldest motifs of American thinking, the *frontier* (where its reach goes from the so-called Virgin West to American politics, financing an industry of cowboy films along the way, extending on up to outer space, always signifying that American holy of holies: a free space beyond culture), but he locates it where no one else has thought (or dared) to: on the body. Burroughs is our cartographer who maps the new world of the body, and he makes us see that the body's traffic is an affair of *entries and exits,* giving us a version of *ecstasy* that is etymologically sound—ex

stasis—and posited as the goal of human activity. Thus it is utterly logical, even if shocking, to read the following: "Gentle Reader, we see God
through our assholes in the flashbulb of orgasm. . . . Through the orifices transmute your body. . . . The way OUT is the way IN . . ." (229).

Ultimately, Burroughs commands our interest as a writer who reconceives the grammar and syntax of our lives, by offering a vision of the
embodied subject and the dance of the species unlike any we are familiar with. If we insist on thinking that such a view is overdetermined by
mind-altering drugs, it is worth remembering that Burroughs said, as far
back as the 1950s, that *Time* magazine is a more powerful hallucinogen
than any chemical you could ingest. His work explodes the polite codes
of speech, behavior, and perception, and urges upon us a chastened (as
well as exalted) sense of our place in the pulsating world: chastened because will and control are for naught as we emit and receive, enter and
exit; and exalted because all those separate spheres of reality—such as
food and drink, sex, drugs, language, media, ideology, politics—are
shown in their radiant unity as a form of intercourse with the body.

Most of us will not be cheered up by the Burroughs model of bodies
in the world. Yet, it would be a mistake to assume that the very idea of
the "opened body" is horrific. Might the rupturing of the body actually
be an entry of the *spirit*? Might it even be necessary to break the body
so that the dross can be removed, and the soul be displayed? Let me
bring into this discussion of pieced-apart bodies one of the strangest
prose writers of the twentieth century, Flannery O'Connor, whose re-
gional focus on rural life in Georgia and whose fierce Catholic beliefs
have tended to position her as all too minor a figure in American letters.
O'Connor reconceives the mind over body dyad by positing the body
(often the grotesque body) as the true locus of grace and miracles. The
religious vision that fuels O'Connor's art is savage: it reminds us that the
sacraments of baptism and the eucharist are inexorably corporeal, and
that the body—far from being "God's temple" in the traditional sense—
is a carnal mystery beyond our knowing.

Perhaps O'Connor's masterpiece along these lines is "The Displaced Person," one of the longest and most ambitious stories she wrote. In this retelling of the Passion play in rural Georgia, she chronicles the odd life and death of Guizac, the displaced person who, with his family, has fled from the Nazi terrors in Poland and has landed on Mrs. McIntyre's farm. Much of the story's pathos, bile, and humor stem from the fact that it is told, in large chunks, from the point of view of the inimitable Mrs. Shortley, the almost white-trash figure who, along with her husband, stands to be replaced by the cost-efficient, incomprehensible Guizac (whom she calls Gobblehook), a man who can handle tractors, believes in hard work, and is so unfazed by the racial givens of life in Georgia that he aspires to bring his niece from war-ridden Poland to the farm, to marry her with one of the black workers. This rich narrative comes into our argument about bodies through the musings of Mrs. Shortley, a woman about to be displaced, who has vaguely heard about the goings-on "over there," in Europe:

> Mrs. Shortley recalled a newsreel she had seen once of a small room piled high with bodies of dead naked people all in a heap, their arms and legs tangled together, a head thrust in here, a head there, a foot, a knee, a part that should have been covered up sticking out, a hand raised clutching nothing. Before you could realize that it was real and take it into your head, the picture changed and a hollow-sounding voice was saying, "Time marches on!" This was the kind of thing that was happening every day in Europe where they had not advanced as in this country, and watching from her vantage point, Mrs. Shortley had the sudden intuition that the Gobblehooks, like rats with typhoid fleas, could have carried all those murderous ways across the water with them directly to this place. If they had come from where that kind of thing was done to them, who was to say they were not the kind that would also do it to others? (196)

In the depiction and reaction of Mrs. Shortley, O'Connor is dishing up for us a Georgia version of "blood and soil" no less virulent than its counterpart in Nazi ideology. The Holocaust is imaged here as an exotic freak show, and this display of severed limbs is coded as plague, as dangerous proof that "others" are infectious barbarians. What is regionalism if not a conviction that one's own stomping grounds and language are special, are not to be invaded? O'Connor is scrutinizing the very ground she stands on, and she finds it hard-hearted, without charity. But, sure enough, this image of genocide as dismembered body parts will reappear at story's end when Mrs. Shortley, in a furious exodus away from the farm, experiences her fateful and fatal vision of grace:

> Fierce heat seemed to be swelling slowly and fully into her face as if it were welling up now for a final assault. She was sitting in an erect way in spite of the fact that one leg was twisted under her and one knee was almost into her neck, but there was a peculiar lack of light in her icy blue eyes. All the vision in them might have been turned around, looking inside her. She suddenly grabbed Mr. Shortley's elbow and Sarah Mae's foot at the same time and began to tug and pull on them as if she were trying to fit the two extra limbs onto herself.
>
> Mr. Shortley began to curse and quickly stopped the car and Sarah Mae yelled to quit but Mrs. Shortley apparently intended to rearrange the whole car at once. She thrashed forward and backward, clutching at everything she could get her hands on and hugging it to herself, Mr. Shortley's head, Sarah Mae's leg, the cat, a wad of white bedding, her own big moon-like knee; then all at once her fierce expression faded into a look of astonishment and her grip on what she had loosened. One of her eyes drew near to the other and seemed to collapse quietly and she was still. (213–214)

Grace comes through the flesh, and the response that O'Connor presents to the pieced-apart, dismembered body is a vision of violent corporeal linkage, a vision that would be *recombinant,* would enlist the old Frankenstein scenario of cobbled-together body parts into a new paradigm of the human family as a collective body, as the sublime gesture of putting the pieces back together. Note that Mrs. Shortley says none of this: her body says it. Like Picasso's nightmarish depiction of sundered flesh and remade contours in *Guernica,* O'Connor shares a reverence for the integrity of flesh, and gives warning that erasing or collapsing or otherwise destroying the contours of the body is tantamount to nuclear fission: an invasion of the existing armature of reality, leading to an explosion of power and violence. (The fierce heat swelling into Mrs. Shortley's face as her body experiences fusion with others says as much.)

O'Connor's fable at once harks back to one of the oldest stories we know—a story of crucifixion in which displacement (Jesus is no less displaced than Gobblehook) becomes dismemberment—and it also looks forward to our culture of genocide and atomic war. Her signature consists in her unswerving focus on the human body as the place where the action is, where love might be, where grace will come. We are all familiar with the fatigued cliché, *the body politic;* O'Connor, Barker, Picasso: so many artists show us the human body as the unacknowledged currency of political discourse, the syntax and grammar through which ideology's story is told.

WRITING THE BODY:
ART, COMMUNICATION, OR TORTURE?

Franz Kafka's dark story "In the Penal Colony" demands inclusion in this chapter as the most troubling account I know about the violated body as a site for knowledge, spirit, or truth. This story has the anthropological sense of estrangement that we have seen in figures like Burroughs, Sacks, and Barker: an explorer arrives at an island to witness their bizarre penal system and to pronounce judgment on it. Prisoners are placed in a "harrow," and for twelve hours the sentence is *written* into the body by the beak of what looks like a monstrous sewing machine. At about the sixth hour, we are told, even the thickest of the condemned begins to understand, to read the body script that is being produced. The system is wildly authoritarian: prisoners are presumed guilty not innocent, no defense is possible, and of course the custom itself looks a great deal like torture. But the officer in charge of the "machine" explains that it has profound religious significance, inasmuch as it displays (to an entire community, with children up front, in the old days) the workings of justice and the attainment of truth on everyone's part: prisoner's as well as society's. We note as well that the prisoner in this exhibition case is described in utterly animal terms: thick-skinned and uncomprehending.

There can be no doubt that the reader is meant to reflect on this frightening model of penal justice, not simply to indict the system as barbaric. But in teaching this story, I invariably find that no one is interested in such reflections, given the unmistakable horror of the system. Kafka, I think, knew all this. Most modern readers and critics are united in feeling that this is torture, not justice; some have even claimed that Kafka's story prophesied the experiments of the Nazi doctors, suggesting that art can be horribly prescient, can even help to produce evil by giving us a vision of it.

But things are not this simple. The story is indeed about justice and truth, and it seems to be asking: how will we know them? where do they reside? what can deliver them? how can they "get" to us? The penal system on show here is actually the penal system on show throughout this chapter: our lifelong imprisonment in a body. Kafka's vision is not all that different from Burroughs's: the human subject must be opened up if truth is to enter. Kafka knows that the human organism lives by ingesting food and excreting waste, that the human species depends on sexual congress of sperm entering uterus if it wants a future. Body life for our species involves entries and exits. Not that Franz Kafka ever made peace with these elemental facts of life. "Coitus is the punishment for human happiness," he once wrote, and no one can fail to be struck by the kinds of incompatibility expressed here: not only are agape and eros different, but the body's needs are disastrously at odds with "ours."

Yet the desire for contact is nonetheless central to Kafka's work, just as it is central to the work of any writer or artist. The great subject of "In the Penal Colony" is human communication. Everything broadcasts it: the desperate effort of the officer to persuade the explorer that the machine is just, the operation of the machine itself as it inscribes its message into human flesh, the modus operandi of the story we are reading. Do any of these (extreme) gestures bear fruit? Kafka is asking us to weigh language as an adequate or inadequate bridge between humans. Yes, food and sex require material entry into the body—the kind of entry that Kafka had trouble negotiating—but human language would seem to promise a finer intercourse, a penetration that does not maim.

Hence the story about communication zeros in on the body. Thick-skinned humans are trapped within their bodies, cannot cross the bridge from me to you. This is what the machine is designed to correct. The beak that rends the flesh of prisoners, that writes into their bodies the "sentence" they receive, is a writing machine. Kafka has devised a kind of fleshly semiotics that aims at no less than a miracle: the production of a language that would be one with what it says, that would collapse the classic sign/referent division. Try to imagine a language that is *immediate,* so that the letters "l-o-v-e" actually *become* "love" rather than a word designating love.

All speakers and writers and listeners and readers negotiate this unbridgeable gulf between words and things every day of their lives. And we all know the numbing feeling that words won't do, or that our words don't get across, or that others' words seem hollow and distant, just sounds. I routinely urge my students to pay real attention to the books I ask them to read, in order that otherwise "dead letters" might come to life. I recall again that moment in O'Neill's play, *Long Day's Journey into Night,* when Mary tells her son Edmund that he may have heard the story of his father going to work at the age of ten some ten thousand times, but that he has never *understood* it; likewise, I acknowledge, in my family a similar story about my father going to work existed—six was the age given—and I too heard it thousands of times; but did I ever understand? *How do words become real?*

These incessant feats of translation constitute the most basic facts of our lives as lingual creatures. (And who can seriously believe that we succeed as often as we fail, in this arena?) But Kafka's machine writes a script that doesn't need deciphering: at the sixth hour the prisoner reads it in his flesh. Kafka is exploding some of the oldest metaphors of civilization: surface and depth. We all know that *deep* is a complimentary term, meaning "profound," whereas *surface* or *superficial* connotes "trivial," "unimportant." We speak blithely of "deep feelings" and we criticize efforts that do not even "scratch the surface." But when a blade approaches your skin, "scratching the surface" matters. We respect human skin as a surface that one is not supposed to penetrate, however much we may like "deep feelings."

Perhaps the pivotal notion in Kafka's story is a word that is not pronounced: *open.* Consider how positive a valence it has: open-minded, open your heart, be open to experience, even open-ended. Now literalize it: the only open end the body knows is an orifice or a wound. Anuses are open-ended. Kafka's writing machine *opens* the body, writes *in* the flesh. And it is monstrous.

And yet . . . Kafka's machine is doing what every writer, at some (doubtless unspeakable) level has dreamed of: creating a language that penetrates, creating a language that actually enters the body of your listener or reader. At some censored level, perhaps we all dream of such potency. In this story we see just how ghastly it can be, when language physically enters the body, when those closed contours so crucial for our integrity and safety are finally opened.

Kafka's penal saga is rough going. Philosophically, it stands as one of the most troubling and provocative stories I know, a story that dares to reveal just how invasive, even sadistic, our quiet terms such as *knowledge* and *communication* might really be. This is because it centralizes the human body. What is utterly missing from Kafka's scheme is *love,* love understood as an embrace of the body, love understood as tenderness and nurturance of the flesh. Could one imagine a work of literature that owned up to the body's authority and vulnerability, its wounds and its pains, but did so in a spirit of love?

TONI MORRISON'S *BELOVED:* THE BODY BELOVED

Toni Morrison's magnificent novel about the legacy of slavery in post–Civil War America, *Beloved,* is unmatched in its tribute to the body as site of our most precious transactions and as target of systematic violence. The evil of slavery has been verbalized and theorized in countless ways in moral discourse, but Morrison is out to write this story somatically. Here the natural preacher Baby Suggs delivers her plaint of pieced-apart bodies and dismembered flesh:

"Here," she said, "in this here place, we flesh; flesh that weeps, laughs; flesh that dances on bare feet in grass. Love it. Love it hard. Yonder they do not love your flesh. They despise it. They don't love your eyes; they'd just as soon pick 'em out. No more do they love the skin on your back. Yonder they flay it. And O my people they do not love your hands. Those they only use, tie, bind, chop off, and leave empty. Love your hands! Love them. Raise them up and kiss them. Touch others with them, pat them together, stroke them on your face, 'cause they don't love that either. *You* got to love it, *you*! And no, they ain't in love with your mouth. Yonder, out there, they will see it broken and break it again. What you say out of it they will not heed. What you scream from it they do not hear. What you put into it to nourish your body they will snatch away and give you leavins instead. No, they don't love your mouth. *You* got to love it. This is flesh I'm talking about here. Flesh that needs to be loved. Feet that need to rest and to dance; backs that need support; shoulders that need arms, strong arms I'm telling you. And O my people, out yonder, hear me, they do not love your neck unnoosed and straight. So love your neck; put a hand on it, grace it, stroke it and hold it up. And all your inside parts that they'd just as soon slop for hogs, you got to love them. The dark, dark liver—love it, love it, and the beat and beating heart, love that too. More than eyes or feet. More than lungs that have yet to draw free air. More than your life-holding womb and your life-giving private parts, hear me now, love your heart. For this is the prize." (88–89)

This moving inventory of the body's sanctity and integrity assaulted by slavery is a prodigious feat of translation, transforming social system into somatic reality, worth more (in my view) than tomes of pious senti-ment or ethical pronouncement. An old mind/body dichotomy, with us since Antiquity and preeminent in Western religious thought since St. Paul—and invariably privileging mind/soul as superior to body/flesh— is overturned here, so that we are struck by the body's centrality, its always/already site as the place where love and war, pain and pleasure, humanity and brutality, do their bidding.

Slavery is the system that, like a brutal sculptor, remakes the black body: collars are there to redesign your posture, bits can be put into your mouth to endow you with a permanent smile, parts can be redis-tributed, so that what is hanging in the trees has "Paul A's shirt on but not his head or his feet." In slavery a man is forced to discover the "dol-lar value of his weight, his strength, his heart, his brain, his penis and his future" (226).

How could you best illuminate slavery, make people see its horror? Morrison has taken a chapter of American history, a chapter that—far from being over—is still playing, in terms of African-American notions of agency, and she has been able to see it as a story of the body. *Agency* or *ownership,* as I have often said, is exactly what none of us has, who live in bodies. But the culture of slavery goes well beyond this generic prob-lem, and reconceives these notions in horrible but familiar ways: the black person's body is owned by the white master. The body is a collec-tion of limbs and organs in someone else's possession. In such a world, the black subject is reduced to being a series of parts and appendages. Wholeness and ownership go out of the picture entirely.

Morrison's genius is to understand the itemized, pieced-apart body as a tragedy that goes beyond flesh. The former slaves at the core of this novel are arguably the poorest, most despoiled creatures in all of Western narrative, more reduced even than Kafka's beetle or Barker's shell-shocked soldiers or O'Connor's displaced Guizac, because they have been systematically deprived of all reach, extension, and connection. Slavery annihilates the family, separates spouses from each other, parents from children, siblings from one another. You are only your physical body, and even that is someone else's property. Not only is there no family, but there is no past, no future either. Morrison has taken the true measure of slavery, has grasped how much inner wreckage, annihilation, and outright *erasure* it entails. Baby Suggs had eight children, and every one of them was taken away: "Four taken, four chased, and all, I expect, worrying somebody's house into evil" (5). She claims she cannot remember: "My first-born. All I can remember of her is how she loved the burned bottom of bread. Can you beat that? Eight children and that's all I remember" (5).

It is not just the children who have been stolen, erased. It is the entire past that is cashiered. Not by any executive order, but because the past that belonged to these former slaves was simply so awful, so lethal, that it had to be jettisoned, had to be blanked, if living was to be possible. The only parallel that I can muster for this would be the mind-set of those who survived the Nazi Concentration Camps; they too found themselves at war with memory, found themselves carrying inside them a record that would kill them, if they dealt with it. Morrison's characters in *Beloved* appear virtually amnesiac, sometimes bordering on autistic, as they hunker down and work at not dying. Paul D, survivor of torture, now lover of Sethe (also a survivor of torture), comes into this story as a man who "had shut down a generous portion of his head" (41), but when he and Sethe are intimate, Morrison chooses a startling image to evoke what this self-inflicted violence and censorship entails: in his chest, instead of the "red heart" that used to be, there is buried a to-bacco tin, "its lid rusted shut." It is a grisly but powerful metaphor: the vital life-giving organ at the center of the human being has been trans-mogrified, altered into something rusty, metallic, and utterly closed.

The novel's elemental project is no less than to reverse this arterial blockage, to restore full circulation to its maimed characters. When Amy Denver, the white girl, saved the life of the escaping slave, Sethe, by helping to deliver her premature child, she massaged also the black girl's monstrously swollen feet, making Sethe cry "salt tears," telling Sethe, "It's gonna hurt, now . . . Anything dead coming back to life hurts" (35). *Anything dead coming back to life hurts.* I have repeatedly invoked the notion of *flow* as central to the life of art, characterizing its connection to us, its depiction of humans as linked and joined, but no novel illustrates the reality of "flow" more richly than Morrison's. It is as if the Emersonian model of Oversoul, of a bloodstream that connects living creatures, were moved out of polite nineteenth-century rhetoric and shown to be the life-saving, corporeal principle it is. Yes, Amy Denver saves Sethe's life, the baby Denver's life, but the larger job is to bring the "red heart" back to life, to restore wholeness to the human soul.

And so the horrors of the past—the stuff that had to stay buried, shut in a tobacco tin or kept in oblivion—are confronted. And it hurts, be-cause anything dead coming back to life hurts. Particularly if the dead themselves come back to life. Particularly if the dead are of your own doing.

Morrison's plot replays the Medea story of a crazed mother who killed her child. Sethe had escaped to freedom, but the slave-hunters found her, one month later, and were about to bring her and her chil-dren back to the plantation. To prevent this, Sethe acted. Here is how Morrison writes it:

> Simple: she was squatting in the garden and when she saw them
> coming and recognized schoolteacher's hat, she heard wings. Little

hummingbirds stuck their needle beaks right through her headcloth into her hair and beat their wings. And if she thought anything it was No. Nono. Nonono. Simple. She just flew. Collected every bit of life she had made, all the parts of her that were precious and fine and beautiful, and carried, pushed, dragged them through the veil, out, away, over there where no one could hurt them. Outside this place where they would be safe. (163)

That was how it looked and felt to Sethe. To the outside world, it looked different: she cut off the head of her little girl, and almost did the same to her baby. For Sethe, it was a matter of saving her children, putting them "over there where no one could hurt them"; for us, this is murder, death. A memory like this is a good reason for amnesia. What could full circulation achieve here?

The book shows us. Years later, Sethe and Paul D—living together, carefully staying on the surface of things—are returning home from a fair, and see a strange girlish figure waiting for them. She says her name is Beloved. And gradually, magically, incredibly, the pieces start to fall into place. This child is possessed of intimate memories that seem unmistakably to relate back to Sethe, to the slavery days, to the impossible incident with the handsaw. And we are obliged to reconsider everything we ever thought possible about reality. Can the dead return? Can this be the murdered child? And if so, was she murdered? Or saved? The book begins with much talk about a baby ghost that haunts Sethe's house, and we recall Baby Suggs's lost children, her comment that each one of them is "worrying somebody's house into evil." Do the dead actually live "on the other side," perhaps as virulent ghosts, in order to come back in the flesh?

Beloved's return makes whole the fissured family; Denver recovers a sister, Sethe a daughter, and Beloved a mother. Beloved is the restored blood flow, the reassembling of all the severed parts, all the mutilations inflicted by slavery. This is borne out even in relation to Paul D, whom she *moves,* whom she comes to at night, imploring: "I want you to touch me on the inside part and call me my name" (116). Paul D resists, begs her to leave, promises to call her by name if she'll leave:

> "Beloved." He said it, but she did not go. She moved closer with a footfall that he didn't hear and he didn't hear the whisper that the flakes of rust made either as they fell away from the seams of his to-bacco tin. So when the lid gave he didn't know it. What he knew was that when he reached the inside part, he was saying, "Red heart. Red heart," over and over again. (117)

Here we see the miraculous view of love that Morrison has presented, a love that at once unites and restores lovers to themselves by means of a generosity and a need so great that the dead limbs come to life, the blood flows again, the "beat and beating" heart is rediscovered. Sexual fusion acquires here the power of a blood transfusion, of opening clogged arteries, of lifesaving. "Red heart" moves out of sentimental or psychological discourse to become a cardiac term, used to denote the creatural pulse and flow of the living body.

Morrison's story is shockingly governed by the logic of the body. When Sethe first sees Beloved, her bladder almost explodes, and as she releases her seemingly interminable flow, she thinks back to the bursting of the water that accompanied Denver's birth. At other times she thinks still further back, to the jagged, precious memories she has of her own "Ma'am," a mother she never knew—slave families were separated—but whom she saw, who spoke a foreign tongue and danced like an antelope, who told her she could be recognized (if dead) by a mark on the breast. Other terrible memories circle around the theft of her milk when, pregnant with Denver, she was caught trying to escape, a scene of torture and quasi-rape that is horribly (unsurvivably?) witnessed by Sethe's husband, Halle.

Toni Morrison shows us how the body speaks, how it expresses it-self in fluids such as urine, milk, and blood, how urine, milk, and blood are the great waterways of human existence, constituting what moves in flesh. The body in this novel can shine when it is ready for mating, just as it can flip a switch and go blank when it is confronted by more horror than is absorbable (as when Denver, worried that Sethe may kill her, since she killed her other child, is without speech for a time). The human body becomes unforgettably eloquent in this story, marked by the depredations of slavery: Sethe carries a "chokecherry tree" in-scribed in her back, as a gift from her white owners. How different this is from Kafka's writing machine. No "truth" written into Sethe at all, just torture; yet these "roses of blood" "blossomed" as Baby Suggs eased her pain and ministered to her wounds. *Ministered to her wounds:* No such human tenderness and solace for Philoctetes. The body in Morrison is marked also by its beauty and power, made precious in its individual integrity; Beloved has nightmares that she is exploding, hence clings to Sethe and Denver, is insatiable for contact. Remember, as contrast, *Guernica* and its fractured forms, its shrieking figures.

Above all, however, in *Beloved* the body is linked, over and over, to the bodies and lives of others. Not through chains but more imperiously through the milk that bonds infant to breast—a nurturance throughout life that is as fluid and unstoppable as the nurturance in utero—and through a love that is so thick that it exposes the fictiveness of weaning, as if, underneath the appearances of separate skin, we were actually one communal body. In this great novel we must question some of our basic facts as to life versus death, individuation versus family. Beloved's fateful return is a triumph of flesh as well as spirit, a way of showing that the mother-daughter bond is indissoluble, unfissurable, all our assump-tions to the contrary.

Whereas Kafka construes writing itself as a penetration of flesh, a rending beak that inscribes meaning onto and into bodies, Morrison, too, hallows flesh as the supreme site of language, but in a radically dif-ferent sense. Her great gift is to write from this site, to eschew abstrac-tions in favor of a writerly vision that seems "cardiac," that understands trauma and repression to be a matter of dead tissue, that treats memory and self-possession as the restoring of full circulation, that understands the mother-child bond to be so viscous that it is "thick love," that dares to reconceive the founding calamity of the Middle Passage that brought blacks to America in slave ships as a uterine passage, a kind of prenatal trauma that haunts black consciousness.

Beloved shows us what a literature of the body might look like, what a culture of physical kindness might be: Baby Suggs kisses Sethe on the mouth when she arrives, all bloody with her baby, gives the newborn to a "young woman in a bonnet, telling her not to clean the eyes till she got the mother's urine" (92); Baby greases Sethe's tortured "flowering" back, eases her pain; Sethe bonds, during the brief twenty-eight days of freedom before the horror, with other women, yielding a radiant new image of family, one of women linked to their children and to one another, of human continuity. This domestic perspective is made possible by a female logic that is as old as the species, a logic that counts out events by monthly cycles in connection with the moon and the womb, a logic that does not shy away from oily fluids and baby spit. This logic finds its purest expression in the creatural flow of mothers and children, showing us in utterly unsentimental ways the very "milk of human kindness."

Morrison's novel seeks to restore a lost tongue to its readers, understood as the prior language of the body, focusing on the profound and unfathomable story of nurturance, of the love that binds the species (as opposed to the hate that butchers it). *Beloved* offers us a version of history unlike any that I have ever seen: the crimes of slavery are actually translated (out of the abstract political discourse we know) back into their natural organic and corporeal language. As in Barker's book and Picasso's painting, we therefore see the carnage in all its horror. But here at last the human body is shown to be the sacred material of life, sacred by dint of its capacity to triumph over death, to nurture, to seed, and to love.

CHAPTER THREE

DIAGNOSIS: NARRATIVES OF EXPOSURE

For now we see through a glass, darkly; but then face to face.

—ST. PAUL, *1 Cor. 13:12*

The wisdom to recognize and halt follows the know-how to pollute past rescue. The treaty's signed, but the cancer ticks in your bones. Until I'd murdered my father and fornicated my mother I wasn't wise enough to see I was Oedipus.

—JOHN BARTH, *Lost in the Funhouse*

DIAGNOSIS: GETTING THE STORY

We live in the dark and go to doctors for light; we call that *diagnosis*. With luck, the fever or ache or impairment we are suffering from is immediately interpreted, and a quick fix is possible. Often enough, things are not this simple: further examination is required, entailing blood work or medical imaging (sometimes of astounding complexity), leading to eventual reports that are deciphered by specialists such as radiologists or pathologists; in complex cases, several expert opinions are needed to interpret the "evidence" and—maybe—to recommend treatment. Often enough, tests and imaging spawn further tests and imaging, so that our hunger for a definitive finding remains thwarted. This is a story.

While it is hard to get clear of the notion that the reality principles of literature and medicine are deeply at odds with each other, I have found that narrative itself is the unsuspected common ground between these two fields. Medicine, which has tended to define itself as a science, with testable truth and empirical knowledge, is understandably reluctant to embrace narrative as one of its constituent principles. I use this term to signal something utterly basic: the telling of a story, the understanding of a story. Our transactions with doctors fall under this heading, and so too do our transactions with the world.

So let me shift gears: you encounter a blush, a giggle, a yawn, a cry—from spouse, lover, child, parent, co-worker, boss—and you don't know why, but you wonder. Or you experience loss of appetite or sleep, bouts of anxiety, spells of fatigue or anomie or rage: and you don't know why, but you wonder. This, too, is *diagnosis,* even though we rarely call it that. We go through life meeting, experiencing, signs and symptoms, and we want to know what they mean. Sometimes it's easy: a simple cold or a strained muscle; the giggle comes from a joke we didn't hear; the yawn from a bad night's sleep. Often enough, it's trickier: the pain isn't new, the odd glances have been going on for a while, the anxiety or anomie has been building. Those signs and symptoms didn't begin yesterday, were not produced overnight, hence they testify to some longer-term event. Sometimes these thoughts can be devastating: from news that we have cancer to tidings that we're headed for a pink slip or divorce or depression, we rightly fear diagnoses of the longitudinal variety. They tell us we are in big trouble.

In exploring the diagnostic impulse, I want therefore to speak about stories, about the surprisingly circuitous ways we come to knowledge, however much we yearn to get our answers immediately. The solution to the mystery that we expect from the doctor or the blood test or the MRI may not be definitive, can be subject to conflicting interpretations; or, worse still, it points to insidious gestations taking place in the dark, over long periods of time. And those other, nonmedical, "readings" that also matter—the state of heart and mind of self, loved ones, friends, and fellows—are equally mysterious, conjectural, puzzling, cued doubtless to a developing rhythm that remains a riddle. In saying "puzzling," I want to suggest that the notion that plays us most false in these matters of body and soul is precisely a *puzzle,* connoting something on the order of a jigsaw arrangement whereby the final correctly placed piece of evidence yields a coherent, satisfying, luminous *truth*, no less than the mythical "big picture" we all yearn for. This moment of clarity when things are sorted out and known in their entirety is the miracle we seek, for it promises to lift us out of the murk, to give us light.

I do not think it exaggerated to say that our belief in answers, in final clarity, in solving the puzzle, is one of the most deep-seated beliefs in human civilization, constituting the driving force not only of science (which you'd expect) but also of personal knowledge and relationships. I feel that this quest (it is no less than that) is as much emotional as it is cerebral, that it drives our love lives as much as our information needs, and that it is underacknowledged in its role as fuel for human endeavor. I believe that the diagnostic impulse, the hunger for light, for the answer and the solution to the mystery, needs to be understood as a *narrative* event, as a process that unfolds over time. This hoped-for *moment of truth* turns out to be something closer to what Borges called (in his most famous story about the enigma of human identity) *a forking path*—circuitous, looping, revisiting—and that path is the temporal trajectory of our illnesses, our bodies, our relationships, and our lives. In short, our quest for truths, at least in the key areas of life that matter, such as illness or even love, hate, and self-knowledge, goes in anything but a straight line.

WHEN DO WE COME TO THE TRUTH?

St. Paul's eloquent words in First Corinthians, chapter thirteen, speak powerfully to this issue: "For now we see through a glass, darkly; but then face to face: now I know in part; but then shall I know even as also I am known." Paul's account of the murky mirror is part of an encomium to love and charity, and he memorably characterizes our faulty knowledge as the knowledge of children—"When I was a child, I spake as a child, I understood as a child, I thought as a child: but when I became a man, I put away childish things"—leading to the conclusion that right perception stems from love, not from reason. We are doubtless expected to also factor God into this equation: God as the clarifying moment that turns dark into light, that makes the mirror give us truth rather than blur, that produces a final *transparency* in the world, a glorious regime in which *knowing* is absolute. This is not a bad version of paradise: the world around us is clear, we ourselves are clear, everything at last can be read. But consider the insistent temporality at work in Paul's words: *now* (clothed in flesh? living in the body?) versus *then* (at death? in heaven?) When do we get to *then*? Is it in our natures to stop being "children"? to achieve at last this miraculous clarity of vision? Is the murk ever dispelled during our lifetime? Could such a path be traced?

No, living in the dark is not news from a religious perspective, since the notion of *revelation* is a familiar one, but Paul's words also have an uncanny relevance for the medical straits that humans find themselves in. I want to tell a story that repeats much of the Pauline fable, but in such a way that we see it as a narrative, as an unfurling in which those keys terms *now* and *then* take on a powerful human significance. You will also see that this becomes a story about exposure, *exposure* meaning at once the diagnostic triumph of turning darkness into light, and also *exposure* as the temporal fact of our lives, of living in the dark.

My mother, in her eighties, began having recurring bouts of skin cancer, nothing terribly serious, but growths that would come and must be removed. She was now paying the bill, her doctors explained, for years of exposure to the sun, done at a time when many of us greased ourselves up and collected as many rays as possible. At that time it was considered okay, even chic, for people to become as tan as possible, and no one had a clue that something untoward was in play. My own dermatologist has let me know that I can expect similar outcroppings in time. Here, then, is one of the chief meanings of *exposure:* to be in the presence of some force without knowing it, to be subjected to some power over time. The range of such exposures can include the sun's rays, but also pollution, smoke, fumes, radiation, asbestos, lead, Agent Orange; in short, what we call the environment, what appears to be outside, we learn now has gone inside of us, working its molecular will on our organism. As people live longer, we will see more and more of these long-term disorders, sicknesses, and growths that have been cooking inside us for decades.

If we are prepared to widen our definition of exposure, to include in it our being subjected to forces other than chemical or biological, then these issues deepen still further. The cultural and personal forces that we are exposed to, that condition our values and assumptions, and that help to construct our subjectivity, may be thought of in equally environmental terms. These forces are potent shapers in our development, but only rarely, and usually only in retrospect, can we illuminate them on some kind of chart or map, so as to say: it is my childhood exposure to X or my marriage to Y or my years living at Z or the teachings of Q or the example of R that have been, usually insidiously, shaping my life ever since. How do we diagnose that? When did it start? When do we know it? Is it knowable? And to complicate matters still further: how does this so-called new knowledge reconceive what you thought you knew, what you thought you were? Feeling no symptoms for years on end, you discover one fine day in a checkup that you are fatally ill; were you sick all along? Let us apply the same logic to our moral and emotional life: being happily married for years on end, you discover one fine day that your spouse has been deceiving you; is all that past happiness bogus? Ford Madox Ford put it beautifully in his intricate novel about delayed disclosures, *The Good Soldier:* "If for nine years I have possessed a goodly apple that is rotten at the core and discover its rottenness only in nine years and six months less four days, isn't it true to say that for nine years I possessed a goodly apple?" (7).

"Narratives of exposure" is my chapter's subtitle, but the point I want now to make, which flows from the examples I have suggested, is that exposure is itself a narrative. If we insist on thinking of exposure in the diagnostic or photographic or even journalistic sense, it may appear to be instantaneous, a kind of on-the-spot illumination that broadcasts a certain knowledge. But in returning to my mother's story, I want to emphasize the importance of temporality: she is not only just now experiencing the "results" of her lifelong exposure to sun, but she is only now making knowledge of it. There is a crucially retrospective cast to this kind of understanding, as if to say: you cannot know exposure until it has done its work, until it is too late. And the corollary is: there is no other way to know. Here, in the mix of night and day, now and then, that governs our understanding of our own lives, in our drama of looking through a glass darkly, here might be where literature's testimony trumps that of the sciences.

THE THREATS OF EXPOSURE
AND THE POROUSNESS OF SELF

I closed my last chapter with a discussion of "readable" bodies, bodies that have a story to tell, a story whose conclusion is often some form of impairment or dysfunction. I want to suggest again that seeing this pattern is invariably a retrospective proposition: it is either too late, or if not, it is certainly after the damage is done, that we are in a position to know. Put more grimly: it is the damage itself that constitutes our knowing. As mentioned, Freud's early view of the etiology of hysteria epitomizes this kind of logic: hysteria becomes the belated confirmation of child abuse. Although Freud has been famously charged with backing away from the cultural implications of this theory, when he proposed the Oedipus complex and thereby transferred the libidinal activity from the parents to the children, we still find the etiology thesis alive and well in contemporary thinking about trauma and post-traumatic stress disorder, as evidenced in the work of Judith Herman and Bessel van der Kolk.

And surely the contemporary concern with recovered memories is cued entirely to the notion of a "founding" trauma that is discernible only later, in its delayed manifestations. In the shower, or on the thruway, you experience a hallucinatory recall; or, your job performance and your capacity to maintain relationships is filled with problems, and you wonder if you are not paying the bill for some earlier disorder. Aside from the epistemological challenge at hand (what is the status of these memories or of the "causes" one comes up with?), there is a prior and even more urgent question: is it possible to have advance knowledge? Can we ever know how we are being harmed? How much will come back to haunt us?

John Barth, in a meditation called "Niagara Falls," wrote the following: "For ages the fault creeps secret through the rock; in a second, ledge and railings, tourists and turbines all thunder over Niagara. Which snowflake triggers the avalanche? A house explodes; a star. In your spouse, so apparently resigned, murder twitches like a fetus. At some trifling new assessment, all the colonies rebel" (101). Causality is real enough, but how often do we see it actually happening? Doesn't it take an explosion, a murderous act, a severe illness, for us to seek explanations and origins? We know that the historian works backward; he starts with effects, and he works toward the causes; the same pattern holds for the detective (who starts, who is brought into existence by, the crime, and then investigates backward) and of course for the doctor (who is confronted by symptoms and must proceed backward, inverting the causal chain, to organic origins). Retrospective is, however, not the same as retroactive, and I cite Barth once again to indicate the inherent futility, the belatedness of our knowledge: "The wisdom to recognize and halt follows the know-how to pollute past rescue. The treaty's signed, but the cancer ticks in your bones. Until I'd murdered my father and fornicated my mother I wasn't wise enough to see I was Oedipus. Too late now to keep the polar cap from melting, Venice subsides; South America explodes" (101).

One of the great hopes of education is that others will not have to endure the determinist sequence, that they might benefit from our retrospective knowledge to create new prospects: no more asbestos pipes, no more frying in the sun, watch your cholesterol, peace rules. Yet, those of us who are teachers or parents or, indeed, policy makers know what an uphill battle it is to impart "advance knowledge," to circumvent disaster by pointing it out. Is it really possible to be in front of the curve?

I cannot help feeling, more on a gut level than a theoretical one, that most of us live in the dark. For each new prescriptive piece of knowledge that comes our way, that could ward off damage, we will have a dozen incidents of measuring the damage already done, learning still more about what is cooking in us, what we have been exposed to without knowing it. A life in time amounts to incessant and incalculable entries within us, ranging from smoke and viruses to the words we hear and the things we see. That such exposure encompasses the moral as well as the somatic is one of the things literature urges upon medicine. All our lazy models of epistemology—starting with the flattering conviction that we are creatures of reason (at the ready) who apply our eyes and brains to whatever comes our way, that we are involved in a fair fight with experience, interpreting appearances and making judgments in response to what gets put on our plate—get skewed once you begin to think that the plate has been filled for years without your being able to know it, that life has been working on you, writing in you, forever, so that your presumably fresh and free stance on things is dubious from head to foot. This is, admittedly, not a happy picture, because it makes our deck look dreadfully stacked, not merely in the genetic ways that we know about, but more insidiously in the entire package of experiences we have been having without knowing we were having them.

To illustrate what these distressing notions might actually look like in the flesh, let me turn to Proust, whose entire work seems cued to this philosophy. One of the early episodes of Proust's monumental novel, *Remembrance of Things Past,* consists in the narrator's recalling his childhood discovery of one of the most potent home truths of his text: the deviant or "alternate" sexuality of folks whom the inhabitants of Combray think they know. In a famous scene, the boy falls asleep at the window of a house in the country, Montjouvain, and when he wakes up and innocently peers into the window, lo and behold, strange things are going on between the two girls inside. This lesbian scene is described with a mix of zoological language (of fowls clucking and sleeves fluttering like wings) and impassioned moral analysis, and it then disappears from view as the mammoth narrative continues.

Many volumes later, years later in the life of the protagonist, and a good deal later in the life of Proust's reader, this scene, which narrative conventions presented as "over," reappears for its shocking curtain call, now ready to reveal its deeper truth. It turns out to be a painfully personal truth for the narrator, Marcel, because he learns from his mistress Albertine that she has long been an intimate friend of these two girls of his past. If Proust is ever reprinted in hypertext or CD-ROM format, here, even more than in the concert renditions of sonatas and septuors, is where one wants to put the music in the text, the well-nigh audible sound of the Proustian subject stripping his gears, following—not leading—the imperious logical translation of this information into its charged personal significance: Albertine is now documentably a lesbian; she is exposed; and so is he. But even this juridical scenario—innocent or guilty—fails to account for the plenitude of Proust's narrative:

> At the sound of these words, uttered as we were entering the station of Parville, so far from Combray and Montjouvain, so long after the death of Vinteuil, an image stirred in my heart, an image which I had kept in reserve for so many years that even if I had been able to guess, when I stored it up long ago, that it had a noxious power, I should have supposed that in the course of time it had entirely lost it; preserved alive in the depths of my being—like Orestes, whose death the gods had prevented in order that, on the appointed day, he might return to his native land to avenge the murder of Agamemnon—as a punishment, as a retribution (who knows?) for my having allowed my grandmother to die; perhaps rising up suddenly from the dark depths in which it seemed forever buried, and striking like an Avenger, in order to inaugurate for me a new and terrible and only too well-merited existence, perhaps also to make dazzlingly clear to

my eyes the fatal consequences which evil actions eternally engender, not only for those who have committed them but for those who have done no more, or thought that they were doing no more, than look on at a curious and entertaining spectacle, as I, alas, had done on that afternoon long ago at Montjouvain, concealed behind a bush where (as when I had complacently listened to the account of Swann's love affairs) I had perilously allowed to open up within me the fatal and inevitably painful road of Knowledge. (II, 1152)

What may initially seem ornate, analogy-crammed prose—Orestes, Avenger, Grandmother's death—is actually as taut and coiled as a steel trap, gathering its power and springing shut in the final, luminous notation of knowledge-as-puncture-wound. The early experience, the exposure to "aberrant" sexuality, enters the mind and body as an image that possesses "noxious power," and it sits there inside of the narrator, imbued with the kind of longevity that we associate with radioactive elements, waiting for its moment to leap out and make its power known; the entire process is shrouded in darkness, does not even exist cognitively, until the moment comes for it to surface and actualize its virulent force. Here is Proust's retelling of the story of Genesis, his version of both the cost and the nature of knowledge, "the road of Knowledge" imaged as a kind of internal pathway—at once somatic, cerebral, affective, and moral—that is arduously opened up, opened up the way life itself punctures us, makes inroads, and deposits within us toxic materials.

Proust invokes Orestes, ordained by the gods to carry out his avenging mission and therefore implacable, not to be deterred, as a way of characterizing the deathless potency of this image that has entered inside. It is an arresting vision of life as exposure, of the subject as porous, permeable, enterable, of experience (even the experience of listening to another speak) as a kind of time-release capsule, a capsule of disease not of medication. It would be no exaggeration to say that Proust's view of all human relations smacks of epidemiology and toxicity: the narrator maniacally seeks to control, even to incarcerate the loved object, but the project goes awry; those whom we love are somehow transplanted inside us, like bacterial agents, foreign bodies, but their presence within us grants us no more power than the power we might have over cancer or bacterial pneumonia. This lack of power, this undoing of hegemony, is an endemnic feature of the story of exposure: our mental life is in a state of perpetual catch-up, reacting to agents and residues that go far back into our pasts. To be sure, new things happen, but they are grafted onto the older things, assessed according to older codes. We are endlessly processing the past, a past that has entered us and works its will as long as we live.

I would argue that all the important discoveries in Proust operate along these lines: the resurrection of the narrator's childhood in Combray hinges on the fact that the famous madeleine dipped in the tea turns out to be toxic as well, having preserved, unbeknownst to the narrator, its indigenous strength and "virtu," ready at last to live and to be made into knowledge. Memory itself now starts to resemble exposure, in that your entire past sits shrouded in the darkness inside, waiting for the right signal to flower and declare itself, to display its continuing life.

One of my college French professors used to drive me mad by claiming that reading Proust was itself a Proustian exercise, that each time he picked up a volume, all of them came bubbling up back into existence, including his memories of his past reading. I fought this view because it suggested navel gazing, endless regress, reading oneself reading oneself reading, etc. Not only do I now think he was right, but he reveals once again the striking temporality of exposure, its crucial dependence on several time frames: the initial encounter or exposure that is often blank and unsignaled, the passing time of gestation, the reexposure which now completes the picture, gives it resonance, all pointing toward still further strata in the future, further readings and exposures. On this account knowledge comes to be a mobile proposition, an affair of sedimentation, of returning to the objects and images within and without us, of unpacking them further. "New knowledge" is, at least in this regard, something of an oxymoron, in that we are always building on our existing stock of information, of exposures; much like our body darkly processes its poisons over the years, our minds too are darkrooms where we are always "developing" the negatives.

With that last phrase, I return to the diagnostic impulse so central to the exposure scenario, especially in its final phase, which is associated with photography and the development of visual images. I have wanted to emphasize our subjection over time, our exposure over time, to forces that gradually and invisibly shape or deform us, both physically and mentally, in order to underscore the primordial role that time plays in this dynamic. Knowledge would then be a kind of temporal narrative, entailing exposure, development, and discovery. Such knowledge is inherently belated, after the fact. Finally, such knowledge is frequently (far more frequently than we realize, given our craving for on-the-spot readings) conjectural, a tentative sighting on a curve, an interpretive construct that is itself conditioned by other contextual forces. It is worth bearing all of these points in mind as we now move more frontally into issues of mapping and imaging, of exposure as a picture of the subject's truth, either somatic or moral.

I think of the remarkable literary invention of the French novelist Boris Vian: a special pistol that he names the *arrache-coeur,* the "heart-ripper"; you aim it at someone, fire, and their heart then moves out of their body, becomes at last visible, and they die. Much to unpack here: our own hearts remain murky to us, despite the EKGs we might obtain on the one hand, or the soul-searching we might do, on the other. Can it be accidental that this key organ of life becomes knowable only at death? Could such "final" readings be lethal? Here would be a grim version of the Pauline fable: not only do you have to die to accede to the truth, but the truth itself kills you. Of course, "reading" the heart means different things for the cardiologist and for the lover, but expectations of transparency in either realm are often dashed.

There are many reasons for being impatient with mystery. Our sanity seems to require that events and acts make sense. Whether it be the news reports on world affairs, the behavior of friends, lovers, and colleagues, or the sensations of our own body and inclinations of our own heart, we want and need to see clearly. Often enough, calling something a mystery simply means that we are, at the moment, ignorant of its cause; we don't have the necessary information. Others are assumed to have this information: experts, police, doctors, politicians, and the like. But are things so coherent? Here, too, Proust has much to tell us:

> I had seen everybody believe, during the Dreyfus affair or during the war, and in medicine too, that truth is a particular piece of knowledge which cabinet ministers and doctors possess, a Yes or No which requires no interpretation, thanks to the possession of which men in power *knew* whether Dreyfus was guilty or not and *knew* . . . whether Sarrail in Salonika had or had not the resources to launch an offensive at the same time as the Russians, in the same way that an X ray photograph is supposed to indicate without any need for interpretation the exact nature of a patient's disease. (III, 953)

In linking together the inscrutability of politics and history and medicine, Proust suggests that there are no keys, no secrets, no bottom line; or rather, that there is endless signifying, that the key to the puzzle is another puzzle, that the X ray is just another document, a construct that can be put together variously and deciphered variously. Kafka, in reflecting over his own tuberculosis and the riddle of its etiology, put it this way: "The origin of tuberculosis is no more to be found in the lungs, for example, than the cause of the World War is to be found in the Ultimatum. There is only one sickness, no more, and medicine blindly chases this sickness like an animal through endless forests" (1958, 320).

Kafka's focus on the blind chase, like the Proustian scrutiny of the X ray, speaks clearly, I think, to our urgent desire to know, to have light and clarity in crucial areas of life, both public and private, somatic and cerebral. "Blind chase" expresses nicely the central plot of most lives: a trajectory at once "driven" and in the dark. To put it that way is to ac-knowledge just how benighted our basic circumstances actually are: we cannot see inside our bodies, we cannot read others' minds, and we are a bit fuzzy about other things too, such as what is really going on in the world around us. Much is closed to human perception: dogs hear and smell better, pigs find truffles, and, in a novel obsessed with reading land and body and mind, Faulkner's *As I Lay Dying*, the mules standing at the floodwaters are not so different from Tiresias, clairvoyant but mute rather than blind: "looking back once, their gaze sweeps across us with in their eyes a wild, sad, profound and despairing quality as though they had already seen in the thick water the shape of the disaster which they could not speak and we could not see" (139). Thus, we live, and have lived, among clairvoyants and prophets and visionaries, ranging from the oracles and soothsayers and medicine men of old to our contempo-rary meteorologists and economists and other witch doctors who are there to read the present and the future, to interpret the signs, whether it be a low-pressure system or a cholesterol count or the NASDAQ Index.

GETTING IT WRONG

Once we consider how much guesswork as well as science is packed into the diagnostic project, it can hardly surprise us that doctors—as well as meteorologists and economists—sometimes get it wrong. For this reason it may be worth remembering what kind of figure the doctor cut in the comic literature of the Middle Ages and the Renaissance. Here we find stories of hilarious misdiagnosis. Molière poked fun at doctors in no fewer than five of his plays, partly because he detested doctors, partly because he knew all too well the power they acquire over the sick, and he could rely on gut laughter from his audience merely by putting the Latin-spouting doctor onstage; how could this fool get it right?

Los Caprichos, plate 40, "De que mal moira?," Francisco de Goya y Lucientes.

Who among us has not sometimes experienced the unpleasant suspicion that the doctor doesn't get it, understands nothing about what one is really suffering from? Goya's painting of a donkey-doctor may be a step further than most of us would go in our anger and dismay, but this evocation registers with rare vehemence just how botched these matters can become. The man trained to decode and minister to our *soma* is himself a crude beast, devoid of diagnostic acumen, pictured almost vampirishly athwart the patient's chest, crushing the poor victim, mocking all scientific pretensions with the jackass ears reflected on the wall.

What are the causes of faulty diagnosis? From a scientific perspective, we'd have to say "insufficient data" or perhaps "skewed assessment." But might the explanation be of a different sort altogether? The literary version of these matters can be, as it were, *environmental,* allowing us to grasp the diagnostic encounter as a cultural event, filled with epistemological challenges, yes, but not necessarily of the sort learned in medical school.

One of the most virulent examples of wrongheaded diagnosis is to be found in Charlotte Perkins Gilman's classic story of 1892, "The Yellow Wallpaper," in which the husband/doctor cheerfully forbids his ailing wife any form of mental or physical activity—no reading, no writing—whatsoever. Gilman herself, in the wake of a depression, had consulted the famous neurologist S. Weir Mitchell, and undergone his "rest cure," which almost drove her mad. She wrote this story in response to this experience, and wrote it from the angle of vision of the suffering wife. Today it is easy to see in the infantilizing behavior of the husband an attitude toward women that derives from nineteenth-century notions of *hysteria,* as they were articulated by the male medical establishment. Thus, we understand his various prohibitions for his patient as so many (unwitting?) patriarchal judgment calls, enabling us to see how much cultural conditioning might be invisibly packaged into doctors' interpretations and injunctions.

Another, still more famous story about male doctors getting it wrong is Hemingway's very early piece "Indian Camp," where the young Nick Adams accompanies his doctor/father and his uncle as they go by rowboat (traversing a distance that is greater than they realize) to attend an Indian woman with a difficult labor. Much of the story's power derives from the "innocent" angle of vision, an innocence that the reader only gradually evaluates; here is what they see upon entering the shanty:

> Inside on a wooden bunk lay a young Indian woman. She had been
> trying to have her baby for two days. All the old women in the camp
> had been helping her. The men had moved off up the road to sit in

the dark and smoke out of range of the noise she made. She screamed just as Nick and the two Indians followed his father and Uncle George into the shanty. She lay in the lower bunk, very big under the quilt. Her head was turned to one side. In the upper bunk was her husband. He had cut his foot very badly with an ax three days before. He was smoking a pipe. The room smelled very bad. (16)

Nick's father explains to him that this woman is going to have a baby, and he goes on to clarify why she is screaming, and what it means: "What she is going through is called being in labor. The baby wants to be born and she wants it to be born. All her muscles are trying to get the baby born. That is what is happening when she screams" (16). The screams continue, and Nick asks if his father cannot give her something to stop it, and the doctor replies that "her screams are not important. I don't hear them because they are not important" (16). The doctor then performs an emergency cesarean for this difficult breech delivery (which Nick queasily watches), and he is feeling understandably upbeat at its successful conclusion: " 'That's one for the medical journal, George,' he said. 'Doing a Caesarian with a jack-knife and sewing it up with nine-foot, tapered gut leaders' " (18). It is only then that they realize there has been no reaction from the "proud father," and upon examination they discover that he has slit his throat from ear to ear with an open razor.

For years I have taught this story as an instance of medical obtuseness, of a doctor who tragically underestimates the significance of pain and screaming, since we must assume that the *husband* simply could not bear it any longer. The doctor's repeated assertion, "her screams are not important," is fatally wrong, and here would be a textbook example of how a scream goes (indeed) through the house. In recent years, however, students have helped me to see this story more "environmentally": the white men from across the water enter the Indian shanty and proceed to do their medical tricks, and we can only wonder what such a spectacle looks like to the woman or her husband.

And it may be that there is also a virulent gender fable on show here: the white male doctor cuts open the Indian woman's body—she can show her resistance only through biting, is called "damn squaw bitch" in return—and we are left to ponder how much murderous horror this might have for the Indian couple. The story closes with Nick, his father, and his uncle making their way back across the water, but readers of Hemingway are entitled to feel that there is no closure whatsoever, in that Hemingway's own doctor/father was to commit suicide many years later, just as Ernest himself would in 1961, leaving us with the eerie feeling that this story was to be dreadfully prophetic in its depiction of pain as something unbearable after all.

"That's one for the medical journal," was the doctor's smug conclusion in finishing his handiwork. On the contrary, as a piece of literature, Hemingway's pithy story urges us to rethink our medical journals, to widen our optic when we take the measure of the challenge(s) at hand. These literary and artistic representations of botched medicine and skewed assessments, from Molière to Hemingway, are themselves tough medicine for readers who seek help, for we all depend on the doctor's scientific gaze. Yet, we see ever more clearly how fraught with libidinal or ideological blinders that gaze might be.

Surely, the supreme literary instance of the doctor's gaze being clouded—usurped—by unacknowledged libidinal forces is Kafka's surreal story "A Country Doctor." The piece begins with a dilemma: the doctor has to get to a patient ten miles away, but he has no horses in his stable; then, as if by magic, two powerful horses "buttock" their way out of the pigsty, followed by a (never before seen) groom who promptly sinks his teeth into the cheek of the doctor's maid, Rosa. The doctor takes off for his patient, intuiting with perfect clarity that the cost of these miraculous horses will be the rape of Rosa. He reaches the sick child, whom he initially diagnoses as not sick at all, but then changes his mind when he sees a blood-soaked towel and discovers a wound that seems off the charts:

In his right side, near the hip, was an open wound as big as the palm of my hand. Rose-red, in many variations of shade, dark in the hollows, lighter at the edges, softly granulated, with irregular clots of blood, open as a surface mine to the daylight. That was how it looked from a distance. But on closer inspection there was another complication. I could not help a low whistle of surprise. Worms, as thick and as long as my little finger, themselves rose-red and blood-spotted as well, were wriggling from their fastness in the interior of the wound toward the light, with small white heads and many little legs. (164)

One need not be a licensed psychoanalyst to feel that something strange is on show here. Is this wound real? If so, how could the doctor not have seen it at once? If it is not "real," what is it? The persistent notations of "rose-red" point us clearly in the direction of Rosa, the maid now (probably) being raped by the groom, an event pulsating in the doctor's mind. On this reading, the worm-filled hole in the boy's side could be a displaced vagina, and indeed the groom himself may be a displaced version of the doctor, doing what the doctor has always wanted to do. Yet, wherever the doctor may be in his fantasy, he is physically in the sickroom, confronting a patient and a wound. Is this a wound of his own imagining? One thing is certain: he can do nothing to assuage it.

Things get worse. The boy only wants to die. The villagers gather around the doctor, strip him naked, and lay him on the bed next to the sick child. At story's end, the doctor crawls back into his gig, but seems permanently stalled now, with spent horses and career up in smoke. It is a bad day for the rule of reason and for the prestige of physicians. The diagnostic project has quite simply exploded into a dreamscape ruled by libido and pulsion, and we see just how subversive literature as an art form can be: it depicts a series of events, but we sense that they are merely a cover, a façade for other, darker forces. Kafka's rendition of doctoring as subjective, oneiric carnival hints at unspeakable motives getting the upper hand, at the absolute failure of compartmentalizing (after all, one could be thinking about a rape and still do one's job; not so here). There does not appear to be much uplift in "A Country Doctor," but there is at least a warning that doctors are no freer of fantasies and obsessions than the rest of us, even when (especially when?) it comes to bedside encounters.

INTERPRETING MYSTERY:
DRIVING FORCE IN LIFE AND ART

Kafka is, admittedly, the most slippery of all authors, and yet his tale is cautionary in its warning about deceptive appearances. These issues have a long history. Medicine and literature are, in some important sense, enlisted in body-reading and mind-reading activities; they are cultural institutions with a mission: to illuminate their respective objects, to reduce or even dispel the originary opaqueness that governs our commerce with ourselves and our fellows. Of course, valuations of this opaqueness, this given mystery, will vary. Not only is the transparent world not to be had—other than in theory, in the academy, in our desire—but it would be a boring place as well, offering nothing to the imagination. Such matters are remarkably present to us in the nineteenth-century novel, a period now seen as the heyday of its generic life. I am thinking in particular of the rich, teeming urban fictions authored by Balzac and Dickens and Dostoevsky, where the modern city moves from assumed backdrop to actual protagonist. These cities were changing at vertiginous speed, and the novel served as a kind of map for its readers, a genial cartography of a world that had become, for many of those who lived there, unrecognizable and unchartable, due to the influx of people from the country, due to the inroads of industrialism, due to the changing physical landscape. *London, Paris, and Petersburg were mysterious.*

What the Internet is today (an information highway), the novel was for that century, which meant that the diagnostic fervor ran high in these texts, to be found in the garrulous authorial voice that placed figures and commented on the action, but also to be found in some of the most striking characters, sphinx-like creations such as Balzac's Vautrin, or Jaggers and Bucket in Dickens. These towering, virtually clairvoyant figures, often possessed of secret information, usually allied to both criminal and police circles, go about their novels turning darkness into light. One could argue that the detective is the quintessential urban hero, for he works in the service of transparency and translation, transforming details into clues. Is it an accident that Sherlock Holmes was created by a man who was also a doctor? Whereas Watson and the reader see a world of random if bizarre features, the diagnostic gaze of Holmes espies plot, design, intentionality, the contours and sequence of events.

The city of nineteenth-century Romanticism is a place where heterogeneity and mystery add vibrancy and richness to life, stir the perceptions of city dwellers and explorers, evoke a plenitude that challenges writing. Wordsworth's depiction of Bartholomew Fair in *The Prelude* is a good example of the poetic bounty that was to be had, a kind of carnival of sights and wonders to behold. No accident, either, that so many of the novels of this period seek to impose some kind of order on this spectacle, whether it be Balzac's sociological theory of Parisians or the elaborate plots that Dickens devises to tie together his mass of disparate figures. The treatment of the *stranger* is particularly instructive here: such a fellow will invariably be yoked into the plot's tight web, perhaps shown to be a protector or a villain or even an unknown parent or child. Baudelaire, in a poem like "La Passante," fashions an erotics of mystery and passing glances—"love at last glance," one critic has called it—entirely dependent on the epistemological merry-go-round that is the city. But let these issues become medicalized, and the tone darkens. In *Bleak House,* Dickens's heroine Esther Summerson has a chance encounter with the sick child of the slums, Jo, nurses him, and catches smallpox from him. I'll return at length to this novel in my next chapter, "Plague and Human Connection," but even now we can note that the mysterious stranger (whose intentions and diseases we cannot espy) may not be so romantic after all. Tony Kushner, writing 150 years after Dickens, picks up the same plot requirements of chance encounter and erotic connection and (potentially deadly) infection to tell his city story in his play *Angels in America.*

James Joyce set out to mock the literary convention of chance encounters in the "Wandering Rocks" chapter of *Ulysses,* where psychology and depth readings are banished from the scene, yielding an anatomy of vectors, with humans randomly intersecting each other on a flat plane. Yet Joyce's hyperrealism—after all, how often do you meet your future spouse or your lost child as a stranger in a chance urban encounter?—gets it wrong about our fantasies and obsessions. Modern societies are filled with people who do not dare to walk the streets alone because of the lurking stranger who may appear; now, however, he appears as homeless beggar (at best) or rapist or murderer (at worst). How much easier it would be if all were transparent. Guessing the intentions of the stranger is indeed a detective-like formula for romance itself, and we have seen that the stakes can change dramatically over time.

You might argue that there are only strangers in the world, in that everyone is opaque when you get down to it. Getting down to it really is the issue, since these matters seem idle as long as we go our merry way and tend to our own affairs (who cares if the taxi driver or the checkout person is opaque?), but what happens when we absolutely need to know more? I am not just thinking of specific secret thoughts, but of the whole terrain, a kind of "heart of darkness" that is not easily illuminated or negotiated. Proust's Marcel embraces the fiercely (insanely, sadistically) desired Albertine, but is obliged to acknowledge that he holds only the "envelope," and that the real (and ungraspable) Albertine reached inward to infinity.

There is something quite wonderful in this cosmic view of intimacy, and I'd argue that the term *infinity* rightly conveys the sheer immensity of dark terrain that the Other is for us, even in moments of so-called fusion. Moreover, erotic and emotional transactions constitute the ideal arena for the diagnostic project: love wants to know, has to know, is tortured by its ignorance, fills in such ignorance with its own fantasizing. But the no less immense flip side of the coin is that love may be thought of as a huge libidinal and experiential network in itself, a kind of inner (hidden) erotic history coded in each body, inaccessible to others. In love, you are also (weirdly enough) on-line. Hence, Freud is quite logical, even though he seems to drop a bombshell in observing, somewhere, that every time two people get into bed, at least six people are involved, in that he points to the invisible but enabling psychic and libidinal displacements that attend emotional and sexual relations, that tend to make all sex a form of group sex. But in an AIDS culture this formula has received a rather more drastic turn of the screw: you are sleeping with your partner's entire sexual history. Mystery is getting priced out of business.

But whatever valuation the unknown is to receive, it seems clear that both literature and medicine have long served (in the metaphor that the eighteenth-century philosophe Diderot prophetically used to characterize the novelist Samuel Richardson) as *torchbearers* illuminating the dark human mind, along with the body that houses it, we may add. It would seem that the Early Modern period marks a moment where literature and medicine become far more interdependent than in the past. Of special interest are the congruences between the evolving medical discourse and treatment of extreme states—from the influential physician Thomas Sydenham's seventeenth-century focus on close observation on through the major reforms initiated by Tuke and Pinel in the next century leading to "moral management" of madness or hysteria on the one hand, and the psychological "inward turn" of the eighteenth-century novel on the other. Consider, in this regard, major prose writers of the period, ranging from Richardson and Diderot on to the more drastic performances of the Marquis de Sade and the subtle, mannered investigations of Jane Austen. What we see on the medical front is a dawning recognition of hysteria, madness, and other dysfunctions as the result of life history, phases of a narrative curve that could be studied and analyzed. No longer "othered" and simply locked away out of sight, the mad and the impaired become amenable to the diagnostic project.

Just how liberating this is, is another question. There is a fascinating synergy here between the goals of scientific research and the strikingly coercive plots of eighteenth-century fiction, imprisoning plots of trapped and explored women providing "knowledge" for their male captors and observers. We know that pornography comes into vogue in this period, with its inherent marketing and objectifying of the female body to elicit hunger or arousal. Richardson's account of a virtuous maiden under siege, Pamela, was long thought to be the "first" psychological novel in English literature, and Diderot's rather more scientific scrutiny of extreme states such as hysteria and aberrant sexual desire (as in *La Religieuse* [*The Nun*], in which the innocent victim is subjected to lesbian advances that she fails to decipher) testify to a diagnostic project of real proportions. The medical ramifications here are both huge and unsettling: the spectacle of a body under siege, conveyed through the immediacy of the victim's thoughts and sensations, is dished up as irresistible and pathbreaking literary entertainment, titillating the reader's appetites, challenging his diagnostic acumen. It could be argued that even Sade's abducted heroines who undergo sexual initiation and/or torture of all stripes likewise have a strange medical tinge to them, on the order of a laboratory experiment in which one tests how the subject/victim will respond to stimuli. Austen's gentler, fine-grained comedies of alliance and misalliance contain massive doses of characters *reading* and *misreading* appearances, in which scenes in drawing rooms, subject as they are to ironclad conventions of what is sayable and what is not, have a distinctly clinical feel to them.

The theorist whom cultural historians invariably invoke here is twentieth-century French philosopher Michel Foucault, especially his work on the birth of the clinic, in that he points to the eighteenth century as the time when the body becomes the legible object of the scientific gaze in ways that were to shape the development of modern medicine, yielding a new episteme about the relation between the visible and the invisible, what he calls "the emergence of the doctor's gaze into a field of signs and symptoms" (91). It is intriguing to note that Foucault the historian of sexuality and Foucault the architect of disciplinary practices are nowhere to be found in his learned study of the scientific gaze, as if he had oddly neglected to factor in some of his own central insights about libido and power into this medical history.

Whereas in medicine it may in fact be possible to pinpoint such a paradigm shift, I am rather more leery about positing a moment in literature when so-called clinical observation moves to the fore. Surely there is much clinical acuity and diagnostic brilliance in medieval romances. And what is one to say of Shakespeare? Iago's entire project depends on his genius in reading Othello, just as Edmund knows how to manipulate Gloucester with consummate skill. As for *Hamlet,* the entire plot might be thought of as everyone's efforts to diagnose the sick prince. What may have historical resonance, however, is the fashioning of a new kind of character, one who uses the "new" scientific gaze in order to control his or her fellows. The figure of the rake who uses his knowledge of physiology and rhetoric for purposes of seduction may have been with us since Ovid, but I think we have to wait until Laclos's *Liaisons Dangereuses,* written in the period Foucault is studying, to see this type realize its full potential. Mme. de Merteuil and her partner, Valmont, are essentially tyrants of intelligence, and their prestige and success derive precisely from their infallible X-ray vision of others, their unerring ability to discern signs and symptoms of erotic interest in their victims who have no idea that they are as visible and on show as if they were waving flags and using loudspeakers.

The gender dimensions of this drama of the scientific gaze are complex and undeniable. Pornography itself, as I have mentioned, is historically related to the triumph of the medical gaze, as it transforms subjects into objects while capitalizing on the libidinal energies and power dynamic that accompany all such transformations. And the familiar plot of such work is that of the reified woman subjected to the machinations of male power and male gaze. From Petrarch to modern film, as Nancy Vickers and Laura Mulvey and others pointed out many years ago, we have become aware of the sublimated violence and control that underwrite this scenario at the heart of much Western art. The notion and presentation of the femme fatale, the assumption that both painting and film will pay "loving" attention to the female body, the utterly predictable cinematic technique of shot/reverse shot that almost invariably *looks* at the woman figure, the virtually unnoticeable device of examining and praising women's body parts (in poetry, in film, in novels, in life): all this displays how irresistible such diagnostic gambits seem to be, and how gendered they are.

Nancy Miller has described the entire eighteenth-century French novel as "feminocentric," and the seventeenth-century *Princesse de Clèves,* with its key scenes of voyeurism where the female is secretly observed in moments of intimacy and sincerity, belongs in this same vein. In fact, Mme. de Lafayette's novel conflates precisely the issues at hand; said to be the first psychological narrative in the French tradition, larded with self-scrutiny on the part of the female heroine, the text nonetheless subjects this analytical woman to the hungry and prying gaze of others, ranging from the man who lusts after her to the entire court world of invading eyes and loose tongues.

DYING OF EXPOSURE

One of my graduate students once wrote that Manon Lescaut, the enigmatic female at the heart of the Abbé Prévost's canonical French novel (1731) of that name, actually dies of "exposure." In using that term, I would like to move more directly into the issues of privacy, violation, and narrative that come together here. It may be recalled that Manon Lescaut is, in all senses, the desired object of Prévost's novel: she is the courtesan who can be bought, and she is the grand love interest of the male protagonist, Des Grieux. Even though there is little physical notation—students are astounded that they cannot answer the question,

"What color eyes does Manon have?"—there is indeed a nonstop, obsessive focus on her mystery, allure, and motives.

After resisting the young man's tireless hegemonic campaign during most of the novel (where she cheerfully takes up with one rich new lover after another), she finally sees the error of her ways, becomes faithful in their final New Orleans stint, sets off with her lover into the American wilderness, and dies. Death by exposure: the harsh American setting, so different from Parisian amenities, kills her; but so, too, does her newly acquired virtue and transparency, as if she were at last domesticated, brought under control, divested of her opaqueness and alterity, and—as the plot shows—no longer of interest. There is a profound narrative law at work here: once opened to scrutiny, once translated or transformed into another's knowledge, the riddling character loses its raison d'être, and the text collapses.

There is food for thought here: narrational energy seems cued to opaqueness, and we must ponder the operation of desire itself. Of course the hungry lover seeks to know and possess. But perhaps the heart yearns—also, even more profoundly—for darkness, feeds on it, and even though human relationships produce, via the passing of time and the agency of understanding, much clarity, it still may be the case that love likes mystery. Put differently, transparency is desire's enemy, and it may well be that the commonplace, quotidian, and tragic facts of life such as divorce and cessation of love reflect the sorry triumph of too much light, too little mystery.

Medically, as well, up until our modern culture of noninvasive imaging, our knowledge was not only dependent on death, but also in collusion with it. Foucault has written eloquently on these matters, in connection with the functioning of the scientific gaze, and enlists the cadaver in a truly baroque play of light and darkness: "That which hides and envelops, the curtain of night over truth, is, paradoxically, life; and death, on the contrary, opens up to the light of day the black coffer of the body" (166). We know that medical history reaches a turning point in the Renaissance with Vesalius's work on anatomy, work enabled entirely by the study of cadavers. The Church lost little time expressing its stern view of such matters, but even in a comic text like *The Adventures of Tom Sawyer,* we see that the practice of robbing the grave is alive and well. Today's debates about the ethics of genetic research and, especially, cloning, suggest that this cluster of issues remains unresolved. My point in coupling the medical and the narrative wars against opaqueness is to underscore their kinship with death; the opening, invading eye does not always await the cold corpse, but rather hastens the process, turns living mystery into dead truth, "the absolute eye that cadaverizes life" (166), as Foucault says.

I am interested in that "absolute eye that cadaverizes life," because all too often our notion of "knowledge" is assumed to be an abstract, innocuous affair, a mere gathering of information. Foucault's formulation is intentionally draconian: seeing cadaverizes, seeing constitutes a form of murder. It is well known that science has been driven by an ocular imperative ever since the Renaissance, and modern medicine is, of course, stamped by this same regime. One logical and overdue reaction against the tyranny of the visual is to restore the primacy of the aural: in particular, in the crucial arena of doctor-patient relationships, in the diagnostic situation, it seems essential to reinstate *listening* as a form of medical knowledge every bit as valuable as seeing or prescribing tests. A listening doctor *restories* the patient. Needless to say, the economics and press of modern medicine tend to work in exactly the opposite direction: talking takes time; doctors have little time. Perhaps more profoundly, talking is about the workings of time, in that talking makes available to the doctor the temporal sweep of a life, at least insofar as the history of the present complaint is concerned.

Less obvious to us is the fact that *looking* is also a story, once we know how to see it. And it is often a story about power. The fundamental curiosity that drives much of science has, I think, an invasively ocular dimension: to *see* what things are made of entails getting inside them. Let me propose an admittedly sensationalist example: William Hogarth's engravings of *The Four Stages of Cruelty*. Hogarth offers a mor-

The First Stage of Cruelty, from *The Four Stages of Cruelty,* William Hogarth, 1751.

The Reward of Cruelty, from *The Four Stages of Cruelty,* William Hogarth, 1751.

alizing allegory of the wretched life and activities of Tom Nero, who moves from young sadist to outright murderer on to his final avatar as specimen for anatomy lessons. What is fascinating is that each of these stints centralizes the scientific gaze, the diagnostic imperative. We need only consider the first and last of these engravings to grasp the argument. *The First Stage of Cruelty* displays what seems almost an epidemic of children torturing domestic animals: Tom Nero (at the center) and his two friends plunge an arrow into the anus of a dog whose owner is trying to beg and buy his pet out of this misery; elsewhere one child deliciously watches another burn out the eye of a bird; other children look at suspended cats clawing each other; another aims a stick at an unsuspecting rooster; another ties a bone to the tail of a dog; from a window above, two people drop a cat with artificial wings. We can all agree that sadism is the unifying feature of the engraving. But so too is scientific curiosity: these children are miniature scientists, not all that different from the psychologists in laboratories today who perform experiments on animals. All of these cruel acts are animated by a powerful desire to know, a "what if?" equation that has genuine intellectual pretensions.

If you find this insistence on science overstated, then you need to examine *The Reward of Cruelty,* in which Tom Nero has come to the end of his career and receives his just deserts. With unerring logic, Hogarth locates Nero's punishment in a medical school setting, with the caveat that Nero himself is now undergoing the same kind of invasive, sadistic, yet scientific investigation that he and his friends meted out to the poor animals. Against a backdrop featuring the emblem of the Royal College of Physicians, a doctor's hand taking a pulse, we see a group of doctors reading, chatting, and laughing, while the main event consists of doctors carving up the corpse of Nero, who seems to be watching in agony. We note the pulley screw in his head, the hangman's rope still around his neck (the result of earlier nefarious deeds), the surgeon gouging out his eye (just as was done to the bird in the first engraving), another pulling out his entrails, which are then put into a tub, still another carving his foot, while a dog picks up Tom's heart on the floor and puts it in his mouth. Yes, this is poetic justice, in that Tom is paying for his misdeeds. But it is also a hallucinatory depiction of the "absolute eye that cadaverizes life," as if Hogarth wanted to link curiosity, sadism, murder, and knowledge, and to say that they are the "four stages" of diagnostic understanding. What we see here is the cruelty that sometimes finances knowing, the drive for power that seems an essential ingredient in our acquisition of knowledge. What is most unmistakable is that ocular knowledge can be horribly invasive, that seeing inside the other may be tantamount to gouging him or her open. There is a great warning here.

EXPOSURE AND THE WILL-TO-POWER

And thus it is no surprise that much narrative literature treats the imperious scientific gaze, the hunger for ever more concealed material to be brought to the surface and transformed into information, with considerable ambiguity. As we shall see later, the relentless drive for clarity triggers a corresponding reverence for darkness, one that is both narrative and creatural. You can die of exposure. All of us know the familiar warnings about excessive X rays, the need for lead aprons, etc. My goal in this chapter is to deepen and extend our sense of such dangers, by radically widening the field of reference, so as to include key moral and emotional relationships where the diagnostic gaze plays a disturbing, sometimes lethal role.

Literature performs a service here, in that it fleshes out these concepts and principles in human stories, and thus helps us to see just how such matters play out in our lives. And I want to emphasize that the predictable gender arrangements of male gaze and female object are often inverted. In Laclos's novel, the supreme controller of the text is the female, Mme. de Merteuil, who practices her art, indeed her science, on victims of both sexes, and delights in reifying and dismantling all those who come into her orbit. Laclos's elegant epistolary novel would seem to have nothing in common with Hogarth's moralizing engravings about Tom Nero, yet they share a conviction that scientific curiosity and diagnostic fervor are often dangerous, cruel, and power-mad.

Or, consider the work of Hawthorne, America's first prose writer of world rank, whose fictions routinely denounce the dangers of the diagnostic project. It has been plausibly argued that Hawthorne was influenced by the new wave of scientism in medical practice, especially the French methods of observation, use of auscultation and stethoscope, impacting on American thinking in the early nineteenth century. Hawthorne famously dramatizes the potential for coldness of heart and scientific violation in the depiction of the satanic physician Roger Chillingworth in *The Scarlet Letter,* and the general theme of the heartless and thus exploitative observer runs throughout Hawthorne's work. Yet, the victims can be of either sex, and Chillingworth significantly plies his trade on the rival male of the triangle, the minister Dimmesdale, whose secret identity as Hester Prynne's lover he is determined to flush out. It is hardly an accident that the vampirish Chillingworth is a doctor, that he is professionally licensed to subject others to his analytic scrutiny. We are a far cry from Molière's impostors and dolts. Hawthorne's plot entails Chillingworth actually moving in with his ailing "client," and although we may sense libidinal reaches in such arrangements today, the community accepts such a move precisely because doctors do such things.

It has been suggested that the entire analytic project in Hawthorne is sexually charged, so that the intimacy of "knowing" another diagnostically becomes an ersatz, even a version of erotic conquest. Readers have often felt that the central love relation between Hester and Dimmesdale remains either abstracted or hidden from view in the novel, a crucial prior event, yes, but never actualized in the prose; I'd argue that the real heat and steaminess of *The Scarlet Letter* are to be found in the Chillingworth-Dimmesdale pas de deux, inasmuch as the *penetration* of the other is hot stuff indeed. Dimmesdale swears to Hester that such penetration is far more sinful than their own sexual liaison: " 'He has violated, in cold blood, the sanctity of a human heart. Thou and I, Hester, never did so!' " (140).

Doctors force their way inside us; but, then, writers do too, and no amount of "satanizing" on Hawthorne's part will blind us to the fact that the doctor's quest is imbued with a kind of hunger and energy that is fueling the entire narrative. Chillingworth is doing Hawthorne's job.

One of the most fascinating literary figures in this regard is Georg Büchner, whose tragically brief career as playwright, lecturer in natural history, and political revolutionary in Germany in the 1830s is entirely cued to the irresistible and inhuman power of scientific analysis. I have already discussed the animality theme in Büchner, but now I want to go further: his sovereign critique of political action (he understands the link between materialism and fanaticism, as he ponders ways to make peasants politically aware, evidence of which we find in his correspondence) stems from the same cold and insatiable curiosity that fuels his groundbreaking doctoral research on the cranial nerves of frogs (research so brilliant that it immediately garnered him a university professorship), and it is just this constellation of analytical intelligence-as-power that is put on trial in his magnificent play, *Woyzeck*.

Büchner puts all the pieces of his life together here, as we watch the antics of the pathetic subaltern, Woyzeck, *armer Kerl* (poor slob) if there ever was one, hounded and mocked by his superiors, most unforgettably exemplified in the machinations of the play's Doctor, who does human experiments with Woyzeck, subjects him to a diet of peas, has him palpated by his medical students, describes his heart-wrenching anguish in the brutal clinical terminology of science, as an affair of pulse rate and heavy breathing. For us, Woyzeck is quasi-crucified; for the Doctor, Woyzeck may be the makings of a professional article. "What makes Woyzeck tick?" is this play's subtext, and whereas we hear in this early proletarian drama the ticking of a time bomb, it is clear that Büchner himself shares the experimental obsessions of his doctor, even though he measures their inhumanity and reductiveness. Woyzeck is reified in front of our eyes, turned into case study, an object of knowledge and horrible exposure.

If Büchner is primitive and brutal in his assault, other writers can be subtle and decorous. No more frightening example of "death by exposure" exists than that of the boy/child Miles in Henry James's novella *The Turn of the Screw,* where the governess relentlessly stalks the little boy in order to find out what he is concealing, and this drama of opening up the other appropriately climaxes in the death of the child. James alters the course of modern fiction by fashioning a narrative theory and repertory that consist, largely, of one quivering consciousness trying to make out what is happening around it, usually found in those other consciousnesses it must deal with. It is hard to convey, in my critical prose, just how decorous yet obscene this kind of thing can be: the governess realizes that the child's lies (if they are that) make up her truth (if it is that), yielding a dialectic of hounding and hunger that moves increasingly from the merely verbal to the corporeal. Take a step back from this decorous story, and you see an older woman systematically closing in on a young boy (everyone else is eventually removed from the house), hot after his secrets, pressing him, more and more urgent in her campaign. One actually feels the awful deliciousness of the contest as she moves in for the kill:

> The face that was close to mine was as white as the face against the glass [the "ghost" that *she* sees, but whose "status" has been the subject of almost a century of critical debate], and out of it presently came a sound, not low nor weak, but as if from much further away, that I drank like a waft of fragrance.
>
> "Yes—I took it." [the child's "confession" of his secret]
>
> At this, with a moan of joy, I enfolded, I drew him close; and while I held him to my breast, where I could feel in the sudden fever of his little body the tremendous pulse of his little heart, I kept my eyes on the thing at the window and saw it move and shift its posture. (85)

The libidinal heat here is overwhelming—the reader measures the almost vampirish feelings of the governess (that "waft of fragrance" she drinks in)—and James has given us a virtually medical notation of the child's condition: a sudden fever, a tremendous pulse. And why not: folded as he is in the arms of this hungry woman, his entire system tells him he is in trouble.

There are few outright detectives in James, but no one surpasses him in sleuthing prowess, and the elegance and fastidiousness of these performances (for they now seem almost operatic to today's readers) convey a wonderful mix of the licit and the illicit, of such ferreting out as the social game par excellence, as well as a test of both intellect and power. The libidinal underpinnings of such probing and digging are unmistakable in both Hawthorne and James, and no reader can miss the sexual hunger that accompanies the epistemological challenge at hand. No less unmistakable, however, is the parallel between this theme of diseased detection and the emerging view of fiction itself, as if storytelling were inseparable from these acts of violation and vampirism, as if the viewing of the human being in terms of signs and symptoms were at once the origin and end of narrative: origin because the speculative, interpretive work of decoding the signs, the hermeneutic drive, is the very pulse of storytelling; and end because the final revelation can kill as well as close.

Nineteenth-century literature is brimming over with comparable scenarios. The heated confections of Dickens and Dostoevsky and the genteel parlor romances like Austen's have been mentioned, but outright teasers like Melville's story "Bartleby the Scrivener" also derive much of their energy from this source. Ibsen's entire enterprise revolves around the exposure of hidden secrets and dirty laundry in the affairs of his Norwegian burghers, but with each successive play he comes to understand the sanctity of secrets, the vulnerability of the exposed human subject. I find Ibsen especially provocative in this regard, inasmuch as the diagnostic imperative is initially seen as the key to his entire dramatic agenda; audiences would flock to see his plays in order to discover what he was going to unveil, unmask, diagnose "this time."

Yet, soon enough in Ibsen's plays, the diagnostician, the man who ferrets out lies and secrets, comes to be seen as monster, not hero, and a sick monster to boot, so that the very urge to get inside gets increasingly understood as at once exploitative and also a cover for one's own neurotic needs. Moreover, as dramatist, Ibsen gradually shifts his focus from secrets themselves to the complex dance of those with secrets, a dance he wonderfully terms the *life-lie,* expressing the view that our dodges and illusions and fantasies are the fuels that get us through life. The brilliance of Ibsen's late dramaturgy derives from showing how we are all the walking wounded, how all of us are using crutches of some sort in order to move at all. In this Ibsen becomes remarkably postdiagnostic, in a way that mirrors the dilemma of modern medicine: not so much what our ailments are, but how we manage to live with them is what we need to know. In the hands of Ibsen, just as in the clinical tales of Oliver Sacks, we come to see just how breathtaking these antics can be.

Ibsen's mad Scandinavian confrère, Strindberg, offers us in *The Ghost Sonata,* his surrealist masterpiece of 1907, Western theater's most astounding send-up of diagnosis. Working with the trusty convention of roof lifting, of exposing what is hidden behind the walls of the prosperous bourgeoisie, Strindberg proceeds surgically to unmask the most diseased and incestuously intertwined group of people in the history of the theater. The great exposer, Hummel, is cast as a version of Thor, the god of war, with a special prowess in crashing through walls, penetrating secrets. Here is how Hummel undoes the Colonel (whose promissory notes he has already bought up):

COLONEL: Are you trying to run my house?

OLD MAN: Yes! Since I own everything here: furniture, curtains, dinner service, linen . . . and other things!

COLONEL: What other things?

OLD MAN: Everything! I own everything! It's all mine!

COLONEL: Very well, it's all yours. But my family's coat of arms, and my good name—they remain mine!

OLD MAN: No, not even those! *(pause)* You're not a nobleman.

COLONEL: How dare you?

OLD MAN: *(taking out a paper)* If you read this extract from the Book of Noble Families, you'll see that the name you bear died out a hundred years ago.

COLONEL: *(reading)* I've certainly heard such rumors, but the name I bear was my father's . . . *(reading)* It's true, you are right . . . I'm not a nobleman!—Not even that remains!—Then I'll take off my signet ring.—It too belongs to you . . . Here, take it!

OLD MAN: *(pocketing the ring)* Now we'll continue!—You're not a colonel either.

COLONEL: I'm not?

OLD MAN: No! You were a former temporary colonel in the American Volunteers, but when the army was reorganized after the Spanish-American War, all such ranks were abolished . . .

COLONEL: Is that true?

OLD MAN: *(reaching into his pocket)* Do you want to read about it?

COLONEL: No, it's not necessary! . . . Who are you, that you have the right to sit here and strip me naked like this?

OLD MAN: We'll see! But speaking about stripping . . . do you know who you really are?

COLONEL: Have you no sense of shame?

OLD MAN: Take off your wig and look at yourself in the mirror! Take out your false teeth too, and shave off your mustache! We'll have Bengtsson unlace your corset, and we'll see if a certain servant, Mr. XYZ, won't recognize himself: a man who was once a great sponger in a certain kitchen . . . (295–296)

There is something adrenaline filled and vaudevillian in Strindberg's handling of the exposure motif, as he cavalierly moves from false papers to false teeth, suggesting that the sleuthing diagnostic gaze operates on the order of PacMan, a voracious mouth that gobbles up everything it encounters, an X-ray machine that delights in shredding every surface it sees through.

Self-Portrait (Night Wanderer), Edvard Munch, 1923–1924.

The maniacal humor here suggests that the ever-so-serious myster-ies confronted in Dickens, Ibsen, and company are now becoming the material for sitcoms. And yet, Strindberg's play is under the aegis of sickness and exhaustion: at the very beginning, the medical student (whom Hummel seeks to use in his revenge scenario) asks the ghostlike milkmaid to cleanse his eyes, eyes that are inflamed, eyes that he cannot touch because his hands have been touching the injured and the dead. We are hard put not to see the aging Strindberg here, a playwright whose eyes are inflamed by so much unmasking of filth and hypocrisy, so much horror. One senses a judgment being rendered on the diagnos-tic gaze itself, as if the capacity to read surfaces, to see what they conceal, to espy the human drama behind the façade, were something grueling, dirtying, finally unbearable.

I'll close this line of reasoning by noting one of Edvard Munch's later paintings, *Night Wanderer,* a self-portrait that seems to relate the horror of having been Edvard Munch, above all of having had Edvard Munch's *eyes* for an entire lifetime. This gaunt, precarious figure, backgrounded by windows giving on to the dark night, has black hollows for eyes, as if what he had seen had gradually eaten up his flesh, a kind of ocular leprosy as it were, offered here as occupational hazard for artists and diagnosticians. Hogarth's sadistic and cruel Tom Nero had his eye plucked out; Hawthorne's Dimmesdale is said (by some, as the savvy Hawthorne puts it) to have an *A* carved in his breast, and although the pious reading would ascribe this to the minister's guilt, I prefer to see it as the fleshly incision caused by Chillingworth's prying eye; Munch finishes our parade and suggests that peering into the mysteries and exposing what is hidden there exacts its toll in your own flesh.

PRESERVING SECRETS, REMAINING IMPENETRABLE

"If looks could kill," the popular expression goes, and it is instructive to reflect on just how damaging looking and being looked at can be. The Lord creates light in Genesis chapter one, but we must wait until Genesis chapter three, when the apple is eaten, before the human subject is endowed with vision—"Then the eyes of both were opened, and they knew that they were naked"—which then introduces both consciousness and shame into the world. The motif of the *evil eye* extends back to folktales and magic, but, often enough, it depicts prying, invading, exposing. Poe's famous short story "The Tell-Tale Heart" is presented initially as a gratuitous act of murder: "I loved the old man. He had never wronged me. He had never given me insult. For his gold I had no desire. I think it was his eye! yes, it was this! He had the eye of a vulture—a pale blue eye, with a film over it. Whenever it fell upon me, my blood ran cold; and so by degrees—very gradually—I made up my mind to take the life of the old man, and thus rid myself of the eye forever" (1951, 244). Gratuitous? We do not need to be Dr. Freud to see that the action is directed against the vulture eye, that the eye seems to be the organ of authority, spying, invasion, consciousness itself, and the speaker cannot bear it.

Ibsen's late play *Little Eyolf* (his greatest, in my view) features a dead child who lies at the bottom of the sea with his eyes open, *evil eyes,* indicting his parents forever. The brilliance of the play consists in the fact that this child has been an evil eye since infancy, when he was left unattended while his parents had furious sexual intercourse, resulting in the child's falling off the table and becoming lame, so that the child's prying eyes seem to haunt this marriage in its entirety, dooming both sexuality and peace. It's worth noting that Ibsen is quite modern in positing the *child* as invading eye, as diagnostic judge for his elders—quite reversing, say, James's treatment of the child in *The Turn of the Screw,* or indeed our familiar (and pious) assumption that children are victims rather than victimizers—thereby giving us an eerie feeling that adults are even more haunted by the Pauline prophecy of being "seen and known" than children are. And why shouldn't they be? They surely have more to hide, as Ibsen well knew. I quite realize I am implying that the nuclear family is a den of espionage, but I suspect that most parents will know what I am talking about.

Privacy, social historians have told us, is not a timeless, universal concept, but rather the construct of particular social arrangements, located within the dynamics and habits of the Early Modern family. There was, we gather, a time when folks had less *pudeur,* were less squeamish about the body and about sexuality, were more on view all the time. But Genesis chapter three also tells us about privacy and exposure, about the cost of being seen. Even Hamlet resists being seen and "played upon," as he informs Rosencrantz and Guildenstern: "You would play upon me, you would seem to know my stops, you would pluck out the heart of my mystery, you would sound me from my lowest note to the top of my compass; and there is much music, excellent voice, in this little organ, yet cannot you make it speak. 'Sblood, do you think I am easier to be played on than a pipe? Call me what instrument you will, though you can fret me, you cannot play upon me" (III.ii.332–338).

Of particular interest, from this perspective, are those figures who refuse to be seen, who remain staunchly closed against the prying eyes of seers and tellers. Laclos's Merteuil once again comes to mind, enigmatic and triumphant in her demiurgic projects despite the lame efforts of the plot to expose and discredit her, a plot that is obliged to give her smallpox and then claim that at last her soul shines forth on her face. Much could be said of Balzac's Vautrin as well, sphinx with an agenda of his own, at least insofar as he remains beyond narrative scrutiny in *Père Goriot,* or of Dickens's inscrutable lawyer in *Great Expectations,* Jaggers, who seems already to know all the dark secrets that Pip must suffer to learn.

Or of Faulkner's magnificent Addie Bundren who lies dying in his novel of that name, Addie who marked all who knew her, desired to whip her pupils so that they would feel her in their very blood, who yet retains a forbidding integrity, rotting in the coffin though she is, an integrity Faulkner calls pride: "that pride, that furious desire to hide that abject nakedness which we bring here with us, carry with us into operating rooms, carry stubbornly and furiously with us into the earth again" (1985, 31). Note how Faulkner unerringly picks up on the medical side of this dilemma, sees the operating room as a rival force for exposure in this book where perception itself is imaged as a water hose that hits you full blast.

Or, consider, for true "good old boy" opacity, the testimony of Flannery O'Connor's mysterious Tom T. Shiftlet in her story "The Life You Save May Be Your Own":

> "Lady," he said, and turned and gave her his full attention, "lemme tell you something. There's one of these doctors in Atlanta that's taken a knife and cut the human heart—the human heart," he repeated, leaning forward, "out of a man's chest and held it in his

hand," and he held his hand out, palm up, as if it were slightly weighted with the human heart, "and studied it like it was a day-old chicken, and lady," he said, allowing a long significant pause in which his head slid forward and his clay-colored eyes brightened, "he don't know no more about it than you or me." (147)

Country ignorance or country wisdom? One thing is clear: Shiftlet's bizarre actions in this story back up his assertion that human behavior often remains a mystery. O'Connor, more even than most writers, honors mystery, regards human motive as opaque; her characters apply the thin grids of reason to their lives (just as we do when we read her stories), but those lives are invariably fitful, animated by dark, imperious, and entirely unpredictable forces. In her work the revelatory and the traumatic are inseparable because grace or horror (or grace as horror) can pop out at any moment. So her stories make for tricky reading. We cannot, as it were, *possess* them.

As a concluding contemporary example, consider the appealing figure of Babette in Don DeLillo's comic novel *White Noise*. Babette, who is married to the narrator/protagonist and whose motivation becomes ever murkier as the text proceeds, comes fully into my argument when she forbids her husband to use words like "entering" to describe sexual congress; "We're not lobbies or elevators," she explains to him.

GETTING IN AT ALL COSTS

I would like to suggest that the narrative of exposure has this funny habit of treating its characters like lobbies and elevators, places to enter, moving places for you to ride in. It can hardly surprise us that medical narratives—whether in the form of fiction or in actual case studies— are full-fledged members of this family.

Consider William Carlos Williams's troubling story "The Use of Force" (troubling to scholars in literature and medicine, because the doctor/writer is stunningly open and unguarded in his account) in which the emigrant girl stubbornly and passionately refuses to open herself to the doctor's ministrations. Attempting the time-honored medical entry of making us go "ahhhhh"—itself an act of forcible rescripting, of making the body speak to the scientist—this doctor runs into problems:

Come on now, hold her, I said.

Then I grasped the child's head with my left hand and tried to get the wooden tongue depressor between her teeth. She fought, with clenched teeth, desperately! But now I also had grown furious—at a child. I tried to hold myself down but I couldn't. I know how to expose a throat for inspection. And I did my best. When finally I got the wooden spatula behind the last teeth and just the point of it into the mouth cavity, she opened up for an instant but before I could see anything she came down again and gripping the wooden blade between her molars she reduced it to splinters before I could get it out again.

Aren't you ashamed, the mother yelled at her. Aren't you ashamed to act like that in front of the doctor?

Get me a smooth-handled spoon of some sort, I told the mother. We're going through with this. The child's mouth was already bleeding. Her tongue was cut and she was screaming in wild hysterical shrieks. Perhaps I should have desisted and come back in an hour or more. No doubt it would have been better. But I have seen at least two children lying dead in bed of neglect in such cases, and feeling that I must get a diagnosis now or never I went at it again. But the worst of it was that I too had got beyond reason. I could have torn the child apart in my own fury and enjoyed it. It was a pleasure to attack her. My face was burning with it.

The damned little brat must be protected against her own idiocy, one says to oneself at such times. Others must be protected against her. It is social necessity. And all these things are true. But a blind fury, a feeling of adult shame, bred of a longing for muscular release are the operatives. One goes on to the end.

In a final unreasoning assault I overpowered the child's neck and jaws. I forced the heavy silver spoon back of her teeth and down her throat till she gagged. And there it was—both tonsils covered with membrane. She had fought valiantly to keep me from knowing her secret. She had been hiding that sore throat for three days at least and lying to her parents in order to escape just such an outcome as this. (59–60)

The critics have had a few problems making Williams politically correct, and many of his doctor stories are quite disturbing in their callousness and unconcealed biases. But of course that is grist for my mill, because this passage pays explicit homage to the uncontrollable, almost ecstatic high that accompanies forcing open the patient. Williams's doctor forces open the girl's throat and finds her secret: tonsils covered with membrane (indicating diphtheria). James's governess corners the little boy, Miles, squeezes him mercilessly for his secret, and he dies. The outcomes are different, but the pride alluded to by Faulkner seems common to both.

Of course, we understand that verbal breaking and entering cannot be flatly equated with physical penetration. And yet everything I have said in this chapter—beginning with the parallel between my mother's exposure to the sun and the Proustian exposure to sexual activity, and continuing to the mystery of Chillingworth's impact on Dimmesdale—suggests that the human subject is invadable both physically and mentally, that the desire to "go in" takes both physical and mental shapes.

Feminists will say that this desire for penetration is a gendered affair (a male fixation), but we need to realize how such hunger constitutes the very pulse of fiction. Some might add, "the pulse of colonialism," as evidenced in the famous image of the ship in Conrad's *Heart of Darkness:* "In the empty immensity of earth, sky, and water, there she was, incomprehensible, firing into a continent" (41). In today's academy, Conrad is now seen along increasingly ideological lines, and citations such as the above offer evidence for the European hunger to colonize and control the non-Western. But the sheer ferocity of the image—"firing into a continent"—also conveys for me an extraordinary appetite of a different sort altogether, a diagnostic and readerly "tracking" that Conrad's famous narrative technique (Marlow "reading" Kurtz) displays to perfection. Marlow's pursuit of Kurtz into the dark continent keeps covenant with the earlier diagnostic projects of Richardson and Diderot, even if Conrad has created a conjectural mode of fiction that accommodates ignorance, guesswork, and outright personal fantasy.

Not that the personal and the ideological are at odds with each other. We have seen that Charlotte Perkins Gilman's version of a male doctor "reading" and "tracking" his sick wife plays entirely into a cultural nexus that infantilizes women and regards any resistance as hysteria. Conrad's Kurtz ultimately resists any definitive reading that Marlow can foist on him; his motives stay shrouded in darkness. But the story of the "target," the human subject slated for "study" and "knowledge," is indeed one that can and must be told.

How does it feel to be on the receiving end of the diagnostic attack? The Swedish artist Lena Cronqvist has left us some remarkable paintings testifying to her stint as caged object of study when she was confined in the mental hospital, St. Jörgens, in the wake of a depression. *Locked Up* (see next page) provides a poignant image of the patient's disarray. All is twisted and tilted in this picture: the subject's dazed eyes and wrenched face, the knife and fork ajar on the plate, the skewed perspective of the entire piece with its sense of both falling and weightlessness, as if the tray were vertical rather than horizontal, the eating surface falling away, the glass insolently perched, the partly eaten sandwich (which looks like a carving) flaunting its reified status—all compounded by the groping fingers that fumble at the (strange, inedible) food. Everything is made alien here, and the inscription of "LOVE" written both forward and backward, as if to signal the awful dislocation and reversal at work here, tells it to us in yet another key. As every spectator immediately notes, the crowning touch of this depiction of consciousness at once amok and under surveillance is the obscene eye in the door, an eye

Locked Up, Lena Cronqvist, 1971.

that could have been imagined by Foucault in his discussion of the Panopticon (in *Discipline and Punish*) and the surveillance strategies used by the State to discipline its subjects.

Cronqvist did an entire suite of paintings about her stint at St. Jörgens, all of them testimony to the estrangement and dehumanizing experience she underwent, but I'd like to focus on an apparently more benign piece from the series, *Private Conversation*. This painting utilizes the same vertical perspective to denote the key pecking order that reigns in hospitals: the sick subject at the bottom, face looking up with trepidation, then the massive table presided over by the two physicians.

Private Conversation, Lena Cronqvist, 1971.

The one on the left looks down at her with the kindness you'd bestow on a lesser specimen, while the one on the right records his findings on the sheet of paper in front of him, likely to produce a document that will be filed precisely in the closed drawer we see on the right.

Against a remarkable backdrop of sky and clouds (where are they? could the patient possibly escape out there if she could get past the doctors?), we nonetheless note the insistent clinical setting, most brilliantly emphasized by the two telephones that are prominently on display. *Private Conversation* is the Swedish title, but there is also a connotation of "Private Confession," implying something on the order of a religious confession, but the telephones (one of which is off the hook) announce just how impeded, "long-distance," and mechanical this consultation actually is. The telephones, the note taking, the complacent professionalism of the two doctors, all speak of the failure of any genuine communication, as well as the imposition of a hierarchical, imprisoning order in which her anguish, although unheard and unalleviated by the doctors' ministrations, keeps her nonetheless imprisoned in the system.

THE VIEW FROM THE PRISON

With Cronqvist's depictions we encounter how the coerced female subject might feel, and there is nothing easy to interpret about it. Cronqvist delivers an image of her prison and her captors that resists easy classifying: tragic? sardonic? mad? But this situation can be imploded still further, inasmuch as narrative might provide a vehicle for rendering the victim's vision that is even more capacious than painting.

Hence, I want to return to Charlotte Perkins Gilman's story "The Yellow Wallpaper," since it provides perhaps our classic depiction of the "colonized" vision. Less noticed, however, is the amazing reversal of power that is staged in this harrowing story, as if, through storytelling from the victim's side, you could show how the institutional bullying that such arrangements routinely conceal—John thinks of himself as loving husband, solicitous physician—might be spectacularly reversed.

Gilman's speaker, denied pen by her husband, nonetheless recounts for her readers her harrowing and hallucinatory descent into madness, as she interacts ever more obsessively with the putative figures depicted in the pattern of the wallpaper of the "nursery" room where she is virtually incarcerated (not for nothing are the windows barred and the floor scratched and gouged and splintered and the bed nailed down). Gilman's story is most remembered for the narrator's fascinating account of the insidious wallpaper: it has curves and flourishes, is figured as "waves of optic horror" and "wallowing seaweeds," resembles toadstools "budding and sprouting in endless convolutions," sports "two bulbous eyes," smells foul.

This imagery seems to signal some sort of fetal fantasia, a landscape of pure (and obscene) spawning that is unbearable. Soon enough, the pattern yields its human figure, that of a trapped woman trying to break through the wallpaper's armature, and this trapped woman then becomes an army of imprisoned women wanting out, "sisters" of sorts to the protagonist who blends with them, perhaps invents them as versions of herself and her plight. Ideological commentary on this story is pale and arid in contrast to the pathos and vibrancy of Gilman's own fable of sisterhood; at one point, the narrator leaps out of bed to help the trapped woman in the paper make her way free, yielding an ecstatic union of subject and vision, of hounded prisoner and emerging escapee: "I pulled and she shook, I shook and she pulled, and before morning we had peeled off yards of that paper" (47).

Gilman was a prolific author, one of the best-known female intellectuals in America at the end of the nineteenth century. The bulk of her fame rested on ambitious treatises about women and economics, about radically reconceiving the family and its domestic trap for women; the other fictions she wrote strike us as didactic. But "The Yellow Wallpaper" is unmatched in its mix of horror, immediacy, and economy, and there is something truly brilliant about a woman trapped in the pattern of wallpaper, for it is a resonant image of societal coercion, of the human subject as incarcerated within the very *design* of patriarchal culture. The story ends with the narrator's final entry/exit through the looking glass, into what we'd probably call madness, but a madness figured as triumphant exit from the patriarchal penal system in which she has lived.

What has gone uncommented on is the fascinating tug-of-war staged within the text, as the female protagonist not only asserts her own personal vision, but does so in wonderfully medical ways: *she* becomes the text's doctor figure, the wily diagnostician who observes her husband, "watches developments," soon finds John "so queer now," and finally becomes suspicious of his prying questions, "As if I couldn't see through him!" True enough, this woman ends up exiting the workaday world, joins the "creeping" women who live in and come out of the wallpaper. Yet, how telling it is that she simultaneously usurps the doctor's position, reverses in some crucial way the power dynamics of the story, makes spectacularly visible to her readers the *huis clos* that her role as wife/hysteric has thrown her into, from which only her empowered, horribly liberated subjectivity can free her. She exits the doctor's prison as mad doctor.

There are simply no terms for assessing the value of this transformation. If self-assertion and agency can go nowhere other than into madness, then we have a Pyrrhic victory indeed. But it is a sign of Gilman's genius that the diagnostic war can shift gears, that the object can become subject by dint of her vision and also of her rigorous observation of the doctor in the house. The dynamic at work here resists easy labels—feminists are divided as to whether this outcome is triumphant or tragic—yet one is grateful for this exploratory fiction that does homage to the explosive shaping power of thought and imagination, most vital when most coerced.

Charlotte Gilman's cautionary fable is a drastic example of analysis run wild, analysis exposed as both ideological terrorism (the doctor's trap) and oneiric outing (the patient's exit). Gilman's woman finds freedom and solidarity in her madness, yielding a visionary richness that *only literature* can articulate. After all, what would *you* have seen, with only your eyes to assist you, had you entered the room with the yellow wallpaper? A woman on the floor? a woman gazing at the paper? a woman shaking and pulling? Or perhaps just a woman locked into herself?

Consider *Melancholy*, Edvard Munch's portrait of his insane sister Laura, painted in 1899. Munch, with all the sympathy and love he can muster, cannot find his way into Laura's mind, cannot show us something rich and strange. What he can do is to articulate her imprisonment in multiple fashion: she sits dead still, hunched over; her eyes seem vacant and inner directed; the reflection of the wall repeats her incarceration; the vivid coloration of the tablecloth (some have compared it to raw meat) contrasts gruesomely with the deadness of the captive. This painting is almost a symphony of lostness, entrapment. This may be

Melancholy (Laura), Edvard Munch, 1899.

why Gilman's deranged woman, no matter how wrecked we know her future to be, enacts a weird triumph of agency and doing, of actualizing her inner world. The madwoman completes her exodus by literally stepping on her husband. Seeing the prostrate doctor lying flat on the floor evokes this response from his "free at last" wife: "Now why should that man have fainted? But he did, and right across my path by the wall, so that I had to creep over him every time!" (50). My students want to cheer at that last line. Here, at last, the doctor gets his comeuppance.

THE DOCTOR: DIAGNOSTIC BULLY OR CRUCIFIED VICTIM?

In some instances, however, one feels that an artist has gone far out of his way to lay low the physician. I cannot imagine a more gripping example of how the prestige of physicians (located both in their social station and in their wise, analytic prowess) can be blasted than by what we see in Ingmar Bergman's painful and punitive film *Wild Strawberries,* which sets out to expose the deceit and sham of an eminent doctor's life and career. Bergman is following in the footsteps of Hawthorne and Büchner in his indictment of coldness of heart, even though the indictment seems severe, sometimes unbearable, because the old physician is so lovingly and seductively depicted by the great actor/director Victor Sjöström.

Bergman's doctor is spared nothing: we witness the nightmare scene where the doctor fails his medical exam, cannot translate the medical formulas, cannot see that the dead corpse is alive and jeering; the sadistic pièce de résistance is provided by the examiner who briskly moves from botched test to a full-scale replay of the doctor's wife's infidelity, enacted in front of him once again in all its virulence, but now explicitly attributable to the doctor's emotional sterility and intellectual arrogance. The film's Dr. Borg has forgotten medicine's first commandment (according to the Swedish filmmaker): "A doctor's first duty *is to ask forgiveness.*" Bergman's brilliant use of flashback and dream sequence displays something of the capacious logic at work here: the successful and omnipotent doctor may have fooled us all these years (in this case, he is en route toward a lifetime's recognition, in the form of a prestigious honorary degree), but the demons will out, the comeuppance will arrive, and it will be unstoppable.

Bergman's cruel vivisection of Dr. Borg has some intriguing parallels with one of Sherwood Anderson's doctor portraits in *Winesburg, Ohio.* The murky story "The Philosopher" focuses on Doctor Parcival, man with a secret, whom Anderson presents as a dark riddle of self-loathing and transgression, yet striving for some kind of utterance. The story is larded with deaths and images of filth and blood, and at a key moment the doctor announces his oracular tidings: "It is this—that everyone in the world is Christ and that they are all crucified."

This tortured story registers the cost of doctoring, the unwashable dirt that is the residue of living with illness and death, that comes from medicine's failure to stop either of these two routine natural disasters. (We know, from the medical literature, that doctors have a significant incidence of psychological disorders, that they are subjected to quotidian levels of stress that are not easily managed.) Anderson's story does not slap around the doctor, as Bergman's film does, but it writes large the mesh of suffering, filth, failure, and blood in which doctoring is caught up. When *we* have performed our diagnostic task—to read this story's odd signs, to see the connection between blood-colored fingers, eyes red from soap-rubbing, unavowable secrets, unstoppable deaths—then we can, I think, assent to its view of crucifixion as the station of doctors.

DIAGNOSIS AND LOVE

The man who was crucified was also a doctor. The New Testament is larded with images of Jesus the physician, Jesus the healer who removes maladies and evil spirits from the bodies of those he meets. The lepers are healed, the bleeding stops, the blind become sighted.

> And Jesus went on from there and passed along the Sea of Galilee. And he went up into the hills, and sat down there. And great crowds came to him, bringing with them the lame, the maimed, the blind, the dumb, and many others, and they put them at his feet, and he healed them, so that the throng wondered, when they saw the dumb speaking, the maimed whole, the lame walking, and the blind seeing; and they glorified the God of Israel. (Matt. 15:29–31)

And we all know that his gift is moral not scientific: he heals by dint of spiritual power, not medical training. It seems fitting to consider the *loving* doctor for a moment, after passing in review so many of literature's cold, heartless, and exploitative types. In "The Surgeon as Priest," Richard Selzer has given us a fascinating picture of the doctor as spiritual hero in his account of Yeshi Dhonden, the personal physician to the

Dalai Lama, making the rounds in Selzer's hospital. In the episode in question, we have the starkest possible of scenes: a fatigued, chronically ill patient lying supine and a physician in safran and maroon gown. No words pass between them; nor does any complex physiological investigation (probing, knocking, squeezing) take place. All we see is a physician taking a woman's pulse. But this he does for a full half hour, "suspended above the patient like some exotic golden bird with wings, holding the pulse of the woman beneath his fingers, cradling her hand in his" (34).

Selzer (and presumably the other Western doctors) is stunned by the depth, intensity, and sheer length of this most routinized of all initial procedures; Selzer calls it "palpitation raised to the art of ritual." As Selzer observes this act of extraordinary intimacy—"his fingertips receiving the voice of her sick body through the rhythm and throb she offers through her wrist"—he feels a sudden pang of *envy,* not of Yeshi Dhonden but of the patient who has been truly *received,* leading Selzer to the realization that he who has palpitated over a hundred thousand pulses has not truly felt a single one. Yeshi Dhonden concludes his examination by whipping up and then inhaling the urine specimen. Later, in the conference room, the Dalai Lama's physician speaks to the American doctors:

> He speaks of winds coursing through the body of the woman, currents that break against barriers, eddying. These vortices are in her blood, he says. The last spendings of an imperfect heart. Between the chambers of her heart, long, long before she was born, a wind had come and blown open a deep gate that must never be opened. Through it charge the full waters of her river, as the mountain stream cascades in the springtime, battering, knocking loose the land, and flooding her breath. (35)

Finally, the "western" diagnosis is requested: "Congenital heart disease . . . Interventricular septal defect, with resultant heart failure."

I have discussed this story with other doctors who express both skepticism and even a sense of anger at the claims made by Selzer here. I am not in a position to judge the medical propriety of Yeshi Dhonden's procedure and pronouncements, but one is certainly struck by several key features of Selzer's account. The description of this woman's somatic disorder in the rich language of winds, gates, eddies, waters, and cascades achieves a kind of grandeur and vibrancy that make the bioscience terminology seem impoverished and inert. The woman is described by Selzer as a person with chronic illness, a person doubtless accustomed to the routinized visits by hospital staff, used to seeing and hearing herself as diseased (but also in some key sense, *unseen* and *unheard*). To be sure, she herself does not overhear Dhonden's report, but I feel that his splendid series of elemental metaphors, figures we tend to associate with exotic places, is a welcome intensification and enlargement, a way of saying that the human body is more majestic and miraculous and even cosmic than our typical medical vocabulary allows.

Beyond the language itself, however, it is the intense, quasi-religious, almost shockingly intimate bond between diagnostic physician and supine patient that most strikes us here. Selzer is not seeking to indict the routinizing of medical rounds, nor does he imply that the Westerners have it wrong, but all his admiration is focused on the rich, pregnant, dense *exchange* that takes place between doctor and patient, a form of *reading* that is at utter odds with the Foucauldian "scientific gaze," inasmuch as its analytic acumen is shown as inseparable from (deriving from?) a closeness that is visceral, existential, indeed spiritual. One might respond that both Yeshi Dhonden and the Western doctor reach the same diagnosis, but what Selzer is showing us is that only one of them reaches the patient.

And beyond that, Selzer is moved, perhaps even threatened, by this quasi-affective model of knowledge gleaned entirely from intimate touching, listening, and smelling. No medical imaging or blood work needed here: just a sufficiently intense one-on-one. Of course Yeshi

Dhonden has his own science, a science that is doubtless so profound and mastered that the simplest forms of human connection, if conducted with requisite concentration, labor, and care, will enable him to read the body he is holding, is receiving. It is hard to imagine a more benign version of diagnosis: the scientific gaze, based on distance and ocular testimony, is replaced by a no less analytic model, but one that inheres in physical contact bordering on fusion (it hardly seems exaggerated to call it that, given the response of the patient, awakened out of her torpor by the immediacy, intimacy, and [one wants to say] charity of this encounter). It is well to remember that Paul's parable of "looking through a glass darkly" explicitly codes ultimate light and knowledge as "charity."

The doctor-patient relation is at the very core of medicine as a humane practice, and yet, much of this chapter has focused on just how much damage (as well as benefit) the diagnostic gaze can bring to that relation. But love and charity are sometimes found where we don't expect them, and for that reason I would like to revisit, briefly, the disastrous situation of Kafka's country doctor. In particular, I want to return one final time to that bed where the doctor lies naked next to his patient. If you are a doctor, I would guess that this prospect fills you with dread. (Doctors have told me that this ghastly story constitutes their worst nightmare.) We have seen that this doctor can control nothing: the horses appear, the groom appears, the wound appears: so unlike the authority and control that most of us laypeople associate with physicians. Yet, there is wisdom as well as punishment in this story. Kafka seems to be showing us, with rare power and surreal images, a story of radical *leveling,* a fable of equality. The doctor is stripped of his accoutrements and protective gear; he is not all that different from the "poor forked creature" that Edgar becomes in *King Lear,* and Lear's hard-earned wisdom at play's end consists in seeing that being a king and being a poor forked creature are the same thing.

Can we not go one step further? Isn't Kafka suggesting that the great diagnostic challenge, the riddle of the wound—the fate of flesh that marks the human creature as far back as Philoctetes—can only be understood along just these lines? That you cannot fathom the wound, heal your patient, until you have lain down naked on the bed with him. One might claim that we see here the purest form of Kafka's metamorphosis: to understand the other, you must become the other. The doctor must, at some level, become the patient. It is a severe lesson, not likely to be popular with physicians, at odds with the prestige of modern medicine, yet suffused with the light of human charity.

MARRYING YOUR PATIENT

Charity, *caritas,* a form of spiritual love, even though keyed (here) to the body, has no libidinal dimension whatsoever. As I suggested in my account of Hawthorne, the diagnostic relationship can indeed be unmistakably charged with displaced sexuality; as we saw in William Carlos Williams's tale of the child who refused to open her mouth for him, affect and libido had their way there as well in the doctor's vehement charge. And Kafka's country doctor is awash in libido.

But what happens when the diagnostician experiences, directly, not subliminally, *eros* instead of *caritas?* When the doctor-patient bond is sexualized? All of us know that this can happen, that physicians can be involved with the patients they treat. And we know something of the damage that can result, for both parties: the ruin of a reputation and career for one, the insidious and exploitative presence of desire (where there should be distance) for the other. It is easy enough to claim that the doctor-patient relationship is violated by such transgressions (as are the lawyer-client or the teacher-student relationships), but what is harder is to ponder the diagnostic paradigm itself along these lines. How much tenderness is right? Does diagnosis inevitably conceal a cluster of emotional tugs, forces? When does concern shade into something hungrier? What are the results?

I'd like to point to two remarkable literary texts that deal with these murky matters, one of them a sibylline, pithy short tale, the other a famous novel: Sherwood Anderson's "Paper Pills" and F. Scott Fitzgerald's *Tender Is the Night.* Anderson's story, drawn from *Winesburg, Ohio,* is, in my view, as perfect and fascinating a piece of writing as we have in American literature. It exhibits to perfection what art and literature have to offer us when we think of nitty-gritty issues, such as sickness, death, and dying, not because of any overt philosophical message, but rather because Anderson seems to have caught (in his four-page piece) the whole beast live: our desire for love, our need for doctors, the fate of flesh, the life of the community.

If his story initially seems a riddle, it is because the dynamics of birthing and dying, sickness and desire, person and place, are unclear even to the cleverest of us, even though we sense that they are the potent forces that punctuate our existence. Hence, the actual story constitutes a diagnostic challenge to its readers: how to make sense of its parts, its metaphors, its strange events? Anderson's hero, Doctor Reefy, is described as a man in whom "there were the seeds of something very fine" (35). Why *seeds*? Listen to the story:

The story of Doctor Reefy and the courtship of the tall dark girl who became his wife and left her money to him is a very curious story. It is delicious, like the twisted little apples that grow in the orchards of Winesburg. In the fall one walks in the orchards and the ground is hard with frost underfoot. The apples have been taken from the trees by the pickers. They have been put in barrels and shipped to the cities where they will be eaten in apartments that are filled with books, magazines, furniture and people. On the trees are only a few gnarled apples that the pickers have rejected. They look like the knuckles of Doctor Reefy's hands. One nibbles at them and they are delicious. Into a round little place at the side of the apple has been gathered all of its sweetness. One runs from tree to tree over the frosted ground picking the gnarled, twisted apples and filling his pockets with them. Only the few know the sweetness of the twisted apples. (36)

This story about apples and seeds harks back to Genesis, to one of the oldest fables we know about carnal knowledge, also redolent of sweetness and delicious apples. And we need to understand that *seeding* is a kind of spawning, a spawning that can be ideational and verbal as well as biological. Note how Anderson's prose moves in every direction at once, so that the "nibbling" in the passage refers backward to Reefy's knuckles as well as forward to the "little round place" in the apple. But then nibbling shades off into something considerably fiercer as Anderson evokes the tall dark girl's earlier love life:

> For a time the tall dark girl thought she would marry the jeweler's son. For hours she sat in silence listening as he talked to her and then she began to be afraid of something. Beneath his talk of virginity she began to think there was a lust greater than in all the others. At times it seemed to her that as he talked he was holding her body in his hands. She imagined him turning it slowly about in the white hands and staring at it. At night she dreamed that he had bitten into her body, and that his jaws were dripping. She had the dream three times, then she became in a family way to the one who said nothing at all but who in the moment of his passion actually did bite her shoulder so that for days the marks of his teeth showed. (37–38)

Desire fuels everything: it lurks under the fine talk about virginity, it animates dreams, it is ravenous for flesh. With sure instincts, Anderson then moves from these teeth marks to still another episode of blood and teeth, forcing us to wonder if perhaps blood and teeth might be nodal points of a story or a life, might be sites where flow and penetration happen, where we actually taste life and other people. The reader simply has to roll with the punches, to grasp the corporeal logic here.

> In the office of the doctor there is a woman, the wife of the man who kept the bookstore in Winesburg. Like all old-fashioned country practitioners, Doctor Reefy pulled teeth, and the woman who

waited held a handkerchief to her teeth and groaned. Her husband was with her and when the tooth was taken out they both screamed and blood ran down on the woman's white dress. The tall dark girl did not pay any attention. When the woman and the man had gone, the doctor smiled. "I will take you driving into the country with me," he said. (38)

Perhaps you wonder why I cite this story, since it may seem incoherent, all over the map. I would suggest that Anderson's manner is poetic, an affair of metaphors and figures that link the disparate parts together. Anderson does not choose this method because he shies away from saying anything directly, but because the things he wants to say can be said in only this way. What are those things? Seeds produce life; biting into apples and into flesh produces sweetness, but also life, and perhaps blood and death as well; sex and birthing may each entail groaning and blood on a white dress. We know that the tall dark girl was "in a family way," and also that she became the doctor's wife, left him money, and died.

And the story's title, "Paper Pills," refers to the scribblings of the doctor, which he stuffed in his pockets in the shape of round paper balls that he then read to the tall girl in the last winter of her life. Why not regard the teeth pulling as a displaced version of either the doctor's friendly abortion or else the sexual intercourse between the doctor and the girl? However you put the pieces together, you end up with the same rich results: the cost of sexuality and pleasure, the making and ending of life, the ceaseless current of energy that moves from seed to flesh to paper to language to seed. *From language to seed:* is this not the magic of literature, the task and delight of reading? "Paper Pills" could be thought of as a shorthand expression for the central vision of this book, the potency of words, the parallels between book shelf and medicine shelf.

Anderson is writing about nothing less than the Tree of Life, the large force field in which pleasure, doctoring, and death take their rightful places. His peculiar rendition of these matters enables us to see the doctor positioned at the very core of this tale, functioning essentially in cardiac fashion, the blood supply and flow for the separate players. This man, whose knuckles invite biting into and whose paper balls are irresistible aborts, marries and buries the tall dark woman; pulls teeth and spills the blood of others; reaches into Winesburg's community like capillaries that carry blood and oxygen into the body's many parts. The doctor is at the heart of the community's arterial life, presiding over its mysteries of seeding and dying.

We never see Doctor Reefy proffer a diagnosis as such. He is not a candidate for the scientific gaze. He is no seeker after power or illumination. Nonetheless, he is unmistakably Winesburg's head priest, the man vitally linked to its prime mysteries of generation and death, of both *eros* and *caritas*. In today's era of cool, distanced, white-coated professionals practicing in shiny, impersonal bureaucratic settings, the sepia story of Doctor Reefy and those seeds and twisted apples is a tonic example of doctoring as the most visceral and intimate of life's events. This loving doctor brings lives into and out of the world, and the medicine he practices, like the "paper pills" of the title, is vital, personal, and existential. Nothing pharmacological in sight here: just a man inscribed in the heat and heart of his living community.

Tender Is the Night, the tragic story of a doctor marrying his sick, rich patient, is a novel that Fitzgerald, America's "golden boy" of the twenties, had great trouble finishing. He wrote as many as seventeen drafts, publishing it only in 1933, at a time when his beautiful but precarious wife was slipping ever more into psychosis, when his own problems with alcohol, nerves, and artistic vision became more complex and urgent. The book opens with the young American film starlet, Rosemary, encountering on the Riviera the charming, charismatic Divers, Dick and Nicole, and much of the early section of the novel is devoted to Rosemary's infatuation with Dick, entailing a full-scale, leisurely writerly account of the Divers's entourage of friends and sycophants— moneyed and less-moneyed Americans gravitating around this magnetic and glamorous couple. Dick Diver, at this point, is the poised, confident lynchpin of a madcap, supremely alluring social carnival; he no longer practices medicine.

We know that Fitzgerald felt, right up to his death, that he had botched the opening of his novel, via his decision to zero in on Diver and company at midpoint, to position Dick as the hero of both the expatriate community and also the idolizing Rosemary. Beginning in medias res was fine for getting Dick in at his apex, but what of his origins, his medical aspirations, his romance with Nicole? All of this would have to be brought in later, as flashbacks of sorts, in subsequent chapters.

Fitzgerald's qualms about where to begin his novel have, I think, a profound parallel with the diagnostic situation itself, as well as the narrative of exposure. When does the illness begin? When you break down? Or when the initial wounds (felt as such?) occur, years, maybe decades earlier? We write our résumés in linear fashion, from birth and early schooling on through higher education right into the list of positions we have held, finally reaching the present moment. Yet, most real human traffic goes the other direction: we possess our past and our formation as retrospective activities. But that's not all: the meaning of early events is rarely signaled as such when they happen, but it often declares itself to us in the fullness of time. To be sure, we only harvest what we have sown, but very frequently we only discover what we have sown at the moment of harvest. Surely, this law governs our understanding of the damage that life metes out to us. Thus, it makes good sense, not only narratively but psychologically, that we first see the Divers intact, and that only gradually, by fits and starts, does the story of their missteps, their fateful choices, their warping experiences, make its way to the light.

Let me insist again: we are not talking about some kind of narrative law here. We are talking about the course of illness and about the shape of a life *as we come to grasp it.* Fitzgerald's story is larded with secrets and cover-ups, not for novelistic reasons, but because that is how the psyche conducts its affairs. The flaw in the design shows up later, much later, in the massive breakdown it has been preparing for years and years. Time is a dreadful bell toller, insofar as it actualizes what has been dormant. Just as more and more men will be diagnosed for prostate cancer by dint of sheer longevity, so too the seemingly manageable features of youthful temperament and character—occasional insecurity, rage, depression—tend to gain weight over time, to gestate into derailing disasters. Even this formulation is too pat and histrionic, as if one fine day the curtain were lifted and the horrors trotted out; on the contrary, this is the dynamic of a lifetime, the skirmishes that we win for years and years before finally losing. That is how it has been with the Divers. That is the challenge for diagnosis. And literature alone possesses the sinuous resources, the narrative strategies, for conveying the temporal roller-coaster that every life constitutes.

Rosemary sees only Dick's magic: "He seemed kind and charming— his voice promised that he would take care of her, and that a little later he would open up whole new worlds for her, unroll an endless succession of magnificent possibilities" (16). But all is not glittery, even in Camelot, as Rosemary first intuits when one of the guests at a party stumbles on strange events in the bathroom concerning Nicole, but is silenced by the Divers' bellicose friend (and Nicole's eventual lover) Tommy, who protects their reputation at all costs. But silence cannot be maintained. Later, this scene will be remembered, this time by Dick himself: "Twice within a fortnight she had broken up: there had been the night of the dinner at Tarmes when he had found her in her bedroom dissolved in crazy laughter telling Mrs. McKisco she could not go in the bathroom because the key was thrown down the well" (168).

But the most explosive and unsettling "breakup" is presented dramatically in the text itself, at the close of the first segment, as a bizarre conclusion to a puzzling, convoluted story about the misadventures of the Divers' friend Abe North. Abe has inadvertently stirred up a race riot in Paris by cavalierly accusing an African of stealing money, but has neglected to get the "right" African, leading to white police tracking four separate black men, themselves seeking Abe North, all of which produces ultimately a black body, dead but still bleeding, on Rosemary's bed in the Parisian hotel they are all staying at. This episode is queasy for the modern reader, inasmuch as its implicitly racist humor and callousness are not very funny today, but no reader anticipates Nicole's reaction to the bloody bedspread. We read that Dick has rushed into the bathroom, and then "Rosemary, too, could hear, louder and louder, a verbal inhumanity that penetrated the keyholes and the cracks in the doors, swept into the suite and in the shape of horror took form again" (112). Nicole is then seen, kneeling by the tub, swaying sidewise, with something to say to her husband:

> "It's you!" she cried, "it's you come to intrude on the only privacy I
> have in the world—with your spread with red blood on it. I'll wear it
> for you—I'm not ashamed, though it was such a pity. On All Fools
> Day we had a party on the Zurichsee, and all the fools were there, and
> I wanted to come dressed in a spread but they wouldn't let me—"
> "Control yourself!"
> "—so I sat in the bathroom and they brought me a domino and
> said wear that. I did. What else could I do?"
> "Control yourself, Nicole!"
> "I never expected you to love me—it was too late—only don't
> come in the bathroom, the only place I can go for privacy, dragging
> spreads with red blood on them and asking me to fix them." (112)

The key may have been thrown down the well, but the emotional doors are opening nonetheless. Nicole's past seeps out of her, not unlike a hemorrhage, in the form of bloody spreads disguised by dominos, all intertwined with her courtship with Dick, the certainty he does not love her, and the pain of violation and exposure. Now we have to go back into the past. Now Fitzgerald takes us there.

Book Two begins brightly: "In the spring of 1917, when Doctor Richard Diver first arrived in Zurich, he was twenty-six years old, a fine age for a man, indeed the very acme of bachelorhood" (115). Dick Diver,

Rhodes Scholar possessed of degrees from Yale and Hopkins, possessed also of overwhelming, radiant charm, a brilliant student and
promising scholar of the burgeoning science of psychiatry, has met, at
the Dolmer Clinic ("a rich person's clinic" . . . "a refuge for the broken,
the incomplete, the menacing of this world") on the Zurichsee, the
beautiful, damaged Nicole Warren.

Dick's colleague Franz regards Nicole's infatuation with Doctor
Diver as "a transference of the most fortuitous kind," and we are treated
to her letters to the dashing doctor, constituting a delicate yet throbbing
portrait of infirmity, desire, and sensitive self-knowledge. The book then
moves still further back, to the admission of Nicole into the clinic. Initially described by her wealthy father, Devereux Warren, to be obsessed
with fantasies of male attackers, Nicole is not long a mystery; soon
enough Warren tearfully divulges the novel's central echoing secret: he
and his daughter were lovers, something that happened when she was
still very young (the mother was dead, she'd often sleep in his bed),
something that is now wreaking havoc with the girl's mental health.

Working his special magic, Fitzgerald evokes the courtship between
doctor and patient, Dick's poignant, passionate sense that Nicole was
"all the lost youth in the world," Nicole's increasing confidence in her
beauty and vibrancy, yielding a twenties lyricist world of falling in love:
"They were so sorry, dear; they went down to meet each other in a taxi,
honey; they had preferences in smiles and had met in Hindustan, and
shortly afterward they must have quarreled, for nobody knew and nobody seemed to care—yet finally one of them had gone and left the other
crying, only to feel blue, to feel sad" (136-137). Today's academy, in its
relentless pursuit of ever keener ideological takes, is embarrassed by
F. Scott Fitzgerald, but you won't understand *Tender*—or *Gatsby,* for
that matter—if you don't thrill a little to the sentimental, lilting, nostalgic
tune he plays, as if to say of course this is illusory, cannot last, but . . . is
it not fine? Isn't young love more splendid than any of those hard-
earned truths that come in its wake? Nicole herself tells Dick as much:
" 'Think how you love me,' she whispered. 'I don't ask you to love me

always like this, but I ask you to remember. Somewhere inside me there'll always be the person I am to-night' " (201).

This is hardly Sherwood Anderson's way of depicting the courtship of Doctor Reefy and the tall dark girl, but for a heartbreaking account of how tenderness and solicitude mix in with desire, for an explanation of why physicians might fall in love with their needy patients, it is very good indeed. Nicole Warren is fabulously wealthy to boot, and her tough older sister, Baby, does not conceal from Dick that the family wants to purchase a doctor ("There was no use to worry about Nicole when they were in the position of being able to buy her a nice young doctor, the paint scarcely dry on him" [153]). Nasty? No doubt about it. Seductive nonetheless, even irresistible? Yes (tragically) also, as the whole novel is to demonstrate.

Against a chorus of warnings (Franz: "What! And devote half your life to being doctor and nurse and all—never! I know what these cases are. One time in twenty it's finished in the first push—better never see her again!" [140]), Dick marries Nicole. Which allows Fitzgerald to explore the real theme he knows only too well: the story of the woman I love; the story of my sick patient; the mix of writerly gold and personal horror that is embedded in this situation. We see, with painful detail, how quickly Dick Diver becomes owned, how trivialized his small income is vis-à-vis her immense wealth, how "his work became confused with Nicole's problems" (170). Of course she seeks to own him: "She had come out of her first illness alive with new hopes, expecting so much, yet deprived of any subsistence except Dick, bringing up children she could only pretend gently to love, guided orphans" (180). Just consider the diagnostic pith of that last formulation: Nicole is subjected to an unblinking moral X ray, exposing her secret drives, her fraudulent mothering. As Nicole's mental instability shows, breaks through the barriers, Dick's role as husband-doctor becomes almost schizophrenic: "The dualism in his views of her—that of the husband, that of the psychiatrist—was increasingly paralyzing his faculties. In these six years she had several times carried him over the line with her, disarming him by exciting emotional pity or by a flow of wit, fantastic and disassociated, so that only after the episode did he realize . . ." (188).

We are a far cry from the spiritual Yeshi Dhonden now: this doctor loves/examines his patient and cannot sort it out, lives on her money, experiences a helpless mix of diagnostic clarity and emotional intensity, is ultimately a contributing factor in his patient's disease. And in a way that no normative code on earth can measure, Dick Diver and this novel find Nicole's madness *interesting,* making me feel that her "performance" is the book's ultimate energy source, the reason Fitzgerald wrote the novel, the thing Fitzgerald knew. We have already noted some of Nicole's breakdowns. There are others: at one point she grabs the steering wheel, forces the car off the road, and jeers at Dick's cowardice for wanting to live; in a carnival she suddenly becomes altered, suspicious and then uncontrollable, shrieking that "the children's ashes are rotting in every box I open" (190). Can the doctor deal with this? Can anyone? The story is wise about psychosis. Madness, we learn, is protean: "But the brilliance, the versatility of madness is akin to the resourcefulness of water seeping through, over and around a dike. It requires the united front of many people to work against it" (191–192).

I have said that Fitzgerald knew this story from the inside. And this unholy mix of the professional and the domestic captures a profound truth about medicine's inherent limits: that we (the sick) live with our diseases around the clock, whereas we see the doctor once a . . . year? Look again at this definition of madness: water that seeps through, over, and around a dike; this is the experiential round of life, the kind of thing one sees because one *lives* with it, but not the sort of specimen one can take to a lab or check out via blood work or easily disclose even through psychotherapy. One reason never to marry your patient is that the medical relation never achieves closure; it is a way of being on call permanently. Add love to the mix and you have something close to a bubbling cauldron. Fitzgerald's critics have alleged that Dick is not truly credible as a physician, but I'd argue that the book is frighteningly convincing as a rendition of what happens when doctors become involved, enmeshed, and ultimately undone by their attachment to their patient. The cold distance that characterized the scientific gaze is lost forever when the diagnostician is wedded to the patient.

Tender Is the Night is a diagnostic masterpiece in still other ways. I have already indicated that it discloses its secrets with narrative savvy, so that we encounter Nicole's outbreaks before knowing why, just as we do in life itself. But Fitzgerald seems obsessed with telling her nasty secret of incest, and he wants us to see how powerfully it still plays. We noted the bloodstained spread, and we gradually understand what Nicole meant when she cried, "I'll wear it for you—I'm not ashamed, though it was such a pity": she is *bloodstained* in such a way that the incest shows forever, not merely as the key thrown down the well but as her permanent self-image. It is possible to feel that Fitzgerald goes over the top to bruit her condition: the film Rosemary is making is called *Daddy's Girl;* one of Dick's patients, Señor Pardo y Cuidad Real (is there any writer who can match Fitzgerald's names?) has a notoriously fey son known as the "Queen of Chili," effectively becoming another version of Daddy's Girl; Dick, in pursuing Rosemary, realizes that "he wanted to sweep away her mother, remove the whole affair from the nursery footing upon which Rosemary persistently established it" (84–85). One comes to realize that the novel's presentation of Nicole is Freudian in its view that hysteria and dysfunction are the belated result of early (and repressed) sexual abuse in childhood. In this light, even Nicole's reference to children's ashes rotting in boxes bears out the same logic: children are despoiled, defiled; that is the story she knows, and the whole novel wants to advertise it.

Why Dick, however? Why should his early interest in Rosemary be painted in these colors? It is here that the true virulence and pathos of *Tender Is the Night* comes into view. Dick Diver, the doctor who marries the rich, sick Nicole Warren, shades increasingly and horridly into a version of Devereux Warren, the incestuous father, the man who preys on little girls. We learn that he is accused of seducing a girl at the clinic, and even though the charge is inflated, Dick admits to having kissed her "in an idle, almost indulgent way" (187). A few pages later, Nicole has the breakdown at the carnival, but its origin seems to be Dick's attentions to a young girl: "Don't you think I saw that girl look at you—that little dark girl. Oh, this is farcical—a child, not more than fifteen. Don't you think I saw?" (190). And then comes the explosive cry about children's ashes rotting in boxes. Whose fixation is this? Is this Nicole espying sexual abuse wherever she looks? Or is this another Dick Diver altogether? Fitzgerald leaves the question tantalizingly open, as he writes Dick's response to Nicole's accusation: "He had a sense of guilt as in one of those nightmares where we are accused of a crime which we recognize as something undeniably experienced, but which upon waking we realize we have not committed" (190).

With a rigor that is almost sadistic, this motif of child molestation reaches its crescendo late in the novel, in Rome, where Dick is at his nadir, vulgar, drunk, beaten up, and suspected of something heinous: "A native of Frascati had raped and slain a five-year-old child and was to be brought in that morning—the crowd had assumed it was Dick." Grotesque irony? Dick, being pulled away by his friends, resists: " 'I want to make a speech,' Dick cried. 'I want to explain to these people how I raped a five-year-old girl. Maybe I did—" (235). Here is the story of the doctor marrying his sick patient rewritten as horror story, written as displaced repetition of the very abuses and sexual violation that made her psychotic in the first place. It is hard to imagine a more cutting indictment of the "loving doctor."

Fitzgerald has remained true to medical logic, but he has surprised us by reversing roles, pirouetting his people, midway in the book. The doctor marries his sick patient. Lo and behold, the patient gradually gets well, but the doctor becomes the novel's sick man, the novel's sexual abuser. Nicole finally starts to bloom, to shake off her illness, to come into her own: "The new state of things would be no more than if a racing chassis, concealed for years under the body of a family limousine, should be stripped to its original self. Nicole could feel the fresh breeze already—the wrench it was she feared, and the dark manner of its coming" (280). That manner is dark indeed: Dick Diver will be replaced by the ever-hard Tommy Barban, as Nicole grows free of her doctor-husband. And he? The book codes him "black," as if his deterioration were some weird continuation of the bleeding black body found earlier on a bed: increasingly alcoholic, mean-tempered, shorn of his glamour, going to seed, Dick Diver becomes a man who now smashes things rather than creating them, a man who muses "I guess I'm the Black Death . . . I don't seem to bring people happiness any more" (219), a man with a "black heart," a man given over to the "black drink."

Readers may feel uneasy at Fitzgerald's fierce story of sickness, loving, and doctoring, may feel unprepared to see the dashing Dick Diver become the "patient etherized upon a table," as T. S. Eliot characterized his figure of Prufrock. One gets well, the other gets sick: this is a diagnostic fable that is uncomfortable. At the end, Dick Diver, prince of the Riviera, the man who was to succeed Freud but married his patient instead, disappears into the American woodwork, at first in Batavia, New York, practicing general medicine, then in Lockport, a man still writing "an important treatise on some medical subject, almost in process of completion" (315), a man no longer in contact with his wife and children, a man snuffed out, extinguished in front of our eyes: "his latest note was post-marked from Hornell, New York, which is some distance from Geneva and a very small town; in any case he is almost certainly in that section of the country, in one town or another" (315). I know of no more cruel closing lines in American literature. Moving his sights from Daddy's Girl, Fitzgerald has placed his own surrogate under the microscope, and he has delivered an autopsy of the American dream, a dream recast as nightmare for the loving doctor.

THE NARRATIVE OF EXPOSURE

I have been attempting to explore the range of issues and values that are packed into our mixed feelings about analysis and diagnosis. Seeing inside the other, whether it be body or mind, is both seductive and empowering; it is also the route toward knowledge. On a more intimate level, who does not experience a secret terror at every visit to the doctor? Surely, a modicum of horror surrounds society's great breakthroughs in the field of imaging, ranging from X rays to mammograms, CAT scans, and MRIs; yes, we understand the miracle at work here, making it possible to "read" the insides of the body without actually invading surgically, but do we really want to know what is going to be found? Even if we have the courage to live with the results, to survive the oracle's prophecy and await its enactment, do we have the fortitude to accept diagnostic findings that outpace any cures, diagnoses for which no therapies exist, a situation that is increasingly likely in our culture of ever more precise and predictive imaging and genetic research?

Exposure is, as I have tried to show, potentially violating and subjugating; but it is also liberating in its conversion of darkness into light, private into public. This can be true medically; this can be true morally. Those of us who see through the glass darkly do desire finally to be seen and to be known. The same Rousseau who, as a young man, exposed himself to passersby on the streets, also wrote *The Confessions,* the great autobiographical text of the eighteenth century, from which I would infer that the organ that is most flagrantly exhibited throughout civilization is the human tongue. We all know the proverbial story of the chance conversation on the park bench that could never happen in the bosom of the family, and we are beginning to see how the electronic highway exponentially expands the possibilities of desired exposure, of shared exposure among support groups and self-help groups that functions as a special therapy that neither doctor nor priest can provide. This same electronic revolution, however, has helped to produce a culture in which your personal medical records, your credit status, your every encounter with authority, is now stored and available, requiring neither God nor Sherlock Holmes to tap into it, retrievable to anyone with a modem and the right code.

How what is private and hidden becomes public and known, what claims to truth such information might have, what the stakes of such "knowing" might be, how such processes are central to both literature and medicine, are the central questions of this chapter. They are explored in a remarkable way by Kathryn Harrison, in her novel *Exposure,* published in 1993. Here is Fitzgerald's fable of child abuse, of *Daddy's Girl,* written some sixty years later, so that the silver screen must now compete with the video camera, drugs stronger than alcohol are now on the scene, and psychotherapy must make its peace with other forms of analysis and treatment. We are no longer in Europe in the wake of the Great War, but in contemporary New York. Harrison writes the story of a young woman, Ann Rogers, whose father, Edgar Rogers, now dead, was a famous photographer whose work is scheduled for a major exhibit at the Museum of Modern Art. His work, however, can be thought of as somewhere between that of Mapplethorpe and Sally Mann, insofar as his central subject was the body of his daughter Ann, photographed from childhood to puberty in scenes ranging from sleep to insulin comas—Ann is a diabetic who brings on these comas to win her father's love by becoming as pliable and docile and helpless a body as he needs for his work—on to episodes of masturbation and sexual activity that Ann did not know were being photographed.

Now, Edgar Rogers is hardly the type of scientific diagnostician we've seen in other texts, yet he truly fits the bill, shows us, in a new key, just how much damage this prying, invasive figure can cause. Edgar represents the allure of possessing the secret life of others taken now to the level of art. His daughter (whom he cannot forgive for causing his wife's death during childbirth) is his artistic material, and although there is no hint of incest itself—unlike what we know from Harrison's other work, such as *The Kiss,* where it figures hugely in her actual life—the relationship between father and daughter is no less obscene and deforming than what transpired between Devereux Warren and his daughter Nicole.

In addition, Ann is a kleptomaniac—the novel opens with an uncommented upon description of Ann changing clothes in a taxi, putting on a skirt that she has just stolen from a posh New York store—and she has a serious drug habit consisting of crystal meth (speed) that wreaks havoc with her insulin shots and skewed body chemistry. There can be little doubt that Ann steals as a frantic gesture for freedom, as a form of self-assertion that no one else scripts; and we see that the drug is there to ease the pain caused by the violations of the past. Like her father, Ann too is a professional photographer—she did graduate work at Yale—but she has no pretensions to high art, works instead with a video camera (employed by Visage Video), someone who records events like weddings and then touches them up to make glistening, harmonious renditions for her clients: "up to Ann to render what she has recorded into a happy if inexact memory."

Yet, the book is out to show that a career or a life of airbrushing is not sustainable. Ann is married to a granola type, Carl, "preserver of history" who restores old brownstones in the city, who senses his wife is coming apart but cannot stop it, and whose ever-positive view about dealing openly with problems is disastrously off base for his wife; in a moment of fury, she screams to him: "I am not a fucking renovation!" Carl later gets back by inveighing, "Isn't it enough that strangers have seen your cunt revealed under brighter lights than I have?" Hence, Harrison's plot comes to a boil because this forthcoming exhibit at the museum, which Ann has agreed to, will be the straw that breaks the camel's back. *Exposure* is the story of a breakdown, of someone whose private past is being turned into public exhibit, someone whose relation to her dead father is every bit as noxious and unprocessed as the Proustian memory of Montjouvain or Nicole Diver's memory of incest.

For starters we note that Daddy is hardly dead at all. He invades his daughter's life no less than he did while living: "*All those years it was you who threatened to eat me up, now I find I have swallowed you, kept you inside me. I went on, I made a life, I thought I wasn't thinking of you. But now I cannot help myself, you've come back*" (113). The novel flaunts his dread presence, not only via his daughter's thoughts and memories, but even in the book's interstices, as in a scene where she is performing (with a tinge of reluctance) oral sex on Carl that is then followed by the catalog-type description of two photographs taken by Edgar of Ann in

1971, one representing sexual intercourse, the other masturbation, leaving the reader to wonder: are these simply mementos of Ann's earlier erotic life? or is Edgar Rogers somehow insidiously present in Ann's intimate marital life?

Like Fitzgerald, Harrison has written her story of abuse "large," stereophonically as it were, so that we see numerous narrative bytes that are strange analogues to the action at hand, replicating it, shoving it down our throat: a young woman belonging to a feminist group protesting the forthcoming exhibit sets fire to herself wearing a T-shirt with the name "Ann Rogers"; with uncanny logic, this woman is blinded by the damage to her optic nerve, signaling Ann (who has eye trouble) once again; in another bizarre episode, Ann as a child is abducted by her science teacher and given what she takes to be insulin (it is really distilled water) so that the teacher can witness firsthand one of her comas (we are told that the teacher has collected untold numbers of photos of Ann, masturbates to them), and we read this horrid episode as a repeat version of Edgar's own mistreatment of his daughter, a mistreatment that reached the level of hospitalization and court case in the past. In a less garish, less lurid mode, Ann's visits to her ophthalmologist, Dr. Ettinger, replay the father syndrome, particularly when he performs laser surgery on her damaged retina, warning her that if she moves at the wrong moment, he could blind her, translating into a medical code the lethal danger she has confronted all her life in the form of an older man with a camera.

Dr. Ettinger's laser surgery, like Ann's work with Visage Video, like her father's famous photographs, spells out the choral dimensions of Harrison's title, *Exposure*. Here, in this ultramodern text, we see state-of-the-art imaging techniques, the fine flower of a scientific practice that can now read the body "uninvasively," and what knocks us over the head is how invasive it all is. Getting your picture, getting your reading, is the bane of this young woman's life, with the added touch that she now does it for a living herself. Ann Rogers is, of course, the text's text, the body that has been photographed forever, with all its poor secrets on view, a body that still wears signs of its history, signs present in the scars left by the times she burned herself, cut herself with a knife, just to know that she could still feel something. She tells Carl she is not a renovation, but she is very much a historical site, an archaeological dig of sorts, and the project of the book consists in excavating all this buried, repressed, unprocessed material. More even than *Daddy's Girl*. Ann Rogers is a palimpsest, a layered artifact, a written-on person, a figure for decoding and diagnosing, a figure who needs a lifetime to come to terms with the poisons cooking inside her.

Now it would seem that Kathryn Harrison has denied herself very little in choosing lurid and sensational themes for her story, and yet the most obscene moment of this text comes midway in the novel, with the reproduction of a contract between Ann's husband Carl and the elegant department store Bergdorf Goodman allowing Ann to steal freely from the store. But the contract provides that she will be under special surveillance by detectives and cameras, that whatever she steals will be billed at 50 percent markup, that any time she spends more than one hour in the store there will a $175 per hour surveillance charge, and that a deposit of $25,000 is required for this contract to be valid.

This entry in the novel effectively pulls the epistemological rug out from under the reader as well as Ann, transforming many narrated scenes (of theft) from private to public, from manic gestures of freedom to controlled exercises of sleuthing. The reader's own take is scrambled: how much of what we've read was, in fact, on camera? Nor is this document alone in its status as rug puller. Harrison has also provided other such materials: the records of the court when Ann was so comatose that her father was brought to trial, the contract and the report of the private detective whom Carl has hired to track Ann, numerous factual descriptions of photographic exhibits and catalogs of Ann's father's work in the past, a final psychological report of bipolar disorder made by the consulting physician to the court following Ann's ultimate breakdown (located appropriately at Tiffany's, where she was walking off with the jewels). Each of these documents is also a form of exposure, and in their mix of detective and medical reporting, as well as their contractual status, they powerfully buttress the novel's major theme of a woman's private life being exposed to public gaze, just as the exhibit of the father's photographs will do.

But that is not all: the sheer variety of these nonfiction materials, impudently taking their place in the narration of a life, flaunts the very constructedness of all such perspectives and representations, making the reader realize that the so-called narrative account of Ann's life is by no means a natural event. We do not expect to see contracts, bills, reports both legal and medical, in a novel; in novels we expect a story. Harrison's mix of documents obliges the reader to understand the factitiousness of any novel's conventions: its day-to-day processing of Ann's life as a story, its confident narration of the past, its cavalier rendition of Ann's thoughts, those concerning the current events and those representing her memories of her father, including her inner italicized voice, which is still speaking to this dead man. These passages, we come to see, are also documents, perhaps as fabricated and debatable as the retrieved memories of abuse that present such epistemological and legal challenges today. But such passages, in a novel, are rarely provocative or disturbing, for they are indeed the conventional means of exposure by which literature presents its people for the inspection of readers. How often have you asked, reading a novel, Who's writing this? who's holding the camera? how is this knowable?

If almost all of this chapter has seemed an attack on the scientific gaze for its assault on the secrets and integrity of the human subject, I'd like now to turn the gaze on literature as well: what is literature if not a diagnostic carnival, a nonstop exploration of human motive, a culturally sanctioned version of going inside? I'd claim that literature constitutes a peculiar form of cerebral hemorrhage, a bleeding *printward* of all that is in the brain (and heart) of its characters. In Kathryn Harrison's hands, all of these procedures have become embarrassingly highlighted and denaturalized, and we grasp just how extensively she has exhausted her theme of exposure. Late in the novel, we read this, in italics, as Ann's yearning: "*I dreamed I was on the autopsy table, that I was dead. When the coroner cut into me he saw that I was empty. I didn't take a thing. It sounds grisly, but it was a happy dream. When I saw the knife slip in, my entrails revealed with nothing inside them, I was so relieved. I felt pure and exultant. Like an angel, I had lived on air*" (205).

Ann's dream has uncanny parallels with Hogarth's rendition of Tom Nero on the autopsy table, and she completes my parade of figures who have been opened against their will. Kathryn Harrison's dazzling repertory of invasive techniques and representational strategies seems to make a gathering statement about the genre itself, obliges us to see that our so-called private story is not very private anymore, but is smeared everywhere, in newspapers and doctors' reports, in business contracts and TV monitors. Harrison's novel closes with uncertainty over Ann's prognosis. Will she be able to live with her poisons?

I too would like to close this chapter on the same note of uncertainty. Literature and medicine are in the business of going inside minds and bodies—not those of angels who have lived on air, but those of opaque human subjects who are crammed full of pulsions and data. Narrative records these interactions, and our richer narratives refuse the blandishments of unitary truths and definitive exposures. I said at the beginning that it takes a lifetime to process what one has absorbed, that the famous Jamesian "figure in the carpet" does not jump out at us like an epiphany, but rather is the pattern on the loom that we ourselves must discover and make and alter and rediscover over time.

Perhaps "exposure" as a kind of on-the-spot discovery of the hidden truth is losing its efficacy, in both literature and medicine. The books we love resist on-the-spot illumination, because they live in time, release their secrets over time, become different as we become different, are ultimately mobile and mysterious. And as for medicine, we are well into an era where the Sherlock Holmes approach, the dramatic and definitive right reading of the mystery, of the disease, is less and less at the center of the stage. The hermeneutic adventure, so central to the detective story and the scientific laboratory, is not likely to be the paradigm for today's hospitals and HMOs. Instead, with heightened longevity, we are more likely to die of chronic disease, or of those slow-moving poisons we have harbored for decades, than of mysterious and lethal infection. But for most of us, as we think about ways of representing our transactions with body and mind, our own and others', we would do best to seek a form that embraces temporality and indeterminacy, that acknowledges the forking path of human lives, that has room for darkness as well as light, that manages a truce between the desired closure of knowledge and the openness and freedom of living—in a word, narrative.

CHAPTER FOUR

PLAGUE AND HUMAN CONNECTION

Thebes is dying. A blight on the fresh crops / and the rich pastures, cattle sicken and die, / and the women die in labor, children stillborn, / and the plague, the fiery god of fever hurls down / on his city, his lightning slashing through us— / raging plague in all its vengeance, devastating / the house of Cadmus! And black Death luxuriates / in the raw, wailing miseries of Thebes.

—SOPHOCLES, *Oedipus the King*

This disease will be the end of many of us, but not nearly all, and the dead will be commemorated and will struggle on with the living, and we are not going away. We won't die secret deaths anymore. The world only spins forward. We will be citizens. The time has come.

—TONY KUSHNER, *Angels in America*

THE MYSTERY OF INFECTION

You board the plane at London Heathrow feeling fine. You still feel okay when you arrive in New York seven hours later, but soon enough you begin to cough and to experience respiratory problems. It turns out, after eventual medical consultation, that you are in trouble: you have contracted drug-resistant tuberculosis. So have six other passengers on that plane. You think back to the trip and you remember the persistent coughing you heard on the plane, although you cannot associate a face to it. You may die. Did you have a relationship with the cougher? Yes, indeed, though you never knew it at the time.

This is a modern story, a story that has happened, that will continue to happen in larger numbers. It has a great deal to do with the failure of antibiotics in their war against bacteria and viruses, driven partly by the overuse of these former miracle drugs. It also has much to do with globalization, with travel patterns that have exploded the whereabouts of virulent bacilli and toxins, putting them on a world tour without precedent since the plane in London had just come from Ankara, and before that from Bombay or Tunis, all the while circulating and recirculating its potent contents for the breathing needs of all passengers. Who is equipped to tell this story? Doctors? The Centers for Disease Control? The Federal Aviation Administration? Your travel agent? What take would any of them have on your peculiar but life-shaping experience?

Now for an ancient version. You are a citizen of Thebes in 600 B.C., and everyone around you is becoming ill; many of the people are dying. Plague is announced. You, like your neighbors and the city elders, ask: where does this scourge come from? The best scientific information available is to be found at Delphi, where the Oracle can be consulted. A leading city official is dispatched to Delphi and returns with the explanation: Thebes is harboring a murderer in its midst, not just any murderer but the person responsible for killing the old king; the Oracle explains that this moral and political transgression is responsible for the mass deaths at hand. (The Centers for Disease Control in Atlanta would never present "hidden crime" as their explanation of the disease; is it so certain they are right?) The vital leader of the city, Oedipus the King, vows to cure the sick city, to bring to light the concealed crime, to do so at any cost, in order to restore the polis to health. In the course of his investigation, it turns out that he himself is the source of the crime, that his violent altercation with an old man many years ago was actually the murder of the old king. It turns out, further, that Oedipus was this man's son, and that Jocasta, the former queen whom Oedipus has married, is his mother as well as his wife. Ultimately, it turns out that Oedipus has been having relationships he did not know he was having—not utterly without parallel to your fatal transatlantic flight—and that the health of the entire community is strangely dependent on these transgressions. Finally, Oedipus learns the damning truth, gouges out his own eyes, and leaves Thebes; we must assume that the plague also leaves Thebes.

Who could tell this story? We know that Sophocles did, and he elected to focus on the detection efforts of the king, giving us the voice and wishes of the people themselves only through the testimony of the Chorus. What might the actual testimony of the dying and the afraid-of-dying have sounded like?

Sophocles must have thought that his play dealt with issues of truth, prophecy, and fate, not with plague as such, which seems merely to be the setting for the plot. Yet, we are entitled to reconceive these matters, so as to posit a more global pattern of logic and causality. That structural pattern tells us that the individual drama of Oedipus' ignorance concerning his most intimate relationships is startlingly replayed at the social and bacterial level: plague itself is a virulent language of connection, a lethal manifestation of ties between people, brought by infection and communicable disease. What interests me in this chapter is the amazing scope of what I want to call the *plague-text:* a story of epidemiological disease, a story of mysterious transmission, a story of community responses and resources, and—last but not least—an individualist story of initially concealed and finally exposed secrets, secrets of moral transgression and taboo.

This same dark logic that links hidden personal transgression to public plague informs a modern film such as Roman Polanski's filmnoir classic *Chinatown,* in which the crucial but concealed incest between Noah Cross and his daughter (played unforgettably by John Huston and Faye Dunaway) is posited as the mysterious cause for the drought that threatens Los Angeles. And it will not do to regard this strange amalgam of private misdeed and public calamity as merely some form of symbolism. The plague-text is generically concerned with secrets, with bringing what is hidden (and censored, toxic, seminal, germinal) out into the open.

For these reasons we stand to learn more about plague and the actual dimensionality of infectious diseases by consulting literature, rather than medical history. Needless to say, the writer is rarely possessed of the key scientific information that explains the transmission of disease. But, then, the human, epistemological, social, and ethical dimensions of plague stem from just this ignorance and blindness. Moreover, science rarely clears up these matters. Understanding the etiology of bubonic or pneumonic plague, comprehending the transmission of the disease via the fleas that got it from the rats, is fine as far as it goes, but it will not advance us in our understanding of society's reactions, nor in grasping the link between individual transgression and public disease. Even these formulations are far too tame. The plague-text intrigues because it broadcasts an entire web of congruences and patterns of causality that mystify our scientific logic, that seem to adumbrate a *networked* universe that, far from being chaotic, may actually be cogent beyond our capacity to explain, may be "rhymed and reasoned" in ways that beggar our rational thinking.

Writing about these matters in America after September 11, 2001, adds a grim factuality to such theories. Calamity strikes via the lightninglike destruction of two seemingly impregnable bastions of American power: the World Trade Center and the Pentagon. Within moments, the plague logic of finding and then broadcasting a credible cause and origin is set into motion: Osama bin Laden's name is instantaneously all over the media, and names that are unpronounceable for most Americans are on everyone's lips, as the key to this horror. Could the key leaders be found, somehow the danger might be contained. Experts explain that there are countless small terrorist cells that are operational all over the globe, but the public is mesmerized by Osama bin Laden, by Mullah Omar, by Al Qaeda, obeying a logic that is closer to magic than to politics, whereby cleansing and protection might be achieved in one fell swoop, so that the nightmare could come to an end.

Right on the heels of the hijackings, the public is treated to mysterious, ominous, lethal outbreaks of anthrax infection. The mysteries abound. One of those mysteries is outright biological, since it will turn out that scientists know next to nothing about how anthrax actually works, how virulent it actually is, how easily contractible it might be. But the other mysteries are such that even Sherlock Holmes could not solve them: what is the connection between the various anthrax-laced letters sent out? How do letters going to a media building, to a TV anchorman, to two senators, fit together? And then there is news of a woman dying of anthrax in New York, who had zero political image and zero known exposure to anthrax; and a second anthrax death of an old woman in Connecticut, she too a mystery, because she is entirely out of any conceivable contamination loop, unlinked to any terrorist or political plot imaginable. With these unexplained deaths, the postal service itself begins to look frightening (as well as frightened), inasmuch as the entire delivery system may have been poisoned, so that the most innocuous routines of the day—such as opening your mail—acquire an unwanted tinge of adventure and threat.

Then the newspapers and talk shows begin to speak of biowarfare, of the possibility of smallpox being spread by some terrorist event, of how easy it is to manufacture biological weapons, of how many people are known to be working on such projects, of how lax security is. A Homeland Security Office is established, in hopes the citizenry will exercise due diligence and caution as they go about their lives. But how can you be diligent about the air you breathe? The water you drink? Can any airplane flight be foolproof against terrorism? Overnight, an entire nation's sense of security is altered. Who has done this? Who might do more of it? Can they be found and, as the saying goes, "brought to justice"? What kind of coherence lies behind these deeds, this menace? Will peace of mind ever return?

Plague-texts are about more than bacterial transmission; they are about the deeper riddles of human connection and social fears. Moreover, the great plague-texts in literature explore the ramifications of physical, emotional, sexual, and political interactions. Plague's terror stems in part from the blindness that limits our individual view, the impossibility of *seeing infection*. More broadly still, plague and epidemic threaten to erase difference or rank along social and political lines. Finally, the outbreak of plague exposes the deepest fears of the state, which then trigger the strategies of containment, the search for explanation and blame. Art that deals with plague is strong stuff, since it depicts the encounter with mass dying, the unpredictable responses and metamorphoses triggered by this encounter, leading ultimately to a new view of self and other.

The interest in AIDS today, the knowledge of old uneradicated diseases such as malaria and exotic new ones such as Ebola, the dawning awareness of bioterrorism as a geopolitical fact of life, tell us that these issues transcend art and literature. But art and literature make us see them differently, give us a different measure of their reach. One of the richest issues that comes into focus has to do with transmission, itself a story that is profoundly social and imaginative in nature.

These matters can be figurative as well as literal. It would be possible to devote this entire chapter to the metaphor of *infection* as it is used to connote the reach of human interactions, the reality of "human transmission." Is it accidental that Shakespeare repeatedly images *lying* in terms of *poison in the ear*? With just a little fantasy, we could claim that all human language is an affair of poison in the ear. My words go into your ear, and if I have made them sufficiently toxic, well then, they work their noxious will on your system. The most famous example of literal ear-poisoning is doubtless the murder of the old King Hamlet by Claudius in exactly this fashion, stealing upon the sleeping king with his vial of hebona, "And in the porches of my ears did pour / The leperous distillment" (I.v.63–64).

But it is to Iago's conquest of Othello that we must turn if we are to gauge the reach of this metaphor. "I'll pour this pestilence into his ear," (II.iii.346) Iago confides to us, confident that it will turn Desdemona's "virtue into pitch," and the magnificent central scene in the play (III.iii) is devoted entirely to this exercise in poisonous infection. It begins with a still believing, still in-control Othello, and by scene's end—after Iago has filled up the Moor with innuendo about Cassio, with dirt about Venetian girls, with insecurity about his own age and alienness ("for I am black / And have not those soft parts of conversation / That chamberers have; or for I am declined / Into the vale of years" [III.iii.260–263]), we have a raging Moor who seals a murder pact with his lieutenant. In all of Shakespeare I know of no richer illustration of how we poison each other with our words, of the quasi-chemical and neurological impact words and thoughts can actually produce.

After all, how would you go about measuring the impact that humans have upon one another? It seems like such a simple question, and yet we have no tools for gauging or even perceiving these lines of force. Language as infection seems scarcely metaphoric. You cough at me, and the bacilli are airborne into my lungs. You speak to (at) me, and the words are airborne into my brain and heart. And why limit these toxic transactions to speech? Why not consider the images we see, the music we hear, all of the cultural sights, notations, formulas, and assumptions that come our way via family and society? Don't all of them invade us, in some unseen, unseeable sort of way?

Or, to return to the more seemly: how would you characterize what is really happening when you read a book? You may recall one of my leading figures in the Introduction: each house has two shelves, a medicine shelf and a book shelf. And I compared works of art to the bodies of warriors eaten by cannibals in order to ingest the strength of rivals. All of these views turn on the notion that word and image have an indwelling power that is active and works its will inside us. Surely you are saying as much each time you claim that you have "benefited" from a book you read, or even "understood" a conversation that took place. It is just that we rarely characterize these exchanges in such charged, penetrative fashion. But I suspect that all writers and artists have, at some time or another, pondered this toxic view of their work, have hoped that their words would indeed enter into their readers or viewers, in order to release their power. The Swedish playwright Strindberg, languishing in

Austria at the home of his in-laws in 1894, speaks perhaps for all writers when he reflects on the possible impact that his play may be having, far away, on Parisian audiences:

> This feeling of power, it's happiness to sit in a cottage by the Danube, among six women who think I'm a semi-idiot, and to know that in Paris, the headquarters of intelligence, 500 people are sitting dead quiet in an auditorium, and are foolish enough to expose their brains to my powers of suggestion. Some revolt, but many will go away with my spores in their grey matter; they will go home pregnant with the seed of my soul, and they will breed my brood. (1979, 23)

To be sure, Strindberg's utterance is larded with occultist notions of hypnosis, telepathy, and the like that were in vogue at the end of the nineteenth century. But, on balance, I find his language quite persuasive and revealing, not about his own manias (of which he had an endless supply), but about the basic, but hidden operation of *exchange,* of how we interact with one another in the world (or how we cannot avoid interacting with one another in the world, which obsessed Strindberg).

I find myself holding forth on this topic to my students as I lecture to them, as I hear numbers of them coughing and wheezing (long winters up here in New England, lots of colds and flus), and I insinuate that my aim indeed is to infect them with my ideas. They usually look up in disbelief (still coughing). Then I say that every instructor in the place is trying to do this, and that we give exams to measure how well we've pulled it off, how much stuff has passed from me to them. We all get a good laugh out of it, but I genuinely believe that education and culture at large can be fairly assessed along these lines of infection, virulence, and toxicity. The truly toxic instruction stays with the student forever, undying, doing its work in the dark, doubtless in the company of other potent microbial/ideological agents carrying out their mission. Surely, the history of the world's misfortunes (as well as its successes) has something to do with these early-stage, poisoning/infecting dramas that we call family, school, and culture.

As you can see, I am drawn to this topic, but issues become richer and deeper when we move from the individual transaction to the larger social container where it happens—because disease can be a matter of life or death for entire societies. Hence the crucial issue of *transmission* turns out to be a fact that is, yes, medical, but also a riddle that is social, ethical, perceptual, and epistemological. Can we perceive infection? What does it mean when A infects B? when A believes/suspects/fears that B might be infectious?

These are weighty matters, since they revolve around the central issue of human contact and therefore impact on the nature of sexual relations, family connections, neighborhood attitudes, and ultimately much else, including racial stereotypes, xenophobia, and scapegoating of all stripes. This welter of concerns is not easily amenable to scientific analysis. And that is why we turn to artistic testimony, because we find, in texts ranging from Sophocles to Defoe, Dickens, Camus, Bergman, and Kushner, a formidably rich depiction of collective illness—plague or epidemic—seen along precisely the lines I have noted: human relations, sexual codes, "othering." In fact, the plague-text is peculiarly eloquent about these moral and political matters, as if disease were the cathartic public experience that made visible, at last, the society's unacknowledged fears and value systems. And it does so because it flaunts *linkage and connection* everywhere, in licit and illicit situations, yielding something like a new map of relationship, an unsuspected network, making notions like individual integrity and hegemony seem more and more quaint.

PLAGUE'S MASTERPLOT: *OEDIPUS THE KING*

Sophocles' play opens with a medical emergency. We are positioned in front of a palace with closed doors, and out of them emerges the king with his "tell-tale limp," to face the procession of priests and suppliants seeking to put a stop to the plague that is decimating Thebes. The old priest describes its plenitude: crops wither, cattle die, women perish in childbirth, children are stillborn, fever is everywhere, "black Death" luxuriates. Oedipus commiserates with the Thebans, his "children," acknowledges that they are "sick to death," and claims that he is even more sick than they are because his spirit grieves for the entire city. The seeds seem planted for the key individual-polis equation.

But Sophocles wants us to realize that this battle is with death itself, death imaged by the Chorus as an invading god, a god of fever and disease who breaks into the human subject. Apollo "the Healer" is urged to save them: "Drive him back!—the fever, the god of death / that raging god of war / not armored in bronze, not shielded now, he burns me, / battle cries in the onslaught burning on— / O rout him from our borders!" Then follow a series of wild and desperate pleas to the other gods in the Greek pantheon: Zeus is begged to "thunder Death to nothing"; Apollo comes in for a second request, to smite them with his "showering arrows"; Artemis, the Huntress, is beseeched to "ride Death down in pain!"; and Dionysus closes the list, urged to come with his "face aflame with wine" and his "raving women's cries," to "burn that god of death that all gods hate!" (218–222).

There is something fierce and primitive in this entourage of deities who are begged to take up battle and repel the invader who is annihilating the community, against whom none of us is "armored in bronze," none of us "shielded." The mystery being explored here is that of massive and invasive disease, of the specter of extinction that will erase Thebes, and it is important to remember these vital matters, to keep them in the front of one's view, before getting too absorbed in psychological and epistemological subtleties. Plague points to apocalypse.

Sophocles' *Oedipus* can be said to stand as our masterplot in this arena, because it prophetically posits mass death and infection as the resonant background for its famous issues of sexual transgression and self-knowledge. It is surprising how little attention has been paid to the medical theme in the *Oedipus,* other than pointing out that the king is significantly referenced as the community's "doctor," the man who is supposed to heal the sick polis. The doctor metaphor ranks as one among many of the Greeks' civilized accomplishments which the play is calling into question. We need to understand the Theban plague here as dreadfully collective, in that the entire community is sick, is contaminated. Greek tragedy frequently centers on the detection and purgation of evil—the miasma that must be uncovered and exorcised—and catharsis itself, the aimed-for, purgative effect that the tragedy (according to Aristotle) was supposed to generate in the Athenian public, is a pharmacological term. Put most reductively, Aristotle implies that seeing the *Oedipus* performed has a therapeutic effect on the Athenian public. But what about the therapies needed within the play itself? Why are the people sick? How will they get well? We know what Tiresias has to say about these issues: a murder and a murderer are concealed in the community, and that is why plague has struck. Is it so simple?

Denis de Rougemont once said that we should inquire of every plot what particular labor it is performing, or indeed what particular fiction it may be confirming. One can say of the *Oedipus* that it is devious indeed along these lines, that it is at war with itself, inasmuch as the overt key to the play—Oedipus is responsible for everything—offers a quick fix for all its echoing problems about disease, death, sexual relations, political order, community behavior, and the like. I say "devious," because Sophocles himself gives us all the ammunition we need to be suspicious here, to query whether indeed "Oedipus" is the sole and satisfying answer to all these puzzles. What, in other words, is being shored up, sustained, by the play's whodunit scheme, which ascribes everything to the king's transgressions? No Western text has received more commentary than this one, and the most influential interpretations look, willy-nilly, into the can of worms that Sophocles has opened, enabling us to gauge how *strategic* the story is, how it seems to be wise about the damage potential its plot possesses.

Freud's famous analysis of the play spells out, along libidinal lines, just how serious the real disease might be, since the actions of the king are now said to express the patricidal and incestuous desires of all male children. To be sure, this interpretation makes the story emblematic, but at what cost? You will note just how utterly this reading distrusts the central character, turns Oedipus himself upside down, since he has no ostensible longing for his mother and he kills his father by accident. Or so it seems to him; Freud—and every psychiatrist after him—would answer (suavely), "But of course he doesn't 'know' he wants to do these things; these desires are unconscious; the proof that they are all-powerful is that he does their bidding anyway." It hardly needs to be said what a cruel and prophetic reading this is. Of course you don't know what you are doing; your libidinal drive is running the show, and you are not even supposed to know it (that is what good repression is all about, yes?).

Moreover, one wonders where Freud got the idea. Perhaps he just paid attention to the text itself. At a key moment in the play, Jocasta herself assures Oedipus that there is nothing new or worrisome about this matter of would-be incest, since our dreams have long confirmed such longings: "And as for this marriage with your mother— / have no fear. Many a man before you, / in his dreams, has shared his mother's bed. / Take such things for shadows, nothing at all—" (1073–1076). Every time I read these lines, I wonder why it is that Freud became famous by cribbing them, since most folks assume, of course, that Freud alone saw that we dream of incest. Sophocles obviously knew it twenty-five hundred years earlier, *but* he has Jocasta scoff at such intuitions, as if, yes, dreams contain such desires, but there is nothing to worry about. Just shadows.

What is going on here? Are these tidings shocking only for Freud (and for the straitlaced Viennese culture that he lived in, that contributed to who he was), whereas they do not daunt Jocasta or Sophocles or the tougher Athenians of Pericles' time? Or should we interpret Jocasta's calming remarks as an effort to put out the fire, to explain away something quite virulent about sexual desire? For Oedipus himself, the murder at the crossroads and the subsequent copulation in the royal bed are unrelated events, but for us, in retrospect, they seem to come together in disturbing ways, as if murdering the older man were somehow the key to the boudoir, as indeed Freud implies. Murder as key? Murder as index?

Furthermore, classicists have investigated the muffled issues of homosexuality and rape that are coded in the Oedipus myth, notably in connection with Laius, Oedipus' father, and his father, Labdacos, each of whom is figured (in other variants of the myth) as brutal and coercive, each of whom is strikingly *marked* physiologically, one "left-sided" and one "lame"—as coded in their actual Greek names—as if to signal something aberrant in the patriarchal line itself. Laius in particular is said to have exerted sexual violence on Chrysippius whose subsequent suicide led to a curse on Laius, damning his house to extinction, and from this comes Laius's "left-handed" sexual relations with Jocasta in order to avoid insemination. Apparently Laius, drunk, failed to maintain "homosexual" arrangements with his wife, planted a seed in her, and hence received the Oracle's plot-enabling prediction that he will be murdered by his son. Sexually speaking, this story has lots of baggage. And remember Lévi-Strauss's insistent emphasis on issues of "walking and behaving straight," his theory that the myth is *thinking about sexuality*. If you put these markers together, you begin to see a parade of figures whose sexuality turns violent, cannot be confined to the norm, wreaks havoc on the body politic. Could there be a link between the many sexual disorders of the myth and its background of plague?

What link, you might say? Plague, after all, is about dying. Think again. One of the most fascinating texts I know in this area is the incendiary thesis put forth by the French theatrical visionary Antonin Artaud, in the 1930s, in his highly influential *Le Théâtre et son double* (*The Theater and Its Double*). Artaud's lead essay is entitled "Theater and the Plague," and in it we find this striking depiction of what happens to a community when plague strikes it:

The last of the living are in a frenzy: the obedient and virtuous son kills his father; the chaste man performs sodomy upon his neighbors. The lecher becomes pure. The miser throws his gold in hand-fuls out the window. The warrior hero sets fire to the city he once risked his life to save. The dandy decks himself out in his finest clothes and promenades before the charnel houses. Neither the idea of an absence of sanctions nor that of imminent death suffices to mo-tivate acts so gratuitously absurd on the part of men who did not be-lieve death could end anything. And how explain the surge of erotic fever among the recovered victims who, instead of fleeing the city, remain where they are, trying to wrench a criminal pleasure from the dying or even the dead, half crushed under the pile of corpses where chance has lodged them. (24)

I will not conceal the fact that Artaud's vision has been thought by many sane people to be unhinged. Moreover, his interests go beyond liberated sexuality, when he goes on to claim that plague is as much a spiritual as a somatic phenomenon, that its "transmission" is far more mysterious than any scientific theory would suggest. In his essay, we learn of a viceroy of Sardinia who *dreams* that plague (in all its dreadful physio-logical virulence) has come to his shores and infected the kingdom, and who then learns that a ship, the *Grand-Saint-Antoine,* coming from Baghdad, has asked for permission to dock; incredibly enough, the viceroy obeys the warning of the dream and denies passage to the ship, which then goes to the mainland and delivers its actual pestilence. Are dreams a viable form of knowledge? Did the plague "contact" the viceroy?

We know that the doctors of the University of Paris were under sig-nificant pressure to account for the origin of the Black Death that hit Eu-rope in the mid-fourteenth century; their best explanation (after a major conference) suggested a conjunction of planets. When plague came to London in 1665, the planet theory was again trotted out. People did not understand *infection,* could not grasp the fact that the fleas fed on the sick rats and then transmitted the disease to the humans. Such traffic was not visible. But, in modern times, in the 1930s, Artaud tells us that the bacteriological explanations are insufficient, that something deeper and larger is binding people, traveling via dreams and thoughts. His world is *networked*.

What most strikes us in the rendition of plague behavior that Artaud offers is its *revelatory* power. Here is a profoundly theatrical model: when plague strikes, the curtain goes up, and we now see a carnival-esque vision of society, a metamorphic tumbling of forms, in which everything you thought you knew (about others, about yourself) goes up in smoke. Small wonder, then, that he claims plague as a kind of "patron saint" for theater, plague as the perfect analogue for the stage, plague as a desirable moment of truth, causing "the mask to fall," revealing "to collectivities of men their dark power, their hidden force" (31–32). Artaud sees the virulence of plague as *beneficial* for the theater because it renews contact with the Dionysian and the divine; at the risk of sounding perverse, it would seem that plague (according to Artaud) *clears the air,* cleanses our sights, removes the dross, exposes our true relations. (It hardly needs to be said that the revelatory view of art put forth in much of this book has some parallels with Artaud's vision.) In the plague-text we see at last the collective dimensions of illness, not only collective illness (plague, epidemic) but also the social responses, the antics of a social group facing death.

The plague-text is profoundly keyed to the epistemological energies of narrative, so that the search for the cause of the disease is inseparable from the name of the transgressor, the secret of his act, the story of his life. The community wants this story told, wants to put a name and a face onto its catastrophe. And the storytelling itself would seem invested with strange healing powers, as if the emerging narrative of Oedipus' life-in-time were oddly therapeutic. The fuller coordinates are at last being graphed. It is odd that the king's life story might function as Thebes' talking cure. Why should this be so, if not because these quests are, at every level, zeroing in on the polis's own dirty laundry? It is a question of public health, in that the society cannot get well until larger stories get told, and the concealed ills and crimes are not only brought to the light but *recognized as the community's business.*

But the unavowable aspect of the community's business, perhaps its driving force, is the push for closure: the play's relentless detective work is in the service of a speedy mass cure. That is what this plot is doing. Its job is to explain (away) plague by nailing it on the king.

Consider, in this light, the anthropological thesis about the *Oedipus* developed by René Girard, whereby the plot is reconceived as a contest among the three head males—Oedipus, Creon, and Tiresias—to see which one of them is to take the rap for Thebes' problems. Girard provocatively argues that the play's fateful breakdowns—parricide and incest—are actually instances of fateful *blurring,* instances where key lines of demarcation and prohibition are erased so that sexual appetite strides across family borders and anger leads to political murder. This is bad news for any society, a small step away from pure chaos, for chaos results when sexuality and violence are no longer "channeled." Oedipus' errors are a formula for social nightmare; and the primary concern "behind" the play, the true rationale for its plot, is to reinstate boundaries, to put a stop to the flux of violence that erases difference. Killing your father, killing the king, sleeping with your mother: these acts erase the sacred lines of familial, social, and political order. According to Girard, the Greeks were terrified of just such calamities, and the unstated purpose of the play is to show the way out, by putting the blame entirely on one man, Oedipus, and thereby "innocenting" the community.

When I present Girard's thesis to students, they are usually incredulous. They remind me that Sophocles has told this story as the account of Oedipus transgressions, transgressions hinted at by the Oracle, articulated more broadly still in the charge put forth by Tiresias, blind prophet who knows the truth, and ultimately validated by the entire plot, which produces all the missing evidence. What's not to believe? the students ask. And they are not wrong: Sophocles has told it this way. But just as the hints of sexual impropriety and virulence are to be found in the story's interstices, so too are there disturbing signs of anarchy elsewhere in the text.

In particular, I have always been struck by the outright ferocity of Oedipus' attack on Tiresias and on Creon. He lambastes Tiresias as "wizard," as "scheming quack," as "pious fraud," and we know that the play is written at a moment when the Athenians are increasingly suspicious of the Oracle, of the claims of prophecy. Could Tiresias be a fraud? (If you, as Athenian spectator, were convinced that the Oracle at Delphi was corrupt—and many people felt it was—what would you make of its predictions? How would you assess Tiresias? Do you ordinarily think that blind men have special access to the truth?) As for Creon, Oedipus accuses him of backstabbing, of wanting to usurp the throne. Is this so implausible? Is he not a thoroughly political animal in the *Antigone*?

Yes, we know that the Athenian public *knew* the myth, thus knew Oedipus to be declared the guilty party; and we too know the myth, know who is shown to be at fault. Yet, try for a moment to bracket this prior knowledge, to put yourself into this play at ground level, and to revisit these scenes of bilious recriminations. Try to imagine this story as open, not foreclosed. And then you see quite a spectacle: each of these hoary male honchos is duking it out with the other, because each one feels the net that is closing in. And that net is precisely the community's not-to-be-denied desire to find a responsible party. Folks are dying like flies. Why? Who is responsible? You can be sure someone will be *produced*. This is ultimately a theory about scapegoating as strategy for "cleansing" the public, and the ideological ramifications are quite fascinating.

In this light, plague is not simply the background mess that Thebes is in; plague is precisely the viral or bacterial version of slippage and erasure that Girard is at pains to articulate in political and philosophical terms. Plague is the physiological language and proof of human linkage and relation; plague is horrendously democratic and egalitarian in its dispensation, broadcasting publicly a new and surprising familial mesh that puts paid to many of the cherished beliefs and fantasies of society concerning order, station, and hegemony. It is thus excruciatingly apt that Sophocles unpacked the strange history of Oedipus, redrew the topography of the king's life, displayed him to have been meshed in ways beyond his ken, revealed that his seemingly normative arrangements were actually transgressive. This is the illumination generated by the plague-text, and even though it traffics in disease, it is also wonderfully salutary, in that it fractures our conventional views about our dealings and schools us toward a more generous and emancipated picture of our place within the scheme of things as well as the place of others, others who are now seen to be inseparable from us.

I said that plague schools us toward a more generous view of our place because it positions us in an ecosystem we had not suspected. But the hallmark of the plague-text is its paranoia, not its generosity. Paranoia that the folks across the water, across the border, across the street, have brought the miasma into our midst. The very notion of the *barbarian*—so indispensable throughout history, denoting the Other wherever he is—seems to have been constituted as the toxic threat that we must combat in the name of preserving our collective health, our purity. There is no barbarian in the *Oedipus,* but Sophocles' plot is a call to arms, a fascinating display of civic cleansing, a determined campaign to lay this disaster on a responsible party. That is what communities do when disaster strikes. Who has caused this? is the clamor.

We also know something about the recurring answers that history provides us with. The oldest one, to be found over and over in the Old Testament, is: God is doing this, and He does it to punish you for your sins. Is this not Job's dilemma: you find yourself covered with boils, know that you are innocent of wrongdoing, and have to hear from your friends that God is punishing you for misdeeds. It is worth noting that Girard has also written about the story of Job, arguing that the very institution of medicine is on the line in this story since doctors should not intervene with illness or plague if they really thought it was God's will. As far back as Hippocrates, we have a denunciation of this view of illness as divine punishment. But the thesis is alive and well all over the world, including in the United States in some quarters when it comes to assessing AIDS.

Susan Sontag has shown us how cubistic such speculations and witch-hunts can be, by remarking that the popular American conception of AIDS having started in Africa, "the dark continent," is matched by a countertheory among Africans (and others) that AIDS is an American export, a virus fabricated by the CIA for purposes of bacteriological warfare. (Note my predictable reference to Bombay and Tunis as possible origins of the disease you caught on your London–New York flight; what might the Africans or Indians onboard have to say?) We also know, to our horror and sometimes to our shame, many of the other answers that have emerged throughout history when people need a scapegoat: the Jews did it; the Gypsies did it; the Catholics or Protestants or Muslims or Russians or Americans or any other group you care to name did it. We call this paranoia. I want also to call it *plot* (in that familiar sense that there is a plot to get you, and in the larger sense that *plot* is about determining causality and responsibility).

We see this logic of cleansing the community everywhere we look. Plague plots abound. Consider what happens in all the detective stories and mysteries. To be sure, the most interesting ones retain some ambiguity and have the courage not to solve everything, but the ironclad formula is well known: at story's end, the criminal is produced (they call it "detected," "discovered," "indicted"). Remember Rougemont's view of plot: we absolutely need to believe that criminals and murderers are caught. Why? Because they'd still be running around otherwise; or, worse still, because they could be anyone, your neighbor, your spouse, yourself. Someone shot down or arrested rids us of this nightmare. This plot is tried-and-true because we crave the security it confers on our lives. Most stories offer a fairly seamless version of finding the murderer, the miasma—so seamless that we hardly question the possible fictiveness of it, so seamless that we hardly see the spadework going on in front of our eyes, or the necessity for such constructions and plots. Sophocles' play fascinates because he gives us a peek into Pandora's box, makes us glimpse the horror show that might just spill out if nobody is found responsible for this mess.

Plague brings out into the open the medical, diagnostic side of this equation. Medicine is as invested as the Oracle is in finding the culprit, in naming the origin of the disease. Diagnosis is not the *neutral* intellectual procedure science would have us believe; a cultural imperative to "solve" problems and to "produce" causes is also in play here. Doctors, especially in an "activist" medical culture like America, are notoriously uncomfortable with the idea of doing *nothing* (despite the recognized wisdom that says intervention may cause more harm than good). Blood work, imaging, tests: so many detection strategies for solving the mystery, pinning it (conceptually) on something. Remember the Sorbonne in the mid-fourteenth century: "conjunction of planets" was the best they could come up with, but you can be sure they had to come up with something.

The plague-text is also wise about flux and mobility, because its infection paradigm is an inherently mobile one, wrecking any fond ideas we might have about stasis or sanctuary; instead, it announces a regime of cancerous activity, in which we turn out to be carriers or receivers, even when we thought we were standing still (or "behaving straight"). This view of "traffic" likewise challenges our conventional views about boundary and hegemony, suggests that we do indeed have strange bedfellows. Oedipus found this out. And it is still being found out in Kushner's *Angels in America*. We need Sophocles, Defoe, Poe, Dickens, Antonin Artaud, Ingmar Bergman, Tony Kushner, and others to tell the story of plague, because they are all drawn to its kaleidoscopic reality, its depiction of the mobile stage we live on, seen at last as a *stage* where the fables of both body and body politic can be acted out. The artist, unlike the scientist or even the social scientist, ponders the jack-in-the-box surprises brought on by plague, sensing that the mix of intimate sexuality, violence, scapegoating, and public health is ultimately a cogent mix, requiring us to rethink our categories and norms.

Whereas the *Oedipus* is Sophocles' premier depiction of these matters, his later play, the *Philoctetes,* warrants further mention in this regard as well. As Edmund Wilson wisely argued long ago, Philoctetes' wound is inseparable from his bow, and we are meant to discover just how binding this sick man's connection with his society actually is. Fine. But we can hardly forget that Wilson's genial reading goes precisely *against the grain,* inasmuch as the entire plot flaunts at us the horror which illness produces, the societal disgust and rejection that the afflicted man produces. I am willing to admit that Philoctetes' special wound is over the top (smell, agony, godlike origin, etc.), but we cannot ignore the brutal social dynamic that set the stage for this play: quarantine this man! exile him! move him out of our midst!

Sophocles' plot entails a brave rethinking of this knee-jerk social mechanism, since it literally revisits this banished man, reconsiders the possible (utterly counterintuitive) utility of the diseased man who has been excised from the body politic. We must assume that the bitten, bleeding, infected Philoctetes had been seen earlier as precisely the miasma that the Greek social system is on the lookout for, almost as if the ideological immune system were brought into play so that the toxic invader can be exorcised. Wilson's handsome thesis has to tackle all of this.

Wilson argues the public utility of Philoctetes by valorizing the magic bow. But there is more to be said about the diseased man's embeddedness in the culture. As if to give still more weight to this theme of civic membership, of widening our view of the polis, Sophocles has powerfully accentuated the father-son connection throughout the play. Hence, it is no accident that Neoptolemus is fatherless (this, against an insistent elegiac backdrop of dead older men—not only Achilles, but where is Ajax? where is Nestor? where is Patroclus? All are dead— which Sophocles rehearses as a form of "current events" for out-of-touch Philoctetes), and that, in this search for a father, Odysseus the master politician is rejected in favor of the sick man with the wound.

It is not merely a question of choosing Philoctetes over Odysseus, but rather a crucial drawing of family lines, a way of saying that the diseased man, the miasma, is no lone wolf (as those who abandoned him turned him into) but a familialized figure, a meshed figure. This is not softness on Sophocles' part; it is part of the collective and social logic that governs this play, a collective logic that has been skewed by the early abandonment of Philoctetes, and which now must be set right by the play's plot. Family and state are reconceived here, showing us that the seemingly islanded sufferer is to be understood as part of a larger gestalt. This is what plague-texts do. We shall see more of it in the pages ahead.

PLAGUE, INDIVIDUAL FATE, AND COMMUNITY RESPONSE: DANIEL DEFOE

In 1722 Daniel Defoe published, anonymously, *A Journal of the Plague Year,* an account of the London plague of 1665 that poses as an eyewitness version of things (even though Defoe was all of five years old at that time). The year 1722 was a good year for this book, given that plague was raging in Provence and the English had reason to fear that it would cross the Channel. This report on pestilence is not as famous as either of Defoe's best-known books, *Robinson Crusoe* and *Moll Flanders,* yet it possesses the same kind of unflinching honesty and tell-it-like-it-is forthrightness that we find all too rarely in fiction. Defoe's single great subject is *survival,* whether it be as a shipwrecked man on a desert island or as a hustling female in early modern London or indeed as a sober citizen surrounded by plague. Defoe presents his material as a kind of warning, as seen through the eyes of his narrator H.F. and as nourished by a significant body of documentary information (some of it explicitly medical) that the voracious reader-author had absorbed. If the *Oedipus* can be read as a symptomatic text about stratagems for scapegoating when mass death occurs, Defoe's text places the real disease, actual plague, front and center. In its freshness and journalistic verve, this book is amazingly readable today, not only because the author describes in detail how the citizens of a great metropolis respond to devastating plague, but because it offers some provocative parallels with our own fears about communicable disease and the paranoia it may produce. Alerted to the dangers of anthrax and smallpox, American readers in the post–September 11, 2001, world have taken something of a crash course on these matters.

Some critics have claimed that the London poor are the true heroes of Defoe's book, and it is undeniably true that they bear the brunt of the attack, since they (unlike the rich) have no resources available to them, such as money, extra provisions, and especially property in the country to which they could escape. Yet, I'd argue that Defoe's concern for the poor is less moral than sociological, inasmuch as he understands to perfection that plague sets the stage for social anarchy. His book shows what a crippled metropolis looks like, what it means when shops and markets close, when exchange has virtually ground to a halt, when there is virtually no money to be made. It is against this vision of economic disaster that we can best understand the remarkable efforts of the Lord Mayor and the city fathers to maintain some semblance of order and decorum. (Here, too, parallels with the New York catastrophe are not lacking.) Defoe lauds the Lord Mayor for his acts of charity, for distributing money and bread to the poor, but we sense that these measures are as political as they are ethical. And we begin to realize just what a powder keg plague can be: when the labor machine stops, when the circulation of goods is frozen, it is only a matter of time before murder and mayhem break loose, and full-scale rioting begins.

Most fascinating of all, we learn what cities must do in this kind of a crisis. Death stalks; how do you stop it? Defoe's book provides eight nonstop pages of Orders from the Lord Mayor, detailing the new kinds of jobs that plague brings into being (Examiners, Watchmen, Searchers, Chirurgeons, Nursekeepers) and the new tasks at hand and the injunctions pertaining to them (Notice to be given of the sickness, Sequestration of the sick, Airing the stuff, Shutting up of the house, None to be removed out of infected houses, Burial of the dead, No infected stuff to be uttered, No person to be conveyed out of any infected house, Every visited house to be marked, Every visited house to be watched, Inmates,

Hackney coaches). Still further rules regard street cleaning, raking, laystalls, disposal of rotting food; and some unsurprising final restrictions concern "Beggers" and "Plays" and "Feasting Houses" and "Tippling Houses," all of which contribute nefariously to the risk factors threatening the polis, and must be curbed or shut down. Even though Michel Foucault never mentions Defoe in his groundbreaking *Discipline and Punish,* his grand theory of the surveillance and penitential arrangements of modern state apparatus that begin to take form in the eighteenth century, we are entitled to consider *A Journal of the Plague Year* as a banner text about the mechanisms for keeping order, about the actual reach of *policing* as the fundamental activity of government and subject formation. Plague brings all of this startlingly, unforgettably, out into the open.

It is all too easy to read Defoe's text as social documentary. The reason it demands inclusion in this book has to do with its visionary thrust. The narrator of the *Journal* prides himself on keeping his feet on the ground, but as you might suspect, plague generates fireworks. As it begins its assault, we see an entire assortment of plague specialists appear, hawking their wares to the threatened public: quacks with their special potions (time-tested, they claim, from other, earlier plagues), astrologers with their cosmic data (with the added windfall of two recorded comets having appeared over London several months earlier), and the usual mix of witch doctors and oracles shrieking disaster and doom for London.

And it is quite a show. Yet the explosions of quackery, prophecy, and lunacy that are annunciatory (look what's coming) pale in comparison to the outbursts that the actual plague produces. Initially, the surprises are of a confessional nature, as if the horror of immediate death were a kind of truth serum: "Many Consciences were awakened; many hard Hearts melted into tears; many a penitent Confession was made of Crimes long concealed . . . Many a Robbery, many a Murder, was then confest aloud, and no Body surviving to record the Accounts of it. People might be heard even into the Streets as we pass'd along, calling upon

God for Mercy, thro' Jesus Christ, *and saying,* I have been a Thief, I have been an Adulterer, I have been a Murderer" (34).

Yet, these self-indictments, dramatic as they are, are tame when contrasted with the actual behavior of plague victims, a kind of collective frenzy that knows no bounds. We read of tormented people raving on the streets, throwing themselves out of windows, shooting themselves. Other notations are hideously familial: mothers become mad, murdering their infants; and still others, dying of grief or turned into idiots, moving into lunacy. Yet, even these responses to imminent death have a "naturalness" to them, in comparison with other, still more grotesque scenes that the narrator H.F. encounters: mockers who taunt and jeer the dying, or crazed figures who see themselves as plague's "emissaries," pouncing on men and women in the street, spreading the disease.

The narrator's own journalistic, commonsensical account of lurid, maniacal events makes them all the more vivid to today's reader, and the upshot of such descriptions of "current events" is a vision of London utterly transmogrified. It is as if all the customary decorous forms went up in smoke, and we now see a carnival of raving, unhinged subjects. Defoe tracks them, follows the trail of those who steal away from the City only to die alone in the countryside, speaks of the dreadful situation for mothers in childbirth (dying in labor, killing their infants, shrieking for aid that does not come), and chronicles the elaborate strategies for survival, such as walking upwind from people who may be infected, speaking to no one, and handling all objects (money, purses, items of exchange) with infinite care (gloves, vinegar, poles, water: all enlisted to prevent skin contact). Paranoia reigns. No reader can escape the chilling thought that plague doesn't simply kill its victims: it upends all civilized behavior, turns people mad, installs a reign of terror. And no reader in the twenty-first century can feel secure that such antics are just a thing of the past.

Plague visits London, and the Lord Mayor calls for the classic community response: quarantine. The greatness of Defoe's book stems, I think, from his profound understanding of what quarantine produces. As we saw in the Orders imposed on London, all infected houses are shut up, and guarded by Watchmen. The penalties are draconian. But the corruption (Watchmen are bribed, fooled, murdered) is widespread. Defoe's narrator is especially drawn to the penitential dramas produced by the severe quarantine laws, and he sees to perfection that the regulations designed to protect public health are little less than death sentences in the private sector, since the barricaded pestilential home betokens doom for those (still) uninfected who tend to their sick relations, who are stuck in this *huis clos.* Infection utterly overturns any fantasies about the safety of home, and the likelihood of lethal contamination poisons family bonds, introduces an element of terror into the enclosed family unit, makes "intimacy" into a deadly nightmare. We have scenes of mothers inspecting their hitherto well, now ailing daughters between the legs, discovering the telltale signs, watching death appear, dying themselves. We have scenes of fathers seeking to get provisions for their sick and dying kin, placing what they get on trays that the infected take in. We have scenes of families plotting their escape, the well tearfully abandoning the ill; still other stories of families being foiled (not by the authorities, but by the plague), united gruesomely in death.

Plague consists of people infecting each other, and this fearsome business wrecks all polite versions of relationship. The threat of infection produces a generic family drama with Poe-like accents of impending doom. And Defoe grapples with the great conundrum of infection: how do you know? when do you know? Yes, the well become the sick, but by the time this is visible and legible, it is too late. Countless Londoners thought themselves well, had (as of yet) no symptoms, but were actually infected to the core, and hence went about their lives infecting others, never knowing it. One might think that the worst of plague is the disease itself, the boils and fevers that take over and annihilate the body; but the truth is considerably darker, because the deeper horror is mental and conceptual, the forced entry into no-man's-land where disease rages everywhere, both around you and (just as likely) inside you, cashiering even the most basic indices of knowing, polluting every area of life. Consider the following passage devoted to the antics of the infected: its sobriety, its depiction of human beings utterly routed by their own bodies, its rendition of death the stalker, its portrait of what bioterrorism might produce, might actually look like on our city streets:

> Now it was impossible to know these People, nor did they sometimes, as I have said, know themselves to be infected: These were the People that so often dropt down and fainted in the Streets; for oftentimes they would go about the Streets to the last, till on a sudden they would sweat, grow faint, sit down at a Door and die: It is true, finding themselves thus, they would struggle hard to get Home to their own Doors, or at other Times would be just able to go in to their Houses and die instantly; other Times they would go about till they had the very Tokens come out upon them, and yet not know it, and would die in an Hour or two after they came Home, but be well as long as they were Abroad: These were the dangerous People, these were the People of whom the well People ought to have been afraid; but then *on the other side* it was impossible to know them. (191)

It is a prodigious passage about what is visible and what is invisible; and the answer is it is almost all invisible, since what you *see* is delusory, because everything is happening *on the other side,* on the inside, in the dark. This is the stark reality of infection, and we see it as the single insuperable obstacle to either knowledge or prevention. Defoe is not known for psychological depths, and these staggering, expiring Londoners are stalwart, poignant in their efforts to retain decorum and sense. *They are trying to behave.* But I read this passage and see in it a very old taboo that has been breached: death has been let loose, death inhabits everything, and all our brave composure is for naught, a whimsy in the face of this devastation.

Defoe makes us see the horrid human side of the infection scheme. In discussing one victim who thought himself hale and hearty, Defoe wonderfully calls him a "walking Destroyer," commenting "how he had ruin'd those, that he would have hazarded his Life to save, and had been breathing Death upon them, even perhaps in his tender Kissing and Embracings of his own Children" (202). This scene is disturbing because we measure the awful ignorance and blindness at hand, the even more awful *economy* which leads you unwittingly to murder those you love, to murder them by your love.

We see, in the course of this book, a gathering diagnosis of plague as paranoia. The well shun the sick, but then the well are simply the not-yet-sick. What does one do in such situations? We read of people locking themselves up, refusing to see or meet anyone. Since human life is inescapably social at some level, such draconian measures cannot be fully maintained, and hence we see the precautions: stay clear of people's breath, avoid their smell, talk to people at a distance, keep preservatives in your mouth (!) and in your clothes, so as to ward off infection and death.

I have called Defoe visionary, even though his narrator is eminently sane and reasonable, because his text shows us what the social ramifications of disease can be, measures just how the social fabric can be systematically *unraveled*. The depiction of plague's inroads and of the pitiful but manic responses of the (still) living returns, in its way, to the theme of quarantine, but now seen as the imprisoned and paranoid self, the self that has come to look upon the entire world as just so much toxic threat.

Defoe is visionary in still other ways also. Drawn invariably to the drama of little people confronting large situations, Defoe gives us, in his narrator H.F., a splendid instance of journalistic integrity and passion, of going fearlessly straight up to the horror in order to report on it and take its measure. At the book's beginning, the narrator and his older brother disagree about whether the right response to the London plague is to flee or to remain. The brother leaves, as do most of the well-heeled Londoners, including priests and doctors. H.F. stays, and even though he frequently chides himself for doing so, I think we can agree that his ultimate motivation is to *bear witness*. He calls this *curiosity*, and nowhere is it more on show than in his maniacal insistence on personally visiting the mass graveyard, the Pit, at night, in order to see for himself, firsthand, what plague is. He is warned by the sexton that this is dangerous, but H.F. insists, claiming that it will be an "Instructing Sight" for him, to which the sexton replies, "t'will be a Sermon to you, it may be, the best that ever you heard in your Life. 'Tis a speaking Sight . . . and has a Voice with it, and a loud one" (61).

"A speaking Sight" is about as good a definition for the visionary as I can imagine. Not in the sense of "sermon" but rather in the sense of art that plumbs our phenomenal world with such intensity that it makes us see and hear it centuries later in textual form, makes us capture the vital life pulsating there, a life at once richer and more labyrinthine than docile notation usually renders. At the very beginning of his tale, H.F. speaks of the initially infected city as a London that is "altered": "Sorrow and Sadness sat upon every Face," as if the citizens sensed the horror that was to come, and it is that sense of things the narrator seeks to capture and to pass on: "I wish I could repeat the very Sound of those Groans, and of those Exclamations that I heard from some poor dying Creatures, when in the Hight of their Agonies and Distress; and that I could make him that read this hear, as I imagine I now hear them, for the Sound seems still to Ring in my Ears" (104). I want to say that Defoe's "sight" still "speaks," and those who read this text do hear the groans of long ago, just as H.F. continues to. *A Journal of the Plague Year* belongs on the short list of artistic texts that convey the actual feel of our history, of where we have been, and—more presciently—of where we might end up.

Not all is dark in Defoe's *Journal*, however, since the author is equally intrigued by the scattered instances of ingenuity and exodus to which these penitential arrangements give rise. One recognizes the author of *Robinson Crusoe* and *Moll Flanders* in the beguiling story of the exploits of the joiner, the baker, and the sailor as they put their wits together and escape London, facing armed opposition and hostility in the countryside wherever they go. Their pluck, their feistiness and survivalist stratagems, their art in fooling others so as to create breathing space and maneuvering room, their ability to work together and to bring others onto their side, their "lifemanship" along straight artisanal as well as philosophical lines, speak for Defoe's deepest values, and announce his faith in the little man's resources when pitted against overwhelming odds. Here is his best answer against quarantine, the exercise of human freedom and creativity, even the making of community. Ultimately, as Defoe well knows from his eighteenth-century vantage point, this plague did not destroy London, and even though he wants to warn about the plague currently ravaging Provence, he is at pains to show how many English citizens rose to the challenge in 1665, not merely by not dying but by devising countertactics of their own.

Nonetheless, just as *Robinson Crusoe* is haunted by the threat of cannibalism and the still darker threat of solipsism and paranoia, so too is the *Journal* stamped by the sweep and even majesty of death. One feels that the onslaught and spectacle of massive dying engages Defoe *as writer,* and that he pulls out all the stops in order to capture these horrible events, producing something of a mixed media work that combines lists, schedules, archival notations, along with close, even daring upfront observations, and more distant reflections, both moral and philosophical. Hence, the narrator, cool and cautious though he is, is mesmerized by much of what he sees, and experiences a kind of siren call, an irresistible urgency to go to the scene of the crime whenever he can, regardless of personal danger or the injunctions of martial law. As noted, he simply must see, with his own eyes, the infamous pits where the dead bodies are delivered, piled up into huge mounds, and then covered with lime. And his visit to this ghastly place, done surreptitiously at night, seems a kind of descent into the underworld, an encounter with mass death and physiological decay, possessed of a starkness and scale that reminds a modern reader of the first accounts of concentration camps or the more recent ones of political massacres and dug-up grave sites.

This new regime has a startling kind of clarity, and one's relations with life and death, with self and other, are reconceived. It is in this sense that Defoe is far more than the note-taking journalist he sometimes appears, because at key moments in his best work, the world suddenly opens up and out, becomes at once larger and more transparent. Here is where metaphysics crashes into the author's pedestrian scheme, and the long view comes into focus. Sickness and death are entries as well as exits, thresholds leading to a radically altered sense of self and world.

Such a vision can have close parallels with the established views of the Church, but it is an index of Defoe's unbribable honesty that he ultimately parts ways with any utopian or doctrinal reading of the plague; we see this most sharply in the book's final pages where the author measures the brevity of London's spiritual transformation and acknowledges that the new dispensation brought about by a glimpse into the beyond is not a lasting phenomenon, but rather a temporary state of affairs. Soon enough the opaqueness, discord, and vice of everyday London life returns to the scene. As for the genesis of the plague or the reasons for its cessation, Defoe remains suspicious of all human intervention and interpretation, claiming that God alone is answerable here. This invocation of the divine may well be the exit perspective of *A Journal of the Plague Year,* but it cannot be said to govern the narrative itself, and we read this book with interest today because it maps out, with great precision, how a huge, secular metropolis comes to terms with massive sickness and death. Defoe's book does honor to the resources of municipal order and medicine, and he makes us realize what it looks like when a bustling modern city is paralyzed, laid low.

But plague itself will be ultimately remembered here as the great *metteur en scène,* the cathartic agent that recasts human doing in shocking ways. Defoe's eyes are focused on the vital but insufficient resources of civic order, and he measures with fascination the equally vital but insufficient resources of the human subject. Ultimately, the behavior of the ants interests him more than the structure of the anthill, so to speak, because he sees in these sometimes creative, sometimes manic explosions of energy and will a precious record of human potential, revealed in both its hideousness and its resilience. Without ever being told, we nonetheless learn that the authorities' policies of quarantine and sequestration were profoundly ineffective and wrongheaded because the living will not be corralled in this manner and because the presence of plague in close quarters—the city, especially the family—catalyzes unheard-of human energies beyond the reach and control of any penal or monitoring system. In this regard, the Foucauldian reading of the *Journal,* with its emphasis on the State's disciplinary practices, gets Defoe right yet backward. One may say, in conclusion, that *A Journal of the Plague Year* is one of our premier descriptions of a city in crisis, arguably valid for numerous decimated cities—Pompei, Hiroshima, Dresden—whose sagas have not been told. But plague is not a volcanic eruption, atom bomb, or fire; deadly infection adds a unique narrative and relational complexity to these grim matters, and no amount of medical advances is likely to make Defoe a dated figure.

On the contrary, Defoe is more than ever our contemporary. His discussion of the paranoia engendered by plague, communicable disease, and above all the invisibility of infection is rich in lessons for our time. Defoe speaks of the anxiety that beset Londoners, of the epistemological horror show that urban life had become. And he also speaks of the origins of plague: human connection, but also trade, exchange, circulation of goods and of people. It is entirely to the point that H.F. discusses England's altered image among other European nations, noting the Europeans' frightened conviction that all English goods are contaminated, noting also their shrewd business sense that such convictions may also improve the Europeans' own bottom line. Reading *A Journal of the Plague Year* in a time not only of AIDS, but also of paranoia concerning mad cow disease, hoof-and-mouth disease, genetically altered grain and foodstuffs for export/import, even smallpox and anthrax—and the furious waves of anxiety and suspicion that accompany these contemporary developments—we may well feel that Defoe saw it all coming.

SOMETHING IS ROTTEN IN
THE STATE OF ENGLAND: CHARLES DICKENS

London does not experience plague during the nineteenth century, and yet Dickens's *Bleak House* demands consideration as one of literature's most powerful and far-reaching accounts of a city threatened by disease, particularly smallpox and typhus, and more generally in the form of a blight that ranges from filth and pollution to brutal socioeconomic conditions. In the neighborhood of eight hundred pages long, this elephantine novel puts off many readers by dint of its sheer bulk, and I have firsthand experience with the uphill battle of getting either students or friends to tackle it. Moreover, Dickensian English—garrulous, slow paced, relishing the syntactical and semantic scope of a leisurely and expansive nineteenth-century literary idiom—is a hard sell today. This is a great pity, because the stupendous fireworks that Dickens routinely pulls off depend entirely on the portentous equipment he is using; not unlike the amount of power necessary to get a 747 or an airbus off the ground, Dickensian plots use a lot of fuel, but they are something to behold when they are airborne. You may still feel that other craft go faster, or that you prefer sleeker, trimmer vehicles, but if the job consists of getting an entire small city into the sky, or an entire large city into language, Dickens is unbeatable. And for our purposes of illuminating the dimensionality of plague, the scale and reach of his fiction are of paramount importance.

In *Bleak House* (which I take to be the author's supreme work) plague comes packaged in its more modern and invisible form: the off-limits slums and ghettos where disease flourishes. Dickens makes us realize that the central slum of the novel, Tom-all-Alone's, albeit shrouded in obscurity and unknown to most London dwellers, is utterly luminous as a kind of barometer for measuring the weather of midcentury Victorian society at large. Like Sophocles, Dickens is drawn to issues of sexual secrets and transgressions, as well as to the threat of social slippage and blurred class lines. His novel resembles the Greek play via its insistent redefinition of family/community and its view of disease as overarching metaphor for denied connections and concealed linkages. Ultimately, Sophocles is Dickens's mentor in the exploration of identity, the reconfiguring of Oedipus' relations and origin as the mystery of the motherless Esther Summerson's birth. I want to suggest that the story of a diseased community inevitably reconfigures the individual subject's self-definition, even though "scientific" thinking would hardly posit this connection. Yet, such larger ramifications are, in some sense, precisely what literature brings to the table.

Bleak House opens with a memorable depiction of London fog, and one cannot fail to see that Dickens's entire story takes place under the aegis of fog, impaired visibility. And it is not far-fetched to posit fog—perceptual and epistemological murk—as a generic feature of the plague-text, something that runs through the genre, as seen in the blindness-sight motifs that Tiresias brings to the *Oedipus* and in the dreadful uncertainty of Defoe's Londoners as to whether they or their kin are infected, as seen in evidence in the mystery surrounding Esther Summerson's birth and all the other mysteries of *Bleak House,* and conspicuously seen even in a filmic version of these matters, Polanski's *Chinatown,* where we are repeatedly told that Chinatown is the place where you don't know who is who. The Sophoclean legacy of hidden linkages is most easily read in Dickens as a vital critique of Victorian façade, so that the drama of illegitimacy that drives the Dedlock plot and exposes the aristocratic Lady Dedlock as the orphan Esther's mother, is Dickens's way of bringing the skeletons out of the closet. A good chunk of nineteenth-century British fiction is cued to this exposure of sexual secrets, and no one surpasses Dickens in his genius for exploiting the sleuthing energies released by such a plot.

But these matters are immeasurably thickened and broadened when we factor infectious disease into this whodunit formula. There is something rotten in London, and the famous fog is also to be understood, more directly, as pollution and material filth—as real dirt in real air—every bit as much as a symbol for blindness. Pollution is a remarkably precise term for *Bleak House* because it too announces the slippage of boundaries, in particular the boundary between inside and outside, so that the germs in the air do not remain there but come into people's lungs and minds to work their spells on the inside. Like Sophocles' play with its incestuously linked figures, Dickens's novel is radically ecological, but whereas the Greek playwright sticks to a few main players, the nineteenth-century writer exploits to the hilt what a modern ecological fiction would look like: a sprawling mix—always picturesque, often grotesque—of human creatures drawn from all walks of life, each with his or her own values and dialects, comprising (when seen together) the ultimate target of the text: London.

But the more potent ecological thrust of Dickens's vision has to do with the interdependence of this mass of people, an interdependence that constitutes the veritable backbone of Dickensian plot—a schema for showing how related and bound to one another all these folks turn out to be. Dickens's characters, like most human subjects, think of themselves as individuals, as contoured creatures with a measure of agency. And some of his characters, such as the aristocratic Sir Leicester Dedlock, assume a great deal more still: their social and economic station, shored up by Victorian class arrangements, confers a form of natural protection and independence to them, making them "lords" in all senses of the term, with unlimited power, but without vulnerability. They have, one might say, immunity. It hardly needs saying that this mind-set was a common one in nineteenth-century European culture, and it is still going strong today.

In an ecological fiction, precisely this atomic mind-set is targeted, and if the fiction is sufficiently virulent, the individualist ethos is blown sky-high. Dickens is out to show us, in his own way, that all immune systems are fictive. Pollution and disease bring bad news to the Dedlocks, not simply by dint of exposing Lady Dedlock's sexual liaison with Nemo, but rather more massively, in terms of a storming of the fortress, an onslaught against all their pretensions of haughty independence. They will be assaulted in their most cherished belief: that they are "untouchable." In the Dedlock worldview, and indeed in the worldview of complacent London assumptions, there can be no connection between the aristocratic stronghold, Chesney Wold, and the disease-ridden slum at the core of the city and at the core of the novel, Tom-all-Alone's. But the wind blows in Dickens's novel, sovereignly traversing geographic and conceptual space, meshing all in its path. In one of the novel's most spellbinding passages, after telling us that Parliament loves to *talk* about reforming the slums while *doing* nothing at all, the author enunciates the new ecosystem at work, yielding a new social result: the community of disease:

> But he [Tom-all-Alone's] has his revenge. Even the winds are his messengers, and they serve him in these hours of darkness. There is not a drop of Tom's corrupted blood but propagates infection and contagion somewhere. It shall pollute, this very night, the choice stream (in which chemists on analysis would find the genuine nobil-ity) of a Norman house, and his Grace shall not be able to say Nay to the infamous alliance. There is not an atom of Tom's slime, not a cubic inch of any pestilential gas in which he lives, not one obscen-ity or degradation about him, not an ignorance, not a wickedness, not a brutality of his committing, but shall work its retribution, through every order of society, up to the proudest of the proud, and to the highest of the high. Verily, what with tainting, plundering, and spoiling, Tom has his revenge. (575–576)

As this stunning passage—with a thrust at once moral, political, and even medical—makes clear, "immunity" is exactly what no one has. "Stop him!" is the suggestive title of the chapter in which these lines ap-pear, and whereas those words refer overtly to the efforts to "catch" Jo (the emblematic child of the slums, more orphaned even than Esther, destined to be her double), they also are nonetheless tragically ironic, in that Jo—and the disease he carries—cannot be stopped, but will indeed be "caught." Jo and Tom-all-Alone's are familializing forces which cannot be naysaid. The ecological fiction teaches us about neighbors we never knew we had, neighbors who are bound to us in ways we need to see.

This, too, means going beyond the retinal illusion of individual self and the still more stubborn social illusion of distance and difference. Nothing proves this argument more forcefully than the experience of infection, for it is here that the never dreamed-of "new family" announces itself physiologically, in the flesh. A great nineteenth-century theme is coming into view here—the remaking of the family, the bonding of disparate figures into a familial mesh—and we can find it in Whitman's democratic poems, Balzac's social critiques, even Baudelaire's city meditations. But nowhere are the consequences more brilliantly drawn out than in *Bleak House*.

On the face of it, this constellation would consist of Esther discovering her long-lost biological mother, Lady Dedlock, which is what the dirty-laundry Victorian plot emphasizes. Yet plague has its word to say as well, and the more far-reaching family paradigm is brought about by Esther's fateful linkage with the orphan child, Jo, exemplary diseased citizen of Tom-all-Alone's. Esther touches and nurses the sick Jo. Next day, the boy has strangely disappeared, and Dickens's prose again rises to the occasion:

> "It's the boy, miss," said he.
> "Is he worse?" I inquired.
> "Gone, miss."
> "Dead!"
> "Dead, miss? No. Gone clean off." (401)

"Gone clean off" turns out to be horribly untrue, since he has infected Charley (Esther's maid), who will infect Esther, who then goes on to live out her dread sisterhood by catching his smallpox, becoming blind (for a while), and then losing (permanently) her beauty. Disease moves. Jo is hounded in this book by London authority, told incessantly to "move on," and we gradually realize that he does "move on," in that he moves into others, alters them, comes close to killing them.

Dickens's book is marked, in all ways, by the imperious inroads of sickness and disease, and like both Sophocles and Defoe, he is out to show that these issues augur life and death for the culture at large. Let us recall those harrowing last lines of Blake's poem "London," "But most through midnight streets I hear / How the youthful Harlot's curse / Blasts the new born Infant's tear, / And blights with plagues the Marriage hearse." Early in the novel, we are led to a squalid hovel where the brick makers live, and we encounter the paradigmatic event of this text: the death of an infant. Dickens does narrative high jinx with this episode, in that Esther places her handkerchief over the dead child, a handkerchief that we discover later as precious possession of Lady Dedlock, as unacknowledged sign of blood connection and motherly love. And perhaps divine love as well: brought into that same hovel, Snagsby the stationer is reminded, in looking at one of the surviving babies, "of another infant, encircled with light, that he has seen in pictures" (287). Yet *Bleak House* seems to center around doomed children: Esther is parentless, the baby dies, Jo dies, Richard dies. Who is responsible, Dickens is asking, for these deaths?

The answer seems to be a large one, including all deficient mothers—Lady Dedlock, Mrs. Jellyby, Mrs. Pardiggle—but clearly going beyond these individual figures to point to the social and economic order itself, the order that produces Tom-all-Alone's. Hence, Esther—a figure of Victorian rectitude and piety who can be impossibly cloying at times, with her sobriquet of Dame Durden—almost dies, becomes pockmarked and permanently scarred, all as a result of her nursing the sick Jo. Dickens makes us realize that this act of contact, motivated by human charity, illuminates, nay determines, Esther Summerson's identity far more fully than the long-hinted mother-daughter link does. "Motivated by human charity" makes it sound as if such contacts were volitional, and in some limited but beautiful sense they are volitional, but the grimmer truth of the novel has little to do with private generosity and everything to do with the tentacular, miasmic vision of a writer who knows that connection is *prior* to individuation, that the simple acts of living and breathing are in truth versions of incessant *traffic,* that no human subject—especially no subject living in a metropolis like London—can claim immunity or think himself or herself safe behind the walls of stone, class, or flesh.

When Esther first goes to the squalid brick kilns, she has a singular thought: "I had for a moment an undefinable impression of myself as being something different from what I then was" (393). When the fateful, deforming smallpox fever comes on, she again becomes confused about identity, "with a curious sense of fullness, as if I were becoming too large altogether" (404). At the height of her pain and transformation, she suffers a visionary redefinition of Self as being exploded: "Dare I hint at that worse time when, strung together somewhere in great black space, there was a flaming necklace, or ring, or starry circle of some kind, of which *I* was one of the beads! And when my only prayer was to be taken off from the rest, and when it was such inexplicable agony and misery to be a part of the dreadful thing?" (447).

Personal disease is translated by fever and delirium into its appropriate cosmic frame—"flaming necklace, or ring, or starry circle"—as the infected human subject is brought agonizingly (there is no other mode of transportation here; agony is the trip) into this brotherhood and sisterhood, initiated into the system by pure pain, as if pain were the ultimate connective tissue, the visceral and neural linkage that explodes all notions of bounded self. There can be no orphans in such a scheme, despite all the social labels we wear. Plague matters for Dickens, one wants to say, even more than sexual secrets or hidden identity, in that it writes on our very flesh the unwitting badge of citizenship in the world. Reformer and passionate student of urban hygiene that he was, Dickens announces that segregation is a myth, that the slum and its ostracized inhabitants actually possess the keys to the City, and that their blighted lives are as uncontainable and unchartable as the Thames that Blake depicted in his version of London, such that their suffering and their venom infects the entire body politic.

But how would you represent this infection, other than by showing people "catch" it from each other? Dickens's novel remains in our minds as a tour de force along just these lines, as he tirelessly finds ways to write plague and contamination. We have already mentioned the filthy London air and the virulent winds that spread infection throughout the city. Could one actually devise a "language" for showing these matters? The very geography of this sprawling plot works in this fashion, since each major figure—Lady Dedlock (twice, fatally the last time), Esther, Bucket, Snagsby—will make his/her way literally into the dreadful Tom-all-Alone's, as if a magnet pulled them there. The "outsiders" are drawn into the pit, but the pit also "moves on," itself. The stunning scene, late in the novel—after the news is out about Lady Dedlock's transgressions and death, when Chesney Wold is invaded by the Beckett-like Grandfather Smallweed, the odious Chadbands, and the crazed Mrs. Snagsby, each rounding out the "dirty laundry" plot right in the aristocrat's drawing room—seems to figure forth the storming of the citadel. There is a weird *translation* of slum and scum into the manor house, establishing a Dickensian parallel to Poe's "The Masque of the Red Death," in which we see the death coded as a lethal affair of unstoppable breaking and entering, disease on the move, against which no fortress can hold.

But the most striking index of spreading sickness is to be found, I think, in the novel's most infamous event: the death of Krook, owner of the rag-and-bone shop, by Spontaneous Combustion. Dickens was understandably testy about this episode, claiming to have it on good medical evidence that such physiological events could take place, that someone actually could *explode*. It is worth remembering that Guppy and Weevle, busily spying on Krook to discover his secrets, had been encountering grease and soot all over the place, prior to the actual discovery of the body, even to the extent of Guppy's very fingers being covered by a strange fluid. A moment later they enter Krook's room, search for him, espy a "crumpled black thing" upon the floor, and then realize with horror that this is Krook, spontaneously combusted. The "thick yellow liquor" coming from the dead man's body but now coating the surfaces of rooms seems a haunting and precise image of Dickensian flux, of the *traffic* that binds seemingly independent figures, of the "inside" wildly emancipated and turned viscous, on the move, indeed "moving on." Germs in air or carried by fleas defy perception, so Dickens has elected to materialize the issue rather hugely, to splatter this secret-filled man all over the environment, to coat others with his residue. Krook, illiterate keeper of secrets, has exploded, has been writ large (as it were), as a kind of oily somatic version of the blood that runs down palace walls in Blake, but brought here to the pitch of actual explosion.

This explosion is to be followed by others. At the end of the book we are told that the nightmarish legal suit, Jarndyce and Jarndyce, responsible for much of the suffering depicted in the novel, is at last to be settled. But when Esther reaches Chancery, she runs into an explosion of lawyers, "streaming out, looking flushed and hot, and bringing a quantity of bad air with them" (796). This purgative moment, akin to the lancing of a wound, is capped by the revelation that no money is left in the centuries-old suit, that the lawyers have gotten it all, and Richard Carstone, whose entire life has been cued to this outcome, must needs speak to the judge; but his words come out like this: "He was stopped by his mouth being full of blood . . ." (798). That mouth full of blood is of a piece with Krook's spontaneous combustion, in that each reveals the human body—its history, dreams, and passions—as fluids that build up, mount to a frenzy, and explode.

A mouth full of blood is also an arresting, frightening image of language itself: can it be incidental that disease in this book is insistently coded in lingual terms? that Charley's smallpox is preceded by her efforts at orthography, that the dying Jo begs Snagsby the law-writer to write his death "uncommon precious large" (594)? that Sir Leicester's agony (upon seeing his life wrecked, his wife departed) requires a slate on which Mrs. Rouncewell translates the stricken aristocrat's gutteral sounds into letters and words? that Krook himself, the other "Lord Chancellor" of the book, has letters galore surrounding him but cannot *read* them? Is this not the perennial challenge of the writer: to bring to legibility all those hidden or obscure forces that bathe and coerce human life? to translate the teeming and tentacular and incestuous life of the city into a language as material and in-your-face as fog?

Spontaneous combustion is Charles Dickens's surreal image of evil and illicit connection turned somatic, then horribly emancipated from the precincts of the body to become pure, spreading flux, a kind of urban pus. Here would be the very script of infection which underwrites Dickens's saga of London transgressions and rot. He achieves a staggering coherence of these materials by insistently linking them to letters, slates, words, and utterance, yielding what we'd have to call a massive diagnosis, a printout, of the polis-in-plague. The wide-angle lens of the nineteenth-century novel captures the diseased antics of an entire culture, as if infection were at last recognized as the essential map of our hidden linkages with one another, providing a kind of luminous urban hypertext with its nodal points and intersections—sites where exchange occurs: exchange of power, money, sex, disease—all on show, inviting our inspection, not even requiring that we click on them.

THE PLAGUE COMMUNITY: ALBERT CAMUS

Camus's landmark novel of 1947, *The Plague,* is at once a modern remake of Defoe's book, a meditation on the inroads of evil, and an allegory of the Nazi occupation. Camus is overtly philosophical, determined to "open up" Defoe's close-to-the-vest narrative, so that the fuller ethical ramifications of a collective scourge can be unpacked. Where Defoe is drawn to the drama of quarantine, Camus is out to measure how such a dispensation—the Algerian city of Oran is essentially under siege, so that no one can enter and no one can leave—redefines crucial humanist notions such as love, memory, and solidarity.

All too often Camus is simply dismissed as Sartre's lesser sibling, the "other" existentialist, and what this gets most wrong is the generosity and warmth that we find in Camus's best work, a kind of creatural seriousness about the goodness of being alive, of inhabiting a body, of living on the earth. (You'll search in vain for any of this in Sartre.) Hence, Defoe's quarantine is reconceived by Camus as separation, as if plague were a systemwide assault on love: "Thus, for example, a feeling normally as individual as the ache of separation from those one loves suddenly became a feeling in which all shared alike and—together with fear—the greatest affliction of the long period of exile that lay ahead" (67).

In this book, as in *The Stranger,* Camus emerges as a writer who richly understands the sensuous, material world, who gives flesh its due. Hence, the character of Rambert, the journalist separated from his lover, is especially poignant, for he has just come to the discovery that he is meant for love, that love is his actual vocation: "The truth is I wasn't brought into the world to write newspaper articles. . . . But it's quite likely I was brought into the world to live with a woman" (85). I can imagine very few novelists capable of this remark. Plague brutally crushes this newfound calling, as we watch Rambert initially seek ways of fleeing the diseased city before finally realizing that his personal happiness must be sacrificed ("it may be shameful to be happy by oneself" [209]), that he must remain with the dying and play what role he can. The pathos of the novel stems from Camus's understanding of the *gravity* of personal happiness—the preciousness of bodies, of human tenderness, of the frail world of love that we construct—and it is, of course, this basic orientation that illuminates the horror of plague. Both Sophocles and Defoe seem, by contrast, untouched by the human tug that animates Camus's novel. Suspicious of postures and posing, the French writer respects tenderness and intimacy, and his people appear in their humbleness, fragility, and low-to-the-ground courage.

The Plague is a sober narrative, and its commitment to human life is all the more profound because the tonality is matter-of-fact and unsensationalist. The body counts in this book: the priest Paneloux, who desperately seeks to bring this reign of death into some kind of alignment with God's will by claiming it to be God's punishment meted out to a secular world, suffers enormously in his struggles, suffers physically, dies of the plague. Camus makes us understand the immense "stretching" and dislocation meted out to this decent man of the cloth who is wrecked by the rift between conviction and experience. The little man of the people, Grand, with his ridiculous literary project and his utterly pedestrian willingness to work for the public good, is proposed as the book's hero, if hero there must be: "the narrator commends to his readers, with, to his thinking, perfect justice, this insignificant and obscure hero who had to his credit only a little goodness of heart and a seemingly absurd ideal. This will render to the truth its due, to the addition of two and two its sum of four, and to heroism the secondary place that rightly falls to it, just after, never before, the noble claim of happiness" (137–138). Note Camus's words: *happiness*—not, say, "wisdom" or "truth" or "soul"—is our noblest claim.

The major protagonist, Doctor Rieux, who cannot accept the religious view of plague as punishment (" 'I've seen too much of hospitals to relish the idea of collective punishment' " [125]), says that the priest would change his views had he ever seen enough dying people. Rieux is the book's pragmatic humanist, the one who does not have time for metaphysics: " 'I have no idea what is awaiting me, or what will happen when all this ends. For the moment I know this; there are sick people and they need curing. Later on, perhaps, they'll think things over; and so shall I" (127). Pure research also must await its turn; late in the book, he says, "a man can't cure and know at the same time. So let's cure as quickly as we can. That's the more urgent job" (210). Once again, Camus's priorities show: metaphysical (or scientific) inquiry must take a backseat to aiding the living. Camus's doctor works feverishly, to the point of sickness, in his uphill battle to save Oran's sick, even when no medical solutions are at hand.

Tarrou, the text's most enigmatic and poetic figure, the one who intuits more deeply than the others what this incursion of death is really about, weakens and lessens before our eyes, dying also at book's close even though plague is finally receding. His is perhaps the most memorable discourse of the novel, as he recounts his past to Rieux and articulates Camus's largest ethical vision: the simple but massive requirement not to be a murderer. In this line of reasoning, all living creatures bear the plague within them, are the cause of others' deaths, and this collusion is insidious, goes by the name of civilization, hence mandating an ethic of resistance: " 'All I maintain is that on this earth there are pestilences and there are victims, and it's up to us, so far as possible, not to join forces with the pestilences'" (253–254).

The allegorical dimensions of Camus's novel are adumbrated in these lines, and some may feel that actual plague is thereby diminished, loses its true virulence by being equated with generalized murder. But one can also see it the other way, as Camus's intuition that collective disease and dying bring an unbearable focus and precision to the human project by illuminating the generic duty of the living to be on the side of life. Such an injunction may seem Olympian and highbrow, but how many of us have truly pondered the reach of such a command: to be on life's side? Who rises every day to this? Plague forces just these issues.

But the match can be horribly unequal, and Camus does not flinch when it comes to bearing witness. To be on life's side means to hallow human flesh, flesh that is essentially tortured by the onslaught of plague. The novel's moment of greatest pathos revolves around the death of the child, a close-up sequence of plague's might and the futility of human defenses, this time focused in the true slaughter of the innocent. The dying child, described with unblinking physiological realism, characterized symbolically in its "grotesque parody of crucifixion" (215), emits a scream that, for the purposes of this study, continues the dirge of human pain that we have seen elsewhere: Blake, Munch, Baldwin, Bergman:

In the small face, rigid as a mask of grayish clay, slowly the lips parted and from them rose a long, incessant scream, hardly varying with his respiration, and filling the ward with a fierce, indignant protest, so little childish that it seemed like a collective voice issuing from all the sufferers there. Rieux clenched his jaws, Tarrou looked away. Rambert went and stood beside Castel, who closed the book lying on his knees. Paneloux gazed down at the small mouth, fouled with the sores of the plague and pouring out the angry death-cry that has sounded through the ages of mankind. He sank on his knees, and all present found it natural to hear him say in a voice hoarse but clearly audible across that nameless, never ending wail:

"My God, spare this child!"

But the wail continued without cease and the other sufferers began to grow restless. The patients at the far end of the ward, whose little broken cries had gone on without a break, now quickened their tempo so that they flowed together in one unbroken cry, while the others' groans grew louder. A gust of sobs swept through the room, drowning Paneloux's prayer, and Rieux, who was still tightly gripping the rail of the bed, shut his eyes, dazed with exhaustion and disgust. (217)

This long citation is not easy going, yet I feel that it reveals what is deepest in Camus. The term *humanist* is frequently applied to him, and I have emphasized the warmth of his vision, but there is also a raw courage that surfaces in his work, a refusal to avert one's eyes or to escape into grand phrases. This courage is anything but steely; on the contrary, it strikes me as arduous, hard to sustain, at the very edge of composure. The author forces us to look head-on at horror because his ethics acquire their meaning in no other way: happiness and life are precious because pain and torture are horrible. This "death-cry that has sounded through the ages of mankind" is little less than an indictment against God, a recognition that all of us live in the penal colony, and that the death of a child is at once natural and intolerable.

Camus's writing in this novel seems largely straightforward and artless, but in this passage, he achieves an unusual eloquence. The power—and the sacrilege—of this event are imaged in almost natural terms as a cry that becomes a plaint that becomes a wave that becomes almost tidal in its sweep and reach. Once again we see how utterly the scream goes through the house. The priest's prayer is blotted out by the force of this child's cry, and the doctor, exhausted and even disgusted, can only struggle for balance and bear witness. *Disgust* in the face of such obscene suffering is, I think, Camus's humanist trademark, his principled rejection of *any rationale* that could justify plague. The great challenge for mankind, stated early on in the story, is entirely secular: how to be a saint in a world without God.

If Defoe is everywhere present in this story of plague, most evident in the novel's sobriety, so too are Poe and Artaud behind the scenes here, as Camus shows us what a necropolis looks like, how anarchy is always kept barely at bay, how much horror subtends this text's even manner. Early on, as if to salute Defoe, we hear of a raving man, marked by the disease, racing outside to leap on the first woman he sees, embracing her, screaming to her that he is the plague. Some rioting occurs, and people are executed, but what force can execution have during plague?

The most Poe-like touch comes as the narrator recounts a performance of Glück's *Orphée* in the plague-stricken city, at which Eurydice's flight from her lover, her return to the realm of death, catalyzed a remarkable exodus beginning with the exit of the singer himself, as he collapsed in the midst of the pastoral decor, and closing with the increasingly hysterical evacuation of all parties:

> For at the same moment the orchestra stopped playing, the audience rose and began to leave the auditorium, slowly and silently at first, like worshippers leaving church when the service ends, or a death-chamber after a farewell visit to the dead, women lifting their skirts and moving with bowed heads, men steering the ladies by the elbow to prevent their brushing against the tip-up seats at the ends of the rows. But gradually their movements quickened, whispers rose to exclamations, and finally the crowd stampeded toward the exits, wedged together in the bottlenecks, and pouring out into the street in a confused mass, with shrill cries of dismay. (201)

In a novel marked by dignity and composure, this baroque scene of collective panic and hysteria stands out for its virulence, and also for its glaring collusion with myth and fable, as if the ancient Orphic story of the battle among love and death and art had jumped the border from representation into reality, had—like the plague—shown itself to be uncontainable. To perform the story of Orpheus and Eurydice in a plague-struck city is perhaps to defy the gods. It is one thing to dine at a fine restaurant before taking in an evening at the opera or theater, to witness onstage the grand gestures of fable and history, and then to take a cab home and go to sleep. But what happens when the carnage and horrors onstage—the sort of fare to which we assign the label of *art*—are of a piece with the world outside the theater?

One remembers Susan Sontag's decision to stage *Waiting for Godot* in Sarajevo, or, for that matter, still earlier stagings of *Godot* back in the 1940s at the prison in San Quentin, all of them moments when the most extreme performances of art come into striking (and sometimes dreadful) synchrony with the places where they are shown, with the people to whom they are shown. We have been told frequently that artistic and media images of violence and pornography can have real social impact, can alter behavior. *Orphée* pushes the Oran audience over the edge; how bearable would the books discussed in this chapter be to us if we were experiencing catastrophe or mass destruction? We are all familiar with the idle question, what book would you want if you were a castaway on a desert island? But what about its opposite number, what would you read if plague or nuclear war struck?

But what we most remember *The Plague* for is the quiet but vulnerable humanism of its vision. Plague is, in every sense, *reductive*. Human happiness—a richer thing by far than heroism—is scuttled; memory is cashiered, made useless, by the new regime of quarantine and separation; love and its life-sustaining egoism are suffocated in the narrow war against lethal disease. The city of plague is a lessening in all ways, a shrinkage of human possibility that goes beyond the actual death tolls.

Camus's reverence for human life shines through this story of systemic butchery, helping us to a sense of how disease dirties us, despoils us, robs us not only of health but of the small, natural miracles that imbue daily life with richness. "*Les hommes meurent et ne sont pas heureux*" ("Men die and are not happy") is the theme song of Camus's absurdist play *Caligula,* but in this book about physical suffering, plague replaces the despotic emperor, and we measure, as a kind of nostalgic backdrop, the immense capacity for happiness and pleasure that life offers the living.

Hence, the late scene, when plague is withdrawing, of Rieux and Tarrou swimming together, breathes a kind of wistful but pagan cosmic order into this text: two men floating in the sea—sustained both by their own efforts and by the tug of the elements, in harmony and solidarity (not only with themselves, but with the planet), swimming soundlessly at the same pace—offer us a radiant image of Camus's belief system. It is a belief system that is sorely tried by plague. Some few may be changed for the better, and Rambert, the journalist for whom love was a vocation, for whom this diseased city was an absurd accident in time and space, actually discovered solidarity: " 'But now that I've seen what I have seen, I know that I belong here whether I want it or not' " (209). Yet, can personal happiness "return," we wonder, as Rambert desperately embraces his lover, who, at story's end, at plague's end, at last has entered Oran? The journalist himself is far from sure, for he senses that he has been permanently altered, that the citizens of this city are deluded in their stubborn belief "that plague can come and go without changing anything in men's hearts" (295).

But for the most part plague betokens an injury that is collective. This is why Tarrou's impassioned protest against complicity with murder and assassination rings true in this book, points to its ultimate concerns, its truest fears. All of Camus's tenderness is visible in the book's eloquent closing lines, as Rieux observes the gaiety and madcap happiness of the city now recovered from plague and realizes that such joy is always precarious, always threatened:

He knew what those jubilant crowds did not know but could have
learned from books: that the plague bacillus never dies or disappears
for good; that it can lie dormant for years and years in furniture and
linen-chests; that it bides its time in bedrooms, cellars, trunks and
bookshelves; and that perhaps the day would come again when, for
the bane and the enlightening of men, it would rouse up its rats again
and send them forth to die in a happy city. (308)

This beautiful closing passage tells us that plague cannot be exterminated. The extermination of men, women, and children, the destruction
of happy cities, seems coded in the very genes of human civilization, always ready to be reawakened. Plague's origins are to be found in our
homes and hearts as much as in our laboratories and slums. Books, the
writer claims, teach us this. Camus's own book was published in 1947,
and he died in 1960, but the latter half of the twentieth century gives
ample evidence of his prophecy. Collective mania and infection punctuate modern history, and the sanctity of human flesh and happiness has
been annihilated on a massive scale, over and over. Prague, Hanoi,
Dubrovnik, Belgrade, Belfast, Baghdad, Grozny, Kabul, countless
cities in Africa and the Third World decimated by AIDS and poverty,
perhaps even pockets of the U.S.A.: many are the cities laid waste by
the rats.

SEEING PLAGUE: OPENING THE SEALS: INGMAR BERGMAN

Exactly a decade after Camus wrote his meditation on plague as a reflection on the recent horrors of World War II and the German Occupation of France, the filmmaker Ingmar Bergman moved into international
prominence by dint of an unforgettable film, *The Seventh Seal.*
Bergman, known until then as a maker of cultish Swedish films, had
been pondering the theme of this gothic work for a number of years
(had earlier written a theatrical script entitled *Wood-Painting,* which
contains virtually the entire plot of the film). The Swedish director is no

less topical than the French novelist: if the Nazi phenomenon was Camus's immediate symbolic backdrop, the specter of nuclear holocaust—a specter increasingly occupying people's fears in the 1950s—was Bergman's subtext. How, Bergman has to have asked himself, could you *show* to a complacent public what the end of the world looks like?

For Ingmar Bergman, son of a prominent pastor, there was an obvious verbal text at hand, the Book of Revelation, describing the famously sealed book of apocalypse. Bergman's gambit is clear: the film is to open up these seals. Hence, *The Seventh Seal* tackles no less than the ultimate, unsurvivable *revelation* that depicts world's end; at both the beginning and end of the film we hear the portentous words, the full script of which goes like this:

6. And when he had opened the seventh seal, there was silence in Heaven about the space of half an hour. (Rev. 8:1)

7. The first angel sounded, and there followed hail and fire mingled with blood, and they were cast upon the earth: and the third part of trees was burnt up, and all the green grass was burnt up. (Rev. 8:7)

8. And the second angel sounded, and as it were a great mountain burning with fire was cast into the sea: and the third part of the sea became blood. (Rev. 8:8)

9. And the third part of the creatures which were in the sea, and had life, died; and the third part of the ships were destroyed. (Rev. 8:9)

10. And the third angel sounded, and there fell a great star from heaven, burning as it were a lamp, and it fell upon the third part of the rivers, and upon the fountains of waters. (Rev. 8:10)

11. And the name of the star is called Wormwood: and the third part of the waters became wormwood; and many men died of the waters, because they were made bitter. (Rev. 8:11)

12. And the fourth angel sounded, and the third part of the sun was smitten, and the third part of the moon, and the third part of the

stars; so as the third part of them was darkened, and the day
shone not for a third part of it, and the night likewise. (Rev. 8:12)

Here is your governing script, but it is not enough; you are producing a
film, not a sermon. But ponder the central image: opening the seals.
Bergman must have understood that this vital metaphor is no less than
the ultimate truth of film itself: to *open up,* to make visible, the secrets of
the world and the self. But this biblical story is still more evocative than
that. One almost hears the "Eureka," hears the gears mesh, as Bergman
ponders the insistent reference to destruction as *the third part,* and then
realizes that this has already happened: *a third part of the world has been
annihilated;* it happened during the Black Plague in the mid-fourteenth
century.

This, Bergman knows, is visual. And he knows it has an iconography
of great boldness and power because he has seen the pictures, seen them
firsthand, when wandering around on his own in the medieval churches
while his father preached (he used to accompany his father on pastoral
duties). This is how Bergman remembered those images many years
later:

Like all churchgoers at all times, I have often become lost in altar-
pieces, crucifixes, stained glass windows and murals, where I could
find Jesus and the robbers in blood and torment; Mary leaning on St
John, woman behold thy son, behold thy mother. Mary Magdalene,
the sinner. Who'd been the latest to fuck her? The Knight playing
chess with Death. Death sawing down the Tree of Life, a terrified
wretch wringing his hands at the top. Death leading the dance to the
Dark Lands, wielding his scythe like a flag, the congregation caper-
ing in a long line and the jester bringing up the rear. The devil keeping the pot boiling, the sinners hurtling headlong into the depths
and Adam and Eve discovering their nakedness. Some churches are
like aquaria, not a bare patch. People everywhere, saints, prophets,
angels, devils and demons all alive and flourishing. The here-and-

beyond billowing over walls and arches. Reality and imagination merged into robust myth-making. Sinner, behold thy labours, behold what awaits thee round the corner, behold the shadow behind thy back! (1988, 274)

I cite this long passage from Bergman's autobiography as an index not only of his germinal vision for his film about apocalypse, but also as a piece of cultural history. American audiences came and come to this film with a sense of astonishment at its exoticism and strange folklore— I know, I saw this film when it first came to America, when I was an undergraduate; and I teach it every year to bewildered students—whereas these images were as old and familiar as mother's milk for baby Bergman.

It all comes together: the Book of Revelation, the biblical images in medieval churches, the Black Plague. To warn us of a future we cannot afford to experience—nuclear war—Bergman goes back to a past where one third of Europe perished. And his supreme concern is *visual:* how to show what this experience feels like? how to merge reality and imagination into "robust myth-making"? how to convey what it is like when "the here-and-beyond billows over walls and arches"? Bergman locates this obsession with *seeing* it squarely within the film itself, so that we have a key scene where the Knight and the Squire stop in a church and encounter a painter of murals, called appropriately *"lilla Pictor"* ("little Pictor") after the famous Swedish muralist of the latter half of the fifteenth century, Albertus Pictus. Perched on a scaffolding, he explains to the Squire that his subject is "The Dance of Death," depicting the terror that plague brings, and he goes on to describe the body's fate: "You should see the boils on a diseased man's throat. You should see how his body shrivels up so that his legs look like knotted strings—like the man I've painted over there" (110). The Squire looks at the tortured figure, and the painter continues his lesson: "He tries to rip out the boil, he bites his hands, tears his veins open with his fingernails and his screams can be heard everywhere" (110). Standing in as a medieval version of

The flagellants.

Bergman himself, the church painter represents the filmmaker's project: to make people see graphically what plague is, to open the seals.

And that is what *The Seventh Seal* does. Plague is a time of torture: that meted out by the disease, and also that which we do to ourselves. Thus, Bergman treats us to the shocking procession of flagellants who whip their bodies in penance for their sins. No single still can convey the sense of mania and crazed behavior on view in this procession: their lips are gnawed and covered with foam, they bite and whip themselves, they sway and fall and jerk in such a way that the "Dance of Death" of the painter's vision seems horribly enacted here in the trancelike spasms of the living. To make certain that we understand their gruesome message, Bergman has them accompanied and led by the crazed monk who lashes out at the stupefied onlookers:

God has sentenced us to punishment. We shall all perish in the black death. You, standing there like gaping cattle, you who sit there

The monk's harangue.

in your glutted complacency, do you know that this may be your last hour? Death stands right behind you. I can see how his crown gleams in the sun. His scythe flashes as he raises it above your heads. Which one of you shall he strike first? You there, who stands staring like a goat, will your mouth be twisted into the last unfinished gasp before nightfall? And you, woman, who bloom with life and self-satisfaction, will you pale and become extinguished before the morning dawns? You back there, with your swollen nose and stupid grin, do you have another year left to dirty the earth with your refuse? Do you know, insensible fools, that you shall die today or tomorrow, or the next day, because all of you have been sen-

tenced? Do you hear what I say? Do you hear the word? You have
been sentenced, sentenced! (124)

These brutal lines, taken from the film script, convey little of the searing
and unhinging power that the actor Anders Ek endows them with in the
film. His look of utter contempt and certainty as he harangues the
crowd, his wailing and damning voice—I still hear his words, "your last
hour" ("*er sista timme*"), turned into God's curse, "er SEESTA
TEEEEMAH," or his scathing jeremiad against these stolid villagers,
moving from one to the next, pointing the implacable finger of damna-
tion at them, focused on their bodily pleasures and excesses—make all
viewers (whether or not they know Swedish) feel the judgment at hand,
a judgment that is being enacted in their flesh, so that pregnancy and
laughter and defecation are all disgusting, nauseating signs of our corporeal shame, and the punishment is nigh. Here then is one of the oldest and most reliable interpretations of plague: God's judgment on
sinners, God's (long overdue) punishment of the body and its carnal appetites.

Bergman is vitally interested in those *revelatory* dimensions of
plague theorized by Artaud, the metamorphoses it produces in the bodies and the souls of those it threatens. Hence we encounter, early on in
an abandoned farm, the renegade priest Raval, who now plies his trade
by stealing jewels and valuables from the dead. Caught in the act by a
young woman, he explains that these days stealing is quite lucrative, that
the rules have changed: "Each of us has to save his own skin. It's as simple as that." He then moves on the girl (in good Artaud fashion) to rape
her, still explaining: "Don't try to scream. There's no one around to
hear you, neither God nor man" (116–117).

All contracts have been breached, it would seem, but this scene is
being witnessed—people watching people watching people happens
often in Bergman—by Jöns the Squire, and he recognizes in Raval the
source of still earlier rot, namely the (fraudulent) Crusades where he has
just wasted ten years of his life: "Your name is Raval, from the theological

college at Roskilde. You are Dr. Mirabilis, Coelestis et Diabilis. . . . You were the one who, ten years ago, convinced my master of the necessity to join a better-class crusade to the Holy Land." Much of Bergman's tonality comes out in that word "better-class," signaling the ironic angle of vision that the Squire introduces into this film; played by Gunnar Björnstrand, the Squire with his occasional bouts of sophisticated, street-smart, Stockholmese language, contrasts wonderfully with the Knight's (Max von Sydow's) existential, timeless, questing voice and manner. The Squire lets Raval off with a warning, "The next time we meet, I'll brand your face the way one does with thieves" (little knaves of your sort, the Swedish says). Sure enough, the Squire will meet Raval again, this time at an inn where he is torturing Jof, the film's lovable but helpless minstrel figure; and Jöns keeps his word, takes out his knife, and slices Raval from forehead to cheek, effectively branding him. Raval is marked; his vicious soul *shows;* the spirit is imaged. Is this not one way of opening the seals: by rending the flesh?

Plague, as Artaud posited, heightens and accelerates these transformations and mutations. Bergman's camera focuses long and lovingly on the faces of his players, conveying the solid, material scheme that we inhabit (our bodies, our world). Yet this hitherto docile universe is drastically menaced by plague: the disease wrecks and deforms your body, the universe itself seems out of phase, amok. Thus, in the scene at the inn, the frightened villagers chronicle horrors: "They speak of the judgment day. And all these omens are terrible. Worms, chopped-off hands and other monstrosities began pouring out of an old woman, and down in the village another woman gave birth to a calf's head" (126–127).

Likewise, we learn that the priests have located the source of plague: "the woman carries it between her legs and that's why she must cleanse herself" (127). Old fears and fantasies are being rehearsed here, as they always are in times of plague, when *causes* must be found. The camera zooms in on these worried but decent faces, but it all changes when Raval starts to taunt Jof. The logic of scapegoating is heating up now, and we see with considerable clarity how "outsiders"—especially those who are marginal and unprotected by law, such as actors and players— are viewed with suspicion, can be subject to outright torture. Raval forces the dazed, frightened Jof to dance on the table like a bear, and the camera again returns to the faces of the crowd, now laughing with sadistic pleasure, ready to see Jof tormented, indeed to see him die. Bergman does not flinch in his depiction of human hardness, of the transformation of an uneasy crowd into a lynch mob.

During plague, Raval can work up the villagers to violence. But in this matter of scapegoating and demonizing, Bergman reserves his real venom for the Church. Some of the film's starkest and most poignant scenes revolve around the ritual torture of Tyan, the girl-child who is branded a witch for confessing to carnal relations with the Devil. The soldiers have already shaved her head and broken her wrists, and they are going to burn her at the stake. Both the Knight and the Squire are moved by her plight, but unable to prevent her calvary. The Knight ultimately gives her a potion to deaden the pain, but his no less urgent goal is to interrogate her himself, to learn what she has seen, what secrets she may possess.

All of Bergman's interests coalesce here, as the drive for visibility, for opening the seals, becomes increasingly frantic. In answer to the Knight's urgent question about God's whereabouts, the girl asks him to look into her eyes, but all he sees is "an empty, numb fear." "No one, nothing, no one?" the girl pleads; "No," is the Knight's reply. As the flames mount, Jöns is consumed with rage: "Look at her eyes, my lord. Her poor brain has just made a discovery. Emptiness under the moon" (148); It is not too much to say that "emptiness under the moon" ("*tomhet under månen*") is Bergman's core article of belief, and against that stark certainty we can gauge the cruel policies of the Church, but also the tragic absurdity of the Knight's quest, a quest that led him to the Holy Land and the Crusades, a quest now to see God in the time of plague. The killing of the girl Tyan is evidence of the sacrificial logic that Girard discerned in the *Oedipus*, and which I have discussed at some

The "witch" Tyan at the stake.

length as frantic communal narrative, as desperate desire to locate the miasma, the source of the disease.

No moment in Bergman's entire cinematic oeuvre exposes the sham and cheat of questing and metaphysics as beautifully as the scene where Jof and Mia and Mikael offer the Knight and the Squire a bowl of wild strawberries and fresh milk. In the presence of a loving human family—unmistakably Bergman's version of the Holy Family—the Knight realizes the folly of his past life and the reality of this dense and rich human moment:

I shall remember this moment. The silence, the twilight, the bowls of strawberries and milk, your faces in the evening light. Mikael sleeping, Jof with his lyre. I'll try to remember what we talked about. I'll carry this memory between my hands as carefully as if it were a bowl filled to the brim with fresh milk. *(He turns his face*

The "sacrament" of strawberries and milk.

away and looks out toward the sea and the colorless gray sky) And it will be an adequate sign—it will be enough for me. (138)

Bergman rings a change on the Artaud formula of plague's dark explosions among human kind, because in this moment the Knight realizes that love and flesh are holy, just as the milk and the wild strawberries are unmistakably given to us as sacraments for the living, every bit as miraculous and transcendent in their way as the bread and the wine of the Eucharist. "*En stor tillräcklighet,*" the Swedish says, "a great sufficiency," as if this dense moment of nurturance and intimacy were *full,* not empty, were not a "sign" (as the English says), did not require "opening up." The world of living flesh and nature's bounty is transformed from closed seal to something radiant and shimmering. Human love alone fills up the "emptiness under the moon." Hence, this family will live, will be spared as plague visits Sweden. Whereas Defoe emphasized the social and emotional horrors of infection, leading to a view of the enclosed family as guaranteed death trap, Bergman has posited human ties as alone enduring.

But plague is real. And Bergman wants to show it in ways that go beyond physical notation. Thus, even if wild strawberries and fresh milk are beautiful evidence of *this life's adequacy, The Seventh Seal* is nonetheless visionary, cued to a world beyond matter, from beginning to end. Jof himself is the film's seer, since it is he who is punished by others for his visions and fantasies, but the film is on his side, and thus all spectators endorse Jof's vision: we too see the epiphany of Mary and Jesus walking on the grass; just as we too see the specter of Death playing chess with the Knight, even if no one else in the film does. These moments of vision are accompanied by music, just as Mia's sweet affirmation of her love for Jof is accompanied by music. Spirit is real.

So too is Death. This film has an assured place in the history of film partly because of Bergman's audaciousness in actually putting Death on the screen as ghastly clown, Death as *visible presence,* Death as chess player and fellow traveler. And although the religious framework of the film incessantly centralizes the presence/absence of God, I'd argue that the actual film does something quite different: it presents Death as the reality principle, Death as black-caped figure who snuffs out all lights, Death as the blackness that usurps the screen (see next page, top). Above all, death is the very personification of plague, the spirit that walks the land and lays waste to all human life. Death is the film's ubiquitous leading actor, as we see in the early shot of the ravaged cadaver on the road whom the Squire gets off his horse to interrogate. Death is in the Church, in the streets, in the forest. And Death is the great lord who besieges the Knight's castle at film's end, whose forcible entry into our sheltered lives cannot be halted, and whose ultimate triumph has become an unforgettable icon in film history: the Dance of Death. This too is, as it must be, a visionary moment that only Jof (and every viewer who has ever seen this film, and many educated people who have never seen this film) perceives:

ABOVE: Death opening his cape. BELOW: The Dance of Death.

I see them, Mia! I see them! Over there against the dark, stormy sky. They are all there. The smith and Lisa and the knight and Raval and Jöns and Skat. And Death, the severe master, invites them to dance. He tells them to hold each other's hands and then they must tread the dance in a long row. And first goes the master with his scythe and hourglass, but Skat dangles at the end with his lyre. They dance away from the dawn and it's a solemn dance toward the dark lands, while the rain washes their faces and cleans the salt of the tears from their cheeks. (163)

There is something utterly exquisite and utterly obscene here. The bodies with the boils, the burned witch, the ghastly flagellants, are now transformed into an image of transcendent beauty, stylized into the measures of dance and hieratic order. The seals have been opened. The medium of film registers, against the backdrop of mass terror and ubiquitous death, a luminous story about the human family in the time of plague, about death's reign and love's salvation: what began as a feisty and baroque bit of filmmaking, even as a warning about nuclear destruction, remains with us as a miracle of illumination.

PLAGUE AND THE BODY POLITIC:
TONY KUSHNER'S *ANGELS IN AMERICA*

Plague comes to contemporary America in Tony Kushner's *Angels in America,* appropriately subtitled "A Gay Fantasia on National Themes." This extravagant play may seem dated already, in that it captures the heyday of AIDS anxiety in 1980s' American culture, and its political references are to Reagan's America, "perestroika," and the momentous end of the Cold War. But Kushner's grasp of both plague and ideology goes deeper than that, sheds light on our themes in such a way as to spell out why these issues matter, and how it is that they illuminate central beliefs about self, illness, and art.

Kushner's play reworks all the motifs we have seen in the plague-text, from Sophocles through Defoe, Dickens, Camus, and Bergman: collective disease tells us, as nothing else quite does, who we are, what our values are, and how we behave in the face of both sickness and death. But in *Angels in America,* what was discrete in the other texts is now revealed in its "fit," its coherence. All of these texts seem to tell us that an epidemic ushers in some dreadful truths about sexuality, identity, and political order, but these truths remain murky. In Kushner's play, it all comes together with brilliance and chutzpah, yielding something like a gathering statement of plague's dimensions, how wide its sweep really is, how deep its take might be.

Let plague be reconfigured as AIDS, and presto: disease is sexual disease, disease is inseparable from sexual desire, but sexual desire now coded (by mainstream America) as deviant because it is homosexual. Kushner's "gay fantasia" is as much about sexual transgression as Sophocles and Dickens are, but it is also cued to the same epistemological crisis each of them records: who is who? how are we actually related? As Lévi-Strauss observed of the Oedipus myth, "walking and behaving straight" are precisely what is at issue here. These tidings constitute a moral test. *Angels* tells the story of gay love's incursions and challenges: the breakup of the Pitt marriage because Joe is a closet gay; the breakup of the Louis-Prior relationship because Louis cannot handle Prior's AIDS. And all of these struggles are interwoven in a meditation about America: Reagan's America of the 1980s, the "me generation," and the maniacal egoism that characterized it. All this comes against a backdrop of millennium and apocalypse. The century approaches its close with unheard-of new developments: communism is dead, yes, but the enemy still burrows within, the membrane does not hold, the ozone is punctured, the family collapses, the bloodstream is polluted, the immune system fails.

Modern America wants none of this sickness discourse, as Roy Cohn, American icon dying of AIDS, confides to the ghost come back to haunt him, Ethel Rosenberg: "The worst thing about being sick in

America, Ethel, is you are booted out of the parade. Americans have no use for sick. Look at Reagan: He's so healthy he's hardly human, he's a hundred if he's a day, he takes a slug in his chest and two days later he's out West riding ponies in his PJs. I mean who does that? That's America. It's just no country for the infirm" (II.58). *Angels in America* is very much about Reagan's America: its bluff and gnarly individualism, its culture of private enterprise, its "feel good" view of the American body politic.

This model is in trouble. The infirm are on the move. And the firm find they are infirm. Joe, the play's good-looking Mormon hero, the American "Ken" who is a chief clerk writing briefs at the (Republican) Federal Court of Appeals, has tried all his life to live the Reagan dream and finds that he has lived a lie. The straight and the narrow, the good and the true, work in Sunday school but not in the flesh, at least not in Joe's flesh. His entire life has been a war zone:

> I had a book of Bible stories when I was a kid. There was a picture I'd look at twenty times every day: Jacob wrestles with the angel. I don't really remember the story, or why the wrestling—just the picture. Jacob is young and very strong. The angel is . . . a beautiful man, with golden hair and wings, of course. I still dream about it. Many nights. I'm . . . It's me. In that struggle. Fierce, and unfair. The angel is not human, and it holds nothing back, so how could anyone human win, what kind of a fight is that? It's not just. Losing means your soul thrown down in the dust, your heart torn out from God's. But you can't not lose. (I.49–50)

It is a poignant passage, evoking not only Joe's futile battle against his nature, but suggesting another reading altogether for the well-known story of Jacob wrestling with the angel, now *seen* as a body-to-body engagement of two males, with erotic dimensions that add a flavor of sexual excitement to the pain of "losing" the battle.

In "coming out," in moving in with Lou, Joe brings great pain to his wife, Harper, whom he still loves, even though their sexual relations have been vexed from the outset of their marriage. Harper, given to Valium-induced dreams and hallucinations, imagines there are men with knives hiding in her apartment, and in a scene of great power, in which Louis's breaking with Prior is systematically spliced with the eruption of truth between Joe and Harper, Joe realizes the grisly truth of his wife's fantasies:

JOE: As long as I've known you, Harper, you've been afraid of . . . of men hiding under the bed, men hiding under the sofa, men with knives.

PRIOR *(Shattered; almost pleading; trying to reach him* [Lou]*):* I'm dying! You stupid fuck! Do you know what that is! Love! Do you know what love means? We lived together four and a half years, you animal, you idiot.

LOUIS: I have to find some way to save myself.

JOE: Who are these men? I never understood it. Now I know.

HARPER: What?

JOE: It's me.

HARPER: It is?

PRIOR: GET OUT OF MY ROOM!

JOE: I'm the man with the knives.

HARPER: You are?

PRIOR: If I could get up now I'd kill you. I would. Go away. Go away or I'll scream.

HARPER: Oh God . . .

JOE: I'm sorry . . .

HARPER: It is you.

LOUIS: Please don't scream.

PRIOR: Go.

HARPER: I recognize you now.

LOUIS: Please . . .

JOE: Oh. Wait, I . . . Oh! *(He covers his mouth with his hand, gags, and removes his hand, red with blood)* I'm bleeding. *(Prior screams)*

HARPER: Mr. Lies.

MR. LIES *(Appearing, dressed in Antarctic explorer's apparel):* Right here.

HARPER: I want to go away. I can't see him anymore.

MR. LIES: Where?

HARPER: Anywhere. Far away.

MR. LIES: Absolutamento. *(Harper and Mr. Lies vanish. Joe looks up, sees that she's gone.)*

PRIOR: *(Closing his eyes):* When I open my eyes you'll be gone. *(Louis leaves.)*

JOE: Harper?

PRIOR *(Opening his eyes):* Huh. It worked.

JOE *(Calling):* Harper?

PRIOR: I hurt all over. I wish I was dead. (I.79–81)

Quoted at some length, this set of exchanges reveals something of Kushner's theatrical magic. Realist boundaries are sovereignly done away with. This scene of double betrayal speaks to the play's deepest moral issues, yet we also see how art speaks its very special tongue: Joe *is* the man with the knives, Harper *exits* this intolerable truth-prison (Kushner understands that Valium and travel agents serve the same purpose), Louis leaves the premises, and Prior emits the scream that goes through the house. Kushner, choreographing pain and ethics in a weird pas de deux, twins his figures and makes their single dramas prismatic, even familial. One remembers O'Neill's groundbreaking efforts to fashion a theater of entanglement and porosity, in which the Tyrone family's collective gestalt becomes ever clearer, in which each figure is embedded in and responding to others. Yet Kushner has gone still further down this road, certain that our escapist fantasies and our secret terrors in fact spill out onto the stage, can be seen and heard and even shared.

In Kushner's hands, the plague-text is inseparable from the plea-sure-text, and with a kind of Strindbergian economy he shows that my freedom is your bondage, my joy your sorrow. Joe leaves Harper be-cause he realizes he is gay; Louis leaves Prior because Prior has AIDS. Each of these relational disasters—as "natural" as the tug of gravity—is going to be plumbed for the moral truths they contain, truths of a very old order having to do with loyalty and human decency. "*Sharfer vi di tson a shlang izan umdankbar kind*" ("Sharper than a serpent's tongue it is, to have a thankless child"), says Rabbi Chemelwitz early in the play, referring (in Yiddish) to Shakespeare's *Kenig Lear* and the rock-bottom sin at hand here: betrayal.

Artaud claimed that the plague-text is brutally unhinging and trans-formative in its surprises and revelations, but Kushner turns metamor-phosis into a structural principle of everyday life: people you work with and think are straight turn out to be gay; private dreams you have turn out to be shared. The results can be delicious, as in the "mutual dream scene" where Louis's lover, Prior, meets Joe's wife, Harper, who is confused:

HARPER: Are you . . . Who are you?

PRIOR: Who are you?

HARPER: What are you doing in my hallucination?

PRIOR: I'm not in your hallucination. You're in my dream.

HARPER: You're wearing makeup.

PRIOR: So are you.

HARPER: But you're a man.

PRIOR *(Feigning dismay, shock, he mimes slashing his throat with his lipstick and dies, fabulously tragic. Then)* The hands and the feet give it away. (I.31)

These lovely stage directions reveal a theatrical imagination of the first order, one that is wise about the acculturated and produced body, wise also about the opportunities for wit and fun that song and dance may provide. Once again, we see the malleability of Kushner's scheme, the kaleidoscopic shape-shifting (and even dream-hopping) that gay culture (and theatrical brilliance) bring to stolid realist appearances. Wit itself, in this play, may be thought of as a kind of last-ditch performance, a dance-of-death (to turn death into a dance is no easy matter), a yoking of disease and determinism into stylistic improvisations and vaudeville routines, whimsical sorties that flaunt life's richness and sweetness in even the narrowest straits.

But AIDS bids to demolish such maneuvering room, to annihilate the actor's song and dance, by positing instead a fiercely anarchic body that resists all control. Louis is available for Joe, at least in part, because his lover Prior is a dreadfully altered figure. Here is the inventory Prior gives to Emily, the nurse:

> PRIOR: Ankles sore and swollen, but the leg's better. The nausea's mostly gone with the little orange pills. BM's pure liquid but not bloody anymore, for now, my eye doctor says everything's OK, for now, my dentist says "Yuck!" when he sees my fuzzy tongue, and now he wears little condoms on his thumb and forefinger. And a mask. So what? My dermatologist is in Hawaii and my mother . . . well leave my mother out of it. Which is usually where my mother is, out of it. My glands are like walnuts, my weight's holding steady for week two, and a friend died two days ago of bird tuberculosis; bird tuberculosis; that scared me and I didn't go to the funeral today because he was an Irish Catholic and it's probably open casket and I'm afraid of . . . something, the bird TB or seeing him or . . . So I guess I'm doing OK. Except for of course I'm going nuts.
>
> EMILY: We ran the toxoplasmosis series and there's no indication . . .
>
> PRIOR: I know, I know, but I feel like something terrifying is on its way, you know, like a missile from outer space, and it's plummet-

ing down towards the earth, and I'm ground zero, and . . . I am
generally known where I am known as one cool, collected queen.
And I am ruffled. (I.97–98)

Perhaps we can begin to put some of the pieces together here, to measure the startling cogency of Kushner's theatrical vision, and to see
how "plague" has become, strangely enough, a sort of "open Sesame"
for the text's diverse concerns: identity, apocalypse, and explosions of
both somatic and cosmic character. Prior's body has gone on a ram-
page, producing liquids, excretions, and fuzz in new, unwanted places,
and this body requires keepers and tenders. "For now" the passage
twice says, to let us know that all physical reports are strictly temporary, that the body is on the move. This somatic outing borders on
metamorphosis: the glands are like walnuts, and the bird tuberculosis
has an almost Ovidian flavor to it, in addition to a scary sense of flight
and flux, so that even the dead body in the casket is disturbingly active
and on the move, a potent agent of transmission. Kushner is wonderfully literal about all this coming and going, and we are to understand
that the dermatologist's stay in Hawaii presents an exodus that is not
unlike the mother's being "out of it," or, for that matter, like Harper's
own Valium trips, which are fabulously assisted by Mr. Lies. Thus it is
rigorously appropriate that this scene closes with mention of a missile
in outer space plummeting toward Earth, so that we understand the
monstrous outings and mutinies of the body to have a cosmic character, to convey, indeed, that the hitherto stable world we knew—both
body and planet—is out of control. Harper sensed as much, at the
play's beginning: "People who are lonely, people left alone, sit talking
nonsense to the air, imagining . . . beautiful systems dying, old fixed
orders spiraling apart . . ." (I.16).

Plague as apocalypse was there in Sophocles, Defoe, Camus, and
Bergman, but Kushner is out to show us new worlds and new vistas. To
be sure, he respects the disasters at home, and Dickens's saga of *sponta-*

neous combustion seems rigorously apposite in the description of Prior's exploding and imploding body. Yet, *Angels in America* wants also to measure the extraordinary velocities and forces now unleashed in this "New Age," wants to see them as expansionist as well as destructive, no less visionary than the opening of the seals. Kushner breaks with realism because the brave new world he is out to chart requires a new stage altogether, one that does justice to the cosmos as well as the id, one that houses private fantasy and political landscape as well as medical dilemma. At times a new code is needed to graph these changes; at other times, a truly older code will do, which is why Kushner chooses, at key moments, to go into Hebrew, to signal that these unheard-of transformations have been adumbrated in the past, are part of the Book.

Kushner's construction of plague has an unprecedented power— utterly beyond the discrete representations of Sophocles, Defoe, Dickens, and even Camus and Bergman—because he centralizes the human body as the war zone itself, the actual terrain for the planetary yet somatic battle. The body is a source of art, wit, and control, as we see in the play's raffish exchanges and pungent dialogue (never perhaps more *saftig* than when Belize, the former drag queen, is on scene), but it is also the site for unparalleled devastation, as Prior comes to learn. And this somatic disaster tests love as nothing else can; Louis fails the test. Prior puts it in sweet living-space terms: "Apartment too small for three? Louis and Prior comfy but not Louis and Prior and Prior's disease?" (I.74).

Perhaps the key to Kushner's vision is his sense, at once lyrical and clinical, of the body as the locus of pleasure. Here is why the sexual element—powerfully present in the formulas of Sophocles and Dickens but nonetheless discrete—is at last foregrounded as the ultimate logic of modern plague. It is very simple: people infect each other sexually. Sexual congress is the most powerful engine in the history of human civilization—the fabulous Angel spells it out: "Not Physics but Ecstatics Makes the Engine Run" (II.39)—and *Angels in America* confers on sexual attraction its rightful place at the center of things. Hence, the seduction scene between Louis and Joe is cued precisely to the mobility of somatic contact, a contact that starts in the air before finishing in the flesh:

> LOUIS: Smell is . . . an incredibly complex and underappreciated physical phenomenon. Inextricably bound up with sex.
>
> JOE: I . . . didn't know that.
>
> LOUIS: It is. The nose is really a sexual organ. Smelling. Is desiring. We have five senses, but only two that go beyond the boundaries . . . of ourselves. When you look at someone, it's just bouncing light, or when you hear them, it's just sound waves, vibrating air, or touch is just nerve endings tingling. Know what a smell is?
>
> JOE: It's . . . some sort of . . . No.
>
> LOUIS: It's made of the molecules of what you're smelling. Some part of you, where you meet the air, is airborne. (II.30)

Theory quickly becomes praxis here as Louis moves up to Joe, close, breathes, and murmurs "Little molecules of Joe . . . ," inhales deeply, says, "Up my nose. Mmmm . . . Nice. Try it" (II.30). Joe now inhales as well, and the lesson continues, moving from smell to taste, quite wonderfully recasting the infection story of noxious bodily transmission as a much older fable still, one of sensory and erotic stimuli, of bodies playing out their timeless mating rituals, now seen up close under the microscope. Kushner offers us something like a poem of the earth, makes us understand the *elemental nature* of human attraction, helps us to actually catch sight of the busy quasi-molecular force field in which desire operates:

> LOUIS: . . . First the nose, then the tongue.
>
> JOE: I just don't . . .
>
> LOUIS: They work as a team, see. The nose tells the body—the heart, the mind, the fingers, the cock—what it wants, and then the

tongue explores, finding out what's edible, what isn't, what's most mineral, food for the blood, food for the bones, and therefore most delectable. *(He licks the side of Joe's cheek.)* Salt. *(Louis kisses Joe, who holds back a moment and then responds.)*

LOUIS: Mmm. Iron. Clay. *(Louis slips his hand down the front of Joe's pants. They embrace more tightly. Louis pulls his hand out, smells and tastes his fingers, and then holds them for Joe to smell.)*

LOUIS: Chlorine. Copper. Earth. (II.31)

This view of sexual desire and sexual coupling is properly elemental, chthonic, and it is the cornerstone of Kushner's play, serving as a basis for the incessant shape-shifting and fusing that constitute reality. The myth of individual hegemony is cashiered, and in its stead, we see a world of interacting bodies, a kind of olfactory and tactile (and emotional and moral) traffic that announces linkage and connection everywhere. One wants to say that his dramaturgy is in this service, a dramaturgy that produces shared dreams and hallucinations, that goes about "familializing" his characters, so that Harper and Prior are almost as much a couple as Louis and Joe (something the double scenes make unmistakable), so that Hannah, the Mormon mother, is pulled from Salt Lake City to New York to play her structural role with Harper. And so that even Roy Cohn, the play's consummate individualist, makes the rounds, is regarded as a putative missing link between Joe and Louis.

The reality of Kushner's play is connection, connection that may start as airborne and genital but then outlasts sexual cohabitation, goes beyond sexual desire altogether. The guilt-ridden Louis tells Emily about Mathilde's fidelity for William the Conqueror: "She waited for him, she stitched for years. And if he had come back broken and defeated from war, she would have loved him even more. And if he had returned mutilated, ugly, full of infection and horror, she would still have loved him" (I.53). Kushner's play may centralize desire, but its view of loyalty has an Old Testament severity to it. Louis comes to understand the enormity, the unforgivability, of his betrayal of Prior, just as Joe finds that he has to walk back into the marriage that he has walked out of.

The reality of linkage and the value of loyalty acquire a special against-the-grain eloquence in Reagan's America. *Angels* is saturated with the egocentric assumptions of 1980s America, and the passages where Roy Cohn and his high-up lackey, Martin, try to lure Joe to Washington should be anthologized for their accuracy in conveying that peculiar American zeitgeist. Kushner seems mesmerized by the muscular individualist creed of eighties America, and he sees the "fall of communism" as part of this ideological high-stakes game; AIDS enters this text in some sense as the missing "theory," the doctrine of connectedness that counters the egoist model. I say "mesmerized," because Kushner seems to live out both sides of his agon, in the sense that the most fascinating figure in his play turns out to be the archenemy, Roy Cohn.

Cohn, like Joe, is seen by us (and by his doctor) to be living a lie. He is dying of AIDS, but insists that it be called cancer. Whereas Joe's Mormon straightness is a mask that must crumble, Roy Cohn not only sticks to his guns (as it were), but goes on to claim the high ground in arguing that power allows you to rewrite the script, that the existential anguish suffered by someone like Joe—should I leave my wife to go to Washington? should I admit I am gay?—is an unnecessary bagatelle if you have enough chutzpah and clout. Thus, Roy explains to his doctor that one must not pay too much attention to labels:

ROY: . . . AIDS. Homosexual. Gay. Lesbian. You think these are names that tell you who someone sleeps with, but they don't tell you that.

HENRY: No?

ROY: No. Like all labels they tell you one thing and one thing only: where does an individual so identified fit in the food chain, in the pecking order? Not ideology, or sexual taste, but something much simpler: clout. Not who I fuck or who fucks me, but who will pick up the phone when I call, who owes me favors. This is what a label refers to. Now to someone who does not understand this, homosexual is what I am because I have sex with men. But really this is wrong. Homosexuals are not men who sleep with other men. Homosexuals are men who in fifteen years of trying cannot get a pissant antidiscrimination bill through City Council. Homosexuals are men who know nobody and who nobody knows. Who have zero clout. Does this sound like me, Henry? (I.45)

Kushner's Cohn is a man of such pluck, resistance, and bile that he threatens to take over the play every time he appears. He is Mephistopheles, the one who seeks to deny the tug of disease and death by sheer force of will, the power broker who personifies the American political id. He exposes the cultural pastime of identity politics as a charade, a house of cards, but he helps us understand the titanism of the moment, the raw creatural appetite that drives the political machine. Wanting Joe to move to Washington to provide some badly needed legal protection, finding that Joe is betwixt and between because of moral scruples, Cohn explodes with the best definition of politics that I have ever come across:

JOE: Well it is unethical. I can't . . .
ROY: Boy, you are really something. What the fuck do you think this is, Sunday School?
JOE: No, but Roy, this is . . .
ROY: This is . . . this is gastric juices churning, this is enzymes and acids, this is intestinal is what it is, bowel movement and blood-red meat—this stinks, this is *politics,* Joe, the game of being alive. And you think you're . . . What? Above that? Above alive is what? Dead! In the clouds! You're on earth, goddammit! Plant a foot, stay awhile. (I.68)

Roy's corporeal vision of life and politics is of a piece with the play's views on both sexuality and plague, as if Kushner were exploring the furthest parameters of a somatic, visceral view of things. The range here can be astonishing. Cohn's interest in Joe carries beyond desired favors and takes on tones of a father-son relationship, a form of spiritual and fleshly mentorship that Cohn believes in, has experienced at the hands of Walter Winchell, Edgar Hoover, Joe McCarthy. And we can recognize strange Sophoclean echoes in this speech, reminiscent of the elegiac paternal theme in the *Philoctetes,* all of which confirms the linkage imperative of the play, a kind of bonding that is every bit as powerful as the paean to individual appetite that is front and center. Even Roy Cohn the militant individualist is familialized by the text: Joe is his would-be son, Belize becomes his reluctant nurse, and Ethel Rosenberg—the nemesis he prides himself for having exterminated way back when—makes a return family visit, seeks to bring news of disbarring to the dying man but ends up instead as Roy's dead mother singing a Yiddish lullaby to her dying son:

ROY: Ma? Muddy? Is it . . . ? *(He sits up, looks at Ethel)* Ma?

ETHEL *(Uncertain, then):* It's Ethel, Roy.

ROY: Muddy? I feel bad.

ETHEL *(Looking around):* Who are you talking to, Roy, it's . . .

ROY: Good to see you, Ma, it's been years. I feel bad. Sing to me.

ETHEL: I'm not your mother, Roy.

ROY: It's cold in here, I'm up so late, past my time. Don't be mad, Ma, but I'm scared . . . ? A little. Don't be mad. Sing me a song. Please.

ETHEL: I don't want to Roy, I'm not your . . .

ROY: Please, it's scary out here. *(He starts to cry) (He sinks back)* Oh God. Oh God, I'm so sorry . . .

ETHEL *(Singing, very soft):*
    Shteit a bocher
    Un er tracht,
    Tracht un nacht
    A gantze nacht:

Vemen tzu nemen

Um nit farshemen

Vemen tzu nemen,

Um nit farsahem.

Tum-ba-la, Tum-ba-la, Tum-balalaike,

Tum-ba-la, Tum-ba-la, Tum-balalaike,

Tum Balalaike, shpil balalaike . . .

(Pause) Roy . . . ? Are you . . . ? *(She crosses to the bed, looks at him. Goes back to her chair.)* That's it. (II.113–114)

This spellbinding passage ends with Roy suddenly sitting up in bed and crowing to Ethel that he fooled her, that he just wanted to make her sing; but this moment of triumph is followed by his death. Ultimately the sequence has significance far beyond Roy's conscious designs because it displays the stunning shaping powers of Kushner's art: much like Prior and Harper enter each other's visions, empowered to do so by the strength of their feelings as well as the genius of the playwright, so too do we have a meeting of the spirits here, and it is strictly within the play's logic that the ghost of Ethel Rosenberg, come back to punish her punisher, can become in her final incarnation Roy Cohn's Muddy, can come back to soothe him to his last sleep. It is also within the play's logic that the plague story be understood as a staging of American history and American myth, that the advent of AIDS and the Gay Movement—far from being some fringe phenomenon—constitutes a *revision* of the entire nation's experience. In this, Kushner displays a kind of ideological hunger, carnival vision, and sheer theatrical bravura that are far removed from the severity of Defoe's and Camus's stories, that take the Dickensian analysis of high and low into almost surreal territory.

Angels in America is indeed a visionary text about the millennium. Tony Kushner makes us see that the plague theme reveals the absolute centrality of the *body* in all human affairs: love, death, politics. Plague leads to an encounter with otherness: with another form of sexual behavior, with a new set of family alignments, with a radical reconception of individual identity, with a rethinking of American politics. Much is unprecedented in its newness: the killer disease, the ozone hole, the alternative culture, the arrival of the Angel. But the old does not disappear: love and loyalty remain as a kind of human syntax that nothing can disrupt. Kushner closes his epic story with humor, tenderness, and visionary wonder. Roy Cohn, "in Heaven, or Hell or Purgatory," finds new work in the area of family law, defending God against the paternity suit that has been building over the centuries. Harper, airborne, is bequeathed a vision of human and planetary healing:

> Souls were rising, from the earth far below, souls of the dead, of people who had perished, from famine, from war, from the plague, and they floated up, like skydivers in reverse, limbs all akimbo, wheeling and spinning. And the souls of these departed joined hands, clasped ankles and formed a web, a great net of souls, and the souls were three-atom oxygen molecules, of the stuff of ozone, and the outer rim absorbed them, and was repaired. (II.142)

This luminous parable counters the familiar Humpty-Dumpty story of plague's ravages, its systematic undoing of body, family, society, and planet. Blithely undoing the routine binaries of life/death, body/soul, even the tug of gravity itself, Kushner's epiphany repairs the ruptured membranes, those of the diseased creature and the polluted planet. And the still living Prior, who has refused the reactionary mission offered him by the Angel, delivers the final paean to life and politics, a vision of existence beyond plague:

> This disease will be the end of many of us, but not nearly all, and the dead will be commemorated and will struggle on with the living, and we are not going away. We won't die secret deaths anymore. The world only spins forward. We will be citizens. The time has come.
>
> Bye now.
>
> You are fabulous creatures, each and every one.

And I bless you: *More Life.*
The Great Work Begins. (II.146)

Angels in America completes my sequence of plague-texts by trumpeting forth in strident, often over-the-top ways, how richly the story of disease turns out to be a story of the culture at large. Prior's final words are to be taken literally: "You are fabulous creatures, each and every one," with emphasis placed on *fabulous,* on the amazingly colorful, variegated and storied existence of all *creatures* who live and love in bodies. Plague is the language of connection, connection now experienced as disease and death, but connection also as the very form, the gestalt, of eros and of politics, and Kushner is mapping a moment of American history when these forms are in crisis, when they are molting. The author's light shines backward to the shtetl and the Mormon pioneers, and it beams forward to the coming world where many of the old paradigms—Marxism, nuclear family, intact ozone layer, walking and behaving "straight"—no longer retain authority. But its most powerful illumination is on the present, the antics of a careening world off balance, trying to reconcile its old beliefs with its new discoveries, experiencing the beauty, the horror, and the sheer power of the body at last placed on center stage, exposed as the driving force of the creature, requiring an ethos and a politics worthy of its needs and yet true to the older codes of decency and loyalty that are the West's irreducible, nonremovable ethical luggage.

Only art can tell the multifaceted story that Tony Kushner has wanted to tell. The reports of both the medical and the social sciences can tell us a great deal about the pathology, demographics, and even therapies for AIDS, but they do not take the measure of *creatures* who are, *each and every one, fabulous.* The scream goes through the house in Kushner's large-souled play, and we understand the house to be the American body politic and even the Judeo-Christian tradition. With humor, pathos, and nonstop brilliance, Kushner takes the stark plague narratives of the past and converts them into a story of our time, our place.

CHAPTER FIVE

SAYING DEATH

*It is not because other people are dead that our affection for them fades;
it is because we ourselves are dying.*

—MARCEL PROUST, *Remembrance of Things Past*

I heard a Fly buzz—when I died—

—EMILY DICKINSON

AVOIDING DEATH

Why speak about death? Most of us spend our lives trying to forget about it, unless we happen to be either undertakers or doctors or professional philosophers. Or sick. Or depressed. The seventeenth-century French philosopher Pascal, who was obsessed with these matters, said that everyone else should be too, concluding that our routine avoidance of the thought of death is the oldest human dodge in history. Our essential dignity, he held, consists in pondering our end, and here is what he then saw: "Imagine a number of men in chains, all under sentence of death, some of whom are each day butchered in the sight of others; those remaining see their own condition in that of their fellows, and looking at each other with grief and despair await their turn. This is the image of the human condition" (165). These penitential arrangements constitute our bedrock truth, Pascal claimed, and we need to face up to them. The classic rejoinder to such a grim injunction was provided by Voltaire, a century later, when he charged Pascal with being at once morbid and useless, claiming that life itself deserves our attention, rather than how it must come to a close. Voltaire had no time for such ultimacies and metaphysics, and he had a point.

Pascal approached death as a religious philosopher, seeking to make his readers embrace Christianity. Voltaire the pragmatist focused on the social tasks that await us in life. I want, in this chapter, to champion Pascal, but to do so on strictly secular grounds: thinking about death, discovering how artists and writers have thought about death, represented death, is exciting and instructive. The excitement is at once intellectual and imaginative: how does the mind make sense of death? of dying? And, how can we imagine, visualize these issues? Responses to this inquiry are stunningly varied, and therein lies what I have called "instruction." Thinking about death and dying brings *life* into focus as nothing else can.

Art's testimony on these matters differs utterly from religious doctrine, in that it seeks illumination rather than conversion: "illumination," the intensifying of *light,* so that we begin to *see* all that these matters entail, so that the elemental darkness that many of us construe death to be is transformed into something luminous and large. I am Voltairean here, in that my sights are indeed on this life, this side of the grave, and I contend that the renditions of death and dying in literature and art are food for the living.

I began by saying that most of us avoid thinking about death, but is this possible? Is our thinking itself not saturated with death? Consider how profoundly death informs all our notions of understanding, wisdom, education, and the like. I do not mean some kind of memento mori, but rather the view that death is hardwired in many of our most basic concepts. Wallace Stevens asks, rather wonderfully, in his poem "Sunday Morning," "Is there no change of death in paradise? / Does ripe fruit never fall? Or do the boughs / Hang always heavy in that perfect sky, / Unchanging, yet so like our perishing earth, / With rivers like our own that seek for seas / They never find, the same receding shores / That never touch with inarticulate pang?" (9). Ripe fruit does fall here on earth, our "perishing earth," just as seeds grow into the fruit that ripens, and rot follows upon fallen fruit. Indeed, just as human development itself is inherently a mobile affair, a linear temporal trajectory that must move from infancy and childhood on to maturation and death. All notions of understanding and value are deeply organicist in nature, tied to a view that recognizes the birth-death tandem as the structure and course of all living things, including wisdom and, perhaps, love.

Consider those clichéd images we have of heaven as some stage set of clouds in a blue sky, bathed in eternity, immutable and unchanging; nothing in life could prepare us for such a realm, a place where the boughs hang always heavy, and this time-free zone seems peculiarly dimensionless, a place without waxing or waning, hence a place where notions such as expectation, desire, and "becoming" are unthinkable. Stevens's famous line "Death is the mother of beauty," properly caps this line of reasoning, not only because the destruction that is death gives beauty its value, but because death truly *mothers* our view of life by installing the very processes that make meaning possible. These are the insights proper to poetry, coming to us as images of things we know—fruit, boughs, rivers, seas—and helping us to a larger sense of death's ubiquitous rule.

While death is the ever-present backdrop against which life achieves focus and definition, ordinarily, mercifully, we do not see this backdrop. Sometimes, however, via art, we do. I think that Edvard Munch's *Self-Portrait with Skeletal Arm,* done in 1895 at the height of his physical and artistic powers, brings this home to us. The elegant, refined face of the artist emerges magically from the brilliant black background—Munch had just learned in Paris how to produce this gleaming, dazzling jet black—and I used to regard this lithograph as a creation myth: the birth of the self as it breaks through the prior nothingness. I now think Munch is trying to position the precarious, miraculous reality of life and self within its ultimate matrix: death. "Who am I?" he seems to be asking, and we see the answers, in three distinct registers: as letters and numerals, "Edvard Munch, 1895"; as two-dimensional figure, the one whose face the painter both saw in the mirror at that precise moment and also had the genius (then, in 1895, in his prime) to convey/construct in his art; but also as skeletal arm, not

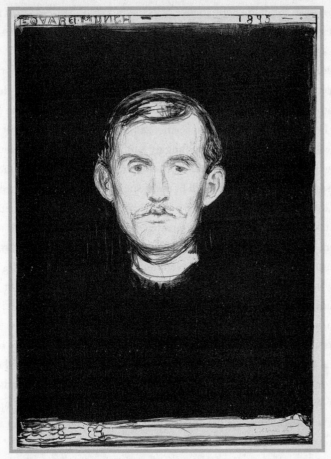

Self-Portrait with Skeletal Arm, Edvard Munch, 1895.

merely the skeleton within the flesh, but rather a material index of who he will be. It is all there: the blackness of Nothing prior to his life, the moment of splendor in/through his work, the fate of death that is inescapable.

This lithograph attempts nothing less than a form of cubist portraiture, a way of representing the human being *in time,* and it thus has the pathos of all death-inscribed phenomena, wise about the evanescence of its human subject (the physical Munch is now, as you read, a skeleton), no less wise about the permanence of its medium (you are looking at this representation now; it cannot die), and immensely moving because it has captured just this dialectic of life, death, and art.

Death, our oldest fact of life, is central to discourses of religion, philosophy, biology, anthropology, and much else that is less self-evident, including politics and art and all creative endeavor. Moreover, it has long been known that religion, science, and literature have constructed stories to make sense of death, ranging from forms of spiritual afterlife and genetic survival, on to fables of reincarnation, moral achievement, and spiritual reward. Almost all of these spend as little time as possible with death itself, but rather move on to disguised life-scenarios, whether they take place in heaven, genetic arrangements, or history. Death as cessation, and dying as entropic fate of living creatures, are severe starting points for any kind of narrative, even though dying itself is a lifelong activity that does have obvious shape and form, as a casual glance at the old and not-so-old makes overwhelmingly clear. Artistic and literary performances both challenge and add to our database in this area by giving us accounts or even renditions that are sharply at odds with the biological ending that awaits us. To be sure, a poem or short story will not stop death, but it may well add furnishings and stock to the minds of those who will die. Above all, art's depictions of death and dying open what is closed, afford us imaginative toeholds and beachheads in campaigns that our bodies are fated to lose.

Hamlet, whose every reflection and meditation (including "to be or not to be") obsessively centers on mortality, refers to death as the "undiscovered country," and no one can disagree. Suicide, the prince muses, rushes us to a destination about which we can know nothing. Death is our common fate, but it has not been charted or mapped out. Hence, all writing about death is radically secondhand; we might even add: radically suspicious, because it is always the account of witnesses and bystanders, never the experience itself. Supposition, projection, and fantasy loom large here. And for those who do not trust literature in the first place, literary accounts of death must be particularly questionable. On the other hand, scientific accounts of the cessation of life seem just as "external" and "locked out" as literary ones do. The body can be described in its agony and subsequent rigor mortis, but is this not just the shell? There is a vein of writing that deals with "out-of-body" experiences, and there are cases of patients who have been "at death's door," and have not only recovered but have left us accounts of what they saw there. But even this is, after all, both liminal and limited, a foretaste of the real thing.

Could you make death speak? Poe, in his "The Facts in the Case of M. Valdemar," offers a grisly scientific version of this imperative: to make the dying body tell its story. But this promised narrative collapses in on itself, as Valdemar's words "dead!" "dead!" are described as "absolutely *bursting* from the tongue and not from the lips of the sufferer, his whole frame at once—within the space of a single minute, or even less, shrunk—crumbled—absolutely *rotted* away beneath my hands. Upon the bed, before that whole company, there lay a nearly liquid mass of loathsome—of detestable putridity" (842). Poe, explorer of the macabre that he is, tries to capture the moment of exit itself and force it into speech, but the decaying body cashiers the tongue, and whatever secret death possesses is one that cannot be transmitted.

Since death itself cancels language, cancels out the speaking or writing subject, what can art possibly know? Where does it find its data? There is, first of all, the immediate issue of *access:* how do you say death if death isn't talking? Is death to be grasped as elemental silence? as riddle? Writers and artists have wondered about these matters, and have often been willing to step into the breach and ventriloquize on their own. I will also investigate what we can and do know: the testimony of witnesses, survivors, and mourners. After all, we do in fact encounter death throughout our lives in a distinctly survivable fashion: the death of others. Here is a lifelong form of exposure to finality, and although I do not want to regard mourning as a kind of trial run, I do want to attend to the complex scenarios—emotional, moral, temporal—that the death of others, especially the death of loved ones, triggers in our own lives.

Memory is especially critical here, in its role in tallying losses, reverencing and referencing the dead, and overseeing the survival of the self. It will be seen that literature sheds a special light on these matters. (How often that metaphor—"sheds light"—appears in this book! My meaning is elemental: literature "discovers," "uncovers" [takes the cover off] the complex reach of issues that are hidden underneath our conceptual tags.) And finally, I will consider the sheer richness and shocking power of artistic renditions of the experience of death and dying, proving just how pulsating and vital this somber topic can be. From personal undoing to national wound, from choreographic endgame to report beyond the grave, writers present their odd findings. Sometimes the angle of vision is private and cryptic; at other times, it is wide-angled and urgently social in its claims. In all instances, these images and visions, far from being snapshots that confirm what we know, jolt and shock us in their strangeness, overturn our received views, disclose a sweep and scale that make us larger than we were.

SURVIVABLE DEATH: MOURNING

We start, then, with the unspeakable nature of death. What can be spoken is the pathos and meaning we ascribe to death. Since one is always outside the experience, what does it mean to be the outsider witnessing a death one can neither stop nor speak? These matters engage us most, take on urgency and pathos when the dead person is a loved one. Already here we can measure the gap between art and science: medically speaking, all deaths are (more or less) alike, but art records "data" about the deaths that matter, the ones we feel. How the bereaved living survive the death of others can be said, and is said, differently in different discourses. The discipline of psychology has theorized these matters, and there is a considerable body of how-to literature that instructs us on the mechanics of mourning and severance. I say "mechanics," because one of the most classic formulations about mourning is very much an affair of determinist laws and rules that govern our experience of the death of loved ones; I am thinking of Freud's "Mourning and Melancholia," and it is worth citing the key passage that spells out how the human subject lets go, how we accept the finality of death:

> The testing of reality, having shown that the loved object no longer exists, requires forthwith that all the libido shall be withdrawn from its attachments to this object. Against this demand a struggle of course arises—it may be universally observed that man never willingly abandons a libido-position, not even when a substitute is already beckoning to him. This struggle can be so intense that a turning away from reality ensues, the object being clung to through the medium of a hallucinatory wish-psychosis. The normal outcome is that deference for reality gains the day. Nevertheless its behest cannot be at once obeyed. The task is now carried through bit by bit, under great expense of time and cathectic energy, while all the time the existence of the lost object is continued in the mind. Each single one of the memories and hopes which bound the libido to the object is brought up and hyper-cathected, and the detachment of the libido from it accomplished. Why this process of carrying out the behest of reality bit by bit, which is in the nature of a compromise, should be extraordinarily painful is not at all easy to explain in terms of mental economics. It is worth noting that this pain seems natural to us. The fact is, however, that when the work of mourning is completed the ego becomes free and uninhibited again. (126–127)

Freud is very much the biologist here, in his conviction that the organism must choose life and that the "ego's attachments" will in due course be redistributed so that the dead can effectively be "cut loose" from the mourning subject. What I have called "mechanical" is the tentacular, string-tying nature of human connection that is imagined here. Each of our memories, our libidinal "linkages" with the dead one, are brought up for review and exposed as futile, as pointless, so that the umbilical cord can be cut; moreover, we understand this process to be slow and incremental, since our linkages are multiple, and it would seem that they cannot be called up at once, but rather require dismantling one by one. It is not unlike jettisoning a huge cargo to which we are bound by countless ropes and ties, and the work of mourning would be the systematic undoing of each knot, so that finally the dead cargo could sink to the bottom of the sea, sink into oblivion. At this point, the "ego becomes free and uninhibited again."

MOURNING: THE DEATH OF A WE-WORLD

There is something at once brilliant, heartless, and tonic in Freud's theory. With the unflinching lucidity of a surgeon, he analyzes the most painful transactions of human life, and seeks to show us how the very muscle and tissue, the tendons of love, must atrophy and die when the loved one is dead. His view is bathed in a higher pragmatism, a shrewd, even profound sense that the "reality principle" must ultimately prevail. We are not constituted in such a way as to deny life or serve death, and even though other Freudian notions about melancholia or the death instinct complicate this thesis, it seems nonetheless to hold true for "healthy" mourning. One recovers. The will puts up a fight, but gradually the *automatic* severing of ties carries the day, educates the will as to its errors. Freud admits to puzzlement as to why this should be so painful, since our "mental economics" governing this redirecting of libido is so clear and unarguable; yet, Freud admits that we take this pain to be "natural."

What does it mean to "naturalize" this pain? Clearly, our moral, emotional, and religious beliefs enter the picture here, since they have their own rival view of mourning, notably that death is unallowable, that our ties to our loved ones are imperishable, that they should be revered. Of course Freud knows this, but he is confident that the ego's imperious need for *living* attachments must win out in the end. We cannot be nourished by dead tissue, he seems to be saying, and sooner or later our system gets the message.

It seems fair to say that prevalent modern theories of mourning essentially toe the Freudian line. The utilitarian flavor of Freud's argument will be put aside, but the basic principles remain valid, as we theorize our encounter with the impossible. The response to death is strangely the same, whether one is the dier or the survivor. Hence, someone like Elisabeth Kübler-Ross, whose work focuses on the stages of resistance and acceptance that mark patients' responses to their own imminent deaths, provides a map that governs grief too. In some sense, Kübler-Ross, who has done extensive fieldwork with the dying and their families, resembles Freud in that she articulates the specific nodal points and passages at work as the ego goes through its *Trauerarbeit* (the work of mourning), a narrative process in itself not unlike a "station drama." This holds for letting go of oneself, or of others.

Kübler-Ross's well-known model—denial, anger, bargaining, depression, and acceptance—lays out a kind of trajectory that can now function as "advance knowledge" for those who confront death (their own or others'), as a kind of compass that alerts them to the phase of the journey they are currently in. This is profoundly educative, and insofar as it draws on Freud's model, it would seem to sketch out a set of laws that apply to all of us, regardless of individual circumstances. Such would be the constitution of the human animal. For the dying, the hoped-for result is a final readiness. For the mourning, it is not far-fetched to view this trajectory as a kind of univeral "pilgrim's progress," but with the guaranteed result that the quest will be successful, that eventually, after each of the hurdles has been passed and the stages gone through, our ego will again be "free and uninhibited."

Literature complicates these matters. We might assume that literature would seek merely to extend the illumination mission common to both Freud and Kübler-Ross, in putting a name and a face on the phases of mourning, in helping us to a more vivid and particularized sense of

the journey we are making. Here is, of course, one of the oldest rationales for art: to give us images and stories where we only have laws and
principles. But things are not this simple. Let us consider Linda Pastan's poem "The Five Stages of Grief," which quite explicitly picks up
the famous psychological principles of Kübler-Ross:

> The night I lost you
> someone pointed me towards
> the Five Stages of Grief.
> Go that way, they said,
> it's easy, like learning to climb
> stairs after the amputation.
> And so I climbed.
> Denial was first.
> I sat down at breakfast
> carefully setting the table
> for two. I passed you the toast—
> you sat there. I passed
> you the paper—you hid
> behind it.
> Anger seemed more familiar.
> I burned the toast, snatched
> the paper and read the headlines myself.
> But they mentioned your departure,
> and so I moved on to
> Bargaining. What can I exchange
> for you? The silence
> after storms? My typing fingers?
> Before I could decide, Depression
> came puffing up, a poor relation,
> its suitcase tied together
> with string. In the suitcase

were bandages for the eyes
and bottles of sleep. I slid
all the way down the stairs
feeling nothing.
And all the time Hope
flashed on and off
in defective neon.
Hope was a signpost pointing
straight in the air.
Hope was my uncle's middle name,
he died of it.
After a year I am still climbing,
though my feet slip
on your stone face.
The treeline
has long since disappeared;
green is a color
I have forgotten.
But now I see what I am climbing
towards: Acceptance
written in capital letters,
a special headline:
Acceptance,
its name is in lights.
I struggle on,
waving and shouting.
Below, my whole life spreads its surf,
all the landscapes I've ever known
or dreamed of. Below
a fish jumps: the pulse
in your neck.
Acceptance. *I finally*

reach it.
But something is wrong.
Grief is a circular staircase.
I have lost you.

Pastan's poem is more than "illustrated" Kübler-Ross. We recall Freud's notion that mourning consists of a laborious but urgent series of severances, of calling up all the memories of the dead one so that the news of death can do its job of cutting the cord. Pastan shows us what this calling up might look like: you are still at the breakfast table when I sit down; the headlines speak of you. Routines die hard, but that is the least of it: we *disseminate* our loved ones into the world, so they crop up in headlines, show up even in the jumping of a fish. This is more than cutting a few cords of memory; it attests to the endlessly creative work of love, namely that it fashions a "we-world," in which objects and places turn out to be saturated with spilled-over feelings, "leavings" that broadcast a life together. Pastan shrewdly enlists a medicalized idiom to convey the damaged life of the mourner: "like learning to climb / stairs after the amputation"; *Depression* is figured both familially and medically as relation whose suitcase contains "bottles of sleep," causing the mourner to lose all sentience. What I have labeled a "pilgrim's progress" is imaged as a mountain climb, an arduous journey (amputees do not climb easily) up the stairs toward recovery and "Acceptance."

Pastan insistently underscores the road markers and labels that guide us in this trek toward healing. These markers are utterly true to the spirit of Freudian inquiry, insofar as private anguish might now be understood generically, so that a map could be drawn, yielding something of great value to those who hurt in the dark. A large Enlightenment project is being played out here, reflecting the elemental hopes we pin on science itself. To "know" that this pain has a form and an end stage is our best weapon for dealing with it. Pastan knows all of this, but her brilliantly imaged account of the trip is hard going for the reader. Each of the five stages is metaphorized into living drama, at first intimate and domestic, later impersonal as a marathonlike climb nearing the longed-for finish line.

As the piece moves toward closure, it opens out into a grand vista—"Below, my whole life spreads its surf, / all the landscapes I've ever known / or dreamed of"—and we begin to see the amplitude of *Trauerarbeit* as the memories of the loved one shade into something enormous and totalizing, the entirety of one's life (and dreams) now at last on show, at last overseen. These lines are eerie in their plenitude, making us realize the reach of this "recovery," entailing nothing less than *all* of one's self that is laid bare. It is as if "you" were everywhere, and to call you up so as to dig you out—the way a surgeon digs under the cancer to see how far it has spread, to gauge how much diseased tissue there really is—were tantamount to leaving one's own life and self. Haven't we always heard that the dying see their entire life unfurl in their last moments? With admirable brevity, Pastan returns from the alpine trek to the domestic stairs, and calls "Grief" a "circular staircase," leading to the devastating conclusion: "I have lost you."

It is at this point we begin to realize how subversive Pastan's poem has been. Far from merely illustrating Kübler-Ross, the poet has wanted to announce the ugly secret that crowns successful mourning: permanent loss, death a second time (now in us). And this loss is a form of diminution, much the way amputation is, so that the recovery is, yes, a victory for life, but also a maiming of the mourner. Pastan is obliging us to ask just what it means when the ego finally becomes, once again, "uninhibited and free." What ego is this? To be sure, the driving engine that fuels our libido and runs our life does indeed come to terms with the reality principle, does indeed finally bury its dead, so as to move on, to find new attachments. But at what cost? The ego continues its fierce life-drive, but the self is permanently altered. Pastan wisely stops here, and does not explore the further ramifications of mourning; instead, she leaves us with a bittersweet image of successful convalescence that is also awful.

Other, more famous poets have written about the death of loved ones, but Pastan's account of mourning seems especially apt for our purposes because of its insistently domestic, insidiously familiar terms. This poem's power derives from its reversals: not only the stunning shift at the end, when I discover that "I have lost you," but the less noticeable, arguably still more painful strategy of inventorying all the accoutrements of domesticity, setting up precisely the familiar icons of shared experience. I call this painful because all this is what now must die, must be seen as illusory, indeed delusory, even mocking in its cruelty. I have lost not only "you," I have lost our life together. Death cashiers a world that is saturated with thick feelings, that shimmers with memories; the camera would merely record a table, a paper, a bottle, whereas the poem registers the intolerable human density of these objects. Is there any wonder that death causes survivors to change surroundings, sometimes even to change mates and lives, in order to get clear of the funereal residue that refuses to die? We sometimes act as if fidelity and memory were some testament of will, some act of virtue, whereas they are also evidence of life's stubborn hold, evidence of the enduring presence of the dead we loved, with us not only in our minds, but in our homes, photos, music, clothes, beds. For the nonreligious among us, this environmental afterlife—half cognitive, half material—may be as good a proof as we are likely to have, that such a thing as "soul" exists.

PROUST: GRANDMOTHER'S DOUBLE DEATH

Perhaps poetry cannot easily manage a longer story than Pastan's account of the five stages. But narrative can, and it may tell us that the Freudian journey toward severance and healing can be murkier, richer, and more complicated than the linear trajectory up the mountain or the stairs. In this regard I would argue that Proust's massive *Recherche du temps perdu* is our premier exemplar for actually rendering the twists and turns that mourning may entail. Now, reading Proust is, in itself, something of a lifelong activity, and the world is full of well-meaning, educated people who will go to their graves with Proust as unfinished business, as a reading task that one never quite completed or got around to. This long book, which opens with the famous phrase "*Longtemps je me suis couché de bonne heure*" ("For a long time I went to bed early"), virtually announces that it is for the insomniacs among us. Only they will find the time for it; and it may even cure their problem. Proust's *Recherche* is almost certainly the great unread classic of the twentieth century, despite his ever-fashionable reputation, as evidenced by the spate of recent books talking about what sort of a personal payoff the author found in tackling such a monster. Most folks would probably still consign Proust to those telling categories such as the book-for-a-desert-island, or its slightly less fantastic analogue: the book I'll read when I either get a humongous vacation near a beach or become permanently bedridden. (Hamlet's "readiness is all" comes into play here.)

As someone who has studied and taught Proust for a good chunk of my life, I have a longitudinal sense of how reading Proust has been rationalized over the years: psychological acuity, social satire, portrait of neurosis, doctrine of art, philosophy of time, nuggets of wisdom. And still more: there are few "ism's" that haven't claimed Proust. He belongs in a chapter about death because his view of life is so insistently and staggeringly vertical, as if people and events presented to the naked eye only their cover, their cover story, whereas one can size them up only by accounting for their historical density. Time is, of course, what fuels this attitude, but death is what parses it and gives it pathos. Moreover, only art can deliver all the substrata that underlie the surfaces we see, and this lesson is meant to teach us humility, to help us toward a more capacious and resonant sense of our fellows and our world, rather than taking them merely for the momentary figures they appear.

In this light, time weaves a special tapestry, so that a glance at a loved one should be four-dimensional, remembering as well as seeing, and if we remember, then the person now seems covered "with the beautiful and inimitable velvety patina of the years, just as in an old park a simple runnel of water comes with the passage of time to be enveloped in a sheath of emerald" (III, 1020). Proustian psychology is often described as narcissist, but I would be hard put to find lines of such generosity in any other writer. It does not seem fanciful to say that Proust's reader is gifted here, for the author urges us to factor "time" into our perceptions and valuations, to discover something of the actual scope and scale of our lives. Routines and habits become silvery (rather than dulling), yielding a layered world of magic and richness; the quotidian world we live in and take for granted—family, friends, lovers—becomes echoing and resonant, rather than the dimensionless silhouettes that habit nastily produces. All this bears directly on how we might understand death.

There are two major deaths in Proust's book: first that of the grandmother, and then that of Albertine. They are handled differently. Proust depicts the grandmother's actual experience of sickness and dying in extraordinary detail, beginning with her first stroke (while out with the boy in the Tuileries gardens) and continuing into her stint with the "medical regime" at the hands of the novel's Doctor Cottard (social nincompoop but shrewd diagnostician), as well as other specialists who come to her bedside. It is worth recalling the remarkable stature of this woman within Proust's narrative world—her sensitivity, generosity, and culture make her arguably the only truly admirable figure in the book, surely the only figure capable of utterly selfless love—if we would measure the stakes of her dying. One cannot avoid the feeling here that this valiant woman—a culture heroine of sorts who can cite Mme. de Sévigné or other classics with ease and appropriateness, who exemplifies moral stature and makes you believe that the work of civilization matters—is somehow targeted in the novel; this woman is to be felled with stunning brutality.

All of us will die. Grandmothers perhaps more than most. Consider the poignant description of Bubeh's dying in Sherwin Nuland's fine recent book *How We Die*. The physician-author describes her entry into dying almost melodically: first we get an account of her increasing bouts of forgetfulness, weakness, and incapacity, as seen by her loving grandson, Sherwin; then we get the grown-up physician's medical analysis of the same episodes, now understood in their terrible physiological cogency as the rigorous and orchestrated breakdown of an old body, with groups of organs and systems beginning to give out. This binary narrative does justice to the human and scientific vantage points, mediates between them, makes us see their terrible congruence.

Yet, the "naturalness" of Nuland's account has none of the horror that Proust's treatment of the grandmother possesses. I say "treatment" advisedly because we feel that the French novel is downright punitive in its assault on this woman. If she represents the noblest virtues of culture, then the novelist is out to show how utterly weightless such virtues are when it comes to dying. To be sure, she dies with valor, but who can forget the indignities that the text visits upon her? There is something systematic in the book's attack: she will be deprived of one sense, then of another, sight, then hearing, then speech; she will be given one protocol, then another. Each will alter her, each will assert its molecular will. She even undergoes leeches, and (to the horror of her grandson) experiences a creatural relief. And throughout this storm, this storming, the lady seeks to hold on to her "self." The pathos of Proust's rendition (which takes up hundreds of pages) lies in the very scandal of flesh which knows only entropy. Proust, unlike Nuland, has an ax to grind, wants us to see how grisly and unfair this contest is, how reductive, coercive, and transformative illness can be. Wakened in the middle of the night to bid her a final farewell, the child does not recognize his grandmother, sees only a "beast" lying on his grandmother's bed, wonders where she really is.

It seems fair to say that this is how many of us experience the death of old people: as systems that are playing out before our horrified eyes. Here is the physiological indignity that comes with age, and one understands the customs of certain tribal cultures where the old and feeble are sent out to die. Any traditional view of maturity and aging as a form of wisdom—a view that has to fight for its life anyway in youth-centered cultures like America—seems particularly vulnerable when physiological deterioration starts to speed up. It is as if the body looms larger and larger in the scheme of things, as if moral or intellectual attainment were crowded out of the picture, so that the spectacle of debility and undoing usurps the stage. Undoing: the seemingly systematic erasure of poise and stature and ease. Ease is when our bodies flaunt their indwelling powers, yet this flaunting hardly registers as such, so natural and effortless it all seems. Most young people inhabit this world of ease, hardly knowing it, never suspecting how time-bound it all is. Sickness puts paid to these arrangements, but once well we mercifully forget how stacked the somatic deck can be against us. Aging and dying make us—all of us, diers and witnesses—excruciatingly aware of this physiological endgame that we cannot win, and they may make us wonder whether all reports of human "mastery" are naïve in character, fair-weather fictions that are destined to fade away when the storm comes. One can well ask what literature has to offer here, since these issues are so dreadfully material and eloquent in their own, nonartistic right. Why invoke literature when the aging body's decrepitude is visible to any and all? These are things we can see.

But is there something to death that we cannot see? To answer this, I want to return to Proust's depiction of the grandmother. In keeping with the downhill trajectory of the body that nature insists on, the old lady dies. The physical horror show is over. But Proust now plays out his own version of mourning, a view that recognizes the survivalist impulse of the mourner, just as Freud and Kübler-Ross do, but which nonetheless offers a rich, rival fable of its own. The grandmother has died as dispossessed beast, as occupant of a body that is held hostage to entropy. In charting her decline, Proust has even saluted Molière by choreographing the comedy of her posturing physicians. No way, Proust tells us, of stopping this journey toward annihilation. But then something quite wonderful happens. The leave-taking that was so brutal and merciless on the physiological front—the helpless spectating that attends the exit of a loved one—gets played out a second time, in different colors now, as the boy is "visited" by the dead grandmother in the beautiful chapter "Les intermittences du coeur." This episode appears in *Sodome et Gomorrhe,* more than a year after the woman's death, and hundreds of busy pages later in the life of the protagonist, now a young man acquainted with various forms of sexuality, now returning to Balbec, the resort area that he and his grandmother had visited many years back. Now, the reader assumes, death is out of the picture.

However, what one needs to remember about that first visit is that it began with utter disarray on the part of the child (a disarray typical of his "neurasthenia" and hypersensitivity to new environments), and the frightened, miserable boy survived this first stint largely through the generous, sustaining love lavished on him by the old lady. Proust had beautifully imaged their intimacy by means of a little semiotic miracle: the boy, when visited by his demons, would rap on the wall that divided his room from that of his grandmother; the raps would be timid and faint, not too strong so as to startle her, not too feeble so as to be unheard. And she heard, understood, rapped back, came, and nurtured, time after time, producing this long novel's only (but radiant) example of pure communication and pure balm. For all intents and purposes, however, the intervening year has done its work, the ties have been cut, the grandmother is dead, gone, and forgotten. But the return visit to Balbec turns out to be "uncanny," in the doubling and displacing sense that Freud gave to the term, because this place is to be the locus of the grandmother's second death—utterly unlike the somatic catastrophe of the first one—as Proust rewrites the rules concerning what lives and what dies, radically challenging the biological and public record.

Tired, in chest pain, bending over gingerly to take off his boots, the narrator is invaded by "an unknown, a divine presence" (II, 273). This presence is, of course, the grandmother who still lives *in* the protagonist, in the form of *mémoire involontaire,* a magic inner space where our past is ever green and vital, which we can only access through the whims of associative connections and serendipitous linkage. Proust's character relives his first visit to Balbec, becomes once again (briefly) the hurting young boy whose pain was alleviated in only one way: through the ministrations of the loving grandmother. This miraculous recall—so utterly unlike the mechanical feats of retrieval and storage made possible by our computer age—completes the early experience, adds to its plenitude, enables the older man to come into his estate by actually possessing what had merely "happened" earlier. And it is only through this re-newed contact with the "reborn," living grandmother that the narrator finally experiences the actual horror: she is dead. It is here that Proust expands and complicates the picture of mourning offered to us by Freud and Kübler-Ross, and it is here that literature amplifies our un-derstanding of what death really might mean. There are two deaths, Proust is saying: the first is the brutal, unstoppable fate of flesh which condemns all living creatures and flaunts its dreadful authority. This is the one on record. But insofar as we are talking about mourning, about the reality of death for a loved one, then the focus must shift to the men-tal and emotional life of the survivor, and it is there that a second death occurs, never really simultaneous with the first one. Traditional mourn-ing acknowledges this much.

But Proust goes on to say that this second death, which may come even years after the first one, constitutes a farewell of remarkable density and richness, unlike the abrupt cessation of the first death. There is something stunningly humanistic in Proust's vision here, and the "*in-termittences du coeur*" register for us just how haunting and beautiful this "second exit" can be. Only now does the narrator measure the ex-tent and depth of his loss, because only now have the extent and depth of the loved one fully reappeared, writ large in this scene of incapacity: he bends down to remove his boots, re-becomes the sick-to-heart young boy of the past, and now knows that the balm-giving grandmother can never again come to his aid, even as he reexperiences her earlier life-saving efforts. Dead though she is, his life is saturated with her presence, and so she still lives.

Memory is life's great double-edged sword: it restores the past to us in all its fullness, while simultaneously flaunting its own virtuality, its status as mere memory, its tidings of absence that mock and undo the miraculous presence. Our experience of the death of others is utterly cued to this delayed-action, double scenario. Whereas the so-called stages of grief map out our incremental severing of ties, Proust reconceives the matter altogether and grants the survivor a bittersweet reprieve: you get a second chance at this death, with the result that your loss is all the more horrible (now that you "know" what you have lost, now that you "know" that you have lost it for good), and yet this second act may have a resonance and volume that do justice to the actual scope of human love. This particular story—this heartbreaking game of hide-and-seek, of finders and keepers, losers and weepers—is not on record anywhere at all. No corpse, no funeral oration, no gravestone, no obituary, none of these markers of mortality, is in on this secret: that the dead haven't died yet, not entirely, not on the inside. Memory knows this story; literature can tell it. This is Proust's quarry.

Now the narrator replays his life with his grandmother, sees with shocking clarity the hurt he has caused her in her life, a hurt that now boomerangs entirely since his very perception of it is self-lodged, self-harming, "for as the dead exist only in us, it is ourselves that we strike without respite when we persist in recalling the blows that we have dealt them" (II, 786). But the bulk of the narrator's leave-taking of the (long) dead grandmother takes place in the dreams that now come to the bereaved man, dreams which refract what Proust calls "the agonizing synthesis of survival and annihilation, once more re-formed, in the organic and translucent depths of the mysteriously lighted viscera" (II, 787). I have repeatedly used the term *illumination* as a way of characterizing the work of literature, and I would submit that nothing can be darker for most of us than our own "viscera." Yes, doctors sometimes shine their light into our orifices and cavities, just as modern imaging provides its own miraculous readout of what is transpiring inside the murky body. We therefore know about the fluids and even blockages that live in our somatic pathways, but how do we account for love? Where does it live and lodge? Isn't memory the body's magic script for reversing entropy? And dreams turn out to be our nightly conduits for a kind of affective traffic that never stops, that outlives the deaths of all players except the dreamer.

Nothing in Proust's long novel quite matches the exquisite oneiric account of the grandmother's second death. The narrator is on a journey in search of his grandmother, embarking "upon the dark current of our own blood as upon an inward Lethe meandering sixfold" (II, 787). Tall, solid forms appear, as he explores this unknown space "beneath somber portals," with the certainty that she still exists, but diminished, so that she is en route to extinction and must be found soon if she is to be found at all. The darkness and the wind increase while the boy remembers that he has forgotten, for weeks on end, to write to the grandmother, thinks of how distressed she must be, living in "that little room which they have taken for her, no bigger than what one would give to an old servant, where she's all alone with the nurse they have put there to look after her, from which she cannot stir, for she's still slightly paralysed and has always refused to get up! She must think that I've forgotten her now that she's dead; how lonely she must be feeling, how deserted!" (II, 788). As happens so often in dreams, the desperate search is continually thwarted; he cannot remember where she lives, his father (who is to guide him) does not show up, the wind picks up still further. Then the father is sighted, and he explains that the grandmother is provided for in her little room, that she has inquired about her grandson, has been told that he was going to write a book, had seemed pleased, had wept.

When one knows about Proust's own carefully guarded sexual secrets and the amount of personal guilt that he harbored vis-à-vis his mother, these lines receive a very personal stamp; yet they also speak a larger, more general story of remorse (has one ever loved enough? does one ever realize it in time? has one ever said one's full to the loved one?). The boy beseeches his father to lead him to the grandmother, but the yearned-for encounter is fraught with problems, is eroding in front of our eyes: " 'Quick, quick, her address, take me to her.' But he says: 'Well . . . I don't know whether you will be able to see her. Besides, you know, she's very frail now, very frail, she's not at all herself, I'm afraid you would find it rather painful. And I can't remember the exact number of the avenue.' 'But tell me, you who know, it's not true that the dead have ceased to exist. It can't possibly be true, in spite of what they say, because grandmother still exists.' My father smiles a mournful smile: 'Oh, hardly at all, you know, hardly at all. I think it would be better if you didn't go . . .' " (II, 789). The dream closes with the boy waking up in his Balbec hotel room, looking out to the sea, then turning away from it toward the wall of his room. And, with perfect circular logic, this wall is the old wall that served as a magic membrane which united (united, not divided) the boy and his grandmother a year earlier, as he tapped his small and frantic message of hurt, and she responded with her answer of love: "those answering knocks which meant: 'Don't fuss, little mouse, I know you're impatient, but I'm just coming' " (II, 790).

This dreamed farewell is neither sappy nor escapist; he never quite finds the dying lady even in the dream. But the pursuit itself, the fashioning of that small room where she lingers, not quite dead, awaiting the boy's communication, pleased and moved that he is writing, the recovery of the grandmother's priceless love, all this constitutes a rival scenario to the specter of the beast on the bed. Just a dream, we might say. Yet this rival story captures something exquisite and profound about his experience of love and loss: the insistently diminished condition of the grandmother, the futile efforts to find her, to tell her how much he still cares, all of this conveys with heart-wrenching detail not only the dismantling of death but the pathos of love, the failure either to save those we love or even to make them know how much we love. We see this as a story, one that adds something to the Little Red Riding Hood saga of the dead woman as beast on a bed whom someone has taken away. Something precious is also being added to the data of our lives here, in that the brutal trauma of death in its somatic form turns out not to be the final act, can be replayed in the mind of the bereaved in gracious and humane fashion. Arguably this second death is far more painful than the first, but it transforms the Gothic tale of abduction ("where was my grandmother?") into a fuller story of leave-taking, it too addressed to the question: "where was my grandmother?"

I want to say that Proust's depiction of the grandmother's "deaths" constitutes precisely that "public utility" that I believe art to be. And this leads to the point of my book. Like any other literary icon, Proust is ordinarily to be found on some ideal library shelf in the mind, filled with other presumable masterpieces that we may get around to reading, if the hustle and bustle of real life ever permits us the time to do so. The very bulk of Proust's novel virtually ensures that it will be given this honorific status: much praise, little reality. At the same time, all of us today are conversant with the host of pharmaceutical, medical, and how-to re-sources that we regard as supremely practical, meant to be consulted or taken if we are in a bad way, located also on some shelf, a real (not ideal) shelf in our medicine cabinet where we go to find help for pain. I am hardly prescribing dosages of Proust for heartache, but I am saying that his depiction of a dreadful common event—no one is without loved ones who will die—is at once visionary and practical in that he shows us something about the way the machinery actually works: our machinery, our processes of mourning and recovery, our own story of love and loss that turns out to have far more twists and turns, indeed far more life, in it than our lazy received notions suggest. How poor and cheating Kübler-Ross's categories look, when contrasted with the odyssey of death-recovery-loss that Proust's narrator undergoes. Not that Kübler-Ross and Freud are wrong, but that life is actually more complex, more wonderful, more capacious than their formulas indicate.

As a professor who has been teaching undergraduates for three decades, I have come to see the "death of the grandparents" as a fre-quent rite of passage undergone by my students during their tenure at university. For many of them, it is the first encounter with death. (In our culture of increased longevity, it may soon be the case that college-age students' first encounter with death will be the death of great-grandparents.) Given the shocking physical contest that such deaths often stage—the entropic endgame—Proust enriches the saga they have witnessed by suggesting that the physiological end is not as definitive as it appears. Whether the young are capable of absorbing this wisdom is another matter. But it is unarguably true that this novel consoles, offers a vision of solace that borders on recuperation in its repeat performances of memory and dream. Wisdom literature? Not really. Rather, a fuller look at some of the stark facts of life through the prism of fiction, jolting us toward a more generous, more imaginative, more surprising view of what life has in store for us.

PROUST: FORGETTING AND REMEMBERING, OR DEATH AND RESURRECTION

But Proust has still more to say about death, and we have still more to learn. His book records a second major death, that of Albertine, the protagonist's mistress, the desired fugitive of the book, the "*être de fuite*," the creature of flight that Marcel can never quite "possess," even though he seeks to with all his might through bullying, blackmail, and even physical incarceration. Along any normative lines whatsoever, this particular love relationship is nasty business, spurred by a maniacal need for control and its corollary: endless anxiety and jealousy. I suspect that many readers lose patience with this part of the book, largely because it has a diseased taint to it, yet we would do well to attend to its aftermath, for that is where Proust demonstrates his sovereign understanding of death's role in the affairs of the heart.

Albertine's dying, in contrast to the protracted illness and death of the grandmother, is narratively offstage. The young man learns, by telegram, that the escaped girl has been killed in a riding accident. Proust handles the following period of *Trauerarbeit* in classic Freudian fashion: the narrator is shown cutting each one of the cords that tied him to Albertine, the object of his libidinal attachment. This is no easy matter: "So that what I should have to annihilate in myself was not one, but innumerable Albertines. Each was attached to a moment, to the date of which I found myself carried back when I saw again that particular Albertine" (III, 498). This death triggers something properly seismic: the narrator revisits the past, scene by scene, to notify his former selves that Albertine is no longer alive. This too turns out to be a dizzying exercise, since there are lots of folks involved: "It was not Albertine alone who was a succession of moments, it was also myself. . . . I was not one man only, but as it were the march-past of a composite army in which there were passionate men, indifferent men, jealous men—jealous men not one of whom was jealous of the same woman" (III, 499).

It is now clear that the death of a loved one is to be understood as a mobile internal theater, virtually unrelated to some body lying in a coffin, and that this process of leave-taking is dreadfully unruly. Inside of us, the dead still live, and in Proust's scheme, they can be horribly free to wreak havoc. Hence, the narrator continues to imagine, with ever more frenzy, scenes of betrayal committed by Albertine, acts of sexual independence that can (now) never be corroborated or disproved because the actress is no longer available for interrogation (not that much was ascertained even when she was). The dead Albertine romps through her imagined sexual repertory, thanks to the prodigiously creative jealousy of her grieving lover.

This is a masochistic story that could go on forever; you might say that such projections, by dint of their sovereign independence from verifiable fact or even a living subject, display a peculiarly horrid form of immortality. This form of grieving is a much grislier, more anxious proposition than the traditional model put forth by the psychologists, in that the mourner still seeks to satisfy his possession-mania; but he finds that the dead, far from being docile at last, are freer than ever to produce mischief and torture. Here is one way of saying that death is not the kind of closure one imagines; on the contrary, it is precisely via imagination that death is negated—not willed imagination, but the imagination of fantasy, prurience, dread, and anxiety—because the seemingly dead actor continues to perform in the *Spielraum,* the theatrical stage, of one's own head.

And it is all too easy for us to pronounce judgment here, to brand such behavior and angst as sick or masochistic, but Proust is merely obeying the central law of his work: we live in our own consciousness, and in those precincts, the public decrees of life and death have zero binding power. What lives is whatever we think about, whatever we give life to. It doesn't take much effort to realize that Proust is reconceiving mourning itself as the continued affective life and agency of the mourner, rather than the cutting of ties theorized by Freud. Dead weight, Freud claimed, must eventually make itself felt as dead weight; not at all, Proust says, because this condition of so-called death merely limits the present maneuvering room of the lost one, but it opens up the gates for endless, unverifiable actions (including betrayals) in our own minds.

Still, Freud had it right. Albertine and Marcel end up playing by the rules. Her show will gradually fade, he will gradually heal, she will be forgotten. For Freud, as I said, this is a question of cutting cords. But for Proust this is a far more intricate and subtle set of transactions. How do we heal, Proust is asking? How do the dead finally die, inside of us? Such a question may appear to be either morbid or idle or both. Proust makes us understand that this issue is shockingly central in our everyday lives, even though most of us have never considered it. This, we come to understand, is what the notion of *forgetting* actually signifies. *Oubli* is the great theme of Proust's work, and its power derives from the fact that it is a cognate of death: our memory of others is tantamount to their life (in us), and according to this same implacable subjectivity argument, our forgetting of others is rigorously equivalent to their death.

At first glance, such a theory seems wildly indulgent, since most of us feel that life and death are the most elemental objective truths to be found in reality, whereas remembering and forgetting appears to be a far lesser, "in-house" proposition that only has to do with consciousness and head games. Proust obliges us to reconsider this. Once we are prepared to accept the two-death model as valid for *Trauerarbeit,* we have already designated the consciousness of the mourner as the terrain where the second death occurs. Such a view of consciousness and *oubli* is profoundly funereal, since it posits the human mind as essentially a graveyard, a place where others lived and now lie buried, forgotten, insofar as we no longer access them. Needless to say, this model cavalierly dispenses with the "actual" condition of the other—in fact, on this heading, many healthy living people continue to die like flies within us, since we "kill" them routinely by dismissing them from our awareness (even this wording is doubtless too volitional; they simply disappear, "die"). There is also a stubborn logic at work here, a logic that recasts the very activity of consciousness as an incessant affair of life and death.

Proust understands this activity to be a story in itself, a story that has gone largely untold. If you actually struggle through Proust's chapters here, it is all too easy to read the long passages devoted to Marcel's slow and painful forgetting of Albertine as a study in minutiae, a maniacally fastidious (and self-indulgent) account of getting over a loss, a pernicious example of excessive psychologizing. My argument goes the other way: Marcel's "mourning" transforms the severance model put forth by Freud and Kübler-Ross into a fable whose richness is a staggeringly large thing, once we are prepared to take it seriously. Far from being esoteric or "literary," this material is as intimate, personal, and universal as anything we're ever likely to read. The author is showing us how the mind actually works over time, and he makes us realize that most of our notions of mind work are snapshots, the sort of thing we gather if we eavesdrop on ourselves, the casual truisms that result from pondering, now and then, how we think.

Proust obliterates this snapshot model by taking the longer view, by examining our behavior longitudinally, and by asking some devastating questions about who we are. What, you may ask, does death have to do with this? Everything, I answer, in that "I" is dying all the time, and this spectacle of death/rebirth is nowhere more on show than in the experience of mourning. Getting past the death of a loved one entails two exits: our loved one's and our own. When mourning, we discover that forgetting and dying are, yes, separated in time (the loved one dies, but we remember, at least for a while), but we also discover that the second death is not merely a form of closure that caps mourning, it is also our own death and rebirth. Even to put it that way is far too static. The beauty of Proust's narrative is that it plays out our innermost emotional transactions in full dress and thereby exposes the poverty of our clinical labels, now seen as reductive shortcuts that have little to do with the true events taking place. The only way to make this case is to cite Proust at work, so we turn now to an evocation of Marcel approaching complete severance. Albertine is long dead, and he is healing, but still able to speak of her; Proust suggests that the mourning figure who no longer hurts in the same way as before is, in fact, someone else, a "newcomer":

> The newcomer who would find it easy to endure the prospect of life without Albertine had made his appearance in me, since I had been able to speak of her at Mme. de Guermantes's in the language of grief without any real suffering. The possible advent of these new selves, which each ought to bear a different name from the preceding one, was something I had always dreaded, because of their indifference to the object of my love. . . . Yet he was bringing me on the contrary, this newcomer, at the same time as oblivion an almost complete elimination of suffering, a possibility of comfort—this newcomer so dreaded yet so beneficent, who was none other than one of those spare selves which destiny holds in reserve for us, and which, paying no more heed to our entreaties than a clear-sighted and thus all the more authoritative physician, it substitutes in spite of us, by a timely intervention, for the self that has been too seriously wounded. This process, as it happens, automatically occurs from time to time, like the decay and renewal of our tissues, but we notice it only if the former self contained a great grief, a painful foreign body, which we are surprised to no longer find there, in our amazement at having become another person to whom the sufferings of his predecessor are no more than the sufferings of a stranger, of which we can speak with compassion because we do not feel them. Indeed we are unconcerned about having undergone all these sufferings,

since we have only a vague remembrance of having suffered them. It may well be that likewise our nightmares are horrifying. But on waking we are another person, who cares little that the person whose place he takes has had to flee from a gang of cut-throats during the night.

No doubt this self still maintained some contact with the old, as a friend who is indifferent to a bereavement speaks of it nevertheless to the persons present in a suitable tone of sorrow, and returns from time to time to the room in which the widower who has asked him to receive the company for him may still be heard weeping. I too still wept when I became once again for a moment the former friend of Albertine. But it was into a new personality that I was tending to change altogether. It is not because other people are dead that our affection for them fades; it is because we ourselves are dying. (III, 607–608)

I have written about this passage in another context in order to emphasize the strange "community of self" which it celebrates: a view of the human subject over time as a kind of parade of disparate figures, an endless dying and birthing, or, as Proust puts it, an insertion of "spare selves" (like spare tires) which life installs on our vehicle when it is in trouble or breaks down (see *The Fiction of Relationship*). My interest here is in the way Proust rewrites our notions of mourning, expands the picture of what it actually means when we "lose" a loved one, shows us how the final acceptance of another's death must be understood as a form of our own dying. There is nothing whatsoever morbid about this model; on the contrary, it is animated by the same vital spirit of survival that fuels the views of Freud and Kübler-Ross, but it spells out for us, as they do not, the human ramifications of such life changes, making us realize that "healing" has its grisly as well as its welcome side. Grisly and yet tender as well. By literalizing issues of discontinuity and oblivion, by arguing that the human subject is reborn and remade via forgetting, by proposing that every "I" is a serial "we" (that should bear a new name each time), Proust suggests that every life-in-time is an incessant, kaleidoscopic affair of death and alteration. But it is "tender," too, in the very act of recuperation that the passage itself illuminates: the man who no longer felt the pain of Albertine's loss is imaged in the passage as a "friend" of the "widower" who "may still be heard weeping." We die over and over, yes, but we remain connected to these corpses, these former selves; we are, in essence, a cemetery, a site where all our past lives—tending to become as alien and evanescent as the nightmares we cannot recall—might still be accessed, are indeed being accessed in this sequence. This is, of course, to be the grand triumph of Proust's book, the ecstatic result of the *recherche* at hand, something on the order of secular resurrection. Such a strangely picaresque view of human feeling seems to me to be possessed of more dignity, to be more commensurate with the realities of love, loss, and survival than the familiar truism that "time heals."

And let me say a word about my term *access* in this context. Proust stuns us with his vision of how stubbornly and uncontrollably the past still lives in us even though we think we are inhabiting a "now-world." His depiction of mourning restores the dead to their proper place, *in us,* and in that locale they continue to live, flaunting the absurdity of any material scheme that would point to a grave in order to prove separation and absence. In this dispensation, we are networked creatures, linked by our loves and ties, doomed to be emotionally and morally *online* as long as we live. True, our electronic culture enables us to log on, to check our e-mail, to travel that new highway wherever we choose. In Proust, no electricity is required (unless it be the electricity that fuels heart and brain), but the connections are stupendous in their immediacy. Above all, the new map of linkages that Proust devises has an amazing economy: it is your life, writ large, not utterly unlike the old TV program *This Is Your Life,* where your old teachers and friends are ghoulishly hauled out onto the stage. No stage necessary in Proust.

I have invoked Proust at considerable length because he radically de-familiarizes our notions of death, and he does so by positing death as the unacknowledged arbiter of all human change, death as the gatekeeper who seals off the infant we were from the child we became, who separates the prepubescent youngster from the adolescent, who marks off the single individual from the later spouse, who delineates the mature professional's edges and thus separates him or her from the old person who emerges. Death is the cessation of each of our avatars. Take a look in your scrapbook, at the photos on your desk, and you will see death at work, especially at work when you sense that these figures of the past are not only alien but strangely independent of one another. Take a look at your résumé, and ask yourself if death is not lurking between each of your entries, lurking there in order to "off" the college student so that the professional could emerge, needed there to "off" the practitioner of career one so that exemplar of career two (or three or four) could ply his trade and prosper.

What is human development but incessant death and birth? It is dizzying to envisage the parade of people we were and are. "Are," be-cause death works laterally as well as vertically, is good at posting electric fences between our fractured selves: the one in the office, the one at home, the one in church, the one at the table, the one in bed. We call this "compartmentalizing," but it is just as accurate to say that every situation mandates a particular self and that all those others who we also are "die." Mourning is how we respond to the serial game and separations that life metes out to us. Mourning is our dirge in the face of discontinuity; it is our nostalgia for wholeness; it is our doomed effort to stop time. Proust, mandarin figure though he is, is also "meat and potatoes," in that he adds something special to our scientific base in this crucial issue of death and mourning. He thus widens our grasp of the narrowest fact of life—death as one-liner, death as "finis"—opens its closed precincts by playing it out and sharing it out, illuminates our emotional trajectory and evolution, and thereby helps us to harness, conceptually, that brute event that co-erces all lives but is mum in the process. Proust "says" death.

The Sick Child, Edvard Munch, 1885.

MOURNING VISUALIZED: EDVARD MUNCH

I have wanted to take a leisurely tour through Proust because his treatment of death upends our truisms about finality and closure. I am tempted to say that he needs all those thousands of pages to get his job done, even though readers (and publishers) are understandably leery of fat tomes that come in multiple installments. Why are we in such a hurry? Why shouldn't art reflect something of the actual twisting and turning, the forgetting and remembering, indeed the living and dying that make up life. Perhaps this is why novels secretly lure us: between front and back cover they package time in such a way that we might retrieve it. Yet, as we saw in Munch's *Self-Portrait with Skeletal Arm,* painting may achieve similar ends. Susan Sontag argued long ago, in her fine book *On Photography*, that photographs have an inherent aura of evanescence and mortality about them, and anyone who has ever owned or looked at a scrapbook knows something about this emotional truth.

Could the complexity of mourning be represented visually? Let me return to Munch, who seems an automatic reference here, as a kind of coda to Proust. The Norwegian painter has acknowledged, in his correspondence, how haunted he was, how powerfully the past shaped him and held on to him: "Disease, insanity and death were the angels which attended my cradle, and have since followed me throughout my life" (Munch, in Hodin, 11). It is no accident that Munch's breakthrough painting *The Sick Child*, done first in 1885 (and continually redone throughout his life), is devoted to the death of his sister Sophie a decade earlier. This early canvas, representing for some scholars Munch's "road not taken" (by dint of its impasto technique and scored surface, all so different from the famous "flat" style developed in the mid-nineties), has a rare emotional vibrancy. One feels that the very technique of the painting (scraping, scouring, gouging) expresses the physiological onslaught suffered by the consumptive Sophie, as if the painter wanted to show disease's inroads, to show how vulnerable skin can be. The face of the girl is serene, almost ecstatic, as she looks at and past the consoling, nurturing aunt (Munch's mother had already died of the same disease years earlier). We can feel the perspiration caused by fever, the weight of the wet hair, all leading to an almost ethereal image of Sophie, as if the crucible of disease had transfigured her, reduced her to pure spirit.

What has always moved me most in this painting, however, is the almost unbearable eloquence of the "mother-daughter" dyad, the older woman who looks down, who *knows* she cannot save the child. And yet, love endows this scene of dying with great beauty, for we see the human family as it is, two figures joined by tenderness and compassion, lending a rich "social" aura to the gloomy depiction of bed, patient, curtain, and medicine. Dying can be shared if not stopped. Munch has painted this scene some ten years after the event, and this calendar speaks volumes:

the painting *is* Munch's mourning, his way of showing that this scene cannot die, this doomed love still lives, this compassion is forever fresh. My terms are not so different from those on Keats's urn—"Forever wilt thou love, and she be fair"—for they point to the same miracle of art: it keeps feeling alive; it vanquishes death.

Munch seems to have been shackled to Sophie's death, so much so that one can scarcely avoid thinking that this obsession was strangely vital to him, acting as a catalyst for his art as much as his memory and love, so that we may now construe mourning to be, at least for this painter, generative. Consider the psychic economy on show here: fidelity to the dead sister is also a cunning pact with one's artistic mission. I find this attitude especially noteworthy when we contrast it with today's "now-cult," most vividly epitomized in that vulgar refrain that all of us hear when we are mired in thought or memory or remorse: *get on with it*. Munch's lifelong cultivation of his early (and later) traumas suggests pragmatism as much as morbidity, and causes us to rethink Freud's notion of the dead as dead tissue (and thus unavailable for cathexis).

Nowhere is the astonishing fruitfulness of mourning/memory more visible than in the most famous canvas Munch devoted to Sophie's death, painted in 1895 (nineteen years after the fact), *Death in the Sickroom*. It is fair to say that this painting *gestated* in Munch, since the figures we see are depicted as young adults, not as the children they were at the time of this event. This painting advertises cohesion as much as separation and presents the family unit as umbilically linked, frozen hieratically at the moment when one of them is lost. The dying Sophie is seated, her back to us, in the chair, attended by the helpless father and aunt, but all the energy and power of the painting is lodged in the posture and experiences of the sibling witnesses, the children who experience *together* this death. The brother Andreas seeks to exit the scene and is caught (forever) at the door, in a posture of foiled escape (foiled by the painting itself) that Munch will return to in his later work. (One does not get away, Munch seems to be saying, one continues to live in, through, and via the deaths of the past.)

Death in the Sickroom, Edvard Munch, 1895.

But the center of the piece is the astounding three-headed mass that registers Sophie's going: Inger, whose face looks like a frozen death mask, stares head-on at us, sphinx-like, defying us to make sense of what we are witnessing; Laura, head angled down with hands folded in resignation, inaccessible to our scrutiny; and Edvard, who has turned his gaze, Medusa-like, fully on the horror, taking in the moment of exit that he will then reproduce in the painting that we are looking at. I do not think these siblings are joined by compassion or sympathy; rather, they constitute a pictorial block, an indissoluble unit (a unit that includes Sophie), welded together by the experience of death. This collective fixation on the moment when one world is left and another entered constitutes a *rite de passage* in more ways than one: Sophie leaves the living, but Edvard becomes an artist. And it doesn't seem fanciful to say that Edvard's journey balances Sophie's, that his homage maintains her

The Midwife, Lena Cronqvist, 1972.

life. The stiff, hushed postures of the witnesses suffuse this portrayal of death with both mystery and majesty, causing us to feel the muffled force that is making its presence known in this family.

WATCHING THE DYING: LENA CRONQVIST

Munch and Proust have often been classified as neurotic, and in some areas, notably their depiction of erotic relations, the charge has merit; but I suggest that their respective fixations on death are ultimately fertile, seeding the art they produce. *Death is fertile.* We all know that our first birth comes from father's seed and mother's egg; in some inarguable way, our "birth" as adults must derive from our parents' deaths, a kind of second seeding that we experience as trauma, but also as fate

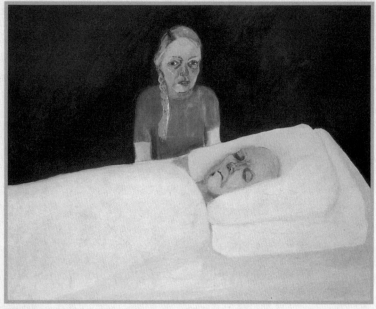

The Wake, Lena Cronqvist, 1980.

and as launch. Artists offer precious testimony here, and I want to draw on the work of Swedish artist Lena Cronqvist to illustrate this point. In her series focusing on the death of her father and mother, we see a kind of narrative, or temporal, imagination that is capable of the same richness we saw in Proust. But let me start, for contrast's sake, with one of Cronqvist's most genial pieces, *The Midwife,* which resolutely treats birth as a natural, organic, indeed botanical event. The woman kneels piously in her garden and cradles the infant who has sprouted out of the earth. Generation seems removed from sexuality, and the production of babies acquires a serene, quasi-horticultural dimension, giving special meaning to our fond notion of babies as "nature's gift."

It is worth remembering this pagan, idyllic side of Cronqvist when we consider what happens at the other end of the spectrum, when father and mother die. The Edenic earlier setting has now become a darkened

Mamma and I, Lena Cronqvist, 1987.

hospital, and in *The Wake,* we see the artist, with her robust flesh tones and red sweater, watching over a gray, horizontal father's corpse. It is interesting to note that this is a scene that Edvard Munch repeatedly depicted, always imagining and positioning himself as the supine corpse attended by the more or less spectral bystanders. Cronqvist clearly occupies the mourning slot here, the helpless onlooker who bears witness to death's hush and stilling of life. Only the father's head shows, but the painting conveys something of the sheer bulk of the dead, in terms at once physical and emotional, rendered somehow all the more palpable by the discreet white sheet. Nothing quite prepares us, however, for the searing series of paintings of 1986–88 entitled *Mamma.* Consider, for instance, *Mamma and I,* where daughter-artist—torso showing, bloodred

The Mother, Lena Cronqvist, 1975.

eyes fixed on us and beyond, body poised and vital—is juxtaposed
against the gigantic death-sculpture of the mother: death's head over
life's head, death shriek against tight living lips, monolithic gray bulk
against artist at the ready, hands prepared to create. Against a sterile
backdrop of imprisoning planes, Cronqvist offers a mesmerizing story
of mourning and creation, of currents that pass between mother and
daughter, suggesting at once bondage, pain, love, and inspiration.

Cronqvist's most famous painting, *The Mother,* was done in 1975,
well before the old woman's death, but it perhaps holds the key to our
interpretation. In this lavish, ceremonial portrait of the artist, with its
salute to grand Renaissance painting, we encounter the mother-
daughter dyad in shockingly inverted form: the daughter holds the tiny

mother (kicking and screaming, one feels) over her womb, thereby signaling not only their link through sexual generation (albeit reversed) but, most crucially, the actual site of the mother. Mother is not yet dead, but the daughter carries her already, over her vagina, yes, but more generally as a parturition that can never take place. Contrary to the upbeat fable of integral and independent babies springing out of the earth (*The Midwife*), this painting advertises enmeshment and inscription as the reality of mothers and daughters, showing just how imbricated we remain with and within one another throughout life. I cannot imagine a painting more in line with Proust's evocation of the grandmother's death, in that we see a moral and emotional geography that no photograph can render, a dispensation that graphs the actual human significance that others have for us. This painting overwhelms us with its imperious displacements, thereby exposing the Newtonian world of docile surfaces to be real enough when it comes to measuring rooms, but delusory when it comes to measuring relationships.

MAKING FRIENDS WITH DEATH

Most writers, great and less great, say death in their fashion, and no argument about literature's testimony in this area can pretend to any kind of adequacy or inclusiveness. The point, rather, is that literature, in being drawn to this grim topic, widens our optic, increases our store of knowledge, enriches our sense of futures. Terrible, awesome texts, such as *King Lear,* have a higher pragmatism in a culture that refuses to dwell on death, and Freud was not wrong when he claimed that Shakespeare's play was about the necessity of "making friends with death." This is no easy friendship. Lear himself does not manage it very well. Modern life seems especially allergic to talk of death, and many people in the United States talk cheerfully and confidently about the possibility of reversing aging, of extending life indefinitely, of getting yourself conveniently frozen until science has gotten its act together, at which time you would thaw out and resume action. The bodybuilding obsession and health mania and wellness syndrome in popular thinking also suggest an un-stated yearning for somatic immortality (soul is not very evident in much of this). Consistent with all of this, of course, is the fact that dying often takes place in special, closed-off precincts in modern industrial-ized cultures, hospitals and nursing homes, places where the old and in-firm live together but that are off-limits to the young and healthy.

Needless to say, these truisms are balanced by a huge suspicion that death is real after all, and that our American way of handling it has much to be desired. The hospice movement is an effort toward bringing death back into a family framework. And the interest in alternative spiritual as well as medical traditions also indicates a reaction against "American death." That Sogyal Rinpoche's *Tibetan Book of Living and Dying* was something of a bestseller tells us that these matters still count, that our resolutely secular scheme is nonetheless death haunted.

My perspective on these matters is largely literary and imaginative, since I believe that it is in our imagination of death that we are most im-poverished and shortchanged. But we all know that the socioeconomic dimensions of dying constitute one of America's great unaddressed problems. These issues, replete with actuarial tables and dollar assess-ments, are increasingly brought to the consciousness of older Ameri-cans by dint of the visibility given to such matters in public health policy as well as by the wake-up calls put forth by insurance companies and re-tirement plans concerning the need to put something away for those last, ghastly expensive years. In every sense of the term, we *pay* for our evasions. There is something economically obscene in the specter of en-tire estates being spent down, or outright ruined, in the (brief!) final stage of someone's life. I think that our engagement with death as a major conceptual "agenda item" deserves a wake-up call, and that the arts can be surprisingly vital here. It is time to realize that death and dying have a kind of imaginative and intellectual majesty and sweep that dwarf our current conversation about estate planning, long-term care, and even hospice arrangements.

If "talking" about death makes many people queasy, this is one good reason why it is useful to see just how prominently and profoundly death figures in literature from antiquity to our time. We will be better armed. I presented Proust's version of mourning as an amplification of what we learn in Freud and Kübler-Ross, but it is obvious that we can go far back beyond Proust. The *Antigone* of Sophocles is entirely cued to issues of appropriate mourning and treatment of the dead, and all ancient cultures had complex rituals and belief systems in place for this final occurrence. We know all too well that these matters are hardly limited to a dispute as to which brother deserves burial rites; events ranging from airplane disasters to the plight of the "missing" and the "disappeared" in many political regimes to the Holocaust itself remind us that modern history is not only corpse ridden but also in search of appropriate forms of mourning and closure. Entire nations and geographical regions—Germany, the Balkans, parts of Africa and Asia and the Americas—have yet to make their way through these matters. It is questionable whether literature or any form of discourse can ever be fully commensurate with such drastic, open wounds, but one might argue that art does emerge from such crises. One remembers Claudel's definition of Greek tragedy as "*un cri devant une tombe ouverte*" ("a cry in front of an open tomb").

THE VOICE FROM THE COFFIN

A modernist classic such as Faulkner's *As I Lay Dying* harks back to Sophocles in this area, focusing on the same scandal of rotting flesh that underwrites the tragic agon in the Greek text, and this twentieth-century novel sets out to give us an entire spectrum of possible views and attitudes toward the dying and dead mother, as instanced in the tortured mind-sets of her surviving family. But Faulkner, like Proust, knows that we can speak this event only as witnesses. One of the most remarkable sequences in his book is when Darl, the visionary son, attends to the discourse of the coffin that contains Mother (a coffin that has been traveling for some days now, in intense Mississippi summer heat), and hears it actually make its utterance: "The breeze was setting up from the barn, so we put her under the apple tree, where the moonlight can dapple the apple tree upon the long slumbering flanks within which now and then she talks in little trickling bursts of secret and murmurous bubbling" (212). I can still remember the angry and shocked response of a student many years ago when I cited this Faulkner passage; this young woman had just lost a parent, and she found that my quotation was inhuman in its brutality. My (feeble) response was that Faulkner is seeking to register this brutality, that his book sets out to orchestrate forms of grieving, including the unhinged cry of the youngest child, Vardaman, who mixes up his horror of Mother in the coffin (won't she suffocate there?) with the memory of the bleeding fish in the pan served for dinner: "My mother is a fish."

When I return to the city where I grew up, I still go to the cemetery where my father is buried, and I look at that tombstone, trying to hear some voice coming out from it; often my mother was there at my side, and she had no trouble at all hearing his voice. I do hear it occasionally, on the other side of the country, mostly in my dreams, where this man long dead continues to live, but entirely according to "his own" schedule, so that I cannot summon him at will, so that I cannot even speak to him as I might, but rather as the dream dictates. And I wonder how I will inhabit the minds of my own children.

One of the ironies of modern culture is its peculiar treatment of high art. Either we subject it to the rigors of modern critical theory, so as to disclose the hidden ideological arrangements it contains; or we piously commit it to the scholar's care, with the implicit view that we "laypeople" do not have the tools of access to frequent such work with any degree of profit. It would be better if we taught our students to view all art as fair game, to approach the most formidable and hermetic works as an aspiring thief might: with intent to break and enter, to discover, steal, and possess what is there. Probably the most revered (and unapproached) work along these lines—excluding, of course, Proust—is Joyce's *Ulysses,* a monument fit for adoration (from afar) or rejection (at once) or lifetime commitment (the scholar's view), but hardly a candidate for pilfering. (When is the last time you saw someone reading *Ulysses* on the bus or subway?) This is a pity because Joyce has a great deal to tell us about death, and we do not need special seminars or esoteric codes to make sense of it. *Ulysses,* it may be remembered, treats us to two memorable chapters in the early pages of the book—the later pages are something else entirely—about the responses of both Stephen Dedalus (the young artist) and Leopold Bloom (Joyce's adult "everyman" figure) to the phenomenon of death. Stephen will be haunted by the ghost of his dead mother (at whose deathbed he refused to pray), and in the sparkling "Proteus" chapter, we see him musing about the dialectic between "Godsbody" and "dogsbody," between the two rival narratives of death itself: either the transcendence of the soul that leaves its perishable carnal envelope, or the story of rot and putrefaction that living matter cannot escape. Joyce's rendition of Stephen's reflections is prodigiously agile and learned, ranging from inscriptions of the church to echoes of Shakespeare's "full fathom five" from *The Tempest* (this, too, a fable of magic "sea change" whereby bones become coral) to depictions of drowned and mutilated corpses.

Bloom—like Stephen, with his own private deaths still to mourn, that of his suicidal father and his son—rehearses these same issues in the "Hades" chapter. But Joyce is wonderfully naturalistic here, as his protagonist, truly a version of *l'homme moyen sensuel,* cashiers all fables of transcendence and paradise by focusing squarely on the somatic transaction at hand: the pump stops, is bunged, and you are dead; the rats make short work of you; any kind of "last judgment" whereby the dead rise and reassume their bodies is visualized as a grotesque vaudeville spectacle. Joyce is especially good at conflating the sonorous claims of the Church about mortality with the all too material fate of flesh:

Mr. Kernan said with solemnity:

—*I am the resurrection and the life.* That touches a man's inmost heart.

—It does, Mr. Bloom said.

Your heart perhaps but what price the fellow in the six feet by two with his toes to the daisies? No touching that. Seat of the affections. Broken heart. A pump after all, pumping thousands of gallons of blood every day. One fine day it gets bunged up and there you are. Lots of them lying around here: lungs, hearts, livers. Old rusty pumps: damn the thing else. The resurrection and the life. Once you are dead you are dead. That last day idea. Knocking them all up out of their graves. Come forth, Lazarus! And he came fifth and lost the job. Get up! Last day! Then every fellow mousing around for his liver and his lights and the rest of his traps. Find damn all of himself that morning. (105–106)

There is something shocking but tonic, as well as hilarious—"come forth, Lazarus! And he came fifth and lost the job"—in this send-up of transcendence and its accompanying fables, and Bloom's suspicion of high rhetoric makes me think of Mark Twain's impatience with what he called "soul butter." But let no one think that such naturalism is reductive; after all, not every pump can manage thousands of gallons of blood every day, and Joyce returns unerringly to this plumbing later in the book, in "Ithaca," when he has Bloom open the faucet in his kitchen, followed by a mind-boggling paragraph that inventories the entire Dublin waterworks. Joyce, like any physician, is wise about the internal pipes and fluids that maintain life, but not many doctors are capable of his brilliant counterpoint. And mind you, Joycean music is possible even here, as, for instance, when Bloom imagines efforts to communicate with the dead as a kind of telephonic relay system that would "network" all corpses with their survivors. It sounds like this: "Have a gramophone in every grave or keep it in the house. After dinner on a Sunday. Put on poor old greatgrandfather Kraahraark! Hellohellohello amawfullyglad kraark awfullygladaseeragain hellohello amarawf kopthsth" (114). Faulkner and Joyce, however different their tonalities, are both drawn to the noise coming from the coffin, and even though each of them can render the suffering, musing, and meditations of the living, they are both stonewalled when it comes actually to eavesdropping on the dead.

That discourse of the living who only interpret death is all we have to go on. I have argued, especially in connection with Proust, that death's so-called finality may be deceptive, essentially because those living interpreters continue to live, continue to process the deaths they encounter and survive. In claiming that Proust exposes many of our casual assumptions as "snapshots," I meant to contrast the instantaneity of our normal thinking with the more sinuous, evolving, dimensional performance that literature produces. Indeed, art deserves our consideration partly for this reason: it is a complex, orderly, layered arrangement, displaying not only a structure but also a sequence and pattern which are hospitable to the play of time. When we scratch our heads and emit "thoughts," they are often of the one-liner variety, and even if they are possessed of profundity, they are rarely strung together or intricately orchestrated. The reasons for this are many: no one cares to listen; life is rushed; we have miles to go before we sleep.

Proust's labyrinthine account of mourning, forgetting, and "healing" derives much of its power from the narrative packaging that the author has concocted. Reading about the young man's return to Balbec, we too have forgotten the dead grandmother, and hence we too are struck by her remarkable return, by the way that this death is not over. What I am saying is that art possesses trumps of exactly this nature: a repertory of strategies and devices for representing experience in such a way as to do justice to its unfurling and destabilizing character. The novel as a form seems particularly well suited to convey the play of time, that "forking path" along which meaning actually travels. Mourning would seem absolutely to require narrative as a way of mapping its peculiar evolution.

Yet, we know that poetry can do this job too, as we saw with Pastan's poem on grieving. But poetry has, I think, obstacles to face, obstacles rarely acknowledged as such in the academy, namely, that poetry is considered rarefied, esoteric, bound by formal and metric conventions, often excruciatingly private and opaque. These are serious liabilities when it comes to my claim that literature provides basic kinds of resources for people in pain, or people pondering finalities such as death and dying. Whereas many are prepared to regard novels as "slices of life," few would approach poetry in the same vein.

Yet, poetry has advantages of its own which endow its testimony about pain, sickness, and death with unique authority. First and foremost, poetry offers us language in its most heightened and thickened form. Unlike the relatively straightforward ciphers that most of us employ when we answer questions or give directions, the words of poetry are frequently cunning, larded with ambiguity or multiple meanings, laid out with considerable savvy as to their impact, and uncommonly empowered: possessed of resonance, of aural and visual effects, chosen and used with frightening precision, out there doing a job. Molière's Monsieur Jourdain, his unforgettable *"bourgeois gentilhomme,"* is stunned to learn that he speaks, and has been speaking all his life, *prose.* Now I have nothing against prose, am even a great admirer of it, but for special effects, for a demonstration of how meanings are made, for the closest possible representation of how the mind encounters experience, for an illustration of how language and life inseminate each other, poetry must be our handbook.

WHITMAN: FROM GRAVE TO CRADLE

Consider, as a first and perhaps surprising example, the manifold ways in which death obsesses even a vital, lusty poet such as Walt Whitman. We rightly imagine Whitman as a kind of titanic promoter of life in all its guises, but he has also left us with some of our most memorable reflections on death, seen from both a personal and a national angle. One of Whitman's most poignant poems, "Out of the Cradle Endlessly Rocking," has a Wordsworthian flavor of retrieved childhood and bucolic reflection, but it unmistakably posits death as the great catalyst for both coming-of-age and artistic vocation. This, in itself, is amazing, since we usually construe death to be the obsession of old age, to be mercifully distant from the reflections and experiences of children.

Of course, Whitman the child has not been heard from, but it is instructive that the mature poet positioned death squarely in his childhood as the determining event. His recollection of wandering on the beach as a child focuses on his encounter with "Two feather'd guests from Alabama," and the ensuing story of the she-bird's death and the subsequent mourning of the he-bird constitutes at once the Ur-saga of grieving and the birth of poetry. At considerable length the poet weaves together the bittersweet call of the solitary bird along with the voices of wind, spray, and water, yielding something melodious and polyphonic, for we understand this spectacle of primal loss to be inseparable from the child's initiation into language: "The colloquy there, the trio, each uttering / The undertone, the savage old mother incessantly crying, / To the boy's soul's questions sullenly timing, some drown'd secret hissing, / To the outsetting bard." The child senses that he is in the presence of revelation, that some defining and definitive utterance is coming into being: "A word then, (for I shall conquer it,) / The word final, superior to all, / Subtle, sent up—what is it?—I listen; / Are you whispering it, and have been all the time, you sea-waves? / Is that it from your liquid rims and wet sands?" (202–203).

Whitman's fable is properly mythic: the child questions the savage sea-mother; the child witnesses death's routine decimation of love; the child seems to grasp that death is the condition of both self and song, that individuation results from the dismantled family, that the experience of loss and grief is what poetry speaks, is why we have poetry. Very little in the Whitman corpus matches the lyrical and haunting beauty of this final illumination that fuses child and bird and sea in a moment of pure baptismal power:

Whereto answering, the sea,
Delaying not, hurrying not,
Whisper'd me through the night, and very plainly before daybreak,
Lisp'd to me the low and delicious word death,
And again death, death, death, death,
Hissing melodious, neither like the bird nor like my arous'd child's
  heart,
But edging near as privately for me rustling at my feet,
Creeping thence steadily up to my ears and laving me softly all over,
Death, death, death, death, death. (203)

In Proust, Joyce, and Faulkner we saw the elemental interrogation: how to speak the dead? how to apprehend the voice from the coffin? Whitman reverses the procedure, shows us that death is speaking incessantly, that the rhythms of birth and death are a kind of systolic-diastolic that structures all human doing, most especially all loving, as if loving came into its own as pathos and richness only through death's intervention. This moment is the poet's liminal experience of vocation, his encounter with a sphinx, from which he emerges with song.

One feels awed by Whitman's poem; it is tempting to see it as a kind of window onto his own formation, and it matters little whether events actually happened this way or that Whitman produced this version of his genesis for the purposes of this particular poem. But there is food for thought here that goes beyond the contours of Walt Whitman. In a culture that is acutely aware of teenage suicide, that increasingly medicates its young against a wide variety of ills, what do we make of this poem's claim that our central apprehension of death may come in childhood? To be sure, Whitman's nineteenth-century Long Island childhood differs considerably from that of young people today in industrialized societies. Yet, the child's encounter with death seems *uncanny,* in the sense that Freud gave the term: a displacement of time and space, whereby one event is telescoped onto, or coded into, another. The older poet looks backward, in search of his origins, and he finds them in this bucolic event that broadcasts aloneness as the condition of both life and song. The child stores information that requires years before it can be decoded or unpacked. The child stumbles on to Nature's "passion play," the cycle of death, separation, and response that structures all reality. The child sees individuation as the product of death and the source of mourning/song.

Whitman himself is a strange case: larger than life, imbued with an aura that all who met him felt, at once utterly available and utterly unavailable, irresistible in his siren song of personal embrace but elusive as a shadow in his roving and restless life, a mystery then and a mystery now. May we not see in this poem about death what might be called a "theory of desire"? The poem depicts a sundering (among the birds) that is inseparable from a weaning (in the child), and from this islanded state comes poetry. Poetry as hunger for connection and knowledge of loss. Poetry as death's child.

The theme of death is frequently sounded in *Leaves of Grass,* occasionally as elegiac plaint, more often with cheerleading pomp and circumstance: "I beat and pound for the dead, / I blow through my embouchures my loudest and gayest for them" (38). For years I believed that such lines were awful, gave poetry a bad name, since who (in his right mind) could endorse such a view? I now think that we see the capaciousness of poetry here (Whitman himself is famously on record for registering his contentedness at being contradictory), poetry as a "what if" exercise, poetry as a kind of affective and imaginative elasticity, a way of "pushing the envelope," as they say today. Nowhere is Whitman more *democratic* than in his championing of death, his confidence that it is not to be valued less than life, that it too needs a singer who can sound its virtues. This is very much the same poet who champions prostitutes and slaves, finds voices for those who were never heard. Could death not be thought of as one of those voices? The poet's hunger for experience and his capacity for empathy and projection (even for ventriloquism, some would say) seem boundless.

But then came the great reckoning. The Civil War tested Whitman's voracious appetites and his emotional elasticity with great severity. This swaggering poet, who seemed to many a kind of portable project of desire, met his match during this bloody chapter in American history, and his experience as a nurse in Washington appears to have exhausted and aged the titan by presenting him with an amount of human suffering and atrocious need that even he could not assuage. A poem like "The Wound-Dresser," with its sober and unvarnished account of maimed and dying soldiers—three out of four operations were amputations—suggests that the encounter with physical suffering and death on a grand scale (no longer that of a lost she-bird) inflicts incalculable damage on the perceiver.

It does not seem too much to say that Whitman the poet was born, as "Out of the Cradle Endlessly Rocking" tells us, in the knowledge of death, but also that Whitman the poet, through his wartime experience, died through the encounter with death. Whitman's gift for journalistic detail and symbolic resonance—so evident in the many unforgettable "lists" that make up "Song of Myself"—serves him also in the depiction of dying soldiers, as we see in "A Sight in Camp in the Daybreak Gray and Dim." This brief piece begins with the poet encountering three forms lying outside the hospital tent, covered by blankets. We feel a weird mix of tenderness, curiosity, and hunger as he lifts the blanket from each corpse—we see the journalist here, but also the invasive and exploitative energies of poetry itself—and we sense as well that this sequence of bodies is going to be allegorical. First comes the elderly man "so gaunt and grim," then the boy, "my child and darling," and one wonders how this countdown will close. Whitman does not disappoint us:

> *Then to the third—a face nor child nor old, very calm, as of beautiful*
>   *yellow-white ivory;*
> *Young man I think I know you—I think this face is the face of the*
>   *Christ himself,*
> *Dead and divine and brother of all, and here again he lies.* (243)

One feels very close to the primal office of poetry in these lines, as the male nurse opens up the scene, shows us that it extends to infinity, that it is rehearsing one of the oldest dramas on record. At the edge of sensationalism, Whitman yet controls his material, invests this realistic account of dead bodies with an aura of both carnage—the old man and the boy are struck down—and spirituality. Perhaps the finest touch is that word *again* which signals that the routine slaughter of war is not routine at all, that the bloody, tedious, daily business of war awaits the poet who can see in it the story of the Crucifixion. It is tempting to posit that wars might end more quickly if more of us could see through Whitman's eyes; the more sobering thought is how could you continue to be a nurse at this time, experience carnage on this scale day in and day out, if you saw Calvary in it? We measure the horror if we project such circumstances into our time, and imagine today's nurses and doctors outfitted with Whitman's sensibilities, translating routine suffering into epiphanic sacrifice.

WHITMAN'S ELEGY TO LINCOLN

If Civil War casualties could be troped in the death of Jesus, Whitman can also work the other way around. One of his most profound poems, "When Lilacs Last in the Dooryard Bloom'd," is dedicated to the death of America's great leader Abraham Lincoln, yet Whitman never names Lincoln in this account of a coffin traveling across the country toward its final place of rest. In electing not to elevate Lincoln but rather to tell a wider story of what his death means—how his death might cap and heal the mighty sundering brought about by the war—Whitman offers a vision that is as epic (reminiscent of Homer's *Iliad*) as it is elegiac. It is here that Whitman reaches furthest, it seems to me, in his exploration of death itself. I want to emphasize the dimensionality and resonance of this poem, for he helps us to a view of death as peace, of a single death as the site of a national healing. Our earlier notion of mourning as private transaction is now expanded into something larger, entailing the rites of passage of an entire nation. In reading Whitman's account today, those of us who were alive in the sixties will be hard put not to think of more recent assassinations, more recent coffins traveling through the land, more recent periods of national division. Might poetry serve here?

Whitman's poem combines earlier motifs such as the poet-warbler (of "Out of the Cradle") with signs of apocalypse (a star that falls out of the western sky) and pagan offering (bestowing of the lilac sprig to the traveling coffin that carries the body of the slain president). These motifs will be orchestrated ever more richly and tightly as the poem gathers speed and density, yet it is this latter feature, the poem's kinetic energy, that warrants our attention. Whitman shows great skill in conveying the pilgrimage of this coffin, so that we see it moving across the great land, betokening the poem's deeper meaning: to bring the divided, fissured land back into some kind of wholeness. Rarely have English syntax and rhythm been more majestically extended, as if the poet were out to bend the very grammar and verbal tools themselves to his totalizing purposes:

> Over the breast of the spring, the land, amid cities,
> Amid lanes and through old woods, where lately the violets peep'd
>   from the ground, spotting the gray debris,
> Amid the grass in the fields each side of the lanes, passing the endless
>   grass,
> Passing the yellow-spear'd wheat, every grain from its shroud in the
>   dark-brown fields uprisen,
> Passing the apple-tree blows of white and pink in the orchards,
> Carrying a corpse to where it shall rest in the grave,
> Night and day journeys a coffin. (260)

These magnificent lines speak the capaciousness and order of poetry, coming to us as a paean to the land and to the ceaseless life that nourishes it, so that death is effectively cradled here, posited as serene and harmonious, rhythmically at home in the round of life, not a catastrophe but a rest, not a cessation but a journey. City and country, fields and lanes, are the composite terrain this dead body must pass, but the poet already hints that nature does not know death, that this seeming end may well be a beginning, just as the wheat emerges from its "shroud in the dark-brown fields uprisen." The poem enacts a countrywide procession, attended by the poet with his lilac sprig, the singing thrush, and the falling star, soon to be joined by death itself, figured as walking companions holding the poet's hands, framing his march. The poem asks what can be retrieved from the night; can we ever have back again what "was lost in the netherward black of the night"?

One answer is, of course, the song, the death-inspired song that constitutes poetry. This much we already know, from "Out of the Cradle Endlessly Rocking," but the stage is dramatically expanded now, encompassing the country at large, a sick country, sick unto death through the loss of Lincoln and the ravages of war. Whitman wants to endow poetry with national purpose by emphasizing that the song, if it is large-souled enough, can bring about healing and renewal, and that the torn country can bind its wounds. Thus, Whitman does more than reference both North and South, he "works through" the disaster (much as, in the next century, Freud was to theorize the work of both mourning and neurosis), rehearses even the slaughter, brings it back horribly into view—note the insistent "I saw"—that it might finally be transcended:

> And I saw askant the armies,
> I saw as in noiseless dreams hundreds of battle-flags,
> Borne through the smoke of the battles and pierc'd with missiles I saw
>   them,
> And carried hither and yon through the smoke, and torn and bloody,
> And at last but a few shreds left on the staffs, (and all in silence,)
> And the staffs all splinter'd and broken.

I saw the battle-corpses, myriads of them,
And the white skeletons of young men, I saw them,
I saw the debris and debris of all the slain soldiers of the war,
But I saw they were not as was thought,
They themselves were fully at rest, they suffer'd not,
The living remain'd and suffer'd, the mother suffer'd,
And the wife and the child and the musing comrade suffer'd,
And the armies that remain'd suffer'd. (265)

In this sequence the poet returns to the scene of the crime and gazes head-on at the horror, seen in utter silence (almost like a silent film), first in the decimated battle flags, shredded and splintered, then in the corpses themselves, now white skeletons, twice described as "debris." But this vision of detritus suddenly becomes a scene of peace, of bodies at rest, just as Lincoln is at rest, and only the living now suffer. Like the shroud of wheat from which life will rise up, these peaceful white skeletons must be transformed into conduits of life so that the grieving can finally be done. Whitman, writing at a moment of unprecedented national hurt, moves well beyond the fables of death-memory-alteration in which Pastan and Proust depict mourning; death, faced fully enough, transmuted into poetry, is the catalyst of healing. And that is the office of song.

Whitman closes his elegy by insisting on this song, a song that "passes," just as the visions "pass," so that the country too can "pass" beyond. The song bestows on life, in the form of the poet's offering, the "lilac with heart-shaped leaves . . . blooming, returning with spring." Songs cannot prevent death, but the songs *of* death are music made of pain, not romantic warbling but "the song of the bleeding throat," as if the real language of grieving were a peculiar form of hemorrhage. Such songs are a kind of human doing set against the monstrous undoing that is death; they are "retrievements out of the night," a raid on that "undiscovered country," a living legacy for the survivors, measuring what has been lost, yet flowering. Death is more than a wound from which the survivors recover; it seeds life.

THE LIFE OF IVAN ILYCH

Death, as is tolerably clear now, is a staple item in much literature, a fertile source of imaginative writing, a subject that seems to authorize language rather than install silence. But what about *dying*? The enabling premise of the texts examined up to now, the enabling premise that underwrites mourning, is that utterance comes from the witnesses, bystanders, and survivors. As Poe's M. Valdemar shows, dying itself holds on to its secrets, yields only a mess of putrescent flesh. If we widen our angle, however, we realize that all of us have a tale of dying to unfold, in the sense that all of us die a little every day. Mercifully it is not a story we like to attend to, nor is the quotidian entropic deterioration of our body easily noted (equally mercifully). Still, the dismantling work of time is hardly a secret for the old and infirm, and toward life's end, it begins to have contours that no one can mistake. But could that crucial *exit*—a generic event if there ever was one, the equivalent of birthing—be spoken? written? storied? What could we learn from such a story?

Arguably the most famous tale of this stripe is Tolstoy's novella *The Death of Ivan Ilych*. The piece begins, cunningly enough, with the announcement of Ilych's death and the ensuing social charade of friends and family who pay their respects. Here is precisely how most of us encounter dying, as obituary, as ceremony where we are the visitors free to leave. Still, it is a sticky situation. With surgical acuity, Tolstoy illuminates the malaise of the living, the downright ignorance that most of us have, vis-à-vis the proper behavior one accords a corpse. Likewise, we note that the grieving widow is mightily concerned with monetary arrangements, with making sure that she gets every last ruble to which she is entitled out of the government's pension. I call the first pages of this story "cunning," in that Tolstoy wants to establish the utterly secular tone of these events right from the outset, a formula that figures death as an affair of mourning clothes, inheritance, and jockeying for position to fill the bureaucratic seat now emptied. It is the secular note that is to be the dominant theme of the story he wants to tell, the story of Ilych's life that preceded his death. It is hardly a stretch to say that little has changed since Tolstoy's time. Death is most prominent in many people's minds as a matter of insurance policies and estate planning. Death destabilizes material interests, and prudent people take measures to see that their survivors will manage. Ivan Ilych, as we first know him, was an eminently practical man, good at marshaling resources so as to get on in his life.

This life, as the author reminds us again and again, is hardly that of a saint or hero, is in fact completely unremarkable, patterned along the lines that characterize the lives and careers of other successful functionaries. Ilych's childhood, education, marriage, and professional advancement read like a textbook primer for getting along and climbing the ladder in his social sphere. Only a few discordant notes are sounded, but we need to attend to them. We learn that Ilych's marriage turns a bit rocky with the birth of his first child. His wife, already in her pregnancy, seems a different woman, impatient, demanding, no longer the comrade he married. With utmost brevity and parsimony, Tolstoy informs us that the Ilyches had several children, that more than one of them died, that the experience of sick or fragile babies, of difficult nurturing, was a hard, disagreeable experience, an experience for which Ilych is unequipped. We read that Ilych throws himself ever more fully into his professional career as a result of the unexpected problems and souring of his domestic life, that he and his wife become gradually estranged. All this is recounted in the third person yet according to Ilych's own perspectives and priorities, inasmuch as his choices—to distance himself from wife and children, to attend ever more assiduously to his career—seem logical, innocuous. Who among us has not seen behavior like this? And so Ivan Ilych succeeds. In a Russia with a labyrinthine bureaucratic system, Ivan Ilych does okay, suffers a few reverses, but manages ultimately to come out ahead. The Ilyches seem fine at story's midpoint.

Unless you want to take account of the odd, quite minor, pain that Ilych has in his side, nothing serious, yet *there*. With this persistent little ache, Tolstoy is going to shift gears in his story. It is here that the logic of the body—a logic seen but not underscored in the travails of pregnancy and childhood sickness and death, tiresome events that Ilych chose to keep at bay—enters the picture and begins to assert its horrid autonomy. It is also here that Ilych is fated to enter what today we call "the medical regime." That pain which he knows to have resulted from a slight "fall" while furnishing his new lodgings takes him to doctors, and in his constantly, maddeningly frustrated engagements with specialists—why won't they simply tell him if it is serious? if he is going to die?—Tolstoy is shockingly of our age as much as of his own.

Ilych is essentially stonewalled by the specialists, fated to try this therapy after that, this protocol after that, as the men of medicine go about theorizing what is the matter with the poor man. Tolstoy makes us see what a guessing game medicine is, how hard it is to illuminate, by dint of scientific knowledge, the dark interior of the body where something is amok. Much worse still, we come to realize (as Ilych himself does) that the song and dance of the medical people is precisely the song and dance that Ilych himself has performed all his life as a successful practicing magistrate. Tolstoy shows us the very antics of professionalism: its codes and protocols, its strictly internal logic, its intricate conventions. The doctors perform the ritual moves of their field, just as Ilych has waltzed through the appropriate categories and precincts of the law. Only now does he understand how independent, hermetic, and free-floating these discourses are, how completely unrelated they are to the plight and misery of the human being who has sought relief or sustenance through them. (This is hardly a quaint nineteenth-century Russian problem; you are likely to encounter it today in any medical or legal emergency.) As patient, Ilych experiences the helplessness and insignificance of all those who appeared in his court, of all those over whom he sovereignly pronounced the rulings of law. Mind you, Ilych was a fine magistrate, one who truly attempted to fit the legal judgment to the situation at hand, one who dealt kindly and graciously with those who were brought to him; in fact, we sense that Ilych's nuanced mastery of the law was akin to his love for bridge, for a complex set of conventions that superior people learn to master.

Tolstoy's novella is insidious because it initially seems so innocuous; it could be an account of our neighbors. By the end of it, most readers are feeling pretty queasy. What we have is a proto-existential fable about the gap between culture and life, between our vast array of models and procedures that govern how we do business (law, medicine, teaching, writing) and our creatural condition. We understand that the purpose of this story is to expose the nullity of a purely secular philosophy of life— Ilych's own dance was like that of his doctors, Ilych's own life has been cued entirely to secular aims—so that the religious vision that gradually makes its way into the story can be seen as a more inclusive picture of what living finally entails. The death of Ivan Ilych is meant to expose the absurdity of Ivan Ilych's life. It was a fine life while he was well; Ilych mastered the rules of the game as it was then played. There is pleasure in such mastery, just as there is pleasure in being promoted, selecting furnishings, making a grand slam, dressing and eating well. Tolstoy's rich sense of the creature comforts, games, and pastimes that occupy most of us most of the time recalls, once again, the rather fiercer argument put forth by Pascal in the seventeenth century; the French philosopher railed incessantly against "distraction," what he called *divertissement,* by which he meant the entirety of secular life, most flagrantly visible to us in the arena of hobbies, entertainment, sports, gambling, and the like.

We need merely factor in television to see how little has changed over time. How much space does the spiritual take up in most modern agendas? With well over a century's distance from this story, we realize that the games played in Ilych's world are still being played today. Can it really make a difference (to me, to you) whose performance gets an Oscar, whose song is ranked number one, whose ball goes first or most into the hole, through the hoop, or between the goal posts? Moreover, the monstrous grip of professionalism is, if anything, more brutal and distorting in our postindustrial, global-marketplace age, than it was in Tolstoy's rural Russia of the nineteenth century. The education that takes place in the elite institutions of the West is not very different from the "training" that Ivan Ilych received: how to master the rules and conventions that regulate secular success. (My university works tirelessly and at considerable cost to furnish its graduates with credentials so that they might find a niche in society; we teach no courses about the soul or about preparing for death.) Death—fear of it, certainty of it—comes as an obscene intruder here, not only crashing the party but exposing the utter nullity of the party. Only now, as Ilych watches the smug complacence of his own doctors, does he grasp the alienness of the entire consort, the mammoth yet intricate web of social custom and action that has been the exclusive focus of his life; he sees, because he is getting ready to fall into it, the abyss that exists between socioprofessional discourse and human fate. As he approaches death ever more closely, he finally asks himself the key question for Tolstoy: have I lived wrong? have I lived at all? At the moment of death, after three days of ceaseless agony and screams, Ilych, we are told, sees the light. Do we?

A proto-existential fable, I said. And also a very unnerving one. I have often wondered exactly what makes this novella so virulent, and I don't think it only has to do with Tolstoy's philosophy. After all, Ilych does see some kind of light, and it has been shrewdly argued that this story is a perennial favorite in "literature and medicine" partly because it presents dying as a positive learning curve. Nonetheless, this story gnaws at us because the author, after ushering us into his decorous narrative, then locks the door and forces us to see these events as Ilych sees them. And what we see gradually builds into a kind of mania. Once Ilych develops what we today would call "chronic pain," the story starts to feel virtually penitential, just as chronic pain itself is penitential. Ilych experiences his gradual dying as an ever-tightening trap, and the tighter it gets, the more absurd and capricious his entire life starts to appear. And neither he nor we get off the hook. All the goodies he has spent his life desiring and acquiring go up in smoke. Why? Because the man is dying. And when you are dying, when you *know* you are dying, what else can possibly be of interest?

Tolstoy makes us squirm, not only because he exposes the evasiveness of all human pursuits but also because he has the bad taste to lock us into Ilych's position. Not only are no dodges possible but everything now appears to be a dodge. We know that the most frivolous, superficial question devised by humankind is: "How are you?" And we also know how distasteful, how obscene, it is when someone actually starts to give a serious and somatic response. Most of us are sufficiently acculturated to rise to the occasion when this question is put to us: we blithely speak of weather, family, or profession. Maybe a hint of our pain or discomfort, but quickly enough we see that this type of response is not much appreciated. Ilych, however, can think of nothing else, can speak of nothing else. He breaks all the rules, and even though he remains largely controlled in his utterances—he does not shriek or truly go off the deep end—he is constantly thinking about the unthinkable, constantly making us think about it, leading us to the horrid conclusion that he is dreadfully logical, that of course we would all obsess about dying if we actually knew it was happening. (How sublimely thoughtful of nature to keep us in the dark here, for years and decades; and how awkward that our current diagnostic culture gets the bad news out to us ever earlier now, even when no adequate therapeutic responses may exist for our now visible maladies.) There is a stench in this brief novella, like a fart in a crowded room, and it reeks of mortality, of somatic thralldom, of a *huis clos* that no one exits.

LONG LIVE THE KING

Literature's testimony about death and dying is most often sought in fiction and poetry. What about drama? Is the stage particularly suited to represent medical issues? We know that medical school (like all schools) is surprisingly theatrical in its actual modus operandi. A professional performs in front of an audience, and this enables learning via spectating. Or consider the doctor-patient relationship as a kind of theater, a (strictly orchestrated) set of roles, punctuated by dialogue, through which, at least sometimes, life-and-death questions are asked and answered.

It is amazing that this dyad—doctor-patient—has not been turned more often into theater: raucous, potentially obscene theater. You lie on a table or sit up straight or bend over, and the (impassive, professional!) physician palpates, listens, probes, inserts. The appointment with the doctor must rank up there with the visit to the barber or the masseur as one of society's few sanctioned opportunities for truly hands-on behavior, for being actually touched and felt and exposed in ways unallowable under any other circumstances. Here is physical intimacy with a vengeance, all in the name of science. And what about the stint at the radiologist's? You sit or lie there with your half-opened gown, freezing and frightened, while folks in white suits calmly read you, follow the barium trail or the nuclear track, print out what is going on there under the skin, foretell your future, terrify you. Sometimes they hand you an imposing manila envelope, sometimes they suavely inform that you will hear from them when the results are known. Drama here.

The great gift of theater, it seems to me, is to offer up a tangible, flesh-and-blood world of living creatures occupying a space in front of our eyes. Here is a form of presence and immediacy that the printed page does not possess. I have been saying all along that art helps us to a more vivid sense of what sickness and death entail, and it is therefore a bit puzzling that so few major dramatic texts with medical subjects come to mind. Some do exist. As I argued in Chapter Two, "Living in the Body," Sophocles' *Philoctetes* is a key instance of injury and pain being at the center of dramatic events, and a number of Molière's best comedies focus on the issues of hypochondria and affectation when it comes to either sickness or doctoring. (The ante is considerably upped when we remember that the ailing Molière himself played Harpagon in *Le Malade imaginaire* and that he was to die shortly after one of the performances.) *King Lear,* as mentioned, is a chronicle of old age approaching dissolution, even if sickness per se is not present. Great tragedy frequently finishes with somebody dead somewhere, and there are always lessons for us. Hamlet muses on the skull he discovers to be Yorick's, and in the light of this longitudinal bad joke that life plays on the living—leading him to ponder the truly egalitarian fates of Alexander and Caesar, now imagined filling up bungholes—he moves toward his sublime moment of acceptance: "If it be now, 'tis not to come; if it be not to come, it will be now; if it be not now, yet it will come. The readiness is all" (V.ii.195–197).

These examples, rich as they are, might be construed uncharitably as foreplay, as preparation for the bloody business truly at hand: dying itself. *Hamlet* finishes with a mess of cadavers, swords, and poisoned chalices. Could we go directly to the quarry? *Angels in America* goes directly into the hospital, as does Margaret Edson's splendid recent play *Wit,* to depict terminal disease, but could you devote an entire play to the *staging of dying*? It may seem that no playwright in his right mind would elect such a severe theme, but the truth is otherwise. The Romanian dramatist Eugène Ionesco—erstwhile prince, along with Samuel Beckett and Jean Genêt, of the theater of the absurd—has supplied us with an answer in his fascinating play *Exit the King.* This full-length drama sets out to choreograph the movements of dying, to show just how spectacular such an exit is. The protagonist, Bérenger, is a king, because the conceit of Ionesco's play is that all of us are kings and that every death is a form of regicide committed by nature. With characteristic wit, Ionesco informs us that this king is a bit special: he has built Rome, New York, Moscow, and Geneva, has founded Paris, is the inventor of gunpowder, of airplanes and automobiles, of harvesters and tractors, is, it seems, responsible for much of the progress of the human race. His death is, well, *absurd.* How can such a figure die? How indeed?

Well, because he has to. King though he is, he will vacate the scene. Ionesco seems to have heeded Freud's view of *King Lear,* for his play is about the necessity of making friends with death. In Shakespeare the death of the king is a seismic event with huge political reverberations; in today's culture as well, we are morbidly attentive to the dying of the high and mighty, as if mesmerized by the final erasure that life metes out to all. As Pascal cheerfully put it, "*Le dernier acte est toujours sanglant, quelque belle que soit la comédie en tout le reste*" ("The last act is always bloody, however fine the rest of the play is").

But, for the twentieth-century Ionesco, the death of the king is a brilliant, often hilarious meditation on kingship of a different sort altogether: the miraculous power that life *lends* us for a while but then takes away. This leads to an unforgettable view of life as an affair of dress and undress, astonishing us with its view of how much clothing we can remove. Theater can tell this story since dress and undress are its basic currency. The playwright achieves stunning effects as we see this all-powerful man systematically and sequentially stripped of his powers. You might expect this to be brutal to the extreme, as we indeed experience it when we visit friends and loved ones who have suffered strokes or who have Alzheimer's, who are *shrinking* in front of our eyes and being divested of all their accoutrements: use of limbs, memory, speech, and the like. But Ionesco surprises us. The leave-taking he chronicles gives rise to a tender kind of poetry, as Bérenger discovers—only through his losses—the miracle of his possessions. Walking upright, speaking, utilizing arms and legs: these are the vestments of kingship, but you don't realize it until they are taken away from you. Even pain is now understood as precious, as we see when the maid Juliette grumpily rehearses all her aches and troubles, while Bérenger rapturously hangs on her words, celebrates the bodily inventory at hand:

JULIETTE: I do all the palace laundry in the wash house. It hurts my
    hand and cracks my skin.
KING *(rapturously):* And it hurts. One can feel one's skin. . . .
JULIETTE: I empty the chamber pots. I make the beds.
KING: She makes the beds! Where we lie down and go to sleep and

then wake up again. Did you ever realize that every day you woke
up? To wake up every day . . . Every morning one comes into the
world.

JULIETTE: I polish the parquet floors, and sweep, sweep, sweep!
There's no end to it.

KING *(rapturously):* There's no end to it!

JULIETTE: It gives me the back-ache.

KING: That's right. She has a back! We've all got backs!

JULIETTE: Pains in the kidneys.

KING: And kidneys too! (60)

Dying is imaged here as a systematic form of dispossession, a rigorous
cashiering—one by one—of the goodies, the freebies, that one has had,
used, and squandered all one's life, without ever thinking about it.
Ionesco's genius stems from this insight that is a brilliant kind of hind-
sight: we cannot value, we cannot even see what we have, until it is being
removed. And theater turns out to be wonderfully apt as a setting for
making this new regime—a regime of raids and losses, a weighing in of
incapacity, a program of sequential dysfunctionalities (what's going to
go today?)—visible. We watch this final striptease that life deals out to
the dying, and there is nothing pornographic about it.

But there are some surprises. The beauty of this unveiling scheme is
that it enables the playwright to show us just how much amazing luggage we have been carrying around all this time. We may have been born
equipped only with appendages and organs, but life has turned us into
shrewd consumers who get hold of all the paraphernalia it takes not to
get too banged up and hurt as we go through. Here too Ionesco achieves
a kind of creatural poetry as he reveals the enormous amount of bric-a-
brac that we have acquired to make our way: the crutches, the weapons,
the shields, all the equipment and armor, that a lifetime of dodging and
slithering through have necessitated. In a feat of theatrical magic,
Ionesco contrives to make us actually *see* this, see the incredible assem-

blage of aids that we have fashioned, all the maniacal but invisible hand-
icraft and bricolage that has been necessary for us to manage.

There are more conventional vocabularies for all this: Freud has
told us about our psychic defenses and the survival strategies and the
injuries we make or sustain in order to live; other, still older discourses
speak blithely of maturation, growth, adapting, coming to terms, and
the like. You will note that there is nothing remotely visual in any of
these concepts. True, the vocabulary is telling: "defenses," "survival,"
etc., but who ever stops to think about what this might look like? The
fact is, we live in the dark, change in the dark, evolve in the dark, and
never have a clue as to what a spectacle our life might be. Try to imagine the sheer quantity of *alterations* you have gone through from infancy to maturity. A scrapbook might reveal a few of the exterior
changes, but what about the others, the ones that take place on the inside? Ionesco creates a theatrical, choreographic language that is
shockingly material to show us these "things," to show just how hoary
and amazing they turn out to be when we come to the end and have to
discard them. The theater as art form is paying its way in full here by
showing us what we cannot see on our own and by suggesting, rather
sublimely, that *dying* (usually thought of as morbid, darkening) is the
source of all this illumination. We see this most clearly in the final moments of the play as Bérenger's queen leads him through his last paces,
helps him in his final bout of disrobing:

> MARGUERITE: There are still some cords that bind you which I
> haven't yet untied. Or which I haven't cut. There are still some
> hands that cling to you and hold you back. *(Moving around the
> King, Marguerite cuts the space, as though she had a pair of invis-
> ible scissors in her hand).*
>
> KING: Me. Me. Me.
>
> MARGUERITE: This you is not the real you. It's an odd collection of
> bits and pieces, horrid things that live on you like parasites. The

mistletoe that grows on the bough is not the bough, the ivy that climbs the wall is not the wall. You're sagging under the load, your shoulders are bent, that's what makes you feel so old. And it's that ball and chain dragging at your feet which make it so difficult to walk. *(Marguerite leans down and removes an invisible ball and chain from the King's feet, then as she gets up she looks as though she were making a great effort to lift the weight.)* A ton weight, they must weigh at least a ton. *(She pretends to be throwing them in the direction of the audience; then, freed of the weight, she straightens up.)* That's better! How did you manage to trail them around all your life! *(The King tries to straighten up.)* And I used to wonder why you were so round-shouldered! It's because of that sack! *(Marguerite pretends to be taking a sack from the King's shoulders and throws it away.)* And that heavy pack. *(Marguerite goes through the same motions for the pack.)* And that spare pair of army boots.

KING *(with a sort of grunt):* No.

MARGUERITE: Don't get so excited! You won't need an extra pair of boots any more. Or that rifle, or that machine-gun. *(The same procedure as for the pack.)* Or that tool-box. *(Same procedure: protestations from the King.)* He seems quite attached to it! A nasty rusty old saber. *(She takes it off him, although the King tries grumpily to stop her.)* Leave it all to me and be a good boy. *(She taps on the King's hand.)* You don't need self-defense any more. No-one wants to hurt you now. (88–89)

Conrad once defined the purpose of his prose as "to make you see," and I can think of no more startling triumph along these lines than Ionesco's transformation of aging, injury, and the small, lifelong deformations that experience has worked upon us, into something dazzlingly *visible*. And yet "visible" only by the magic of theater, as Marguerite "speaks" this inventory of weaponry and defenses, "pretends" to remove it, and thereby gives it presence.

Dying as *illumination* is a familiar concept, that moment when all at last becomes luminous. But there is still more happening here because Ionesco's art is showing us things with words and gestures that we would not have without the words and gestures. This play causes us to realize how inert and lame our customary labels are; yes, we have talked about defenses and injuries forever, and we have always known that life works its will on the living, that the damage done by experience is somehow on show, in our mannerisms, our dodges, perhaps in our very postures and tics and body movements. Even a cursory glance at a body that has lived for any period of time can be a scary proposition in that we see the toll that life exacts, the traces, marks, and scars left by experience. But who has ever seen it quite as explosively and materially as it appears in the King's final disrobing? This affair of ball and chain, rifle, machine gun, and saber constitutes an unforgettable portrait of civilized man, of what we might call the "cost of living."

With perfect logic, Ionesco carries out the striptease to its necessary end, as still more accoutrements and "aids" are now seen and discarded, but we are now in the end zone, and we have moved from weaponry to even more basic equipment. Marguerite carries out Death's decree: naked you came into the world, naked you shall leave it; from dust you came, as dust you will exit. All of us "know" this; Ionesco actually *shows* it happening as Marguerite helps lead the dying King to his final throne:

MARGUERITE: Higher, up again, up you go, still higher, higher, higher! *(The King is quite close to the throne.)* Now turn and face me! Look at me! Look right through me! Gaze into my unreflecting mirror and stand up straight! . . . Give me your legs! The right one! Now the left! *(As she gives him these orders, the King stiffens his legs.)* Give me a finger! Give me two fingers . . . three, four . . . five . . . all ten fingers! Now let me have your right arm! Your left arm! Your chest, your two shoulders and your stomach! *(The King is motionless, still as a statue.)* There you

are, you see! Now you've lost the power of speech, there's no
need for your heart to beat, no more need to breathe. It was a lot
of fuss about nothing, wasn't it? Now you can take your place.
(92–93)

Those are the play's last words, but its last act—our last act—is shot
through with mystery and beauty: Marguerite disappears, the King is
seated on his throne, the doors, windows, and walls now disappear as
well, and then the King and his throne disappear, slowly but implacably,
even serenely. This disappearance act, which is the culminating moment of all somatic beings—far from being the nightmarish removal and
abduction that many of us suspect it to be—is invested with grandeur.
And this grandeur, this final occupancy of the throne, is revealed as the
exact opposite of conventional kingly arrangements: no pomp, no circumstance, no possessions whatsoever. Bérenger dismantles into
majesty. His dying, we understand, is a form of purification, a return to
basics, a putting aside of all dross, not unlike a spring cleaning or an existential scouring that gets rid of all the clutter and rubbish that has collected over a lifetime. Bérenger's final state has an austere freshness—on
the far side of heroics, on his part, on the far side of mourning, on ours.
He has completed his trajectory.

I am not such a fool as to believe that many secular readers are prepared to regard dying as a triumph. I believe that Ionesco, like Tolstoy,
writes about death in order to speak of life. Life is imaged here as a
miraculous gift, or more precisely, a series of miraculous gifts, such as a
functional body and mind. The rationale of this chapter on death and
dying as reflected through literature turns on the key notion that we are
poor at imagining death, that literature adds to our stock. I want now to
say that our greatest poverty is the laziness with which we approach *life*,
the insidious way in which routine and blankness bathe so much of
what we do. Ionesco's play is about the discovery of life: its quotidian
splendor, its dazzling plenitude, its muffled drama. Berenger's dying
constitutes an explosive burst of light not entirely unlike the "Let there

be light" of Genesis, which is also a story about coming into one's estate. The playwright has taken on and has then reversed the oldest of
metaphors about death, "night" and "darkness." Remember Othello's
grave line as he stands before Desdemona's sleeping body: "Put out the
light, and then put out the light: / If I quench thee, thou flaming minister, / I can again thy former light restore, / Should I repent me; but
once put out thy light, / Thou cunning'st pattern of excelling nature, / I
know not where is that Promethean heat / That can thy light relume"
(V.ii.7–12). In Ionesco's play dying produces light and life.

EMILY DICKINSON: THE FAR SIDE OF DYING

If Ionesco clothes dying in regal colors, there is a poet who presents it in
the widest array of tones and tropes, but always with a stamp of utter familiarity, sometimes whimsical, sometimes pedestrian, sometimes virulent; I am referring to Emily Dickinson. Today Dickinson is the darling
of the academy, and for good reason: unrecognized in her moment, she
is seen now as arguably the boldest American voice in the nineteenth
century, employing a sibylline writing style—reordering English grammar to suit her needs—in the service of a powerful philosophical vision.
But the other side of the coin is this: her poems are grounded in daily
experience, in the domestic routines of her time, but they subject this
world of habit and manners to a veritable crucible of fire and feeling,
yielding a visionary world that is at once recognizable and wondrous
strange. Nowhere is this more the case than with her poems about
dying. As much as anything else, I want to focus on the *example* of Dickinson, the artificer who remakes the world, who ceaselessly transforms
the known (our own familiar, fatigued, clichéd arrangements) into
something arresting, unsettling, often unforgettable. We can use her to
rethink our lives. And our death.

Writing at a time when death was a household item, especially for
women who were expected to tend to the sick and dying, Dickinson
manages, time after time, to infuse the quotidian occurrence with a

dosage of wit, indeed of madness and genius, that stands as her signature in the poetic tradition. Poems such as "There's been a Death, in the Opposite House" (no. J389) are almost anthropological in their scrupulous notation of the local signs by which death is signaled: doctor's visit, mattress being aired, minister's arrival, milliner on the scene, and finally the arrival of you-know-who: "the Man of the Appalling Trade." Okay, this is the side of death we know about, even if Dickinson's cool report has the earmarks of the census taker or statistician—or of a Martian who happened to witness this odd parade of stuff coming out the window and people going in the doors, and who then wondered what it all signified. At least we are not threatened, since the trouble is in the "opposite house."

Usually, however, there is a bite, and sometimes more than that, as the death poems go through their paces. Therefore, it is worth acknowledging how vicious and sadistic the demure Emily can be with this (usually sober, high-minded) theme. One little ditty begins, "If I shouldn't be alive / When the Robins come" (no. J182), and goes on to say that she would like to thank the birds for their visit, but that it is hard "With my Granite lip!" Camille Paglia, in her provocative book *Sexual Personae,* has explored the nature and limits of Dickinson's nastiness, and has persuasively argued that it is time to recognize the sheer violence and savagery of this poet's imagination. The dead, lying in their tombs, are frequently characterized as victims of industrial accidents such as "soldered mouth" or "rivets" or "hasps of steel" that considerably hamper their maneuvering room. Paglia's version of Dickinson as "Amherst's Madame de Sade" is often over the top (and not much loved by the scholars), but it is also salutary as a way of peeling off the layers of Victoriana and maidenly decorum that, like cobwebs of yesteryear, sometimes coat these poems in misleading prissiness and that obscure their pith and rage.

Other pieces express their malice more finely, as in " 'Twas just this time, last year, I died" (no. J445). The title alone (merely the first line) leaps out at us with its tidings of Dickinson's mind-wrenching breakthrough.

Every text we have considered up to now views death as a limited situation, as a state that can be spoken by others, but never from the inside, from the angle of the dier. Dickinson blithely cashiers that silly notion and proceeds to write from the grave. As you might guess, it is a fascinating sight/site, offering a perspective that stands alone in American literature (or any other literature that I know). The speaker in this poem remembers the trip to the grave, remembers wanting to get out ("But something held my will"), and then goes on to evoke the harvest time and the grand get-togethers at Thanksgiving and Christmas, family gatherings where she will be absent.

We feel in the presence of a kind of narcissist fantasy here, a mix of "oh, won't they be missing me" cut with undertones of Perry Como's "I'll be home for Christmas"; but just wait, this is Dickinson, and so the final stanza releases all the held-back venom: "But this sort, grieved myself, / And so, I thought the other way, / How just this time, some perfect year— / Themself, should come to me—." It is not easy to get your mind around the closing vendetta staged in folksy tones here, but it adds a bit of spice and vinegar to the grieving models put forth by Freud and company. Yes, we miss each other, but I'll have my chance to play hostess soon enough when *they* die and come for dinner. Here is a zinger for our time, wise about the warfare that informs love no less than hate, that pirouettes genteel nineteenth-century notions of hospitality with such oomph that we can almost taste the Schadenfreude that finances the poem's conclusion. Pyschologists have told us that anger is a necessary stage to go through when loved ones die; it's not nice, they say, but you have to accept the fact that you have trouble forgiving people for dying. But who ever had the wit to turn this logic full circle, and to propose that the dead themselves, angry lot that they are, are so unseemly as to hunger for our arrival among them?

Dickinson's registers in this arena are varied. "Because I could not stop for Death" (no. J712) is probably her most famous poem about dying, and it too invokes the perspective of the tomb. This time, Death is a courtly gentleman caller who escorts the dying one to her final destination, past the school, past the "Fields of Gazing [!] Grain," to arrive at "a House that seemed / A Swelling of the Ground." The topographical realism of this charming coach ride to the grave closes with a jolt as we realize this memory goes back "Centuries," constitutes the last remnants of an earthly existence. One finds no shocking exposé of what death is like, merely a blow-by-blow rendition of the trip to the cemetery, but a rendition infused with a wit and gentleness and mellow wisdom that are not so far from Shakespeare's "The readiness is all." This often anthologized piece—I remember it as one of the first poems I ever read in grade school—soothes more than frightens, invests dying with a school-girlish charm that would not be out of place in describing a hayride. Yet, reconsider the first two lines, "Because I could not stop for Death— / He kindly stopped for me—," and try to measure what kind of kindness is expressed in that shocking adverb, "kindly." The slow, measured pace of the rest of the poem applies to dying, but living, confined to the first verse, is an altogether more hectic and busy proposition, a time when we cannot stop for death, when we cannot stop at all. Not to worry: death will do the stopping.

Many Dickinson poems recount the trajectory of dying and then being buried, as if she wanted to redo Edgar Allan Poe, but with more acid as well as more philosophy. Poe specializes in the horror of being buried alive, as his classic stories such as "The Fall of the House of Usher," "The Black Cat," and "The Cask of Amontillado" all suggest; Dickinson also finds burial stimulating, not just because the grave is our last dwelling place (hence worthy of our consideration), but also because some of us are doomed to imagine this itinerary over and over. *Being buried* starts to resonate as a figurative experience of great reach insofar as it adumbrates an immense voyage through time and space.

Now we all know that graves are rather small spaces, but of course that is just the literal side of the equation, and in Dickinson the grave becomes a portal, capping the first stage of a life and beckoning toward the unknown. What happens next? "Whereto?" is the question. Religions offer their otherworldly scenarios; we have also seen how Joyce's Bloom can't get past "the fellow in the six feet by two with his toes to the daisies," and well before that, Hamlet discoursed on Polonius's final destination as a kind of "supper," a feast for worms. Even at her nastiest, Dickinson eschews the decomposition route; instead, she heeds Hamlet's other voice, the nobler one that muses about death as the "undiscover'd country." That country is about to be mapped.

One of her very strongest poems, "I felt a Funeral, in my Brain" (no. J280), explores just this territory, showing us just how far you can go once you see death as something imaginatively open rather than materially or doctrinally closed. This poem seems to burst clear from any recognizable nineteenth-century framework, as it offers its picture of dying. What we have is a full-dress burial *on the inside.* Burial as mental event. Here is victory number one: death is imploded; death is metaphorized. According to this logic you could die several times a day, even more often. (Isn't this true to our hidden feelings?)

There is no way to posit for certain the ontology of this poem, in that we cannot determine whether the "experience" of dying is co-opted as a metaphor for other forms of distress (depression? misery? headache? hangover? all of these viable candidates for invoking "dying" as the way we feel), or whether the "event" is to be understood as a real burial (i.e., realism, à la Dickinson). Whatever the referent may be, the event itself has the relentless clarity of a nightmare. The mourners "in the Brain" are described as "treading—treading—till it seemed / That Sense was breaking through—," and the next stanza echoes this same pounding, figured "like a Drum— / Kept beating—beating—till I thought / My Mind was going numb—," inviting us to see this as both the funeral ceremony it appears to be, and also as the insistent pounding of either head or heart, the somatic syncopation that punctuates our mental and physical terrors. All of us have experienced these somatic symptoms; but who has translated this "beating" into the tread of mourners or the beat of a drum?

It is through such figuration, such mind travel, that Dickinson opens up the sensations of the body or, indeed, the smallness of the grave and transforms them into something large and rich. With characteristic intrepidity, Dickinson goes all the way, she will be fully buried indeed: "And then I heard them lift a Box / And creak across my Soul / With those same Boots of Lead, again / Then Space—began to toll." Note how materially exact this torture is, how excruciatingly precise this language of oppression is (the creaking, the boots of lead), and yet how horribly "multiplied" and displaced the speaker/sufferer is: both in the box and yet also the very terrain where it's happening, the floor-soul that is being tread upon and pounded. Again, I call upon my readers' sensory experiences (of distress, horror, pain) to validate the poet's extravagant notations.

Given the (understandable) claustrophobia of the burial scenario, one initially feels a sense of freedom and liberation at the stanza's closing notation about space tolling, as if death were a surprising exit, not a carceral entrapment but a flight into space. Think again. The last two stanzas open up the scene in ways that intensify still further the terror of the poem, as if the brutalization of being stepped on and pounded were just a prelude for the fuller, more unbounded torture now to come:

> As all the Heavens were a Bell,
> And Being, but an Ear,
> And I, and Silence, some strange Race
> Wrecked, solitary, here—
>
> And then a Plank in Reason, broke,
> And I dropped down, and down—
> And hit a world, at every plunge,
> And Finished knowing—then—

Critical commentary is humbled in the face of these luminous lines. But so too are our mundane notions about death and dying humbled, routed by the fierceness and magnificence of this interplanetary drama of exile and hurt. Yes, we tell ourselves, the "Bell" is that of the church that marks the burial, but what we see is a series of awful transformations, a turning inside out that spells pure vulnerability ("And Being, but an Ear"), the sort of capacity for being hurt that would come if our entire body were a membrane being struck and bruised, so that the noise itself is pure violation. Then, it is over. Silence. But she is still here, lost beyond finding, broken beyond fixing. And the final plummet starts: a surreal roller-coaster ride that makes us yearn for the low-tech journey in a coach with Death as gentleman caller.

Once again, the stunning figures speak: a "Plank in Reason" beautifully tells us that reason *is* a plank, the plank that enables us to stand up and be grounded, the sustaining base of any fiction of agency or knowledge. It breaks. And down she goes; but no free fall, rather a continued saga of trauma and brutality, hitting a world at every plunge. A "world," Dickinson says, making us realize that death is a horrid form of cosmic travel, in which you are struck incessantly, producing a kind of repeated torture that puts paid to any notions of rest or peace at last. Or? That last line is a marvel of ambiguity: the nonstop violations we have just witnessed may also be understood as the very modality of knowing, yielding an epistemology that is closer to trauma than mental event. Or, just perhaps, knowledge is really about to be achieved, on the far side of "then," maybe. This poem wrecks all received views about death, and although it can lead us "to make friends with dying," it does at least establish the final event as a trip unlike any other we've ever taken.

Why, you may ask, make the arduous trip that Dickinson's death poem proposes? I have tried to accentuate the sheer brilliance and intellectual reach of her language and metaphors. Dying, as imaged here, has a kind of punch and insolence that stretches our thinking to the breaking point. Yes, this view is horrible, but I would argue that it is even more mesmerizing; you negotiate this piece in increasing disbelief: what on earth is this woman saying? What starts as a still familiar sense of oppression and misery ends up in a no-man's-land that is pure Dickinson territory. Such imaginative travel is good for the soul, and it is particularly surprising as a description of how life ends. If that is not enough, consider that what Marshall McLuhan many decades ago termed the "global village" has shrunk, imaginatively, still further in today's Internet culture, whereby the mere act of logging on will transport us instantaneously through space. We can explore the great museums and wonders of the world without leaving our study. But in no case does it make available to us the splendors glimpsed and (vicariously) experienced in Emily Dickinson's death voyage. Dickinson's surreal metaphors enact a staging of death unlike any that we have hitherto imagined, and it does so by harnessing our own most basic sensations (treading, beating, hearing, dropping) in order to subject them to her special alchemy, whereby they are transmuted into "knowing." This is the knowing of poetry: it provides no answers for any test that you or I are ever likely to take, but it rocks our understanding nonetheless.

My final Dickinson entry returns us to earth (as a chapter on dying should), to an experience of dying that is supremely pedestrian, without any of the fireworks we just witnessed: "I heard a Fly buzz—when I died" (no. J465). We are now at the antipodes of the cosmic fireworks of "I felt a Funeral, in My Brain," are returned to the conceptual murk that most of us pass our days and nights living in. Epiphanies and visionary experiences move us in literature precisely because we have so few of them in life. Would you know "truth" if it hit you on the head? (Maybe that is how one knows it?) Art in general is held in suspicion because it trucks too easily with genius and beauty and all those other ultimacies, seems to proffer its brilliant never-never schemes for the twilight zone so many of us live in. Perhaps this poem will set the record straight. At last Dickinson appears to set her sights on the confusion and static that bathe our existence.

In this bizarre poem Dickinson challenges perhaps the oldest and most revered of all death myths: death as *revelation*. Not only do religious belief systems tap into this model, but proverbs and folklore also valorize the exit from life as a kind of visionary moment, the viewing of one's entire life in one fell swoop, just before the leaving of it. Death would be the instant of clarity, the dispelling of the murk. We remember that Tolstoy's Ilych saw the light in his final seconds, that Ionesco's Bérenger at long last mounted his real throne and assumed his full kingship. So it cannot surprise us that this poem of dying appears invested in, and preparing for, the coming radiance that is to cap the agony. Dickinson emphasizes the stillness in the death chamber, a quiet that is akin to the stillness of the storm, the eye of the hurricane, "Between the Heaves of Storm—." There is a hush that is tinged with awe and fervor, a step beyond grieving toward initiation and ecstasy: "The Eyes around—had wrung them dry— / And Breaths were gathering firm / For that last Onset—when the King / Be witnessed—in the Room."

Evoking the same topos of majesty that Ionesco will use a century later, Dickinson retraces the Pauline journey of First Corinthians, chapter thirteen, the move beyond the blurred reflection of the glass toward the sacral encounter with the godhead, an encounter of pure light and truth when all parties are at last transfigured and known. There is also a distinctly theatrical cast to the story: not just the dier, but the funeral party itself collectively assume the role of audience so that the prime player can be witnessed, can make his august appearance. Again we see the cleansing and disrobing that characterized Bérenger's initiation, the removal of all that would be secular or dross, as readiness is achieved ("I willed my Keepsakes—Signed away / What portion of me be / Assignable"), as the rigorous logic of divine revelation is enacted.

And then comes the bomb, a bomb announced in the title, but one that goes off only now: "and then it was / There interposed a Fly—." No other poet could have written this line which annihilates all the reverential and ceremonial machinery in full gear. You almost hear the wreckage of an entire visionary project in this line. With maniacal integrity, the poet stays true to her insect spoiler, evokes to perfection the blurry, devastating performance of the fly that usurps the entire stage: "With Blue—uncertain stumbling Buzz / Between the light—and me—." Dickinson is sovereignly undoing Genesis here: let the light be stopped, let there be impediment. All notions of revelation are going to be put paid, as the poet completes the saga of failed vision: "And then the Windows failed—and then / I could not see to see—." Paul's story of illumination is turned on its head: we see, once again, through a glass darkly. The hunger expressed in those repeated notations, "and then," underscores the magnitude of this disaster, "windows" dysfunction, for nothing is transparent any longer. This fly may be thought of as the messenger of contingency, the "fly in the ointment" that spoils all dreams of transcendence and truth. Heaven may be there, but, as Kafka said in his own way, it is not for us.

In offering this poem as my final example of what literature can tell us of dying, I am acknowledging the skepticism of those who remain dubious about my central thesis. The poet herself seems to say, "transcendence is a myth"; our real lives and our real deaths are an affair of muddled vision and buzzing flies. At last, one might say, a poet who owns up to the pretensions of the entire enterprise of poetry. Dickinson does possess that kind of honesty. And yet, readers who feel that this poem is not about tragic failure, but rather about some kind of (twisted) victory, are not wrong. The buzz of the fly may also be interpreted as the very noise of consciousness, the static of the brain that is continuing right up to the final shutdown. If we can see it this way, then there is a precious triumph of sorts in this poem, a kind of mad and heroic journalistic impulse that refuses to be cowed or to cease operations; the mind thinks its way right into death and beyond. The human subject is perhaps not equipped with organs that would apprehend the godhead, but it has consciousness instead, and that is where its ultimate loyalties and heroics lie, that is the quest which may be extended right into the grave. Dickinson functions as reporter in this poem, as indeed she has in so many of her poems, and her job is to issue a report about the final phase of human existence. And she does. She notes every step of this last voyage, right up to the buzzing of the fly and the brain that are the final event. Not bad. Death be not proud.

To write right on through dying is to display, with rare power, the rival testimony of literature when it comes to saying death. Dickinson's "postdeath" poems do honor to the human project of gathering knowledge, and they evince a mix of courage, hunger, humor, madness, and duty which restores our faith in the project of art as testimony. The history of civilization is marked by those special milestones when some brilliant mind starts to challenge all the givens of his or her time, starts (as we say today) to think outside the box. Emily Dickinson's poems exploring death obey a profound cosmographic impulse, share some of the curiosity and passion that informed the cartographers of the Renaissance who had to map new worlds. Death, as I have repeatedly said, seems for the secular among us portentous, tragic, and to be avoided (even, especially, in thought) because it must appear to be the end, our end. But writing suggests otherwise. Writing opens what seemed closed, grants us a measure of freedom within the prison our bodies inhabit. The French poet Chateaubriand called his autobiography *Mémoires d'outre-tombe* (A Record Beyond the Grave); we may think of Emily Dickinson's poems as raids into that "undiscover'd country," as versions of Whitman's "retrievements out of the night," as territorial ventures that expand the estate of each of her readers.

HAMLET AND HIS PROGENY

I have of late—but wherefore I know not—lost all my mirth, forgone all custom of exercises; and indeed it goes so heavily with my disposition, that this goodly frame the earth seems to me a stale promontory, this most excellent canopy the air, look you, this brave o'erhanging firmament, this majestical roof fretted with golden fire, why it appeareth nothing to me but a foul and pestilent congregation of vapors.

—SHAKESPEARE, *Hamlet*

ENDING WITH THE MELANCHOLY PRINCE

Could there be something worse than death? I want, in this last foray, to move beyond physical death in order to address what is arguably the most urgent social and medical issue facing us today: *depression.* You will hardly be surprised by my conviction that art and literature offer the same shocking and eye-opening testimony about depression as they do in all the other areas of life discussed in this book, and I wish to invoke the single best-known figure in Western literature to make my case: Hamlet. His is a story we know; I think it is also one from which we have much to learn about a disorder that seems distressingly of our special moment.

Why, however, end this book with this topic? Can depression "follow" death? Handsome view of afterlife that would be! Depression is, in America at least, doubtless a better candidate for modern plague than AIDS is, inasmuch as the real numbers of people who suffer from it are probably well in excess of the statistics we possess. Moreover, whereas I argued that mourning is the healthy person's survival-experience of death, it does not seem exaggerated to say that depression is the other side of the coin, a way of dying without dying, of leaving the living while still dwelling among them.

Depression seems to be nature's scheme for letting us experience death ahead of time, for letting some of us experience it on virtually a chronic basis. Often enough, as we know, depression can lead to physical death, not infrequently by means of suicide as an exit that is preferable to the state of mind that living entails. I feel that depression tests my thesis as nothing else does. What is depression if not that *unheard* "scream that goes through the house"? And what is the basic certainty of those who are depressed if not that their scream goes nowhere, that no one can hear or help them, that their life is dispossessed of beauty or value, that they are bereft of resources? Could *Hamlet* illuminate here?

First of all, is Hamlet depressed? The question is not as frivolous as it may appear. The term that would have come to mind to an Elizabethan audience looking at this young man's behavior and mind-set would doubtless have been *melancholy,* a medical term denoting the "black bile" that caused an excess of sullenness or moodiness or even violence according to the Renaissance humoral scheme of personality. This may not be our view of serotonin deficiencies or bipolar disorder, but it accords with a pharmacological view of the human subject, which leads me to think that the contemporary running joke that Hamlet needed only Prozac or Zoloft to solve his problems would, if translated into Elizabethan medical terminology, have made sense to those folks.

But Shakespeare's pharmacy had no magic bullets, and even if it did, the play is not about *curing* Hamlet, but about displaying him, indeed displaying him and his strange temper as a subject of endless fascination. It has been noted that virtually everyone *in* the play—Gertrude, Claudius, Polonius, Ophelia, Rosencrantz, and Guildenstern—is mightily invested in *diagnosing* the sick prince. It is not far-fetched to say that we have had some four centuries of diagnostic work devoted to the enigma and infirmity of this (mesmerizing) single young man who exists only as a character in a play. Can any "living" creature (with a "real" case history) claim as much? Therefore, to use Hamlet as a "guide" for what depression looks like is not in the least wrongheaded, and I agree entirely with the view argued recently by Harold Bloom that Shakespeare *invented the human,* that his plays offer the most capacious map for what it is to be human that civilization has ever devised. Literature, especially Shakespeare, may well be our most authoritative source when it comes to the behavior of the human psyche; his works are the literary version of the human genome.

Listen to Hamlet describe to his friends how he feels, and ask yourself if a better description of clinical depression has ever been written:

> I have of late—but wherefore I know not—lost all my mirth, forgone all custom of exercises; and indeed it goes so heavily with my disposition, that this goodly frame the earth seems to me a sterile promontory, this most excellent canopy the air, look you, this brave o'erhanging firmament, this majestical roof fretted with golden fire, why it appeareth nothing to me but a foul and pestilent congregation of vapors. What a piece of work is man, how noble in reason, how infinite in faculties, in form and moving, how express and admirable in action, how like an angel in apprehension, how like a god: the beauty of the world, the paragon of animals. And yet to me, what is this quintessence of dust? (II.ii.282–292)

Loss of joy, loss of pleasure, loss of exercise, a disposition turned heavy: it would be hard to improve on Hamlet's words for characterizing the anomie, dullness, and general mix of torpor and doldrums that spell out the behavior of the depressed. But note how mind-bogglingly eloquent this young man is in his inventory of disappointments; most of us, when depressed, would be hard put to see our everyday sky as a "majestical roof fretted with golden fire," and even though such a person would agree that the universe has become "but a foul and pestilent congregation of vapors," the very words bespeak a kind of visionary sharpness beyond the energies of the depressed.

Hamlet evokes a world of grandeur—the purest expressions of Renaissance idealism: man as "noble in reason," "infinite in faculties," "admirable in action," even "like a god"—in order to close with the most reductive formula imaginable, "this quintessence of dust," as if to display the hubris of all the Humanist huffing and puffing. We are looking at a *before / after* picture that seems at once personal and historical, as if this young man's experience of *fall* were not merely individual but also representative. It is also the very cartography of depression, the graphing of what we were, what we are potentially, and now what we have become. Measures are being taken here. This is the backdrop against which depression must be seen, the *bas-relief* which enables us to gauge heights and depths, yielding essentially a *four-dimensional* portrait of depression, including length, width, depth, and time. Yes, Hamlet beggars most of us through his verbal splendor, but, then, that is one reason to turn to him, because he is mapping the very itinerary of melancholy.

The sheer vitality of this speech is of a piece with the stunning vibrancy, physical as well as verbal, of the character throughout the play—as seen in the derring-do of the Mousetrap, the brutal attacks on Gertrude and Ophelia, the murder of Polonius, the leaping into Ophelia's grave, the fencing with Laertes—and it will hardly do to read Hamlet as some sluggish, moping creature who would prefer to stay in bed or live in a closet. It won't even quite do to call him *manic depressive,* since his mania seems of a piece with his blues (rather than alternating with it), since he seems hyperactive right on through, perhaps most of all when he is just *talking,* as exemplified in the showdown with Gertrude, where he elects words as his weapon: "I will speak daggers to her, but use none" (III.ii.359). And even though this play closes with crossed swords and poisoned chalices and many cadavers, its profoundest message has just been adumbrated: *words are cutting,* speech enters into us, just as it does into Gertrude when she begs her son, "O, speak to me no more! / These words like daggers enter in my ears." (III.iv.95–96). How else to account for the fact that a literary text some four hundred years old penetrates us even today, limns for us the contours of human behavior? I repeat Mallarmé's definition of the poet's mission: *"rendre plus purs les mots de la tribu."* ("purify the words of the tribe"). Hamlet is a living portrait of the self out of sync, a reflecting mirror of our woes.

Hamlet's predicament is no less than a roll call of the gathering ills and crises charted in each of my chapters: the autonomous body with a will of its own; the enigma and capriciousness of motive; the metamorphic self; the view of hidden transgression as social toxin, as plague; the discovery of death as pure corrosion, not so much of life as of meaning itself. More on stage than any other character in Shakespeare, this young man articulates a nonstop scream that goes, from his initial encounter with the ghost to his final exit, through the house. All that is left is to understand his hurt.

Yet, this is the play's riddle: who understands Hamlet? One of the most persuasive explanations of Hamlet's problem is indebted to Freud, as relayed through the offices of Ernest Jones: Hamlet has an Oedipal complex. On this heading, he unconsciously desires his mother, hence unconsciously identifies with Claudius—the man who has killed his father and is sleeping with his mother—since this is what he (or his id) would like to do. I have put this libidinal thesis a bit bluntly, because I think it has its undeniable share of the truth and accounts for the twisted sexuality that seems to drive this young man. By "twisted sexuality," I mean an overpowering disgust for sexual intercourse, a disgust that leads him to indict Ophelia (told to get herself to a nunnery) with the same diseased, lecherous desires that he equates with his mother, whose lovemaking with Claudius is evoked with venom and fury: "Nay, but to live / In the rank sweat of an enseamèd bed, / Stewed in corruption, honeying and making love / Over the nasty sty—" (III.iv.92–95). There is a generalized kind of hot nausea about female sexuality that makes up a good bit of Hamlet's problem.

But this won't quite do. If we think back to passages such as the immortal "to be or not to be" speech, we find that sexuality is nowhere to be seen, whereas the obsession with death appears central. It has been argued that death is indeed the play's great theme, and that Hamlet is its ambassador. This interpretation gives us a Hamlet who has seen through humanity, who is like Mephistopheles in his brilliance, cynicism, and nihilism. G. Wilson Knight (whose thesis I am rehearsing) goes on to claim that all of the play's other characters are essentially decent, life-affirming creatures (so that Claudius, Gertrude, Polonius, and Laertes are glimpsed as they might appear in another world, a world uncontaminated by Hamlet), but that Shakespeare has so powerfully sided with his death-obsessed, death-dealing protagonist that the others—at least in the eyes of the audience and of the play's readers over time—never have a chance. He torments them, terrorizes them, sees through them, has them see through themselves (as in the case of his mother), all this as part of a merciless truth crusade. Hamlet's encounter with the grave digger, and the number of corpses at play's end, help to shore up this interpretation. So we have identified two major problems, each quite recognizable today as well: sex and death, the body's pleasure and the body's end.

Now you may well be wondering, what does all this have to do with depression? So let me begin to put some of this together. Shakespeare is out to offer us a portrait of dysfunctionality, and it is for us to see both "how" and "why." As mentioned, Prozac may be good for alleviating your symptoms, but has little to actually *say* about your problems. The old school of psychotherapy might produce a narrative for you, but it could take years of analysis to get to it. Shakespeare's play is *thinking* about depression. It is thinking about what saps our belief in life, thinking about why a young man in his prime becomes dysfunctional, thinking, ultimately, about what lives and what dies. In its peculiar way, it is wrestling with that familiar riddle of the Sphinx, about the transition from animal to human, about whether it can be done. But it is no longer a question of walking straight, nor is Hamlet's *wound*—for he is wounded—like that of Philoctetes. Let me then say straight out: what is infected and dying in this famous play is the notion of a *unified person-*

ality. Even more bluntly: *self is dying* in this play. The behavior of this prince is new in the way that entire continents were new in the Age of Exploration. Hamlet comes to us as the victim of a disease without name, but I think the play offers a gathering, essentially choral, assessment of his ills.

Let us begin with sex. Sexual appetite transforms his mother and his betrothed into unrecognizable creatures: the first he sees, the second he imagines; to Ophelia, he rants, "God hath given you one face, and you make yourselves another. You jig and amble, and you lisp; you nickname God's creatures, and make wantonness your ignorance. Go to, I'll no more on't, it hath made me mad" (III.i.139–143). But sexual transformation is only the most blatant crime committed by nature; metamorphosis itself—the view of identity as a merry-go-round—is the terrifying truth of things. Take another look at the scene where Hamlet berates Ophelia; you will note that his indictment of her is inseparable from his self-description as kaleidoscope:

HAMLET: Get thee to a nunnery. Why wouldst thou be a breeder of sinners? I am myself indifferent honest, but yet I could accuse me of such things that it were better my mother had not borne me: I am very proud, revengeful, ambitious, with more offenses at my beck than I have thoughts to put them in, imagination to give them shape, or time to act them in. What should such fellows as I do crawling between earth and heaven? We are arrant knaves all; believe none of us. Go thy ways to a nunnery. Where's your father?

OPHELIA: At home, my lord.

HAMLET: Let the doors be shut upon him, that he may play the fool nowhere but in's own house. Farewell.

OPHELIA: O, help him, you sweet heavens!

HAMLET: If thou dost marry, I'll give thee this plague for thy dowry: be thou as chaste as ice, as pure as snow, thou shalt not escape calumny. Get thee to a nunnery, farewell. (III.i.119–134)

There is something quite fascinating in the double accusation put forth here, well on this side of madness. Hamlet indicts himself by rehearsing his repertory, walking through the many scoundrels he knows himself (also? yet?) to be. Hamlet's diatribe is profoundly inscribed in time as well as in interiority—not simply that he acknowledges his potential as villain, but that he knows time may actualize his parade of selves. Thus his words to Ophelia are especially ominous and disturbing in their sense of futurity: yes, you are pure now, but. . . . And this is the plague he offers: you will alter, I will alter, we will alter. You may want to say: he does this because of what he has seen in his mother. To which I answer: his mother is a representative figure here.

Let us recall the original accusation against Gertrude: she sins because she is made of flesh, is ruled by carnal desire: "Fie on't, ah, fie, 'tis an unweeded garden / That grows to seed. Things rank and gross in nature / Possess it merely" (I.ii.135–137). Sex and death, I said; the play is about what lives and what dies. Flesh lives, lives its own life, lives in ways having little to do with our moral distinctions. The beast that makes its way throughout this book—synonymous with our anarchic body, defying diagnosis, mating and infecting in the dark, programmed for an entropic exit—is *real*, and we, well, we are phantoms. Yes, this spells out death, death of who we are, who we want to be, but Hamlet's awesome truth is life, not death. He has discovered the all-powerful, amoral principle of life, endless life, creation without form or meaning. He has seen that the world is precisely "an unweeded garden / That goes to seed," thereby exposing the hubris of weeding itself, indeed the hubris of gardens in a world not at all so fine and proper, a place where "Things rank and gross in nature / Possess" everything. Especially somatic creatures.

Thus it is, he tells Polonius: "For if the sun breeds maggots in a dead dog, being a good kissing carrion—Have you a daughter?" When told yes, he goes on: "Let her not walk i' th' sun. Conception is a blessing, but as your daughter may conceive—friend, look to't (II.ii.150–151, 153–154). To focus on the bawdiness of these last lines is to miss the more generic principle at work: ceaseless generation, in the earth, by the sun, upon dead flesh, within live wombs. It is hard to surpass "The sun breeds maggots in a dead dog" as a tribute to the spawning principle that animates all matter, that metamorphoses dead dogs into live maggots, that tells us that rot itself is pure life, a kind of cellular or molecular fiesta. Flesh lives; photosynthesis knows nothing of morality or of human design. In this logic, gangrene would be just another form of life, just as cancer would, just as infection is. The famous joke about the dead Polonius's whereabouts—"Not where he eats, but where 'a is eaten. A certain convocation of politic worms are e'en at him," leading to the final zinger, "But if, indeed, you find him not within this month, you shall nose him as you go up the stairs into the lobby"—conveys the same cashiering of spirituality in the name of rotting matter.

Hamlet is the fellow who is thinking incessantly about this fleshly carnival, about the avatars of human flesh that make a mockery of all design, all notions of personality. But mortality is not the only threat; you can also die while still living. Ophelia, become mad, is described as "Divided from herself and her fair judgment, / Without the which we are pictures, or mere beasts" (IV.v.83–84). What does it mean to be either pictures or mere beasts? Hamlet is wondering about just this. There is indeed a plague settling into Denmark, and it announces the collapse of all human self-possession and agency. For this is hardly just a matter of decomposition after death. As I said, Hamlet's discovery is of life, of discovering that one is amorphous and metamorphosing at the same time, that chastity today leads to vice tomorrow.

We know that Shakespeare inherited a view of human inconstancy and indeterminacy from Montaigne, whose splendid term *ondoyant* (wavelike) perfectly captures the fluid nature of identity. In *Hamlet* this view of transformation is bruited from every corner of the play. The mad Ophelia expresses it in folktale terms: "They say the owl was a baker's daughter. Lord, we know what we are, but know not what we may be." (IV.v.41–42). Claudius, urging Laertes to take action, espouses this same dark wisdom: "That we would do, / We should do when we would; for this 'would' changes, / And hath abatements and delays as many / As there are tongues, are hands, are accidents, / And then this 'should' is like a spendthrift's sigh / That hurts by easing" (IV.vii.116–121).

Considered as a philosophic proposition, Claudius's words utterly recast Hamlet's own dilemma, since "procrastination" is irrelevant and meaningless here, in that the failure to act stems more disturbingly from a changed actor. "Would" is an enormous fiction, a fiction of constancy and immutability, in the kaleidoscopic view of emotion and character presented here, and willpower is exposed in all its promiscuity and capriciousness since the willer is altered. Claudius's advice has nothing to do with cowardice or falseness; it is, in a far more radical sense, about a human subject who should be wary of making promises because he may not be around any longer, i.e., still be the same person, when it is time to deliver on them.

We see this theme everywhere. At play's end, Hamlet begs pardon of Laertes, saying "Was't Hamlet wronged Laertes? Never Hamlet. / If Hamlet from himself be ta'en away / And when he's not himself does wrong Laertes, / Then Hamlet does it not" (V.ii.207–210). Of course, these lines have been facilely glossed as bad faith (It's not my fault, it wasn't me), but their full force is felt if we realize that Shakespeare is showing us a world in which a person "from himself be ta'en" is a natural event. I repeat: a *natural* event. "Madness" is, in some sense, the great alibi of the play, the convenient cover term that seems to account for human absenteeism, for vacating the premises, for being yanked off the stage while still on it, for being picture or beast.

The metaphysician of this doctrine of alterations is unquestionably the Player King whose response to his wife's assertion of fidelity unto death is among the most stunning speeches in the play: "*I do believe you think what you now speak; / But what we do determine oft we break. / Purpose is but the slave to memory, / Of violent birth, but poor validity; / Which now, the fruit unripe, sticks on the tree, / But fall unshaken when they mellow be*" (III.ii.169–173). "Memory" is the guarantor of our pledges, but its "validity" is "poor," is subject to time, which Shakespeare wonderfully expresses in the organic metaphor of unripe fruit that sticks on the tree (is firm in its commitment) only until ripeness comes, at which point it can "fall unshaken," i.e., collapse or change without any external force applied.

This "ripeness"—which will later be famously expressed as "readiness"—is an evolutionary process governed by nature, not by man, not even by the most well-intentioned man. Later in that same speech we have the marvelous line, "*Our thoughts are ours, their ends none of our own,*" buttressing an ongoing disconnect between other binaries in which we want to believe: "fortune" and "love," "will" and "fate." The glue that holds these things together—that makes us keep our promises, remain ourselves—is being dissolved in *Hamlet.* The ultimate ramifications of such a view are unhinging, because what is unseated is any proprietary view of self, any view that we can claim ownership to our acts. On the contrary, "our" is a sort of verbal conceit here—possessive pronouns have gone out of business—because the actor is different from the willer, shares only a name.

I want now, at long last, to say that Hamlet's melancholy is to be understood in the light of this devastating view that time undoes self, that all our notions as to who we are and what we would are quaint fictions, as whimsical as soap bubbles that the air dispels, dissolved simply by the act of living. This is what is rotten in Denmark. This is why Polonius's paternal, immortal advice to his son—"This above all, to thine own self be true, / And it must follow as the night the day / Thou canst not then be false to any man" (I.iii.79–81)—is a formula for disaster: there is no firm self to be true to, no "own" self to serve as compass, and hence, Hamlet, in all his multiplicity, is the truest man in the play.

Shakespeare everywhere measures the reach and price of this vision. We are to understand the touching account of poor Yorick in this fashion: that exhumed skull suggests the current status of Alexander and Caesar, imagined now to be stopping a bunghole or keeping the wind away, but this physical grotesquerie, the bad joke that life plays on the (now) living, is but a lead-in to the harder truth that is spiritual: a recognition of one's absurd metamorphoses, of what it really means to be *on-doyant.* "I did love you once," Hamlet tells Ophelia; why so he did, just as Gertrude did love her husband once. The immensely theatrical vision expressed later in *Macbeth* of the human subject as a player that struts and frets his hour upon the stage is fully adumbrated in *Hamlet,* and the earlier tragedy measures even more deeply how much wreckage such a vision entails. One has no command over one's repertory. One cannot know how long-lived or short-lived one's feelings are to be. "To be or not to be," that is indeed the question. Life is change.

Hence there is wisdom, humility, and also fatigue in Hamlet's final great recognitions, the pact with change and fortune that he makes in the fifth act of the play. "There's a divinity that shapes our ends, / Rough-hew them how we will" (V.ii.10–11) and the even more sublime, "The readiness is all. Since no man of aught he leaves knows, what is't to leave betimes" (V.ii.196–197). The famous preceding lines about a "special providence in the fall of a sparrow," along with the meditation on death's certain arrival and uncertain schedule ("If it be now, 'tis not to come; it if be not to come, it will be now; if it be not now, yet it will come"), have led us to think in terms of the body's fate, but the lines are even more powerful if we consider that the "aught" that one leaves may also be oneself, a prior self, left because one is willy-nilly en route to being someone else, something else.

"Readiness is all" unmistakably sounds a note of acceptance and reconciliation, but those valedictory lines do not erase the sound and fury of the earlier Hamlet's astonishment and upheaval that the self is kaleidoscopic and decentered, that its cogency and projects are transitory and frothlike. In saying this, I have returned to the theme of melancholy and depression, and I want now to characterize depression as a state in which one's cogency and projects lose their validity, in which the things one has done, perhaps for decades, all of a sudden appear emptied out, mere constructs: one's work, one's relations, one's beliefs.

Here is a ghostliness that many of us have either known or seen, and it has little to do with the specter of a dead father seeking revenge. The entire argument that I have sketched out about the unraveling of self, about the discovery that the world is made of cardboard and that what we are today is no augur for how we will wake up tomorrow: all this has common cause with depression. And I have chosen *Hamlet* as my test case for another reason, no less crucial: *depression turns reality into theater.* Not theater as something multicolored and vital, but theater as hollowness and artifice, theater as unreality. The old debate as to whether Hamlet is *acting,* is *playing a role,* needs to be reconceived and turned on its head. One fine day you *discover* how theatrical your life is, how what seemed natural and spontaneous and self-evident is now somehow different: mechanical, a role, a construct. This can apply to everything: having a meal, loving a spouse, going to work, writing or reading a book. Let us recall the clown's way of parsing the verb *act* at the graveyard scene: "an act has three branches—it is to act, to do, to perform" (V.i.9–10). Depression is when that middle term *do* loses its innocence and spontaneity, becomes *act,* in the sense of playing a role, and *perform* in the sense of pleasing a public. Depression is when this most unwelcome change of life simply declares itself, and that is when Humpty-Dumpty enters your life. And it may well be that all the king's horses and all the king's men—the tender ministrations of analysts or loved ones, the prescribing of lithium or Prozac or other wonder drugs—fail to put you back together again.

Hamlet has long been recognized as a "revenge tragedy" that goes amok, a play where the obvious work to be done—kill the king, stupid—becomes undoable, is put off and rationalized. Generations of schoolchildren have been taught that Hamlet's "tragic flaw" (thanks to good old Aristotle) is *hesitation.* Shakespeare's play is indeed a revenge tragedy, but the revenge is of a different order: it is the revenge of life—sprawling, amoral, bestial, haphazard, anarchic—over design, over purpose, over self. To borrow from the old TV show, it is the announcement that the play's mission—kill Claudius—is impossible, that every mission is impossible.

Hamlet is about the discovery of living death, not in the trumpeted soliloquies about the virtues of suicide, but in the quotidian experience of alteration, dissolving, imploding. Yes, this play has a kind of fire and frenzy that are hardly what comes to mind when we think "depression," but then Shakespeare is not that kind of realist. Instead, he has given us a portrait of a *new man,* a man for whom reality has just become pure histrionics. *All the world's a stage:* for years, I took this phrase simply to denote a delightful, baroque picture of life. In the light of *Hamlet,* in the light of what depression is and does, I now perceive the sheer horror of those lines, the horror of being "ghosted," of discovering that all is spectral and factitious, that our most personal feelings are hideously time-bound, regulated by a clock we did not set, just as prone to stop or explode as our bodies are prone to stroke and heart attack. But unlike those somatic time bombs, this one is scandalously invisible, goes off on the inside, rending the fabric of our life and self in ways that no camera or blood work is likely to show. That is why we turn to literature.

To be sure, the Renaissance prince neither dresses nor speaks as we do. But his antics and his brilliant sorties illuminate the galaxy where we keep house. Galaxies are larger than houses, especially the cramped quarters of depression, and this is good to know when we feel cornered and lessened, since it offers us living space. Moreover, his problems are just as intimate as those which unhinge us today. "Sex and death," I claimed. I could just as easily say, "Mother and Father," since Mother's sexuality is unbearable, and Father's expectations are unmeetable. Shakespeare has not put his young man on a couch, nor does he have any medications to offer. Instead, he has staged his dilemma and made us see its unforgettable fireworks and vistas. This is no happy picture. It is no accident that Claudius refers to Hamlet in outright medical terms, as a scourge, a pestilence, a disease that needs extinguishing (which task he asks England's help in accomplishing); nor is it happenstance that Ophelia goes certifiably mad just by dint of observing this man's sickness and "fall."

But where modern thinking would seek to trace causes and derive an etiology, as indeed I myself have done in my remarks on sex and death, on Mother and Father, as the "origin" of the disease, Shakespeare seems to have a darker, virtually absurdist view of the human project. It is a view that is in line with the haphazardness of all things concerning the creature who moves from four legs to two legs to three legs, suggesting that fixity is illusory, that explanations are frivolous, that appearances are deceptive, and that knowledge is unattainable. Reflecting on the senselessness of soldiers giving their lives for a small plot of land, Hamlet proffers a spellbinding assessment: "This is th' impostume of much wealth and peace, / That inwards breaks, and shows no cause without / Why the man dies" (IV.iv.26–28). I am not sure even today that I completely understand these lines; the glosses tell us that "impostume" means "abscess," and hence this medical idiom seems to be about the impossibility of diagnosis, the utter misfit between appearances and reality, between surface and depth. Hamlet seems to be saying that no equation is imaginable between this piece of land and the "value" ascribed to it in war (either in terms of money or soldiers' lives).

But the image of an abscess that breaks *on the inside,* beyond our scrutiny or knowing, and kills its man forthwith, well, this image carries the venom of the entire play. Yes, the self is dying in *Hamlet,* but it is all taking place in the dark, according to rules we cannot know, just as our impending heart attacks and strokes are coming to meet us along paths that we (mercifully) cannot see. But the illness here is not stroke or heart attack; the abscess envelops the mind, the soul, and it can simply *pop,* leaving us not so much dead as other. This is Shakespeare's tragic insight, that identity and personality are not only constructs but capricious constructs that can come undone at any moment, without warning, showing absolutely "no cause without / Why the man dies." With this formulation, we measure in full the horror of all mental and psychic disorders, all those alterations and inner deaths whose coming cannot be charted, whose legacy is wreckage (of "I"), whose dimensions constitute that larger dread territory to which the word *depression* points.

HAMLET'S PROGENY

Depression has its writers. Coleridge had his own demons to wrestle with, and hence had much to say about *Hamlet,* conceiving him as one of the first great intellectual heroes, and getting in trouble for just those reasons. In fact, Hamlet does not truly mystify or mesmerize readers and audiences *until* nineteenth-century Romanticism. It is no surprise that Dr. Johnson has little to say on the figure, whereas Goethe, acutely aware of the changing philosophical weather in Europe, reflected long and hard on Shakespeare's prince, found him too tender for the brutal charge laid upon him, and offered countless, rich reflections on him in *Wilhelm Meisters Lehrjahre.* Or one could evoke the French Romantic playwright Alfred de Musset whose hero, Lorenzaccio, is unmistakably conceived as a jaded version of the Shakespearean prince with an existential dilemma.

One thinks especially of Dostoevsky's "Underground Man" who seems to have inherited Hamlet's decentered self. Dostoevsky goes on to assure us that the nineteenth century is full of such sick creatures, people without a compass, chameleon types who know themselves to be all role. It even seems to be a virtue: "Yes, an intelligent man in the nineteenth century must and morally ought to be a pre-eminently characterless creature; a man of character, an active man, is pre-eminently a limited creature" (5). By the end of his bitter story, Dostoevsky has illustrated the poverty and pain of this mind-set, this modern condition, and we especially measure the toll exacted in the area of human love and charity. The Underground Man's self-loathing resembles Hamlet's, and his torture of Liza (the prostitute whose heart he has touched) seems modeled on Hamlet's treatment of Ophelia.

Doubtless the most extravagant twentieth-century rendition of Shakespeare's prince would have to be James Joyce's Stephen Dedalus, peerless razor-sharp intellectual with his own share of sexual and parental problems, and possessor of a "Hamlet-theory" of humongous complexity, upon which he famously expatiates in the "Scylla and

Charybdis" chapter of *Ulysses*. Stephen's meditation on the melancholy prince targets fatherhood itself as the supreme fiction of history and religion, as well as family. Moreover, Hamlet's shadow is sensed also in the character and rendition of Bloom, where Joyce has tried to create a staggeringly *indeterminate* character, at once various and evolving, reminiscent of the randomness articulated by Shakespeare. Yet Joyce's temperament is essentially radiant in this book, a kind of *gai savoir,* drawn to the prince's cerebral high-wire act, but rather less attuned to the dark side of the Hamlet story, the life-sapping side.

And of course we have our contemporary figures who have set out to chronicle their bouts with depression, their *saison en enfer.* I am thinking of the moving accounts left by Kay Redfield Jamison, William Styron, Andrew Solomon, and others, who offer a report from the actual battlefield, so that those of us who are intact might at least have a glimpse of what it feels like when one goes under. But I'd like to conclude by focusing on the single modern writer (in my view) who can sustain a comparison with Shakespeare along these lines: William Faulkner, and his depiction of Quentin Compson, melancholic young Mississippian who commits suicide at Harvard at the end of his first year. My text is, of course, *The Sound and the Fury,* a title that advertises Faulkner's debt to Shakespeare, to the famous speech in *Macbeth* that closes with this cheerful definition of life: "It is a tale told by an idiot, full of sound and fury, signifying nothing." The first segment of Faulkner's novel is the interior monologue of Benjy, the idiot son, but the second sequence, giving us the inner thoughts of Quentin, the Compson family intellectual, seems ready-made for our purposes. Quentin's dilemma is that of manifold impotence: son of a decaying Southern family, he is powerless to prevent its decline, to stop his father from drinking himself to death, and, above all, powerless to protect the honor / chastity of his sister Caddy in accordance with the chivalric code he has inherited.

I invoke Faulkner's novel in full awareness that it is a notoriously difficult read. What makes this book so hard to negotiate? The most likely answer has to do with the narrative achievement for which Faulkner is most credited: the use of the interior monologue. His novels seem to defy us at every turn, because they appear to be written from the *inside* of the minds of his protagonists, and as readers we are thrust—without guide or guidebook—into these unruly, often anguished and capsizing interiors. This is not a voyage that every reader is prepared to make, even in the best of days, but to expect a reader who is conceivably suffering from depression to perform the labor necessary to sidle up to Quentin Compson—well, that may well seem quixotic. So, let me say why I choose to close with Quentin. Yes, he is depressed. Further, he seems exiled in his own mind, and this matters for two reasons: (1) it is what makes the interior monologue so riveting, for it conveys Quentin's consciousness with a rare immediacy, and (2) being exiled in the mind is the very signature of depression.

Remember Hamlet once more. The most famous speech in English literature, which starts with the words "To be or not to be," closes with something very close to an indictment of *thinking,* thinking (or "conscience") now understood as a paralyzing force: "Thus conscience does make cowards of us all, / And thus the native hue of resolution / Is sicklied o'er with the pale cast of thought, / And enterprises of great pitch and moment / With this regard their currents turn awry / And lose the name of action" (III.i.83–88). On this head, Hamlet's dilemma is that he thinks too much, has too much consciousness. Shakespeare is particularly modern in the medical idiom he offers here: our indwelling power of volition and agency, figured as "the native hue of resolution," is subject to something almost like pollution, a kind of advancing fog that blurs things and saps resolve, so that "sicklied o'er with the pale cast of thought" seems very close to what we might term "neurosis" or "depression," a mind-induced disorder that robs us of strength and the power to act.

William Faulkner's genius consists in finding a new narrative language for just this consciousness, the incessant *thinking* that can be a feature of depression. Hence, the Shakespearean device of the soliloquy, brought in to cargo the thoughts of the mind in a shockingly direct way to a Renaissance audience, now becomes precisely the interior monologue, the stream of consciousness, in which the repressed thoughts, damning affective material, and general garbage of one's past rise to the surface and to language. I am saying that Faulkner may indeed be difficult but that you should listen in because you could well be eavesdropping on the very music of your own mind.

But the Mississippi Hamlet has none of the vigor of Shakespeare's prince. He does indeed strut and fret his hour upon the stage, but we sense early enough that this young man is soon going to be down for the count. He is, I think, more damaged, more undone in his inner wiring, more a portrait of distress and depression than anything we see in Shakespeare.

Here is what a typical byte of Quentin's consciousness sounds like:

Sometimes I could put myself to sleep saying that over and over until after honeysuckle got all mixed up in it the whole thing came to symbolize night and unrest I seemed to be lying neither asleep nor awake looking down a long corridor of gray halflight where all stable things had become shadowy paradoxical all I had done shadows all I had felt suffered taking visible form antic and perverse mocking without relevance inherent themselves with the denial of the significance they should have affirmed thinking I was I was not who was not was not who. (211)

This is, in my view, what Hamlet might sound like in American modernist prose. The condition of being neither asleep nor awake, the long corridor of gray half-light, these are the vistas of depression. Moreover, Quentin's dirge records a series of collapses: a discovery of the world as perversely theatrical, as a dumb show that mocks one's designs and hopes; as a turning inside out of the forms of coherence, culminating in the most drastic collapse and implosion of all, that of the self, "thinking I was I was not who was not was not who." It would be hard to improve on these lines for saying the erasure that depression entails.

Quentin is still further Hamlet in the sexual malaise he experiences. Expected to protect the honor / chastity of his sister Caddy, Quentin finds this to be difficult for many reasons. The external obstacle is Caddy herself, a feisty, strong-willed girl who is not to be stopped in her hunger for sexual freedom; but there are internal problems also, notably that Quentin himself harbors sexual desire for Caddy, and if this were not enough, Quentin also happens to be deeply fearful about sexuality, a trait that is beautifully exposed when Quentin remembers a story he heard about a man found in the woods who had castrated himself, then muses:

> He went into the woods and did it with a razor, sitting in a ditch. A broken razor, flinging them backward over his shoulder the same motion complete the jerked skein of blood backward not looping. But that's not it. It's not not having them. It's never to have had them and then I could say O That That's Chinese I don't know Chinese. (143)

We have come a far piece from the sexual bawdiness and brutality Hamlet evinces with Ophelia and Gertrude, inasmuch as sex itself seems a plague to the modern young man. The longing for innocence is seen as the absence altogether of genitals ("It's not not having them. It's never to have had them"), and this is in turn coded linguistically: Oh, "testicles"? what are they? Chinese? I don't speak Chinese. Welcome to modernity.

Quentin's most powerful and unhinging relation to Hamlet comes from their joint recognition that love can die, that time at once alters us and cancels us out. Whereas Hamlet looked straight on at these tidings and expressed his reconciliation by claiming that "readiness is all," Quentin cannot bear such news of human promiscuity. Moreover, he has not figured it out on his own, but must hear it from his own father, who offers him this nihilistic medicine (which goes by the name of *temporary*) in hopes that he will cheer up and stop being depressed and sui-

cidal over the fate of his sister and his own vexed feelings about her.
This too comes to us via Quentin's interior monologue, in the form of a
long-remembered conversation with his father about whether or not to
end his life. The dialogue itself (consisting of *i* and *he*) reveals how powerfully and even fatally others can live inside us; it is not so different
from the Ghost's "Remember me" in *Hamlet,* a terrible sign of the father's law that cripples the son. This magnificent passage stumps far too
many readers because it is written without punctuation or capital letters, so I shall take the liberty of using bold letters to show the remembered dialogue (and a few italics to emphasize what is crucial), and you
will easily see just how clear it really is:

> **i** [Quentin] *temporary* and **he** [Father] you cannot bear to think that
> someday it will no longer hurt you like this now . . . you wont do it
> [commit suicide] under these conditions . . . no man ever does that
> under the first fury of despair or remorse or bereavement he does it
> only when he has realised that even the despair or remorse or be-
> reavement is not particularly important to the dark diceman and **i**
> *temporary* and **he** it is hard believing to think that a love or a sorrow
> is a bond purchased without design and which matures willynilly
> and is recalled without warning to be replaced by whatever issue the
> gods happen to be floating at the time no you will not do that until
> you come to believe that even she was not quite worth despair per-
> haps and **i** i will never do that nobody knows what i know . . . and **i**
> suppose i realise what you believe i will realise up there next week or
> next month and **he** then you will remember that for you to go to har-
> vard has been your mothers dream since you were born and no
> compson has ever disappointed a lady and **i** *temporary* it will be bet-
> ter for me for all of us and **he** every man is the arbiter of his own
> virtues but let no man prescribe for another mans wellbeing and **i**
> *temporary* and **he** *was* the saddest word of all there is nothing else in
> the world its not despair until time its not even time until it *was*
> (220–222)

It seems to me that Faulkner is spelling out the dreadful consequences of this view that nothing lasts, that our loves as well as our hates are invisibly time-bound, can be "called" and "replaced" by "whatever issue the gods happen to be floating at the time," with the result that you wake up and simply discover, one fine day, that it is all over, it just *was,* although you said, thought, and needed it to be eternal. All is *temporary,* including self.

There is a heinous kind of mutiny on display here, a rebellion on the part of our deepest feelings, as if they wanted to show that we do not own them, that they live and die an indigenous existence of their own. Once again we see the "impostume" "That inward breaks, and shows no cause without / Why the man dies," but we also see, in Faulkner's novel, that this news is simply unbearable. We may feel that Quentin Compson chooses to commit suicide precisely in order to avoid the shameful metamorphosis that has been prophesied here. He fights "temporary" the only way he knows how. He kills himself to remain faithful to his deepest feelings, to remain himself. He acts on the famous "To be, or not to be" in the name of self-preservation.

I do not want to suggest that all suicides resulting from depression are secret forms of self-assertion. Many are doubtless final exits in order to leave pain behind. Nor do I have illusions about the arduousness and accessibility of Faulknerian prose as a tool for showing the utility of literature. I close with Faulkner's Quentin Compson because he is the modern age's rival to Hamlet in just this sense: *inside, it is all sound and fury.* Interior monologue thrusts us into the minds of tortured protagonists, and this difficult trip seems enormously worthwhile to me. First of all, it writes large for us what the tempest is like. And, even more significantly, it offers an exit from *our* penitential arrangements into the field of vision of a character in literature. I do not know how to overstate this last point: art and literature provide for us a unique means of travel, of vicarious experience, of seeing the world with new lenses, of vacating— at least for a bit—the cramped quarters where we keep house. There can be no better medicine against depression.

It has long been said that Faulkner's world—unlike that of so many American writers who are future-oriented—is past-haunted, saturated by a sense of determinism. His characters are excruciatingly conscious of their doom. Robert Penn Warren once revised this notation quite memorably: Faulkner's characters, he said, are not simply conscious *of* their doom; their consciousness *is their doom.* Is it too much to say that depression can be understood along just these lines: consciousness as doom? Is this not precisely our modern fate?

Shakespeare wrote that "something is rotten in the state of Denmark," and I believe that what is rotten about modernity, what constitutes our own special plague, is excessive consciousness, a lifelong jail sentence in our own minds, the dreadful condition of being locked into our perceptual system and hence locked out of everyone else's. This is the death of love as well as the shrinkage of life. This is poison in the ear and in the heart.

And this is why literature matters. Art is that other place that can become ours, those other selves we also are. The experience of art is a precious exercise in freedom, in negotiating subjectivities and lives that are not our own. Strange as it may initially seem, Faulkner's tortured novel about a tortured young man is therapeutic and liberating along just these lines: as a magic venture *out* of our own precincts and *into* something rich and strange. The gift of emancipation that art offers is arguably most intense and most exhilarating when it comes to novels such as *The Sound and the Fury,* because Faulkner's very depiction of Quentin Compson is only readable if we agree to make the voyage, if we are prepared (in heart as well as mind) to make the great leap into his daunting text. There is no middle ground here. You do not browse Faulkner. Either you make the plunge (and inhabit Quentin's mind, "endorse" his sensations), or you are left where you started: on the outside, looking at prose that looks like gibberish. Should you, however, go *in,* you will encounter something not utterly unlike what Ali Baba found when he entered the cave: great treasure.

That treasure does not consist of nuggets of wisdom. Quentin has little of that to offer. The treasure is the trip itself, for it is perforce a trip outside yourself, outside the doom that is your consciousness, and into the capacious structures of art and literature, into the imagined world. Faulkner's novel is not a cheerful affair, but it is deeply life enhancing (even though Quentin dies), inasmuch as it operates like all the other artworks discussed in this book: it is an extension of your life, a way for you to partake, as Emerson said long ago, of the commonwealth, to enter into the great bloodstream that courses through history in the form of art. Yes, art is arterial. Bon voyage.

ACKNOWLEDGMENTS

"Nobody . . . I spect I grow'd," Harriet Beecher Stowe's character Topsy replies, when asked who made her. It seems to me that this book too just "grow'd," evolving from a more academic study in the burgeoning field of "literature and medicine" into a broader account of the way feeling and pain are expressed in literature and art. But that evolution has its history and its helpers, and it pleases me to acknowledge them.

My work in literature and medicine began more than a decade ago, and I owe a debt to Dr. Timothy Rivinus who team-taught with me the first actual course I had ever given in that area. Since then, I have had the pleasure of working on these issues with the editors of the journal *Literature and Medicine,* most especially Rita Charon, who offered her encouragement and keen critical eye when I began writing in this field. I am also grateful to Carl J. Gerber of East Tennessee State University Medical School, Burke A. Cunha of the School of Medicine at Stony Brook, and Larry Zaroff of the Medical Humanities Program at Stanford for opportunities to present my ideas to medical audiences. I was fortunate, as well, to receive a research grant from the National Endowment for the Humanities, which enabled me to devote further time to this study; some of that time was spent in Stockholm where I had fruitful conversations with Carl Magnus Stolt and Rolf Ahlzén of the

Karolinska Institut in Stockholm, both of whom believe passionately in the connection between medicine and the arts.

Closer to home, I have had a chance to try out these ideas on a repeated basis with Brown University undergraduates, many of them pre-meds, all of them lively and critical, well versed at keeping their professor on his toes. Brown University has provided material as well as intellectual support, and I am grateful to Charles Auger and to Laurence Vanleynseele for the unstinting assistance they provided me in the preparation of my manuscript; I want also to acknowledge the grant made available to me by the Dean of the Faculty, in order to offset some of the expenses entailed in marshaling the visual images that make up part of my study. In that regard, Gun Lundberg of the Svensk Filminstitut, Lotta Edoff of Svensk Filmindustri, Tytti Soila of Stockholm University, and Karen Lerheim of the Munch Museum in Oslo were instrumental in helping me get the Bergman and Munch materials and permissions I needed. Another debt I am happy to acknowledge is to Thomas Rollins and The Teaching Company, where I had a chance to offer a series of lectures on these issues entitled "Using Literature to Understand the Human Side of Medicine," providing, like my Brown courses, something of an early trial run for this book.

Some of my debts are more far-flung. Asked by the Shakespeare Society to lecture on *Hamlet,* I had an opportunity to try out many of the ideas on depression that now appear in my conclusion; I am grateful to both Adriana Mnuchin and Nancy Becker for their encouragement in approaching the Bard along these lines. Shakespeare's entry into this book typifies the way it "grow'd" from a discussion of literature and medicine into a much wider and far-reaching inquiry about feeling itself, as the motor-force of art and literature. In that sense, this book constitutes, for me, something on the order of a culminating vision of why the arts matter, and what kind of role they play (or might play) in the most vital areas of our lives, especially in connection with pain, illness, and dying, but illuminating ultimately the entire arena of human sentience. Here, too, in seeing the larger picture, I have debts.

First and foremost, as my dedication suggests, I owe more than I can say to my wife, Ann, whose belief in literature as a fount of experience has been a guiding force throughout my career and my life. All of my books reflect her presence in my life, and none more so than this one, where her sanity, wit, and measure were indispensable. The tenor and scope of this book are what they are also because of the great good luck that I had in working closely with Kate Medina at Random House, who saw—often more sharply than I did—what the larger stakes and issues of this book were and might be. Kate's vision of the book, along with the equally illuminating and generous commentary offered by Sally Arteseros, have played a signal role in the "growing" of this book, and have at once stimulated and sustained me through the long editing process. Likewise, Kate's very able colleagues at Random House, Jessica Kirshner, Deborah Foley, and Vincent La Scala made much of the inevitable labor of turning a manuscript into a book something palatable and civilized. Here, too, I have been lucky, and can only hope that the final result is commensurate with the help I received in achieving it.

SELECTED BIBLIOGRAPHY

Anderson, Sherwood. "Paper Pills." In *Winesburg, Ohio* (London: Penguin, 1976).

Artaud, Antonin. "Theater and the Plague." In *The Theater and Its Double,* tr. Mary Caroline Richards (New York: Grove Press, 1958).

Baldwin, James. "Sonny's Blues." In *The Urban Muse. Stories on the American City,* ed. Ivan Stavans (New York: Delta Trade Paperbacks, 1998).

Barker, Pat. *Regeneration* (New York: Penguin, 1993).

Barth, John. *Lost in the Funhouse* (New York: Bantam, 1969).

Bergman, Ingmar. *The Seventh Seal.* In *Four Screenplays of Ingmar Bergman,* tr. Lars Malmstrom and David Kushner (New York: Simon and Schuster, 1960).

———. *Fanny and Alexander,* tr. Alan Blair (New York: Pantheon, 1983).

———. *The Magic Lantern,* tr. Joan Tate (New York: Viking, 1988).

Blake, William. "London." In *The Selected Poetry of Blake,* David V. Erdman, ed. (New York: New American Library, 1981).

Brontë, Charlotte. *Jane Eyre* (London: Penguin, 1966).

Büchner, Georg. *Woyzeck.* In *Woyzeck and Lenz,* tr. Hedwig Rappolt (New York: TSL Press, 1988).

Burroughs, William. *Naked Lunch* (New York: Grove Press, 1959).

Camus, Albert. *The Plague,* tr. Stuart Gilbert (New York: Random House, 1948).

Conrad, Joseph. *The Heart of Darkness* (London: Penguin, 1985).

Defoe, Daniel. *A Journal of the Plague Year* (Oxford: Oxford University Press, 1990).

Dickens, Charles. *Bleak House* (London: Penguin, 1994).

Dickinson, Emily. *Final Harvest: Emily Dickinson's Poems* (Boston: Little Brown, 1961).

Dostoevsky, Fyodor. "Notes from Underground." In *Notes from Underground & The Grand Inquisitor,* tr. Ralph E. Matlaw (New York: Dutton, 1960).

DeLillo, Don. *White Noise* (New York: Penguin, 1986).

Eggum, Arne. *Edvard Munch: Paintings, Sketches, and Studies,* tr. Ragnar Christophersen (New York: Clarkson N. Potter, Inc.: 1984).

Emerson, Ralph Waldo. *Essays and Lectures* (New York: Library of America, 1983).

Faulkner, William. *The Sound and the Fury* (New York: Modern Library, 1956).

———. *As I Lay Dying.* In *William Faulkner: Novels, 1930–1935* (New York: Library of America, 1985).

Fitzgerald, F. Scott. *Tender Is the Night* (New York: Scribners, 1933).

Ford, Ford Madox. *The Good Soldier* (New York: Vintage, 1951).

Foucault, Michel. *The Birth of the Clinic,* tr. A. M. Sheridan Smith (New York: Vintage, 1975).

Freud, Sigmund. "Mourning and Melancholia," tr. Joan Rivière. In *A General Selection from the Works of Sigmund Freud,* ed. John Rickman (New York: Anchor, 1957).

Gilman, Charlotte Perkins. *The Yellow Wallpaper* (New Brunswick: Rutgers University Press, 1993).

Harrison, Kathryn. *Exposure* (New York: Random House, 1993).

Hawthorne, Nathaniel. "The Birthmark." In *The Celestial Railroad and Other Stories* (New York: New American Library, 1963).

———. *The Scarlet Letter* (New York: Norton, 1978).

Hemingway, Ernest. "Indian Camp." In *In Our Time* (New York: Scribners, 1970).

Hodin, J. P. *Edward Munch* (London: Thames and Hudson, 1972).

Ionesco, Eugene. *Exit the King,* tr. Donald Watson (New York: Grove Press, 1963).

James, Henry. *The Turn of the Screw* (New York: Norton, 1966).

Joyce, James. *A Portrait of the Artist as a Young Man* (New York: Penguin, 1992).

———. *Ulysses* (New York: Vintage, 1961).

Kafka, Franz. *Briefe, 1902–1924* (New York: Schocken, 1958).

———. "A Country Doctor." In *The Penal Colony,* tr. Willa and Edwin Muir (New York: Schocken, 1971).

———. "The Metamorphosis." In *The Penal Colony,* tr. Willa and Edwin Muir (New York: Schocken, 1971).

Kushner, Tony. *Angels in America, Part One: Millennium Approaches* (New York: Theatre Communications Group, 1993).

———. *Angels in America, Part Two: Perestroika* (New York: Theatre Communications Group, 1994).

Morrison, Toni. *Beloved* (New York: New American Library, 1988).

O'Connor, Flannery. "The Displaced Person." In *The Complete Stories* (New York: Farrar, Straus and Giroux, 1983).

———. "The Life You Save May Be Your Own." In *The Complete Stories* (New York: Farrar, Straus and Giroux, 1983).

O'Neill, Eugene. *Long Day's Journey into Night* (New Haven: Yale University Press, 1956).

Pastan, Linda. "The Five Stages of Grief." In *The Five Stages of Grief* (New York: Norton, 1978).

Poe, Edgar Allan. *Selected Poetry and Prose of Edgar Allan Poe* (New York: Modern Library, 1951).

———. "Facts in the Case of M. Valdemar." In *Edgar Allan Poe: Poetry and Tales* (New York: Library of America, 1984).

Proust, Marcel. *Remembrance of Things Past,* tr. C.K. Scott Moncrieff and Terence Kilmartin (New York: Random House, 1982).

Rilke, Rainer Maria. *The Notebooks of Malte Laurids Brigge,* tr. Stephen Mitchell (New York: Vintage, 1985).

Rowling, J. K. *Harry Potter and the Sorcerer's Stone* (New York: Scholastic, 1999).

Sacks, Oliver. *The Man Who Mistook His Wife for a Hat* (New York: Perennial, 1987).

Selzer, Richard. "The Surgeon as Priest." In *Mortal Lessons* (New York: Touchstone, 1987).

———. "Imelda." In *Letters to a Young Doctor* (New York: Harvest, 1996).

Shakespeare, William. *Othello* (Harmondsworth: Penguin, 1968).

———. *Hamlet* (New York: Norton, 1992).

Sontag, Susan. *Illness as Metaphor* and *AIDS and Its Metaphors* (New York: Anchor, 1989).

Sophocles. *Philoctetes.* In *Electra and Other Plays,* tr. E. F. Watling (London: Penguin, 1953).

———. *Oedipus the King.* In *The Three Theban Plays,* tr. Robert Fagles (New York: Penguin, 1984).

St. Paul. *Corinthians 13* (New York: Abradale, n.d.).

Strindberg, August. *Inferno/From an Occult Diary,* tr. Mary Sandbach (London: Penguin, 1979).

———. "The Ghost Sonata." In *Strindberg: Five Plays,* tr. Harry G. Carlson (New York: New American Library, 1984).

Stevens, Wallace. "Sunday Morning." In *Poems Wallace Stevens* (New York: Vintage, 1959).

Weinstein, Arnold. *The Fiction of Relationship* (Princeton, N.J.: Princeton University Press, 1988).

————. *Nobody's Home: Speech, Self, and Place in American Fiction from Hawthorne to DeLillo* (New York: Oxford University Press, 1993).

Whitman, Walt. *Leaves of Grass and Selected Prose by Walt Whitman* (New York: Modern Library, 1950).

Williams, William Carlos. "The Use of Force." In *The Doctor Stories* (New York, New Directions, 1984).

INDEX

A SCREAM GOES THROUGH THE HOUSE

Arnold Weinstein

A READER'S GUIDE

To print out copies of this or other Random House Reader's Guides,
visit us at www.atrandom.com/rgg

AN INTERVIEW WITH THE AUTHOR

Q: What made you want to interrupt your academic work to write *A Scream Goes Through the House*?

Arnold Weinstein: One reason for writing *A Scream Goes Through the House* was to *demystify* the reading and study of literature. We know that educated people love to read: we see it on planes and trains and buses, we see it on beaches and in book clubs, and we know it is a major activity where we can't see it: happening on sofas and in comfortable armchairs, being the routine event between getting in bed and falling asleep. Yet folks are very, very uneasy and suspicious around "literary critics" and professors of literature.

Q: Why do you think that is?

AW: I think it is largely our own fault. We professors have created a specialized language and set of interests, as well as a massive theoretical scaffolding, in order to discuss our field. Like all specialized languages, the language of literary criticism or literary theory serves as common currency between the specialists themselves, and serves as an insurmountable barrier for everyone else. We seem to live in an "era of expertise," and it is taken for granted that "you," the lay people, do not have the tools to understand many of the issues of our time. How knowledgeable are folks about the environment, or about the geopolitical consequences of foreign policy developments? Most of us do not have the background.

Q: What makes literature a different kind of endeavor?

AW: Literature is about life. Everyone lives, has a body, has loves and losses, dreams and fears, work and leisure, illness and health, and finally dies. These are the basic issues dealt with in literature. But you might not know that in glancing at the titles of the books we write or the conference papers we present. And it might not be all that evident even in the courses routinely taught today in English departments. For all these reasons I wrote my book, to show that literature is not esoteric or only for specialists. I have always felt that it deals with the meat and potatoes of life, with the gut issues that all thinking and feeling people experience, wonder about, and grapple with.

Q: What did you hope to achieve in writing this book?

AW: People read, many people read voraciously, and thus it is all the sadder that we professors have lost our way to this larger public. But I also believe that this great hunger for reading is an innate force that we have not truly measured or understood. Folks read hungrily, not for evasion, but for fulfillment, perhaps even for wisdom. It is almost as elemental as breathing, and needs to be seen as such. But I am not sure they get much help from the credentialed people who are the supposed experts on books, and that is what I thought I could do in this book. Especially in this book that deals with so many dark issues: pain, illness, depression, death.

Q: As both a professor and someone who generally loves to read, to what do you attribute the disparity of thought and the lack of communication between academia and the general public?

AW: Published literary criticism and literary scholarship are understood as a scholarly pursuit for information, so that the scholar can show how his or her in-depth research over the years has led to specific discoveries or data about, say, Shakespeare or Dickens or Postmodernism. There is a crucial "informational" dimension here, a sharing of the fruits of one's professional labors. What is not found—and not sought—in such publications is the personal relevance of either the literature itself or the scholar's experience of that literature. I do not want to overstate this; of course the best scholarship often has a personal tinge to it. In teaching literature, I have come to understand that the far richer and more engaging story is *not* informational, but personal, tied over and over to our own private lives, wants, needs, dilemmas, and hopes. In short, I think the academy has it wrong—we go through the wrong motions, talk about the wrong things, and simply walk right by the actual treasures in front of us. We are warned to be "professional," and above all not to be "confessional"; yet I have noted, over and over, the surprised look of interest and excitement in students' eyes each time I become personal, each time I relate a point to my life, to their life. There is an elemental logic in play here, the logic of a species that is seeking the best nourishment it can find, that inevitably asks of what it encounters: What good will this do me? What is of sustenance here? And very often, we the professors come up short.

Q: In your own course work at Brown University, you focus on the relationships between literature and medicine. What, for you, is the allure of this combination of pursuits, and how did you decide that this relationship would provide the right road map for *Scream*?
AW: When someone would ask me about the current work I was doing, and I answered "literature and medicine," I would get expressions of puzzlement and mystification. Literature and medicine? What does that mean? How do you possibly connect those two areas? And that was when the fun began for me, because it was astonishingly easy to convince people that these two fields *do belong together,* must be brought together, if we are ever to have a richer understanding of those fundamental life issues, those which I have chosen to deal with in *A Scream Goes Through the House:* the reign of *feeling* in human life, the strangeness and the anarchy of our bodies, the siren song of diagnosis and *reading* body and mind, the threats of disease on a large scale such as AIDS or bioterrorism, the fear and mystery of death, the dread of depression.

These are issues that everyone thinks about, and yet—where can we actually learn about them? My answer—an answer that had been building for three decades of teaching and writing—was: The great books from the Bible and Greek tragedy on through Shakespeare all the way to the Moderns tell us precisely about these issues. And they can be stupendously eloquent and challenging, calling into question our received views, adding to our "stock," our "repertory," just by dint of our having read them.

Q: In translating your academic work for a trade publication, what challenges did you face? How did you move between the languages of academic investigation and general criticism?

AW: When I decided to write a book that would make sense for nonspecialists, I didn't anticipate it would prove as difficult a job as it did. In each successive draft of this book, I tried to remove what was too "academic," too specialized, too narrow, in order to keep my eyes on the central matters at hand. It was hard to wean myself entirely from "professor-speak." But then something unpredictable happened: By foregrounding the human aspects of the literature at hand, I somehow managed to loosen my own tongue, to feel freer about offering my personal vision, about drawing on my personal experiences as child, student, husband, father, and grandfather. And the more I did this, the more dimensional my book became, since I was no longer so bound to particular texts, but able now to weave a more personal, even intimate kind of tapestry, to bring my readers into what was more a conversation than an analysis, more an exploration than any kind of argument.

Q: Since you've opened yourself up to this new way of looking at your work: How did this shift in professional perspective make you feel?

AW: I had a strange sense of being in a "win-win" situation, since the fuller and more evocative my words might be, the better chance I had to win over my reader to the central matter at hand: the richness of literature as guide to the human heart, as magic resource for tracking human feeling over the ages, as even more magic opportunity for time travel and self-enhancement for all readers. Oddly enough, I discovered that my "personal" digressions were not digressions at all, but the meat of my argument, since I was actually showing how literature feeds life.

Q: What did you learn about yourself and your work through writing this book?

AW: I wrote this book hoping, initially, to find some wisdom for myself by revisiting these writers, and discovered that the best role I could play was that of Guide: As someone who has worked with these books over a lifetime, I could be the fellow who revisits this or that novel or poem in order to "unpack" it and muse over it, who mulls over and plays out the often staggering ramifications of these books and paintings and films. In short, I could bring, not so much my expertise, as my deep familiarity and love for literature into play here, by taking a more leisurely, more probing, more extended look at these works of art than most rushed readers would be likely to do on their own. And maybe my fuller account of these books would whet the appetite of my readers, make them also feel that literature can be profoundly gratifying, a resource for the long haul.

Q: Did you take anything away from the experience of writing *Scream* that surprised, excited, or inspired you?

AW: While I do not think I found any wisdom (I am still as afraid of pain and death as I was before), and while I cannot be sure how much help I can truly give the hurting and dying with my book, I am sure that I have succeeded in packing a lifetime of encounters, feelings, and thoughts into this book about literature and life, and there is true exhilaration in that. By opening my sights, by including my feelings, by speaking directly to my reader, I hope to have shown that reading books is in fact an affair of feeling, a human exchange. That would be a satisfying achievement.

In writing *Scream*, I also learned to "open up" my texts, my arguments, and above all myself. I learned to descend more directly and ambitiously into my own depths. I felt an injunction to approach each page of my book with the terrifying question: Why say this? What's in it for my reader? And I found, to my amazement, that I had real answers, full excursions, even extended vistas that I could unfurl to address these central existential issues. I found that a lifetime of teaching and loving books had prepared me for just this kind of opening, this kind of adventure. *Scream* is punctuated by the motif of "trip," "adventure," "journey," and, indeed, that expresses my own extraordinary voyage as writer, my own act as self-explorer and as guide for self-exploration. While I had often done this in passing in my courses, I was now doing it systematically, full throttle, and I found it exhilarating, remarkably fruitful, gratifying, like a fabulous dessert that followed my lifetime meal of teaching and writing.

Q: What overall impact has the experience of writing *Scream*, and the self-discoveries associated with it, had on your work and on your life?

AW: It is hard to overstate the significance of these discoveries for me. At sixty-two, I had already begun to wonder how much longer I want to teach, to work full time. In some utterly unanticipated way, the writing of *Scream* has been a revelation for me about these matters, because I now know that there are more books I want to write exactly along these experiential lines. I know that whatever my "gift" is, it has to do with making exactly those connections between life and art that I made in *Scream*, connections that I now feel poised to make in newer ventures, on other themes, about other books. It is as if I myself have gone through the looking glass.

Q: What are you, the Guide, reading now?

AW: I am currently rereading Proust. He's rather applicable to this conversation, in fact. One of his central, daunting insights is that we may well die before coming to true self-knowledge or self-possession, and that the goal of life is to reach that stage so that at least that one possession—the only one Proust believes in—may be brought about: the possession of our life. It sounds exalted and over-the-top to compare myself to Proust, but in some sense, the writing of *Scream* has led me to a startling sense of my own rich quarry, the materials that I am now prepared to mine, exploit, and share.

Q: What are you currently working on?

AW: I am at work on a book that could open the way for readers to enter some of the greatest but most mystifying books of the twentieth century, books that everyone knows but that few feel comfortable with: Proust's *Remembrance of Things Past,* Joyce's *Ulysses,* Woolf's *Mrs. Dalloway* and *To the Lighthouse,* Faulkner's *The Sound and the Fury* and *Absalom, Absalom!,* Morrison's *Beloved.* I do not profess to have any "key" to these marvelous books, but I have spent a lifetime reading and teaching them, and I am convinced that they tell us about the most basic human issues: consciousness, love, self, desire, fear. These writers broke radically with the nineteenth-century realist novel in order to create a style and a vision that are startlingly new. My goal is to show how intimately and explosively these books tell *our story*. Once again, as in *Scream,* I want to clear away some of the academic cobwebs surrounding these novels so that we can see these dazzling performances for what they are: an unprecedented picture of how the mind works, how feelings live, how the past and the might-have-been dance in our heads. Such writing jolts us out of the often narrow and tidy views we have of life—of our own life—by showing us how prancing, kaleidoscopic, and incomparably rich it actually is. It is going to be fun to write this.

QUESTIONS FOR DISCUSSION

1. In the Introduction, Weinstein asserts that the bookshelf is comparable with the medicine shelf, because of the way that each can serve as a basic resource for the body and the mind. This analogy fuels a great deal of what is to come. Do you agree with the parallel? Do books have therapeutic value for you? If not, might they? If so, what kinds of books have this value? Familiar favorites or new discoveries?

2. Weinstein claims that science does not deal with pain and illness in terms of how we experience them, how they make each individual feel. Does this ring true in your own experience? Do you feel that doctors do or do not address these matters? Should they? How could the literary testimony which this book presents have a bearing on your own doctor/patient relationship?

3. It has been claimed that "happy love has no history," meaning that great literature tends to dwell on the problems and crises of life. Yet happiness and pleasure are certainly real. Does this book scant them? Is it over-focused on the dark side of things?

4. Weinstein argues that through art we discover that we are not alone. Is this an exaggerated or romantic claim? How do you connect with other people by sharing the experience of reading a certain book, or

looking at a certain painting? In your experience, can art counteract loneliness?

5. Weinstein's discussion of William Blake's poem "London" closes with an assertion that this poem offers its readers an experience of eighteenth-century London that no other source could match. What about history? Or painting? Or actually walking the London streets with a good guide or guidebook?

6. The account of James Baldwin's "Sonny's Blues" mentions Ken Burns's recent TV documentary on jazz as an example of what Baldwin is trying to do. What do you make of the familiar notion that the "blues" are "pain turned into music"? Do you subscribe to the notion that suffering produces art? What other artists or writers come to mind as exemplars of this notion?

7. Weinstein says that the paintings of Edvard Munch are not depressing. Given the very dark subject matter of so much of Munch's work, do you agree with the author's claim?

8. The chapter "Living in the Body" asserts that art and literature *defamiliarize* our received notions about our bodies. What does that mean? Is it true? If so, might it be a general feature of successful art? Do such "surprises" strengthen or undermine your sense of who you are?

9. Weinstein focuses a good deal on the authority, even the tyranny, of the body. Are you persuaded by this view? Could you argue that we do control our own bodies? How do you feel these issues are seen in contemporary culture? What might be said about the beauty or pleasure of the body? What do you make of the "I/It" correspondence that the author discusses? Do you experience your body as an "It"? When?

10. Weinstein's chapter on "Narratives of Exposure" is much taken up with the issues that go into *diagnosis*. Do you feel that literature is a diagnostic enterprise? Do books help you "see more clearly"? Could one argue the opposite: that books often confuse us, make the world a murkier place than it was? Would that be good or bad?

11. To what extent do you believe modern life in America—with its regular medical checkups, routine testing of children for disorders, and huge array of imaging procedures—is a diagnostic culture? Do you see a risk in the enormous advances made possible by diagnostic imaging and testing? With the advent of ever-improved genetic research, some have argued that our lives will be a kind of readable "blueprint" from infancy on; will this be a benefit or a curse? Are we now able to diagnose beyond our capacity to heal?

12. In his chapter on plague and contagion, Weinstein quotes the French visionary Artaud, who argues that plague is revelatory, and that it has a kinship with theater. Is this a mad claim? What could be said for it? What might be said against it? What can we learn about plague or epidemic from artists and writers that we cannot learn from epidemiologists?

13. We are familiar with the spate of films and books that deal with "coming plagues." Does this topic have a new resonance in post-9/11 America? Has your own sense of vulnerability been altered? Can we learn something about our own time from a book like Defoe's *Journal of the Plague Year*, written almost three centuries ago? If so, what? Are there modern poems or novels that speak to this dilemma?

14. We usually think of grieving as a private experience connected to the loss of our loved ones, but Weinstein also deals with public grieving, as reflected in Whitman's poem about the death of Lincoln. Does an

entire society go through the work of grieving? Do you think the assassinations of John and Robert Kennedy and of Martin Luther King catalyzed a national mourning experience? We know that holidays and memorial events commemorate these deaths, but might literature or art or film play a role here?

15. Weinstein's chapter "Saying Death" closes with a discussion of the "post-death" poems of Emily Dickinson. Is Dickinson's perspective whimsical? Mad? None of us knows anyone who has died and come back to tell about it; what are we to make of poems that seem to do that? What can we the living learn from material like this?

16. Given that depression tends to shut down one's appreciation of life, can there be a literature of depression? How can we square the grayness and anomie of clinical depression with the fireworks, the "sound and fury," of performances such as Hamlet's and that of Faulkner's Quentin Compson? Weinstein alleges that the collapse of "I" is central to the experience of depression. Could you argue that it is also central to every chapter in this book? Can art help us in this dilemma?

SUGGESTED READING

Many of the primary texts mentioned in *A Scream Goes Through the House* are discussed only in passing, and they too belong on the following list.

Chapter 1. A Scream Goes Through the House

Works of art in which the flow and power of feeling are central, carrying over time and space.

Stephen Crane, *The Red Badge of Courage:* a coming-of-age story set in the Civil War, written in impressionist, hallucinatory prose

Euripides, *The Bacchae:* collective hysteria, trauma, psychological extreme states

Romantic poetry: Wordsworth, Coleridge, Keats, Shelley, Byron, Whitman, Goethe

F. Scott Fitzgerald, *The Great Gatsby:* tender, lyrical account of the American dream, and the power of belief

Gustave Flaubert, "Un coeur simple": moving story of a servant's passionate need to find a love object

William Faulkner, *Light in August* and *Absalom, Absalom!:* spellbinding yet arduous novels about race and violence in the South, both present-day and in the Civil War era

Zora Neale Hurston, *Their Eyes Were Watching God:* lyrical story of a tumultuous love relationship and female self-assertion in a paroxystic natural setting

Arthur Miller, *Death of a Salesman:* heartbreaking account of Willy Loman's "fall" and the collapse of an entire ethos

Jean Rhys, *Wide Sargasso Sea:* modern "prequel" to Brontë's *Jane Eyre* which focuses on the tragic life of Bertha Mason Rochester, "the madwoman in the attic"

Tim O'Brien, *The Things They Carried:* searing Vietnam War counterpart to Crane's Civil War story

Chapter 2. Living in the Body

Works in which the human body is depicted with power and strangeness, and the culture's grip is inseparable from the body's fate.

Lazarillo de Tormes: anonymous sixteenth-century picaresque tale of starvation and coming of age

Ernest Hemingway, *In Our Time* and *The Garden of Eden:* early and late works of the master of desiring and injured bodies, the first about violence and trauma, the second about self-creation and gender-bending

James Joyce, *Ulysses:* the paramount modernist fiction in the English language, with unforgettable somatic notations in the representation of Leopold Bloom; a very difficult "read," with commensurate rewards

Toni Morrison, *Sula:* gorgeous and troubling story of female rites of passage, written in the style of "magical realism"

Francisco Quevedo, *The Swindler:* seventeenth-century picaresque story of hunger and street life, written in almost surreal fashion

François Rabelais, *Gargantua and Pantagruel:* rollicking, bawdy sixteenth-century French account of giants with giant needs and ways

Philip Roth, *Sabbath's Theater:* dazzling, over-the-top story of Mickey Sabbath's insatiable erotic and intellectual hunger; an American version of Rabelais

the Marquis de Sade, selected novels: these cruel and often pornographic texts from the late eighteenth century are hard to read, but go a long way toward sketching the geography of the body, its wants, and the horrible abuses that can be imagined; some treat Sade as a huge bad joke, but others see his work as exploring the limits of self and power

Harriet Beecher Stowe, *Uncle Tom's Cabin:* classic account of the institution of slavery in which others own your body; the key precursor to Morrison's *Beloved*

Whitman, *Song of Myself:* hypnotic breakthrough long poem celebrating the body and acknowledging its frailties as well as strengths, with which American poetry came of age

Chapter 3. Diagnosis: Narratives of Exposure

Works in which issues of diagnosis—reading the body, reading the mind—are both central and problematic.

Arthur Conan Doyle, Sherlock Holmes stories: the chronicler of the deductive feats of this great genius of detective fiction was a doctor, and the clinical tone of these stories is no accident

Atul Gawande, *Complications:* restless, probing contemporary examination of how medicine moves forward and how all diagnoses are keyed to an evolving paradigm of what the body is and what doctors do

Henry James, *The Ambassadors* and "The Beast in the Jungle": two vintage Jamesian tales about reading and misreading the other's motives, and the consequences

Pierre Choderlos de Laclos, *Les Liaisons Dangereuses:* classic eighteenth-century French account of erotic warfare and diagnostic prowess; unrivaled psychological fiction

Thomas Mann, *The Magic Mountain:* classic German novel of the 1920s set in a Swiss sanatorium, in which "reading the body" and diagnosing its ills becomes tantamount to diagnosing the health of European culture

Sherwin Nuland, *How We Die:* compassionate, informative discussion of how lives end, and how we go about understanding the process, culled from the life experiences of a distinguished surgeon

Edgar Allan Poe, "Murders in the Rue Morgue": the beginning of the detective story genre, written by a master of psychology

Hjalmar Söderberg, *Doctor Glas:* brilliant turn-of-the-century Swedish story of a doctor who spends his life "reading" and "controlling" his patients, with echoes of our own Dr. Kevorkian

Alexander Solzhenitsyn, *The Cancer Ward:* allegorical but hard-hitting account of medicine, death, dying, and politics, often seen as successor to Mann's opus

William Carlos Williams, *The Doctor Stories:* candid account of the trials and joys of diagnosing and treating poor emigrant patients, by America's best-known doctor/poet

Chapter 4. Plague and Human Connection

Works that either focus on the impact and ramifications of plague or deal with the mysteries of transmission and contagion.

Boccaccio, *The Decameron:* contemporaneous account of the antics of those seeking to escape the Black Plague in Italy; said by many to represent the birth of narrative literature

Gabriel García Márquez, *Love in the Time of Cholera:* sultry yet surgical treatment of the mix of eros and death in times of crisis; reminiscent of Artaud's thesis about plague as revelatory

Henrik Ibsen, *Ghosts:* Ibsen's most scandalous play, about inherited disease; theme of infection as something destructive happening in the dark now seen as metaphor for what was wrong with nineteenth-century Scandinavian society

Jerzy Kosinski, *The Painted Bird:* harrowing account of a Jewish child's efforts to survive in World War II Poland, revealing the scapegoat logic of plague with considerable horror

Roman Polanski, *Chinatown:* film noir classic about a drought in Los Angeles, in which concealed private incest is inseparably linked to the public dilemma; a stylish, beautifully acted modern version of the Oedipus story

Susan Sontag, *AIDS and Its Metaphors:* brilliant assessment of how deep the scapegoating logic cuts when it comes to understanding and dealing with the impact of infectious diseases

Bram Stoker, *Dracula:* fascinating story of outside threats, in the form of disease and blood-sucking, arriving in London and the heroic efforts to combat them as well as the social anxieties brought to the fore

Chapter 5. Saying Death

Works in which the experience of dying—whether that of the dying person or the mourner—is front and center, as well as works that explore the meaning of death.

Aeschylus, *The Oresteia:* classic Greek dramatic trilogy about the processes of grieving and revenge, seen as a fatal cycle of violence requiring some counterforce such as the law

Ingmar Bergman, *Cries and Whispers:* Bergman's most exquisite and most unbearable film about the dying of Agnes, who is surrounded by her two loving/hating sisters with heavy pasts of their own; a unique effort to choreograph dying as something at once painful, social, and imaginative beyond our expectations

Jorge Luis Borges, *Ficciones:* wry, metaphysical, mind-bending short stories by the Argentine master, many of which show that dying may not be the final act of a life, inasmuch as that life continues to unfurl in history and in the minds of others

Anatole Broyard, *Intoxicated by My Illness:* moving narrative of a well-known journalist's fatal bout with cancer, filled with insights, courage, humor, and eloquence

Don DeLillo, *White Noise:* DeLillo's comic masterpiece about the antics of the academy, the threats to the environment, and the culture of death, as seen both in the Hitler phenomenon and in our never-ceasing anxiety and search for a "cure" for dying

Henry James, *The Wings of the Dove:* rich, elaborate late novel depicting the complex moral issues involved in the friendships and entanglements of the dying female protagonist, Milly Theale

Michel de Montaigne, *Essays:* this sixteenth-century French philosopher wrote about death and the need to face it with a clarity and humor that were to influence Shakespeare, Emerson, and many others

Blaise Pascal, *Pensées:* seventeenth-century French perceptions and beliefs about the scandal of flesh, the certainty of death, and the need for religious belief; searing, eloquent, often called a proto-existential document

Philip Roth, *Patrimony:* moving, unpretentious account of the death of Roth's father, told with humor and pain and a relentless willingness to look the ultimate straight in the eye

Sophocles, *Antigone:* foremost classical text about burial rituals and the tug-of-war between one's duties to the living and to the dead; also the story of a young woman who chooses self-assertion to the point of death

Paula Vogel, *The Baltimore Waltz:* zany yet intensely moving play about a sister attending the last act of her dying brother

Concluding Thoughts on Depression

Works in which the theme and experience of depression are prominent.

F. Scott Fitzgerald, "The Crack-Up": lucid and unsparing account of what it feels like to come apart, written by someone who knew

Adam Haslett, *You Are Not a Stranger Here:* stunning collection of contemporary short stories focusing on a variety of nervous disorders, including depression, through the lenses of both family and sexual orientation

Kay Redfield Jamison: selected works on madness, bipolar disorder, and the connection between psychological distress and artistic creation

Andrew Solomon, *The Noonday Demon:* recent large-scale investigation of depression's manifestations, written by an author who has gone through it

William Styron, *Darkness Visible:* narrative of the author's "descent into Hell" via his experience of depression, written with flair, honesty, and a sharp eye for the reverberations of his theme in other works and other lives